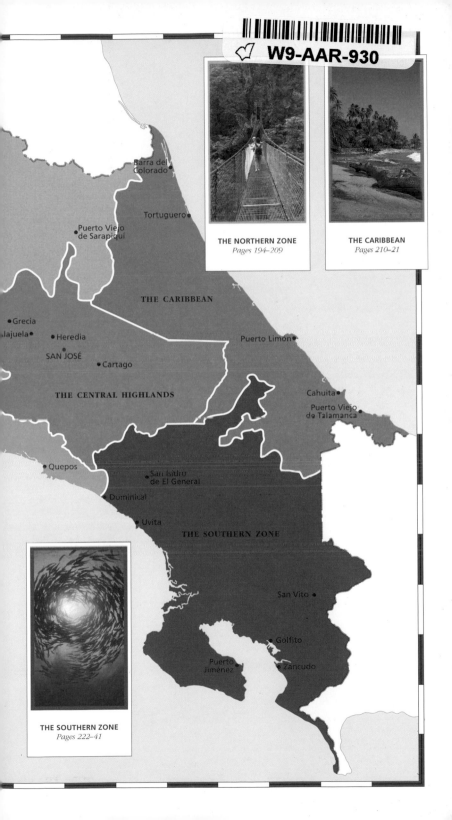

W9-AAR-930

Barra del Colorado

Tortuguero

Puerto Viejo de Sarapiquí

THE NORTHERN ZONE
Pages 194–209

THE CARIBBEAN
Pages 210–21

THE CARIBBEAN

Grecia

lajuela

Heredia

SAN JOSÉ

Cartago

Puerto Limón

THE CENTRAL HIGHLANDS

Cahuita

Puerto Viejo de Talamanca

Quepos

San Isidro de El General

Dominical

Uvita

THE SOUTHERN ZONE

San Vito

Golfito

Puerto Jiménez

Zancudo

THE SOUTHERN ZONE
Pages 222–41

EYEWITNESS TRAVEL
COSTA RICA

EYEWITNESS TRAVEL

COSTA RICA

MAIN CONTRIBUTOR: CHRISTOPHER P. BAKER

DK

DK

LONDON, NEW YORK,
MELBOURNE, MUNICH AND DELHI
www.dk.com

MANAGING EDITOR Aruna Ghose
ART EDITOR Benu Joshi
SENIOR EDITOR Rimli Borooah
SENIOR DESIGNER Priyanka Thakur
EDITOR Ankita Awasthi
DESIGNER Shruti Singhi
SENIOR CARTOGRAPHER Uma Bhattacharya
CARTOGRAPHER Kunal Kumar Singh
PICTURE RESEARCHER Taiyaba Khatoon
DTP COORDINATOR Shailesh Sharma
DTP DESIGNER Vinod Harish

MAIN CONTRIBUTOR
Christopher P. Baker

PHOTOGRAPHERS
Jon Spaull, Linda Whitwam

ILLUSTRATORS
P. Arun, Ashok Sukumaran, T. Gautam Trivedi, Mark Warner

Printed and bound by L. Rex Printing Co. Ltd, China

First American Edition 2005

Published in the United States by:
Dorling Kindersley Limited, 80 Strand,
London, WC2R 0RL, UK

12 13 14 15 10 9 8 7 6 5 4 3 2 1

Reprinted with revisions 2008, 2010, 2012

Copyright © 2005, 2012 Dorling Kindersley Limited, London
A Penguin Company

A CATALOG RECORD FOR THIS BOOK IS AVAILABLE FROM THE
LIBRARY OF CONGRESS.
ISSN 1542 1554
ISBN 978-0-75668-565-2

*Front cover main image: stream flowing through Tabacon
Hot Spring Resort and Spa, Costa Rica*

MIX
Paper from
responsible sources
FSC
www.fsc.org FSC™ C018179

CONTENTS

INTRODUCING COSTA RICA

A performance of traditional
dance near Cartago

WILD COSTA RICA

Exquisite orchid

Playa Chiquita, the Caribbean

Fresh produce at the Santa Cruz
market, Guanacaste

COSTA RICA AREA BY AREA

TRAVELERS' NEEDS

Traditional carved and
painted Bribri gourd

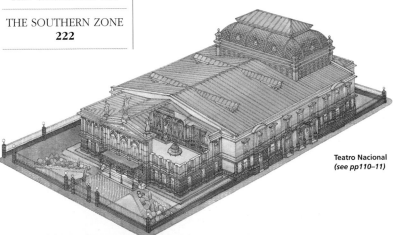
Teatro Nacional
(see pp110–11)

INTRODUCING
COSTA RICA

DISCOVERING COSTA RICA

Costa Rica can be divided into seven regions, corresponding to well-defined geographic criteria. The capital, San José, occupies a broad valley enfolded by the mountains of the Central Highlands. The Central Pacific and Southern Nicoya region is a transition zone between a dry ecosystem and a humid one. To the northwest, the dry plains of Guanacaste and Northern

Macaw made of wood

Nicoya are framed by volcanoes and, to the west, by gorgeous beaches. Northward, the land slopes down to the sprawling lowlands of the Northern Zone. The Caribbean's coastal plains are unique for their African culture and endless beaches, while the rugged Southern Zone is covered in dense rainforest. Below is an overview of the distinctive highlights of each region.

Centro Costarricense de Ciencias y Cultura, San José

SAN JOSE

- **Fascinating museums**
- **Teatro Nacional**
- **Top-notch dining**
- **Splendid shopping**

A large, bustling conurbation with few historical buildings, San José does not have many sights of interest: two days are sufficient for exploring the city. Most attractions are concentrated downtown within walking distance of one another in the compact city core. With fine hotels for every budget, the city center is easily accessed on foot, while the taxi system is efficient. Some localities can be dangerous (see p316), but police patrol the tourist areas.

One day should be spent concentrating on San José's **Museo del Oro Precolombino** (see pp112–13) and **Museo de Jade** (see p117), as well as the **Teatro Nacional** (see pp110–11), Costa Rica's Neoclassical architectural gem. The Mercado Central

and Edificio de Correos (see pp108–9) are close at hand. The small squares that anchor the city core can also be taken in.

Day two should be given to the Museo Nacional and Parque Nacional (see pp120–21), and to exploring Barrio Amón (see p117) and the **Centro Costarricense de Ciencias y Cultura** (see pp112–13). If time remains, check out the artwork at the

Museo de Arte Costarricense (see p124) and shop for quality arts and crafts – the **Centro Comercial El Pueblo** (see p289) is recommended.

San José has many fine-dining restaurants serving food from all corners of the globe. **Restaurante Grano de Oro** (see p274) offers great nouvelle Costa Rican cuisine, with an ambience to match.

THE CENTRAL HIGHLANDS

- **Scenic journeys**
- **Drive-up volcanoes**
- **Exhilarating whitewater rafting**
- **Charming country inns**

With its fabulous scenery, charming towns, and colonial churches, the Central Highlands region is tailor-made for scenic drives. It offers delightful touring through coffee *fincas* (farms) and

Rafting down one of the rivers in the Central Highlands

◁ Ceramic wall mural in San José's Barrio Amón created by local artist Fernando Matamoros

lush valleys, culminating atop towering volcanoes. Two active volcanoes are accessed by paved roads that lead through lush cloud forest to the crater rims. Encompassed within **Poás** and **Irazú** national parks *(see p140 and p153)*, these volcanoes offer superb opportunities for hiking and birding, as do relatively hard-to-access Turrialba National Park *(see p153)* and the rugged trails of Braulio Carrillo and Tapantí-Macizo national parks *(see p141 and p151)*.

Wildlife is also displayed at several sights near Alajuela *(see p134)*. Particularly recommended are the Butterfly Farm, Zoo Ave *(see p134)*, INBioparque *(see p142)* and the World of Snakes *(see p136)*.

Heredia *(see p142)* makes a good base for exploring the coffee country, including a visit to the Doka Estate and Café Britt *(see p140 and p142)* to see how Costa Rica's coffee is produced. **Sarchí** *(see p136)* – a must-visit center of crafts – lies along an exquisite drive taking in Grecia *(see p136)* and Zarcero *(see p137)*, known for their metal church and topiary respectively. Some of the best scenery lies along the **Route of the Saints** *(see p147)*, while east from San José, a separate drive leads through the Orosi Valley *(see p148)*, revealing some fine colonial churches. Nearby, Turrialba *(see p151)* is a gateway to **Monumento Nacional Guayabo** *(see pp154–5)*, the nation's

The blue expanse of the Gulf of Nicoya

foremost pre-Columbian site, and also a base for exciting rafting on the Reventazón and Pacuare rivers *(see p152)*.

Four days should prove sufficient, although a week would be required to explore in-depth. Convoluted roads and lack of road signs can make for frustrating touring. However, a large choice of appealing boutique hotels, some set amid coffee estates, makes up for this.

THE CENTRAL PACIFIC AND SOUTHERN NICOYA

- **Parque Nacional Manuel Antonio**
- **Incredible surfing**
- **Relaxing Isla Tortuga**
- **Thrilling crocodile safaris**

With two of the nation's most popular and easily accessed national parks, and a fistful of other coastal wildlife reserves, this region appeals most strongly to wildlife lovers. Refugio Nacional de Vida Silvestre Curú *(see p160)* and Reserva Natural Absoluta Cabo Blanco *(see p162)*, both compact reserves along the shores of Southern Nicoya, offer diverse habitats and a plethora of wildlife. **Isla**

Tortuga *(see pp160–61)*, offshore from Curú, is an idyllic escape that plays host to boat excursions departing the port town Puntarenas. Youthful travelers are drawn to the tiny community of Montezuma and the surfers' haven of **Malpaís** *(see p162)*, which enjoy spectacular settings along rugged shorelines.

Popular with surfers, the beach resort town of **Jacó** *(see p164)* boasts casinos, nightclubs, and a range of hotels. Immediately north, Parque Nacional Carara *(see p164)* extends inland from the coastal highway. Excursions, including crocodile safaris on **Río Tárcoles** *(see p165)*, are offered from Jacó. Explore a rural community in the Fila Chonta Mountains with the **Santa Juana Mountain Tour** *(see p165)*.

Most travelers in this region head for the **Parque Nacional Manuel Antonio** *(see pp168–9)*, accessed via the sportfishing town of Quepos *(see p166)*. This lovely park combines superb beaches with a coral reef, fabulous wildlife viewing along easily accessed trails, and some of the finest hotels in the country.

Picturesque terraced farmland in the Central Highlands

Tropical dry forest in Guanacaste's Parque Nacional Palo Verde, which boasts diverse habitats

GUANACASTE AND NORTHERN NICOYA

- **Scintillating beaches**
- **Exciting horseback rides**
- **Mysterious cloud forests**
- **Rare dry forest reserves**

The most diverse of Costa Rica's regions combines montane cloud forests and lowland dry forests – both full of wildlife – with lovely beaches. At least one week is needed to explore this region, with two weeks required for a full tour.

The key destinations are connected by regional air services. Exploring is easy overland, with main sights accessed by spur roads that branch off the Pan-American Highway. However, a 4WD is recommended, not least to reach **Monteverde** *(see pp174–8)*, acclaimed for its cloud forest reserves. Farther north, Parque Nacional Rincón de la Vieja *(see p182)* offers spectacular hiking, as well as horseback riding and mountain biking at ranches that double as rustic hotels.

Situated beneath the shadow of Volcán Orosi, **Parque Nacional Santa Rosa** *(see pp184–5)* is a dry forest reserve where wildlife is easily seen. Although not as accessible as some other parks, Santa Rosa is well worth the effort. In contrast, **Parque Nacional Palo Verde** *(see p180)* has wetlands unrivaled for birding. Chorotega Indian traditions live on in the potters' hamlet of Guaitíl *(see p193)*. The **Nicoya Peninsula** is known for its profusion of beaches. Playas del Coco and Flamingo *(see p186)* have great scuba diving and sportfishing. Tamarindo *(see p186)* is the most developed resort, while nesting marine turtles can be spotted at **Playa Grande** *(see p186)* and **Ostional** *(see p190)*.

THE NORTHERN ZONE

- **Volcán Arenal**
- **Active adventures**
- **Fabulous bird-watching**
- **Centro Neotrópico SarapiquíS**

With Costa Rica's most active volcano, an A–Z of active adventures, and a choice of nature lodges and rewarding birding, the Northern Zone is a booming latecomer to the tourist scene. The attractions

Tabacón Hot Springs Resort and Spa, Northern Zone

are concentrated in two distinct regions centered on the towns of La Fortuna and Puerto Viejo de Sarapiquí.

Bustling La Fortuna *(see p198)* is the gateway to **Parque Nacional Volcán Arenal** *(see p199)*, and offers several dozen lodges, most with vistas of the soaring volcano that erupts almost daily. Activities such as spelunking in the Cavernas de Venado and superb birding at **Refugio Nacional de Vida Silvestre Caño Negro** *(see p204)* lie close at hand. Soaking in the thermal waters at **Tabacón** *(see p198)* is a great experience, as is a ride on the Arenal Aerial Tram *(see p199)*, which combines excitement with grand views of both the volcano and of Lake Arenal *(see pp200–2)*, popular with windsurfers and anglers.

Farther east, Puerto Viejo de Sarapiquí *(see p206)* is a departure point for nature excursions on the Sarapiquí and San Juan Rivers. A short distance away are eminent rainforest reserves such as Selva Verde *(see p206)*, **Rara Avis** *(see p209)*, and Tirimbina *(see p205)*. Adjoining Tirimbina is an excellent educational facility, **Centro Neotrópico SarapiquíS** *(see p205)*, which is dedicated to a celebration of pre-Columbian and contemporary indigenous cultures.

Heavy rainfall is possible at any time of year. A 4WD is essential for successful touring. Local airlines fly to La Fortuna.

THE CARIBBEAN

- Wildlife-rich Parque Nacional Tortuguero
- Afro-Caribbean culture
- Close-up turtle-viewing
- World-class sportfishing

Mangrove swamp at Puerto Jiménez, southern Costa Rica

The Caribbean offers three of Costa Rica's premier rainforest reserves, plus splendid sportfishing and a uniquely laid-back ambience deriving from its Afro-Caribbean culture. The heritage is most colorfully alive in the village of **Cahuita** *(see p218)*, where spicy Caribbean dishes are served at rough-hewn restaurants that reverberate to the sounds of Bob Marley. Steps away is **Parque Nacional Cahuita** *(see p218)*, with trails that include one for snorkeling. Farther south, Puerto Viejo *(see p220)* appeals to lovers of surf and an offbeat lifestyle. Its beaches unfurl southward, culminating in **Refugio Nacional de Vida Silvestre Gandoca-Manzanillo** *(see p220)*, good for hikes, turtle-watching, and trips in search of dolphins and manatees. Excursions inland provide an opportunity to learn about the lifestyles of indigenous communities *(see p221)*.

The highlight of any Caribbean itinerary is a visit to **Parque Nacional Tortuguero** *(see p217)*, where exploring by boat unveils a rainforest menagerie unsurpassed in the nation. A minimum three-day stay is suggested – longer if you wish to combine Tortuguero with Cahuita and Puerto Viejo. Drawbacks to the area include the heavy year-round rainfall. Be aware that drugs are a problem in coastal communities, and you may find that locals exhibit, at times, a surliness not found elsewhere in Costa Rica.

THE SOUTHERN ZONE

- **Parque Nacional Corcovado**
- **Intriguing indigenous reserves**
- **Challenging hiking**
- **Unsurpassed scuba diving**

Encompassing Costa Rica's premier rainforests and most rugged mountains, this region, with its exceedingly diverse terrain, requires a 4WD for travelers exploring on their own. Come prepared for high humidity and heavy rain. Inland, the Talamancas offer a challenge to hikers. While well-developed trails lead to the summit of Cerro Chirripó *(see p229)* from San Gerardo de Rivas *(see p226)*, access into the more remote portions of the mountains to the south is along seldom-trodden trails within **Parque Internacional La Amistad** *(see p227)*.

Farther south is **Las Cruces Biological Station** *(see p227)*, a superb destination for birders and individuals with a botanical interest. Nearby, a number of indigenous reserves are opening up to the tourist trade *(see p232)*.

The rugged coast is known for high surf and some splendid diving. **Dominical** and Zancudo *(see p230 and p240)* are popular surfing beaches, while **Parque Nacional Marino Ballena** *(see p230)* has fine whale-watching possibilities. Whale- and dolphin-viewing boat excursions are popular from Bahía Drake *(see p238)*, where many lodges specialize in scuba diving.

The big draw is **Parque Nacional Corcovado** *(see p239)*, which offers hiking and superb wildlife-viewing. Linked by water-taxi to the sportfishing town of Golfito *(see p240)*, **Puerto Jiménez** *(see p238)* is the gateway to Corcovado. To the southwest is the hard-to-reach UNESCO World Heritage Site **Isla del Coco** *(see p241)*.

Beachgoers at Parque Nacional Cahuita in the Caribbean

Putting Costa Rica on the Map

Washed by the waters of the Caribbean Sea and
Pacific Ocean, the republic of Costa Rica lies wholly
within the tropics, between 8 and 11 degrees north
of the Equator. Bordered by Nicaragua to the north
and tapering gradually southward to Panama,
it covers 19,650 sq miles (50,900 sq km). Much
of this extremely mountainous country is
uninhabited and overlaid with several types
of tropical forest; almost one-third of the
land area is protected within reserves.
Administratively, the country is divided
into seven provinces and 81 *cantones*
(counties). It has a population of 4.5
million, heavily concentrated in the
Central Highlands, with some 350,000
people living in the capital, San José.

LAGO DE
NICARAGUA

Isla
Mancarrón

San
Carlos

La Cruz

Isla Bolaños

Los Chile

Aguas
Claras

Islas
Murciélagos

Golfo de
Papagayo

Liberia

Daniel
Oduber

Río Temisque

Río Corobicí

Laguna
de Arenal

Cañas

Tilarán

| 0 km | 50 |
| 0 miles | 50 |

Tamarindo

GUANACASTE

Las
Juntas

Santa Cruz

Nicoya

Isla Chira

Miram

Golfo
de Nicoya

Ostional

Río

Nosara

Carmona

Puntarenas

Sámara

PUNTARENAS

Isla
Tortuga

Malpaís

Montezuma

Isla Cabo
Blanco

Aerial view of the capital city, San José

ISLA DEL COCO

Isla Manuelita

Isla Pajara
Bahía Weston
Isla Cascara
Bahía Wafer

Bahía Chatham
Punta Paceco
Isla Conico

Cabo Barreto

Punta
María

Parque Nacional
Isla del Coco

Cabo
Atrevida

Cabo Lionel

Isla Montagne

Isla Dos
Amigos

Bahía Yglesias

Isla Juan Bautista

Punta Turrialba

Isla Muela

| 0 km | 3 |
| 0 miles | 3 |

Cabo
Dampier

PACIFIC OCEAN

Isla del Coco
(310 miles)

Nueva Guinea

NICARAGUA

Punta Gorda

Río San Juan

Río San Juan

Río San Carlos

Río Chirripó

Barra del
Colorado

ALAJUELA   **HEREDIA**

Río Toro

Puerto Viejo
de Sarapiquí   • Tortuguero

a Fortuna

CARIBBEAN SEA

Ciudad Quesada
(San Carlos)

LIMÓN

Zarcero   Guápiles

Sarchí   Sacramento   Siquirres

Río Reventazón

Alajuela
Heredia   **SAN JOSÉ**   Puerto Limón

Juan
Santamaría   Cartago   32

Río Grande   Turrialba   10

Río Banano   36

Tárcoles   **SAN
JOSÉ**   Orosi   Tapantí   **LIMÓN**   Cahuita
Puerto Viejo de
Talamanca

Jacó   **CARTAGO**   Bribri

Manzanillo

**COSTA
RICA**

San Gerardo
de Dota

Quepos   34   San Isidro de
El General

Río Urén

Río Teribe

Dominical   Río General   Buenos
Aires

PANAMA

Palmar
Norte

Isla
Boca Brava   Río Colón

Isla Violín   San
Vito

PUNTARENAS

Bahía Drake
Isla del
Caño   Rincón   Golfito   14   Ciudad Neily

Coto 47

Zancudo   David

Puerto
Jiménez   Golfo
Dulce   La Cuesta

KEY

✈	International airport
✕	Domestic airport
⛴	Ferry
▬▬	Pan-American Highway
▬▬	Major road
– –	International border
– –	Provincial border
– –	Ferry route

UNITED STATES OF AMERICA   *ATLANTIC OCEAN*

MEXICO   *Gulf of
Mexico*

CUBA

DOMINICAN
REPUBLIC

HAITI

BELIZE

GUATEMALA   HONDURAS   *Caribbean Sea*

EL SALVADOR
NICARAGUA

COSTA
RICA   PANAMA   VENEZUELA

*PACIFIC
OCEAN*   • *Isla Del Coco*   COLOMBIA

ECUADOR   BRAZIL

PERU

A PORTRAIT OF COSTA RICA

*D*ominated by mountain ranges and verdant forests, gouged by fertile valleys, and flanked by lovely beaches and the ocean, Costa Rica is undoubtedly one of the most beautiful places on earth. Vivid colors of nature, a virtually unmatched range of outdoor activities, friendly, hospitable people, and the subtle charm of an essentially rustic lifestyle – all combine to make the country one of the world's favorite tropical holiday destinations.

Straddling the Meso-American isthmus at the juncture of North and South America, this diminutive nation is barely 300 miles (480 km) north to south and 175 miles (280 km) at its widest point, near the Nicaraguan border. Occupying one of the world's most geologically unstable areas, the country is subjected to powerful tectonic forces that trigger earthquakes and punctuate the landscape with smoldering volcanoes. With scores of micro-climates, the emerald landscape is a quiltwork of 12 different life zones, from coastal wetlands to subalpine grassland

Costa Rica is characterized by a homogeneity of culture unique among

Costa Rica's official emblem

Central American nations, with the Spanish influence being all-encompassing and indigenous culture having little impact. However, non-Spanish cultures exist in a few pockets, such as the Jamaican ethos of the Caribbean coast.

Another distinctive feature is the nation's conservation ethic, as evidenced by its nationwide network of wildlife parks and refuges, which embraces about 30 percent of its area, more than any other nation on earth.

CONSERVING NATURE'S WONDERS

The greatest appeal of Costa Rica is its astonishing wealth of flora and fauna, protected within more than 190 biological reserves, national parks,

A farmhouse on the flanks of Volcán Arenal, in the Northern Zone

◁ A milkman pushing his cart along a street in one of San José's residential districts

The guanacaste tree, Costa Rica's national tree

wildlife refuges, and similar entities. The Reserva Natural Absoluta Cabo Blanco was created as the first protected reserve in the country in 1963. Since then, more parks and reserves have been set up every year.

However, destruction of the natural habitat continues, even in some protected regions. The park service is understaffed and lacks the funds to compensate owners for expropriated land. Thus, the wetlands of Refugio Nacional de Vida Silvestre Caño Negro are imperiled by landowners reclaiming precious marshlands for farming. Animal populations are declining in Parque Nacional Manuel Antonio due to loss of habitat. Illegal hunting menaces the populations of jaguars, tapirs, and wild pigs in Parque Nacional Corcovado. Logging, however, has been tamed and forests, which diminished by two-thirds since

Columbus stepped ashore in 1491, are increasing in area once again.

Fortunately, there are several conservation organizations that are unstinting in their efforts to save flora and fauna. Also, the government's focus on integrating protected regions by grouping them into 11 distinct regional units within a Sistema Nacional de Areas de Conservación (National System of Regional Conservation Areas) is a giant step in the right direction.

THE GOVERNMENT

A democratic republic, Costa Rica has a government headed by an elected president, who is assisted by two vice-presidents and a cabinet of 17 members. The Asamblea Legislativa (Legislative Assembly) is a single chamber of 57 popularly elected *diputados* (deputies), limited to two terms. The president appoints regional governors, who preside over the seven provinces of San José, Alajuela, Cartago, Guanacaste, Heredia, Limón, and Puntarenas.

Two parties dominate the political scene and have traditionally alternated in power with each election. The social-democratic Partido de Liberación Nacional (National Liberation Party) champions welfare programs, while the conservative Partido de Unidad Social Cristiana (Social Christian Unity Party) is pro-business. All citizens between 18 and 70 years of age are mandated to vote. A Special Electoral Tribunal

The famed Reserva Biológica Bosque Nuboso Monteverde (Monteverde Cloud Forest Biological Reserve)

appointed by the Supreme Court oversees the integrity of elections.

Costa Rica declared neutrality in 1949 and has no official army, navy, or air force, although branches of the police force have a military capability. Citizens proudly proclaim that since the late 19th century, only two brief periods of violence have marred the nation's democratic development, and the country has avoided the bloodshed that has afflicted neighboring countries. However, it has not been aloof from Latin American issues: in 1987, President Oscar Arias won the Nobel Peace Prize for brokering peace on the isthmus.

Papayas being sorted for sale in a town market

THE ECONOMY

Costa Rica's thriving economy is today powered mainly by tourism. With its stupendous landscape of mountains, beaches, and forests full of exotic flora and fauna, the country offers opportunities for outdoor life and active adventures. The focus is on ecotourism, promoted by the Instituto Costarricense de Turismo (Costa Rica Tourism Institute) under the advertising slogan of "Costa Rica – No Artificial Ingredients." Another factor aiding tourism is the country's reputation for stability in an area rent by political upheavals. Well-planned specialized lodges, large hotels, and beach resorts serve the spectrum from budget to deluxe markets.

Resident in Costa Rican colors

THE PEOPLE

Costa Ricans are known as Ticos because of their habitual use of this term as a diminutive – for instance, "*momentico*" for "just a moment," instead of the usual "*momentito*." The majority are descendants of early Spanish settlers. Indigenous peoples account for a fraction of the population, and live tucked away in remote reserves. Concentrated on the Caribbean coast, Afro-Caribbeans are mainly descended from Jamaicans who came as contract labor in the 19th century, and form a large community. A sizeable

San José is one of Central America's major financial centers with a burgeoning high-technology industrial sector. Beyond the capital, the country is still largely agricultural. Land ownership is widespread, except in Guanacaste, where large-scale cattle *fincas* (farms) prevail. Coffee, pineapples, and bananas are Costa Rica's three main crops.

The bustling capital city, San José

Traditional oxcart used for farming in the Costa Rican countryside

Chinese population also exists, mainly in the Caribbean province of Limón. Tens of thousands of North Americans and people of other nationalities have also settled in Costa Rica, drawn partly by its fabulous climate.

About eight out of ten Costa Ricans are nominally Catholic, and a significant portion of the population are regular practitioners of the faith. The most venerated figure is La Negrita, the country's patron saint, who is believed to grant miracles. Although proselytizing is illegal, the influence of evangelical Christians is growing, especially in poorer areas and among the indigenous communities.

The country has the highest rate of literacy and life expectancy in Latin America. Internet access is relatively widespread, and cell-phone use is the highest in Central America. Roads and electricity extend into even the most remote backwaters, and today few communities are entirely isolated from the modern world. In fact, Josefinos (residents of San José) lead a typically modern urban lifestyle, and the capital has a well-developed and entrepreneurial middle-class. However, old traditions survive in the countryside, where a peasant lifestyle still prevails, the horse is the main form of transport, and oxen are used as day-to-day beasts of burden.

Life revolves around the family – usually headed by a matriarch – and an immediate circle of *compadres* (friends and fellow workers). Individuals tend to guard their personal lives closely and are more inclined to invite acquaintances to dine at restaurants than to welcome them into their homes. However, Ticos are a warm-hearted people and always treat strangers with great civility.

Costa Ricans are proud of their country's neutrality and stable democracy. Although a recent influx of immigrants with "Indian" features from neighboring countries has caused much resentment, Ticos are generally a liberal, tolerant people with a concern for societal harmony and welfare.

Effigies carried along a street as part of Good Friday celebrations

THE ARTS AND SPORTS

Crafts dominate the artistic scene, mainly because of the tremendous creativity displayed by artisans. Woodcarvers such as Barry Biesanz produce hardwood bowls of immense delicacy. The indigenous influence lives on in the creation of gold jewelry, which adopts the pre-Columbian motif of animist figurines. Other native crafts include the pottery created by the community of Guaitíl in the style of their Chorotega ancestors.

A traditional dance performance near Cartago

In the 20th century, the arts scene was dominated by the nation's *campesino* (peasant) heritage, which found its most influential expression with the Group of New Sensibility in the 1920s. Headed by Teodorico Quirós Alvarado (1897–1977), the movement evolved a stylized art form depicting idyllic rural landscapes, with cobbled streets, adobe dwellings, and peasants with oxcarts against volcanic backgrounds. Their influence remains to this day, notably in miniature paintings that are a staple in many homes and souvenir stores.

Exceptions to the insipid art of the mid-20th century were the powerful depictions of peasant life by the internationally renowned sculptor Francisco Zúñiga (1912–98). Contemporary artists such as Rodolfo Stanley and Jiménez Deredia have invigorated the scene with compelling avant-garde works.

Carlos Luis Fallas's novel *Mamita Yunai* (1941), about the plight of banana workers, is the sole literary work of international note. Costa Ricans are great theatergoers, however, and theater venues are scattered all over San José and some other cities. Josefinos dress up to hear the National Symphony Orchestra perform in the Teatro Nacional and at the less formal annual International Festival of Music, while the young dress down to dance to fast-paced Latin *merengue* in clubs and bars. Virtually every town has a bandstand where people enjoy folk music featuring the *marimba*, a form of xylophone. The guitar is the main accompaniment to the *punto guanacasteco,* the national folk dance performed by men and women in traditional costume.

Played on weekends by local teams throughout the country, soccer is the national obsession for men. Rodeos and *topes* (horse parades) are a focus of general festivities, while *corridas de toros* (non-fatal bull-running) are popular with men eager to prove their *machismo*. Most Costa Ricans are passionate about activities performed in the open air such as running and cycling, which is only to be expected in this land of nature and the outdoors.

Corridas de toros

A local soccer match in progress in Heredia

Landscapes of Costa Rica

One of Costa Rica's butterflies

Few countries on earth can rival Costa Rica for diversity of flora and fauna. Despite its tiny size, the nation is home to almost 5 percent of the world's identified living species, including more types of butterflies than the whole of Africa. This astonishing wealth of wildlife is due to the country's great variety in relief and climate, from lowland wetlands to cloud-draped mountaintops. As a result, Costa Rica boasts 12 distinct "life zones," each with a unique combination of climate, terrain, flora, and fauna.

Perfectly conical Arenal, Costa Rica's most active volcano

LOWLAND RAINFOREST

Rainforests *(see pp22–3)* cloak many of the plains and lower mountain slopes of the Caribbean lowlands and Pacific southwest. These complex ecosystems harbor a large proportion of the country's wildlife. Tapirs and jaguars inhabit the understory, while birds and monkeys cavort in the treetops.

MONTANE CLOUD FOREST

More than half of Costa Rica is over 3,300 ft (1,000 m) above sea level. Much of the higher elevation terrain is swathed in cloud forest *(see p179)*, where mists sift through the treetops and branches are festooned with bromeliads and dripping mosses. Bird and animal life is profuse.

Ceiba trees *are giants of the rainforest, often towering 230 ft (70 m) tall. Their thick trunk is covered with conical thorns.*

Poor man's umbrella *is a common name for* Gunnera insignis *due to its leaves' huge size.*

Labios ardientes, *or "hot lips", is named for this lipstick-red flower's resemblance to pouting lips.*

Aguacate, *or wild avocado, is a favorite food of the resplendent quetzal.*

Heliconia flowers *grow from long, erect, brightly colored bracts that in many species resemble lobster claws.*

Tank epiphytes *are bromeliads whose waxy whorled leaves hold water, like a cistern.*

COASTS

The total length of Costa Rica's coastline is over 800 miles (1,290 km). On the Pacific, promontories and scalloped bays are common, while the Caribbean coast is almost ruler-straight. Small patches of coral reef fringe the coast off the Central Pacific and southern Caribbean shores. Many beaches provide nesting grounds for various species of marine turtles.

Mangroves, *which thrive in alluvial silts deposited by rivers, form a vital nursery along the coastline for marine creatures, such as the olive ridley turtle, and avian fauna, such as the frigate bird.*

Beaches *in Costa Rica come in every color, from white and gold to chocolate and black. Most are backed by forest.*

DRY FOREST

Once covering most of Guanacaste and Nicoya, dry forests *(see p183)* today cover only about 200 sq miles (520 sq km) of Costa Rica. The mostly deciduous flora sheds its leaves during the seasonal drought, making wildlife easier to spot. Conservationists are trying to revive dry forest ecosystems.

WETLAND

Wetlands range from coastal mangroves *(see p233)* such as the Terraba-Sierpe delta in the Pacific southwest, to inland lagoons such as Caño Negro in the north. Many habitats are seasonal, flooding in the wet season from May to November; wildlife gathers by waterholes in the December–April dry season.

The poró, *or cotton tree, blazes brilliant yellow in January and February. Its blooms resemble buttercups.*

Raffia palms *are associated with swamplands and grow leaves up to 25 ft (7.5 m) long.*

Corteza amarilla *trees typically burst into bloom the same day toward the end of the dry season.*

Water hyacinths *choke lagoons and canals and are a favored food source for manatees.*

Gumbo limbo *is often called "naked tourist tree" for the way its bark peels, like sunburned skin.*

Water lilies *are found in shallow lakes and can clog slow-moving waterways.*

The Rainforest Ecosystem

The lowlands of Costa Rica are enveloped in tropical rainforest, its canopies forming an uninterrupted sea of greenery. Hardwood trees, such as mahogany and kapok, may tower 200 ft (61 m) or more, and rely on wide-spreading roots to support their weight. The forests comprise distinct layers, from ground to treetop canopy. Each layer has its own distinct microclimate as well as flora and fauna, with the vast majority of species concentrated at higher levels. Animals such as kinkajous, sloths, and arboreal snakes are adapted for life in the branches, which are weighed down by vines, epiphytes, and other vascular plants.

MAJOR RAINFOREST RESERVES

- PN Carara *see p164*
- PN Corcovado *see p239*
- PN Tapantí-Macizo la Muerte *see p151*
- PN Tortuguero *see p217*
- RNVS Gandoca-Manzanillo *see p220*

Bromeliads *adorn the branches. These epiphytes ("air plants") have nested leaves that meet at the base to form cisterns. Leaf litter falling into these tanks provides nourishment for the plants.*

Creeping vines *of many varieties grow on the tree trunks, and use grappling hooks and other devices to reach sunlight.*

Buttress roots *have evolved to hold towering trees steady. These thin flanges radiate out in all directions from the base of the trunk, like the fins of a rocket. The largest can be 10 ft (3 m) high and extend 16 ft (5 m) from the base.*

Heliconias grow abundantly on the forest floor, and draw hummingbirds, insects, and other pollinators to their flaming red, orange, and yellow bracts.

Walking palms literally migrate across the forest floor over decades atop stilt roots only loosely attached to the ground.

The soil of rainforests is thin since leaf litter decomposes rapidly and nutrients are swiftly recycled. Heavy rainfall further leaches the soil.

Emergent trees *rise above the forest canopy where their crowns are often buffeted by high winds. Many species bloom flamboyantly in season.*

The upper canopy forms an unbroken stretch of foliage. About 80 percent of rainforest vegetation is concentrated here, as is most wildlife.

Orchids

Understory *species, adapted for varying amounts of sunlight, may grow to 80 ft (24 m) tall. Many are genetically coded to grow rapidly whenever a large tree falls, which opens a space for new growth.*

The forest floor is sparsely vegetated. Rain on the canopy can take up to an hour to reach the ground.

FAUNA

Rainforests shelter many of the largest and most endangered mammal species, such as tapirs, peccaries, and jaguars. Most animal and bird species are well camouflaged and difficult to spot in the shadows of the dark, dappled forest.

Squirrel monkeys, *or titis, are the smallest as well as the most endangered of Costa Rica's monkeys, and are found only in Pacific southwest rainforests. They live in large bands and are omnivorous.*

The jaguar, *known locally as tigre, requires a large territory for hunting. It is endangered, mainly because of illicit hunting and loss of rainforest habitat.*

Pit vipers *are well camouflaged and perfectly adapted for stealthy hunting in the understory, where they feed on small birds and rodents.*

Toucans *are easily recognized by their distinctive calls and colorful beaks. These predominantly fruit-eating birds are found in all of Costa Rica's rainforests.*

The harpy eagle, *the largest member of the eagle family, clings to existence in the rainforests of Corcovado and Gandoca-Manzanillo.*

Canopy Tours

Costa Rica is the world leader in "canopy tours," which allow active travelers to explore the forest canopy more than 100 ft (30 m) above the jungle floor. Facilities such as suspended walkways and rappels by horizontal zipline cable, which usually link a series of treetop platforms, offer a monkey's-eye view. "Aerial trams" (modified ski lifts) are a more sedentary option. Such experiences can be a fascinating way to learn about treetop ecology and compare various forest environments, from rainforest to montane cloud forest. Zipline tours are more for the thrill – it is unlikely that wildlife will be spotted while whizzing between trees at high speed. The one drawback of canopy tours is that they often disturb the local ecology, scaring away many creatures.

Treetop platforms *are usually built around the trunks below the treetop canopy, and are supported by branches. Some tours offer the option of overnighting on the platform.*

Aerial trams *operate like ski lifts, using similar technology. Naturalist guides accompany visitors on the Rainforest Aerial Trams (near Jacó and Parque Nacional Braulio Carrillo) and Arenal Rainforest Tram to educate visitors about forest ecology.*

All forest types in Costa Rica, from dry forest to montane cloud forest, host canopy tours. By going on several tours, visitors can experience diverse habitats.

Trails *with interpretive signs, found at most canopy tour sites, provide insights into life at ground level. Combined with the tours, they provide a broad understanding of the interrelationships between ecology at different levels. Most trails are slippery – sturdy footwear with good grip is recommended.*

Zipline tours *follow "trails," comprising a series of steel cables that run between trees or span canyons, and can exceed 1 mile (2 km). Sped by gravity, the visitor "flies" between the spans, securely attached in a harness.*

LOCATIONS OF THE BEST CANOPY TOURS

- Bahía Culebra *see p186*
- Bahía Drake *see p238*
- Jacó *see p164*
- Laguna de Arenal *see p199*
- Monteverde *see pp174–8*
- Montezuma *see p162*
- Pacific Rainforest Aerial Tram *see p165*
- PN Rincón de la Vieja *see p182*
- Rainforest Aerial Tram *see p209*
- Tabacón *see p198*
- Termales del Bosque *see pp204–5*
- Veragua Rainforest Research and Adventure Park *see p218*

Towers and cables made of reinforced concrete and steel are built to the highest standards according to government regulations.

Suspended walkways *held aloft by steel cables permit the best wildlife viewing. Visitors can follow their own pace and stop at will to watch a creature. Many sites have "trails" formed from a series of walkways.*

Visitors' centers are located at some sites, and often feature restaurants, exhibits, and gift stores.

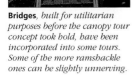

Bridges, *built for utilitarian purposes before the canopy tour concept took hold, have been incorporated into some tours. Some of the more ramshackle ones can be slightly unnerving.*

THE BEGINNINGS

The American scientist Dr. Donald Perry pioneered the concept of the "canopy biologist" in the 1970s, when he developed a system of ropes, pulleys, and a radio-controlled cage to move through the treetops at his research site near Rara Avis. Perry's successful "automated web" led him to eventually build an aerial tram that would permit the public the same privileged access for educational purposes.

Dr. Donald Perry exploring the forest canopy at Rara Avis

Beaches of Costa Rica

Most of Costa Rica's shoreline, which extends for 800 miles (1,290 km), is lined with beaches in a range of colors, from sugar white to varying shades of gray and brown. On the straight Caribbean coast, beaches stretch for miles, while the ones on the serrated Pacific coast are separated by rocky headlands. In most places, thick forest edges right up to the shore, lending a dramatic beauty to even the dullest brown sands. The coastal waters are relatively murky due to silt washed down by numerous rivers and there are few coral reefs. Beaches run the gamut from developed areas, with resorts and various amenities, to isolated, virtually undiscovered stretches of sand. Dozens of beaches offer great swimming and surfing *(see p187)*.

Playa Naranjo, *hemmed by tropical dry forest, is difficult to access, but offers tremendous wildlife viewing, including sightings of leatherback turtles. Mangroves nearby harbor caimans and crocodiles (see p187).*

Playa Conchal, or "Shell Beach," is acclaimed for its snow-white beach, comprised of billions of minute seashells. The turquoise waters are unusually clear *(see p186)*.

Playa Flamingo
(see p186)

Los Chiles

THE NORTHERN ZONE

• Liberia

GUANACASTE AND
NORTHERN NICOYA

La Fortuna •

Ciudad
Quesada
(San Carlos)

Playas del Coco
(see p186)

Nicoya •

• Puntarenas

THE CENTRAL PACIFIC
AND SOUTHERN NICOYA

Playa Ostional is one of about 12 beaches worldwide where endangered Pacific ridley turtles crawl ashore en masse to nest *(see p190)*.

Playa Jacó, popular with surfers and lined with hotels, is a lively beach resort *(see p164)*.

Playa Grande *is Costa Rica's most important nesting site for leatherback turtles. This long, scalloped beach of coral-gray sands is also a famed surfing destination, attracting hundreds of surfers every year* (see p186).

Playa Montezuma is a beautiful, coconut-fringed, cream-colored beach. Its rough waters are unsafe for swimming *(see p162)*.

Playa Guiones is *several miles long and extremely deep at low tide* (see p190). *It has tidepools, and it has been identified as a site of* arribadas (see p191) *of Pacific ridley turtles.*

Playa Carrillo is *virtually undeveloped, despite the hotels dotting the nearby hills. Fishing boats gather in a cove at the southern end of this palm-shaded beach, which is backed by an airstrip.*

Tortuguero's beach *is an unbroken, 23-mile (37-km) long stretch of gray sand backed by forest. It is a prime nesting site for green turtles, who emerge glistening from the surf to lay eggs in the sand (see p217).*

Cahuita's beaches – *Playa Negra with its black sands and the golden Playa Blanca – are edged by rainforest. The forest and the coral reef bordering Playa Blanca are protected within Parque Nacional Cahuita (see p218).*

Playa Cocles *is a popular surfing center. Splendidly scenic, it is perfect for sunbathing, although swimmers should beware the riptides.*

Tortuguero

Puerto Viejo de Sarapiquí

THE CARIBBEAN

lajuela
●Heredia

Puerto Limón

SAN ●Cartago
JOSÉ

THE CENTRAL HIGHLANDS

0 km   25
0 miles   25

●Quepos

San Isidro de El General

THE SOUTHERN ZONE

Playa Zancudo has miles of gray sand and excellent surf *(see p240).*

Playa Manuel Antonio *(see p168)*

Golfito●
Puerto Jiménez●

Bahía Ballena is an unspoilt bay fringed with a mile (1.6-km) long gray sand beach. Dolphins and whales congregate offshore, where a coral reef offers fine snorkeling.

Gandoca-Manzanillo, *a remote reserve with gray-black beaches, also contains swamps and mangroves inhabited by crocodiles, manatees, and varieties of birds. Four species of marine turtles nest in the beach sands (see p220).*

The Story of Costa Rican Coffee

A cup of Costa Rican coffee

Costa Rica is famed for its flavorful coffee. *Coffea arabica* – a bush native to Ethiopia – was introduced to the country in 1779. For more than a century, beginning in the 1830s, the *grano de oro* (golden grain) was Costa Rica's foremost export, funding the construction of fine buildings. The nation's mountains provide ideal conditions for the coffee plant, which prefers consistently warm temperatures, distinct wet and dry seasons, and fertile, well-drained slopes. More than 425 sq miles (1,100 sq km), concentrated in the Central Highlands, are dedicated to coffee production.

Guided tours *of plantations and* beneficios *(processing factories) give visitors a chance to see beans being processed, as well as offering demonstrations of "cupping" (tasting).*

COFFEE PLANTATIONS

After being raised in nurseries, 8 to 12 month-old coffee seedlings are planted beneath shade trees in long rows perpendicular to the slope to help avoid soil erosion. They require precise amounts of sunlight, water, and fertilizer.

Coffee seedlings ready to be planted

Worker weeding in a coffee plantation

Shade trees allow the proper amount of sunlight to filter through.

Elevations between 2,650 and 4,900 ft (800–1,500 m) are ideal for coffee estates.

The volcanic soil contains the nutrients that coffee bushes require.

THE EARLY DAYS

Before the construction of the railroads in the late 19th century, coffee beans were packed in gunny sacks and transported to the port of Puntarenas in *carretas* (oxcarts). Trains of oxcarts loaded with coffee traveled down the mountains of Costa Rica in convoys. From Puntarenas, the beans were shipped to Europe, a journey that took three months.

Carreta **(oxcart) transporting sacks of coffee**

BERRIES TO BEANS

Typically it takes four years for the shiny-leafed coffee bush to mature and fruit. With the arrival of the rains in early May, small white blossoms appear, giving off a jasmine-like scent. The fleshy green berries containing the beans gradually turn red as they ripen. Each berry contains two hemispherical seeds, or beans. Well-tended bushes produce *cerezas* (cherries) for about 40 years.

White coffee
blossoms

Green and red
berries

The harvest normally begins in November. Traditionally, entire families would head into the fields to help with harvesting. Although children can still be seen picking coffee, today Nicaraguans and indigenous peoples form the majority of the labor pool.

The red berries are hand-picked by workers.

Handwoven wicker baskets are usually used to hold the berries.

Coffee workers *wait in line to measure baskets of freshly harvested coffee. The berries are shipped to a* beneficio *for processing.*

At the beneficio, *the berries are cleaned. The fleshy outer pulp is then stripped off and returned to the slopes as fertilizer.*

The moist beans *are dried, either in the traditional manner by being laid out in the sun, or in hot-air ovens.*

The dried beans *have their leathery skins removed before being roasted.*

PACKAGING

The roasted beans are sorted by quality, size, and shape. Export-quality beans are vacuum-sealed in foil bags and typically come in light roast, dark roast, espresso, decaffeinated, and organic varieties. Lower grade beans for the domestic market are sold loose at local markets as *café puro* (unadulterated) or *café tradicional* (containing 10 percent sugar).

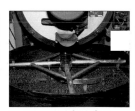

**Coffee packed
for export**

Roasted coffee beans

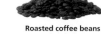

Different varieties of coffee

Ground coffee

Coffee bags

Coffee liqueur

The Indigenous Groups

Sparsely inhabited at the time of Columbus's arrival, the country today has 40,000 indigenous inhabitants, who account for less than 1 percent of the total population. They belong to seven main tribes – Chorotega, Boruca, Bribri, Cabécar, Guaymí, Guatuso/Maleku, and Huetar. Living relatively marginalized from mainstream society in 22 remote reserves, the tribes sustain themselves by hunting and farming; and some continue to create traditional handicrafts. The aboriginal way of life is under constant threat by missionary activity and by the government's habitual espousal of logging and mining interests over those of indigenous peoples. Few tribes speak their native language, and even fewer have been able to keep their religious traditions free from outside influences.

The Guatuso/Maleku *retain their language and customs. They are known for bark cloth* (mastate) *painted with the fingertips.*

The Bribri *today comprise 10,000 individuals, who cling to their collective faith in Sibú, the creator of the universe. They welcome visits to the Reserva Indígena KeköLdi (see p221), where some Bribri continue to live in traditional huts.*

Carved and painted gourds, called *jícara* by the Bribri, are used as vessels and objects of decoration by most indigenous groups. Pictured here is a Bribri *jícara.*

Motifs depict natural elements. To preserve tribal identity, names of the elements are carved in traditional languages as well as in Spanish.

Huts are thatched to the ground.

A traditional Bribri hut – a
windowless, conical structure

INDIGENOUS ARTIFACTS

Many of the traditional crafts of Costa Rica's indigenous peoples emphasize their relationship with the rainforest. Age-old techniques continue to be used in contemporary works. Crafts, clothing, and musical instruments of several tribes, as well as shamanic totems, are displayed in the Museo de Cultura Indígena *(see p205).*

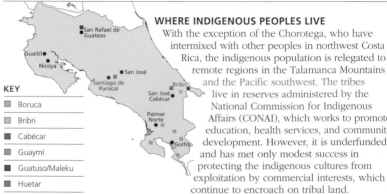

WHERE INDIGENOUS PEOPLES LIVE

With the exception of the Chorotega, who have intermixed with other peoples in northwest Costa Rica, the indigenous population is relegated to remote regions in the Talamanca Mountains and the Pacific southwest. The tribes live in reserves administered by the National Commission for Indigenous Affairs (CONAI), which works to promote education, health services, and community development. However, it is underfunded, and has met only modest success in protecting the indigenous cultures from exploitation by commercial interests, which continue to encroach on tribal land.

San Rafael de Guateso
Guaitíl
Nicoya
San José
Santiago de Puriscal
Bribri
San José
Cabécar
Palmar Norte
Golfito

KEY

- Boruca
- Bribri
- Cabécar
- Guaymí
- Guatuso/Maleku
- Huetar

The Chorotega *of Guanacaste and Northern Nicoya were the largest tribe in the pre-Columbian era. Today, about 1,000 true-blood Chorotegas live in matriarchal families, and take pride in their distinctive pottery.*

The Boruca *cling precariously to ancestral lands in the hills west of the Terraba valley. They are famed for their balsa-wood masks (mascaras) of animals representing supernatural beings, used in the Fiesta de los Diablitos (see p232).*

Chorotega pottery, *with its characteristic earth-tones, continues to be produced in Guaitíl (see p193).*

Designs are created by pecking tender green gourds with a needle. The residual skin surrounding the design is then scraped away. As the gourd dries, the skin turns dark brown.

The Huetar *of the Puriscal region still practice the ancient Festival of the Corn but in many other aspects have been integrated into mainstream society.*

Ulú (healing cane) used by shamans

The Cabécar *live in the Talamanca Cabécar Reserve (see p221) and today consist of about 5,000 individuals. Shamanic rituals remain an integral part of Cabécar culture.*

The Guaymí *retain a strong cultural identity, including the Guaymí language. Uniquely, women still wear the traditional garment with decorative triangular patterns, as well as collares (necklaces) of colorful beads.*

Guaymí painters *experiment freely with scenes of daily life, images of natural forms, and spiritual symbols.*

Traditional Guaymí dress

COSTA RICA THROUGH THE YEAR

A major factor in planning a visit to Costa Rica is the weather. The dry season (December–April) offers the best climate and draws the most visitors. Christmas and New Year, as well as Easter, when Costa Rica celebrates its most colorful festivals, are the peak periods: schools and offices close, and the nation goes on holiday. Late April and May are relatively less crowded. Promoted by the tourism department as the "green" season, the wet months (May–November) see fewer visitors

Ticos in traditional dress

and lower prices: for those willing to brave the rains, this is a good time to visit. Religious ceremonies and folk festivities are held year-round, though the celebrations usually lack the color and vitality of Mexico and Guatemala. *Topes* (horse shows) and rodeos are the staples of provincial events. Note that while many rodeos include bull-baiting, visitors can choose not to view the events. The Caribbean moves to its own beat, and a strong Afro-Caribbean heritage influences its festivities.

Floats depicting Costa Rican fauna, Fiesta de la Luz, San José

DRY SEASON

The cooler, drier months are ideal for beach holidays, especially in Guanacaste and Northern Nicoya, where it hardly rains. Town squares are ablaze with jacaranda and flame-of-the-forest. With coastal waters in the south at their clearest, scuba diving is excellent. Wildlife viewing is also at its best, with deciduous trees dropping their leaves. Dirt roads with river fordings are more easily passed, although off-road driving can kick up billowing clouds of dust. However, this is peak season throughout the nation, with high prices and fully booked hotels and car rentals.

DECEMBER

Fiesta de los Negritos
(Dec 8), Boruca. The indigenous Boruca peoples celebrate their traditions with costumed dancing and drum and flute music.
Fiesta de la Yegüita *(Dec 12)*, Nicoya. The Festival of the Little Mare recalls a Chorotega legend and blends Indian and Catholic rituals. Villagers carry an image of La Virgen de Guadalupe in procession, and there are *corridas de toros* (bull runs), as well as fireworks and concerts *(see p192)*.
Los Posadas *(Dec 15)*. Before Christmas, carolers go house to house by night and are rewarded with food and refreshments.

Tope Nacional de Caballos *(Dec 26)*, San José. During the nation's most famous *tope*, the country's finest horsemen show off their skills in a parade of more than 3,000 horses along Paseo Colón.
Fiesta de la Luz *(Dec 26)*, San José. The nocturnal Festival of Light features floats decorated with colorful Christmas lights. The "Parade of Lights" passes from Parque Sabana to downtown via Paseo Colón. Fireworks light up the night sky.
Carnaval Nacional *(Dec 27)*, San José. Locals don costumes and dance in the streets to live music. A competition of brightly decorated floats is the highlight of the procession.

People dressed as devils at the Fiesta de los Diablitos

Carretas (oxcarts) gather for the Día del Boyero celebrations, Escazú

Fiesta de Zapote *(late Dec)*, Zapote. Citizens flock to this suburb of San José for the fairground, fireworks, *topes* and rodeos.
Fiesta de los Diablitos *(Dec 31–Jan 2)*, Buenos Aires and Boruca. Men dressed as devils rush through the two villages in the Boruca Indian community's reenactment of battles between their forebears and the Spanish *(see p232)*.

JANUARY

Fiesta de Palmares *(first two weeks of Jan)*, Palmares (near Alajuela). Concerts, rodeos, fireworks, and music highlight this festival, which also features fairgrounds and sporting events.
Fiesta Patronal de Santo Cristo *(mid-Jan)*, Santa Cruz. Rodeos, folk dancing, street festivities, and a parade of *carretas* (oxcarts) mark this two-day celebration honoring Santo Cristo de Esquipulas.
Festival de las Mulas *(late Jan)*, Playas Esterillos (near Jacó). Popular festival with mule races on the beach, as well as a crafts fair, *corridas de toros*, and music and dance.

FEBRUARY

Expo Perez Zeledón *(early Feb)*, San Isidro de El General. Cattle fair and orchid show, also featuring *topes*, rodeo, beauty contests, carousels, and displays of agricultural machinery.

Good Neighbors Jazz Festival *(mid-Feb)*, Manuel Antonio. Jazz ensembles perform at hotels and other venues through the area.
Carnaval de Puntarenas *(last week of Feb)*. Parade floats, street fairs, music, and dancing enliven this coastal city for a week.

MARCH

Día del Boyero *(2nd Sun)*, San Antonio de Escazú. A parade of colorfully decorated traditional oxcarts honors the *boyero* (oxcart driver). The streets come alive with music and dance.
International Festival of the Arts *(2nd week)*, San José. Theaters and other venues bustle with live theater, dance performances, music concerts, visual art exhibits, and conferences
Semana Santa *(Mar or Apr)*. Easter Week is the most important holiday celebration of the year, with processions nationwide, notably in Cartago and San Joaquín de Flores near Heredia. Costumed citizens reenact Christ's crucifixion in passion plays.

APRIL

Día de Juan Santamaría *(Apr 11)*, Alajuela. Marching bands, a beauty pageant, and *topes* are part of the celebrations honoring the young national hero who was killed fighting against William Walker in the War of 1856 *(see p43)*.
Feria del Ganado *(mid-Apr)*, Ciudad Quesada. The nation's largest cattle fair also features a horse parade and *corridas de toros*.
Feria de Orquídeas *(late Apr)*, San José. Hosted in the Museo Nacional, this orchid festival exhibits prize specimens, including some for sale.
Romería Virgen de la Candelaria *(3rd Sun)*, Ujarrás. A pilgrimage from Paraíso to Ujarrás terminates with games and celebrations to honor the supposed miracle attributed to the Holy Virgin that saved the town of Ujarrás from pirate invasion in 1666 *(see p150)*.
Semana Universidad *(last week)*, San José. The campus of the University of Costa Rica is the setting for weeklong free activities, including open-air art shows, concerts, and the crowning of the university queen.

The San José Symphony performing at a music festival

WET SEASON

The onset of the rains marks the beginning of the off-season. Mountainous parts are prone to landslides, and many roads are washed out. Nonetheless, mornings are typically sunny, while afternoon rains help cool off sometimes-stifling days. This is the best time for surfing in the Pacific, and olive ridley turtles begin their *arribadas (see p191)*. Sportfishing is also at a premium, especially in northern Pacific waters. Toward the end of the wet season, Costa Rica is at its lushest, and swollen rivers provide plenty of white-water thrills. The Pacific southwest is subject to severe thunderstorms in October and November.

MAY

Día de los Trabajadores *(May 1)*. Trade unions organize marches in major cities to honor workers on Labor Day.
Fiesta Cívica *(early May)*, Cañas. Cowboy traditions are displayed at *corridas de toros* and *topes*. Street fairs feature folkloric music, dance, and traditional food.
Día de San Isidro Labrador *(May 15)*, San Isidro de El General. A celebration of

Pilgrims at Cartago's Basílica de Nuestra Señora de los Angeles

the patron saint of farmers, with an oxcart parade and an agricultural fair.
Corpus Christi *(May 29)*, Pacayas and Cartago. The two towns hold religious parades and church services.

JUNE

Día de San Pedro y San Pablo *(Jun 29)*, San José. St. Peter and St. Paul are honored in religious celebrations around the city.
Compañía de Lírica Nacional *(mid-Jun–mid-Aug)*, San José. The National Lyric Opera Company presents a two-month long opera festival in San José's sumptuously decorated Teatro Mélico Salazar *(see p108)*.

JULY

Festival de la Virgen del Mar *(mid-Jul)*, Puntarenas. The "Sea Festival" honors Carmen, Virgin of the Sea, with religious processions, a carnival, fireworks, and a boating regatta.
Día de la Anexión de Guanacaste *(Jul 25)*. The annexation of Guanacaste by Costa Rica in 1824 is celebrated nationwide with music and folkloric dancing. Rodeos and bullfights are held at Liberia and Santa Cruz.
Chorotega Tourist Fair *(late Jul)*, Nicoya. This celebration of traditional Chorotega culture features artisan displays, indigenous foods, and several educational activities.
International Festival of Music *(Jul–Aug)*. International musicians perform predominantly classical music at venues around the nation.

AUGUST

Día de Nuestra Señora de la Virgen de los Angeles *(Aug 2)*, Cartago. Costa Rica's most important religious procession to honor its patron saint, La Negrita, draws the faithful from around the nation. The devout carry crosses or crawl on their knees to Cartago's famous basilica *(see p144)*.

Recorrido de toros (bullfight) at a fiesta in Parque Nacional Santa Rosa

A San José parade celebrating Día de la Independencia

Liberia Blanca Culture Week *(early Aug)*, Liberia. Cowboys come to town, and citizens don traditional attire to honor local traditions with music, dancing, and food.

Día de las Madres *(Aug 15)*. On Mother's Day, everyone honors their mother, who is usually taken out to lunch or dinner and serenaded by hired mariachis.

National Adventure Tourism Festival *(late Aug)*, Turrialba. Mountain biking, whitewater rafting, and kayaking are among the activities highlighted.

Dia de San Ramón *(Aug 31)*, San Ramón (near Alajuela). The local patron saint is carried in procession. Tico culture is celebrated with marimba music, *topes*, processions, and regional dishes.

Semana Afro-Costarricense *(Aug or Sep)*, Puerto Limón and San José. This week-long festival celebrates Afro-Costa Rican culture. Activities range from art shows and lectures to musical performances and beauty pageants.

SEPTEMBER

Correo de la Candela de Independencia *(Sep 14)*. Runners carrying a Freedom Torch from Guatemala travel from town to town, arriving in Cartago at 6pm, when the entire nation sings the national anthem. At night, children carry home-made lanterns in procession throughout the country.

Día de la Independencia *(Sep 15)*. Costa Rica's independence from Spain in 1821 is celebrated nationwide with street festivities, *topes*, and school marching bands.

Orosi Colonial Tourist Fair *(mid-Sep)*. Cultural events and exhibits celebrate the region's colonial heritage.

OCTOBER

Carnaval *(2nd week)*, Puerto Limón. Ticos flock to the coast for a vibrant, no-holds-barred, Caribbean-style Mardi Gras with parade floats, street fairs, live reggae and calypso music, and beauty pageants *(see p215)*.

Día de las Culturas *(Oct 12)*. Columbus's discovery of America is celebrated with cultural events throughout the nation, notably in Puerto Limón; the city's Carnaval culminates on this day.

A band at Puerto Limón's famous Caribbean-style Carnaval

Fiesta del Maíz *(mid-Oct)*, Upala (near Caño Negro). Locals craft clothes out of corn husks and make corn-based foods in a traditional celebration of *maíz* (corn).

Día del Sabanero *(Oct 18)*. *Topes* and celebrations mark Cowboy's Day. Liberia and Parque Nacional Santa Rosa have the most lively festivities.

NOVEMBER

Días de Todos Santos *(Nov 2)*. All Souls' Day is celebrated nationwide with church processions. Families visit cemeteries to remember loved ones and lay marigolds and other flowers on graves.

La Ruta de los Conquistadores *(mid-Nov)*. This week-long, coast-to-coast mountain bike championship, which aims to retrace the route of the Spanish conquerors across Costa Rica, is considered one of the world's most challenging.

Feria Agroecoturística *(mid-Nov)*, Atenas (near Alajuela). Log-felling contests, tractor tours, horseback rides, and an orchid show at the Escuela de Ganadería reserve.

Fiesta de las Carretas *(late Nov)*, San José. Oxcarts are paraded from Parque Sabana and along Paseo Colón.

The Climate of Costa Rica

Most of Costa Rica experiences distinct dry (December–April) and wet (May–November) seasons, which Ticos call *verano* (summer) and *invierno* (winter). There are dozens of regional microclimates: San José and the *meseta central* (central plateau) are delightfully warm year-round; the eastern lowlands are swept by rain-laden Caribbean breezes; the southern Pacific coast has high precipitation; and in the dry season temperatures regularly rise above 35° C (94° F) in the parched northwest. Temperatures are affected by the varying altitudes, and can drop to below 0° C (32° F) on mountain summits. However, the sun is strong at all times of the year across Costa Rica, with sunrise at about 6am and sunset at 6pm.

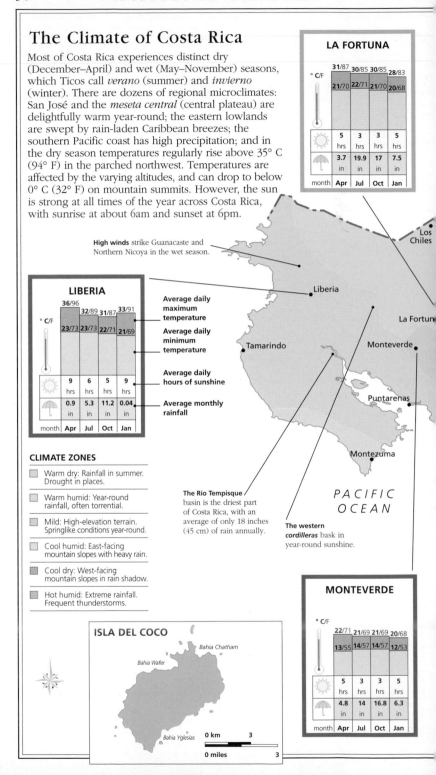

LA FORTUNA

° C/F			
31/87	30/85	30/85	28/83
21/70	22/71	21/70	20/68
5 hrs	3 hrs	3 hrs	5 hrs
3.7 in	19.9 in	17 in	7.5 in
month Apr	Jul	Oct	Jan

Los Chiles

High winds strike Guanacaste and Northern Nicoya in the wet season.

Liberia

La Fortuna

Monteverde

LIBERIA

° C/F			
36/96	32/89	31/87	33/91
23/73	23/73	22/71	21/69
9 hrs	6 hrs	5 hrs	9 hrs
0.9 in	5.3 in	11.2 in	0.04 in
month Apr	Jul	Oct	Jan

Average daily maximum temperature

Average daily minimum temperature

Average daily hours of sunshine

Average monthly rainfall

Tamarindo

Puntarenas

CLIMATE ZONES

- Warm dry: Rainfall in summer. Drought in places.
- Warm humid: Year-round rainfall, often torrential.
- Mild: High-elevation terrain. Springlike conditions year-round.
- Cool humid: East-facing mountain slopes with heavy rain.
- Cool dry: West-facing mountain slopes in rain shadow.
- Hot humid: Extreme rainfall. Frequent thunderstorms.

The Río Tempisque basin is the driest part of Costa Rica, with an average of only 18 inches (45 cm) of rain annually.

Montezuma

PACIFIC OCEAN

The western *cordilleras* bask in year-round sunshine.

ISLA DEL COCO

Bahía Chatham

Bahía Wafer

Bahía Yglesias

0 km		3
0 miles		3

MONTEVERDE

° C/F			
22/71	21/69	21/69	20/68
13/55	14/57	14/57	12/53
5 hrs	3 hrs	3 hrs	5 hrs
4.8 in	14 in	16.8 in	6.3 in
month Apr	Jul	Oct	Jan

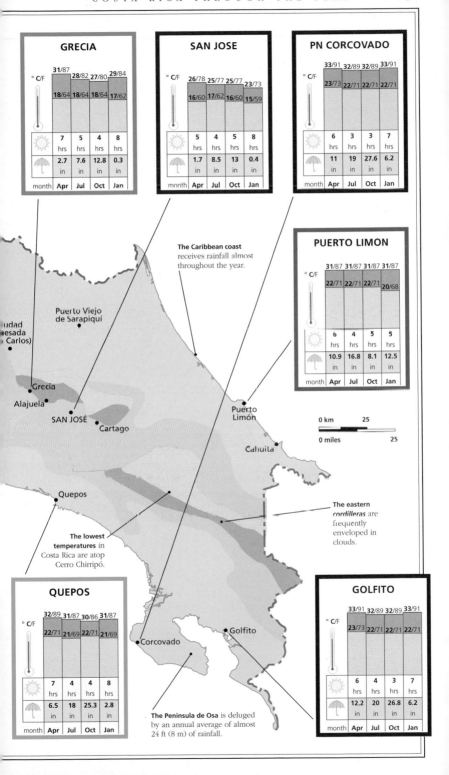

GRECIA

°C/F			
31/87	**28**/82	**27**/80	**29**/84
18/64	**18**/64	**18**/64	**17**/62
7 hrs	5 hrs	4 hrs	8 hrs
2.7 in	7.6 in	12.8 in	0.3 in
month Apr	Jul	Oct	Jan

SAN JOSE

°C/F			
26/78	**25**/77	**25**/77	**23**/73
16/60	**17**/62	**16**/60	**15**/59
5 hrs	4 hrs	5 hrs	8 hrs
1.7 in	8.5 in	13 in	0.4 in
month Apr	Jul	Oct	Jan

PN CORCOVADO

°C/F			
33/91	**32**/89	**32**/89	**33**/91
23/73	**22**/71	**22**/71	**22**/71
6 hrs	3 hrs	3 hrs	7 hrs
11 in	19 in	27.6 in	6.2 in
month Apr	Jul	Oct	Jan

PUERTO LIMON

°C/F			
31/87	**31**/87	**31**/87	**31**/87
22/71	**22**/71	**22**/71	**20**/68
6 hrs	4 hrs	5 hrs	5 hrs
10.9 in	16.8 in	8.1 in	12.5 in
month Apr	Jul	Oct	Jan

The Caribbean coast receives rainfall almost throughout the year.

Puerto Viejo de Sarapiquí

iudad esada Carlos)

Grecia

Alajuela

SAN JOSÉ

Cartago

Puerto Limón

Cahuita

0 km   25

0 miles   25

Quepos

The lowest temperatures in Costa Rica are atop Cerro Chirripó.

The eastern cordilleras are frequently enveloped in clouds.

QUEPOS

°C/F			
32/89	**31**/87	**30**/86	**31**/87
22/71	**21**/69	**22**/71	**21**/69
7 hrs	4 hrs	4 hrs	8 hrs
6.5 in	18 in	25.3 in	2.8 in
month Apr	Jul	Oct	Jan

Corcovado

Golfito

The Peninsula de Osa is deluged by an annual average of almost 24 ft (8 m) of rainfall.

GOLFITO

°C/F			
33/91	**32**/89	**32**/89	**33**/91
23/73	**22**/71	**22**/71	**22**/71
6 hrs	4 hrs	3 hrs	7 hrs
12.2 in	20 in	26.8 in	6.2 in
month Apr	Jul	Oct	Jan

THE HISTORY OF COSTA RICA

C ontemporary Costa Rica has been shaped by a relatively benign history devoid of the great clash between pre-Columbian and Spanish cultures that characterized the formative period of neighboring nations. Following the colonial era, Costa Rica evolved stable democratic institutions that permitted sustained economic development. The nation's declaration of neutrality in 1948 continues to help forge its identity today.

When Christopher Columbus landed off the coast of Central America in 1502, the region had a history that went back 10 millennia. The indigenous peoples who inhabited the thickly forested and rugged terrain were relatively isolated from the more advanced and densely populated imperial cultures of Meso-America to the north and the Andes to the south. They were divided into several distinct ethnic groups and further subdivided into competing tribes ruled by *caciques* (chiefs). These peoples left no written record.

Pre-Columbian hunter

The semi-nomadic Chibchas and Diquis, who occupied the southern Pacific shores, were hunters and fishermen. They were expert goldsmiths as well, and also produced granite spheres of varying sizes for ceremonial purposes. The highland valleys were the domain of the Coribicí, subsistence agriculturalists skilled at using the "lost wax" technique to create gold ornaments. These groups had affinities with the Andean cultures, with whom they traded. The Votos of the northern lowlands were matriarchal and, like most other groups, used shamans to assist in the fertility rites that dominated religious belief. The agriculturalist Chorotega of the northwest lowlands were the most advanced. They traded with Meso-America, were famed for their elaborate jade ornamentation, and created a written language and calendar of Mayan origin. Most tribal names were ascribed by the Spanish and often indicated individual *caciques*.

Inter-clan warfare was common. Slaves from neighboring tribes were captured for labor and ceremonial sacrifice, while women were taken as concubines. Gold ornamentation indicated status. High-ranking individuals were interred with their wealth; their slaves were often killed and buried alongside to serve them in the afterlife. Each tribe lived communally in large thatched huts, and although modest urban settlements have been discovered, principally at Guayabo on the southern slopes of Volcán Turrialba, nowhere did elaborate temple structures result.

TIMELINE

15,000 BC	500 BC	AD 1	AD 500	AD 1000

10,000–8000 BC The first known inhabitants settle the region

800 BC Guayabo established on the slopes of Volcán Turrialba

Granite spheres

AD 400 – 1000 Diquis culture produces granite spheres for ceremonial purposes

AD 1400 Guayabo mysteriously abandoned

1000 BC Olmec influence extends southward from Mexico

Jade pendant

500 BC–AD 800 Jade is crafted into pendants and figurines using the cord-saw technique

AD 500 Gold begins to replace jade

AD 800 The Chorotegas arrive in Nicoya

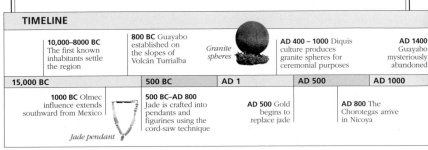

◁ **A detail of a fresco by Diego Rivera (1886–1957) depicting the Spanish conquest in Central America**

THE SPANISH CONQUEST

Columbus arrived in Bahía de Cariari, on the Caribbean coast, while on his fourth voyage to the New World. He spent 17 days in the land he called *veragua* (mildew), and his descriptions of the gold worn by the chiefs spelled doom for the indigenous population. Spanish conquistadors soon followed in his wake, driven by the quest for silver and gold. However, they failed to find any local source of the precious metals.

Colonization was initiated in 1506 when Ferdinand of Spain dispatched Diego de Nicuesa to settle and govern the region. Nicuesa's expedition north from Panama proved a disaster, as his troops were decimated by tropical diseases and guerrilla attacks. In 1522, a second expedition led by Gil González Davila explored the Pacific coast, converting the natives and seizing vast quantities of gold. Davila named the region *la costa rica* (rich coast). Many natives were enslaved under the *encomienda* system that granted Spaniards rights to native labor. Villa Bruselas, inland from today's Puntarenas, was Spain's first permanent settlement in Costa Rica, founded by Francisco Fernández de Córdoba in 1524. Davila's group and Córdoba's township, however, succumbed to tropical hardships and violent resistance by the natives. Despite this, by 1543, when the region was incorporated into the Captaincy-General of Guatemala, which extended from Yucatán to Panama, most lowland areas

Bust of Columbus and his son, Puerto Limón

had been charted and Spain's conquest was assured. Many natives were shipped to work the gold and silver mines of Peru and Mexico, while thousands died of smallpox, measles, influenza, and other European diseases that culminated in a 17th-century pandemic.

In 1559, Juan de Cavallón founded the settlement of Castillo de Garcimuñoz, with Spaniards, black slaves, and Indians brought from Guatemala and Nicaragua. Appointed governor in 1562, Juan Vásquez de Coronado penetrated the fertile Central Highlands and established El Guarco (today's Cartago) as capital of the region. For the next 250 years Costa Rica was a neglected colony of Spain, virtually forgotten by the governors of New Spain, based in Mexico.

THE SUBSISTENCE ERA

By the 17th century, the relatively small supply of gold had been shipped to Spain, and the country had nothing to trade. Settlement was

Theodor de Bry's (1528–98) copperplate print depicting gold being seized by Spanish conquistadors

TIMELINE

1502 Columbus lands on September 18	**1522** Davila successfully explores the Pacific coast	**1559** Philip II issues royal edict ordering the conversion of the native population	**1611–60** A great pandemic kills thousands	**1655** Spain closes port of Puerto Limón following pirate raids

1500	1525	1550	1575	1600	1625	1650

| **1506** Diego de Nicuesa named governor. Attempts colonization | **1542** *Encomienda* law repealed to little effect; indigenous peoples remain in servitude | **1563** Governor Coronado founds Cartago and explores much of Costa Rica | *Juan Vásquez de Coronado* | **1641** Survivors of a slave-ship establish a free community of Miskitos |

concentrated in the central valley of the interior highlands, where the absence of a large indigenous population and near total neglect by colonial authorities forced the Spanish settlers to work their own land. As a result, most of the land remained sparsely developed and agriculture existed at barely more than subsistence level. Moreover, the *mestizo* population (of mixed Spanish and Indian parentage) was small and the majority of inhabitants were predominantly Spanish. Thus, unlike the rigid feudal societies of its neighbors, Costa Rica evolved a fairly egalitarian social structure dominated by the independent farmer of meager means.

A 19th-century etching of Hacienda Santa Rosa, Guanacaste

The northwestern regions of Nicoya and Guanacaste on the Pacific coast were exceptions. Spanish landowners established large cattle estates here, and exacted harsh tribute and labor from Indians and *mestizos* through the *encomienda* and *repartimiento* systems. The densely forested Caribbean coast, meanwhile, was part of the "Spanish Main," the domain of pirates and smugglers, who traded precious hardwoods, such as cocoa and mahogany, through the small port of Puerto Limón (it was closed by the Spanish in 1665 to combat smuggling). All through the 17th century, English buccaneers such as Henry Morgan and

Buccaneer, 17th century

autonomous bands of Miskitos (a community of mixed-blood Indian and African slaves) regularly marauded inland settlements.

By the 18th century, exports of tobacco and hides to Europe began to boost national fortunes. Simple townships of adobe structures developed: Heredia (1706); San José (1737); and Alajuela (1782). Immigration from Europe gathered pace, and in the 1740s the increased demand for labor led to the forced resettlement of natives who had fled enslavement in the initial years of colonization and established communities in the Talamanca Mountains. On the whole, far-flung Costa Rica's parochial citizenry was spared the harsh taste of monopolistic, bureaucratic colonial rule; lacked an elite social class; and remained divorced from the bitter fight for independence from Spain that engulfed Central America at the end of the 18th century.

1723 Volcán Irazú erupts, destroying Cartago

1747 Talamanca Indians are forcibly resettled in the highlands

1808 Coffee introduced from Jamaica

1675	1700	1725	1750	1775	1800

1706 Heredia founded

1737 Villanueva de la Boca del Monte founded. Later renamed San José

1782 Alajuela founded

Coffee beans

THE FORMATIVE YEARS OF THE REPUBLIC

The news that Spain had granted independence to the Central American nations on September 15, 1821, reached Costa Rica a month later. The country was torn between the four leading townships: the progressive citizens of San

General Francisco Morazán

José and Alajuela favored total independence, while the conservative leaders of Cartago and Heredia preferred to join the newly formed Mexican empire. Although the four city councils met and drafted a constitution, the Pacto de Concordia, the discord erupted into a brief civil war in which the progressives triumphed. Costa Rica became a sovereign state of the short-lived Federation of Central America, formed by Guatemalan General Francisco Morazán. Under a law called the Ley de Ambulancia, the capital was to rotate between the four cities every four years.

Costa Rica's independence from Spain coincided with a boom in coffee production and the evolution of a monied middle-class dedicated to public education and a liberal democracy unique on the isthmus. Juan Mora Fernández was elected the first head of state in 1824. In 1835, Braulio Carrillo came to power. A liberal autocrat, he set up legal codes, as well as promoting a centralized administration in San José and large-scale coffee production. San José's growing prominence under Carrillo led

to great resentment, which culminated in the War of Leagues (La Guerra de la Liga) in September 1837, when the other three townships attacked San José but were defeated. In 1838, Carrillo declared Costa Rica's independence from the Federation, but was ousted by Morazán, on behalf of the emergent coffee oligarchy. Morazán was briefly named head of state in 1842, before being executed for attempting to conscript Costa Ricans to revive the Federation.

THE COFFEE ERA

Costa Rica's smallholding farmers benefitted immensely from Europe's taste for coffee. Thousands of acres were planted, while income from the exports of *grano de oro* (golden grain) funded the construction of fine edifices in San José. This economic prosperity went hand in hand with a rare period of aggression, starting in 1856 when William Walker, a Tennessean adventurer, invaded Guanacaste. President Juan Rafael

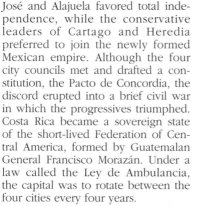

Costa Rican workers picking ripe coffee berries, woodcut, 1880

TIMELINE

1821 The Central American nations gain independence	**1830s** Coffee boom	**1835–7** Ley de Ambulancia establishes rotating capitals
		1837 San José becomes permanent capital

1856 William Walker invades Costa Rica

President Juan Rafael Mora (1814–60)

1820	1830	1840	1850	1860	1870

1824 Guanacaste secedes from Nicaragua to join Costa Rica

1823 Federation of Central America proclaimed. Civil war

1838 Costa Rica withdraws from the Federation, declares independence

1849 *Cafetaleros* elevate Juan Rafael Mora to power, initiating political dominance of coffee barons

1869 General Tomás Guardia establishes compulsory, free education for all

Mora raised a makeshift army that repulsed Walker but also created a group of ambitious, self-styled generals who from then on meddled in politics at the behest of their *cafetalero* (coffee baron) patrons. The most significant was General Tomás Guardia, who seized power in 1870. Guardia proved a progressive reformer,

Bas-relief in San José's Museo de Arte Costarricense

who promoted the construction of the Atlantic Railroad, which linked the highlands with Puerto Limón. The prodigious feat of hewing a railroad through the forested, rain-sodden, mountainous terrain was achieved by New York-born entrepreneur Minor Cooper Keith (1848–1929). Part of his terms for the project was a 3,100-sq-mile (8,050-sq-km) land lease in the Caribbean lowlands, on which he set up a banana plantation, and eventually established the influential United Fruit Company.

By the end of the 19th century, Costa Rica had evolved into a modern nation-state in which its citizens were active participants. When Bernardo Soto lost the presidential election in 1889 and refused to step down, street demonstrations forced his resignation. Similarly, students and women toppled war minister Federico Tinoco Granados, who staged a coup in 1917. However, the inter-war years were beset with labor unrest and social problems, which were exacerbated by a widening rift between the wealthy elite and impoverished underclass. Although the 1940–44 administration of President Rafael Angel Calderón established several bold social reforms, including a social security system, tensions rose as the country became increasingly polarized. The Calderón administration formed an anti-Nazi alliance with the Catholic Church and the Communist Party. This pitted itself against an equally unlikely anti-Calderonista alliance of intellectuals, labor activists, and the rural elite.

WILLIAM WALKER

In 1860, when he was executed, Walker was only 36. He was born in Nashville, and graduated as a doctor before starting to pursue a dream of extending slavery all over the Americas. In 1855, he rallied mercenaries and, with the blessing of President James Buchanan, invaded Nicaragua to establish a pro-US government. He went further, though, and proclaimed himself president. A year later he unsuccessfully attacked Costa Rica. Walker fled to New York, but returned to Central America in 1857, still filled with ambition. After a brief time in jail, he met his fate in front of a Honduran firing squad.

William Walker (1824–60)

	1890 Atlantic Railroad completed		**1917** Federico Tinoco Granados seizes power	**1925** Sigatoka disease devastates banana fields	**1940–44** Calderón sponsors social reforms and founds the University of Costa Rica	

Atlantic Railroad

1880	1890	1900	1910	1920	1930	1940

1889 Liberal constitution drafted

1897 A coffee tax finances construction of the Teatro Nacional in San José

1930s United Fruit Company expands its political and economic influence

1934 Workers win the right to unionize

1942 A German U-boat sinks a Costa Rican cargo vessel on July 2, leading to anti-German riots

THE 1948 CIVIL WAR

In 1944, Teodoro Picado succeeded fellow party member Calderón after a violent and fraudulent election. Calderón ran for office four years later, but was defeated by a journalist, Otilio Ulate Blanco. Calderón objected, and the building housing the ballots was set ablaze by unknown arsonists. The Calderonista-dominated Congress annulled the election, and Ulate was arrested. This explosive situation paved the way for José "Don Pepe" Figueres, a radical utopian socialist. On March 11, 1948, Figueres declared the War of National Liberation to purify national politics. The badly trained and poorly equipped government forces were no match for Figueres' highly motivated guerrillas and, after 44 days of fierce fighting that claimed about 2,000 lives, the government was toppled.

Figueres entered San José in triumph on March 29, and established the "Second Republic." He nationalized the banking system and enacted enlightened social reforms. In 1949, Figueres forced congressional passage of a new constitution that disbanded the army, declared Costa Rica neutral, and extended universal suffrage to the Afro-Caribbean population. Still, key opponents and communists were executed in a bid to further consolidate his power. After 18 months as provisional president, Figueres handed the reins of government to Ulate.

YEARS OF PROSPERITY AND TERROR

The 1950s, 60s, and 70s witnessed accelerating prosperity along with the rapid expansion

President José Figueres leading the parade of victorious civilian troops, San José, 1949

of the welfare state. Costa Rica's stability was severely threatened, however, by developments in Nicaragua, where on July 19, 1979, the Somoza regime was toppled by left-wing Sandinistas. Somoza's right-wing supporters, the Contras, set up clandestine bases in Costa Rica and were supported by the CIA in their attempts to overthrow the Sandinistas. These activities turned the northern border into a war zone. Meanwhile, Costa Rica's banana and coffee crops failed, while a transfer of capital out of the country led to an economic freefall. The Reagan administration pressured President Luis Alberto Monge to show support for the Nicaraguan right-wing paramilitary operations on Costa Rican soil in exchange for economic aid. Costa Rica's neutrality was dangerously compromised.

In 1986, Figueres' protegé Oscar Arias Sánchez became

Revolutionary soldier

TIMELINE

1949 New constitution adopted; Figueres later hands power to the winner of the 1948 election

1963 Volcán Irazú erupts during President John F. Kennedy's visit

1981 Costa Rica defaults on international loans

1950	1955	1960	1965	1970	1975	1980

1948 Figueres launches War of National Liberation

1955 Nicaragua invades Costa Rica but is repulsed at Santa Rosa

1950s Pan-American Highway (Carretera Interamericana) connects Nicaragua and Panama

Social security symbol

1970s Expansion of social security system

1980s Costa Rica-based Contras destabilize the country

president of Costa Rica. The youthful leader protested against the activities of the US-backed Contras, and negotiated a peaceful resolution of regional conflicts. As a result, in August 1987, leaders of five Central American nations signed a treaty committing to free elections and a cessation of violence. Arias was awarded the Nobel Peace Prize for his role as mediator. He was succeeded in 1990 by

Pedestrians crossing Avenida 2, San José

Rafael Angel Calderón, son of the great reformer. The conservative Calderón administration introduced reforms to alleviate the country's international debt. Austerity measures helped, to some extent, to regenerate the economy. In a curious twist of

fate, Calderón was replaced in 1994 by José María Figueres, son of Don Pepe, the elder Calderón's political nemesis.

THE ENVIRONMENTAL ERA

The 1980s had seen the beginning of a huge tourism boom, which was fueled by Costa Rica's stewardship of its natural resources. The government committed itself to environmental protection, but economic scandals, anti-government demonstrations, and a series of natural disasters bedeviled the administrations of Figueres (1994–8), Miguel Angel Rodriguez (1998–2002), and Abel Pacheco de la Espriella (2002–6). In 2004, Rafael Angel Calderón and Miguel Angel Rodríguez were arrested on charges of corruption. (In October 2009 Calderón was sentenced to five years in prison.) Meanwhile, in 2004, José María Figueres was forced to resign as chairman of the World Economic Forum for receiving kickbacks. However, none of this has slowed the development of Costa Rica's eco-tourism. Oscar Arias Sánchez successfully lobbied for a reversal of a law preventing former presidents from running for office again, and in 2006 he became the first ex-president to be elected to a second term. In 2010, his successor, Laura Chinchilla Miranda, became the first woman elected president in Costa Rica. Her early term has been marked by tensions with neighboring Nicaragua.

JOSE "DON PEPE" FIGUERES

"Don Pepe"
(1906–90)

Figueres, born on September 25, 1906, to Catalan immigrant parents, was largely self-educated. He studied in the USA in the 1920s, and returned to Costa Rica inspired by utopian ideals. After the 1942 anti-German riots, Don Pepe denounced the Calderón government in a radio address, during which he was arrested and subsequently exiled to Mexico. On his return in 1944, he set up a guerrilla training camp at La Lucha Sin Fin (The Endless Struggle), a farm high in the mountains south of San José, before launching the War of National Liberation. He founded the Partido de Liberación Nacional and was elected to two terms as president (1953–7 and 1970–74). He died on June 8, 1990.

Oscar Arias

	1990s Costa Rica established as a world leader in ecotourism	1994 Banco Anglo Costarricense declares bankruptcy		2003 Supreme Court rules that former presidents may be re-elected	2009 Large earthquake devastates Poás region	
1985	1990	1995	2000	2005	2010	2015
	1991 Earthquake in April causes great damage	1990s Large-scale immigration strains the social system. Drug trafficking accelerates.	2000 Attempts to privatize electricity and telecommunications generate civil unrest		2007 Costa Rica joins the Central America Free Trade Area (CAFTA)	
	1987 Arias wins Nobel Peace Prize					

WILD
COSTA RICA

THE WILDERNESS EXPERIENCE 48–57

FIELD GUIDE 58–97

THE WILDERNESS EXPERIENCE

Many come to Costa Rica to spot the resplendent quetzal; others for the thrill of close-up encounters with monkeys, sloths, and scarlet macaws. With so many diverse habitats, Costa Rica never disappoints nature lovers, largely because its wildlife is so abundant and easily seen. Visitors are captivated by a fascinating assortment of creatures that creep, crawl, prowl, and fly amid magnificent landscapes enshrined in national parks and reserves that cover almost one-third of this beautiful country.

Costa Rica prides itself on being one of the most biologically diverse countries on the planet. With a surface area of 19,730 square miles (51,100 sq km) and 801 miles (1,290 km) of coastline, this tiny tropical nation is barely as big as the state of West Virginia and only half the size of Iceland. However, Costa Rica boasts an estimated one million or more plant and animal species, including 10 percent of the world's butterfly species and an equal percentage of all known species of birds.

The graceful ocelot

By the late 1960s, after decades of severe deforestation and dwindling animal populations, an appreciation that something precious was being lost began to develop. Today, multiple ecosystems – and the vast diversity of living creatures they support – are protected within a network of almost 200 national parks and reserves. Costa Rica has evolved from being a pioneer of ecotourism – promoting ecologically sensitive visits with the purpose of viewing wildlife in its natural habitat into a world leader in this industry, with a dizzying array of tour companies specializing in birding and wildlife viewing, and an ever-growing number of Costa Ricans making a living as nature guides.

The wide range of options available permits visitors to stitch together a medley of distinct experiences and habitats. Whether it be viewing marine turtles laying eggs by night at Tortuguero National Park, or watching spider monkeys leaping through mist-shrouded trees at Santa Elena Cloud Forest Reserve, Costa Rica is sure to enthrall.

A diver photographing yellow tailed surgeon fish, Cocos Island National Park

◁ Walking along one of the many trails lining Monteverde Cloud Forest Biological Reserve

PRACTICAL INFORMATION

Tiny Costa Rica has such a rich diversity of parks and reserves – each with its own highlights – that it is easily possible to see a large percentage of its wildlife in as little as a week. Organizing and booking a visit is straightforward, since there are many reputable tour operators, both in-country and abroad, that can assist in planning a trip

A creek tour in Tortuguero

according to any budget and taste. The biggest difficulty may be deciding upon which regions and reserves to visit, and whether to opt for a DIY approach or go with an organized tour. Consider all available options before booking. The following pages will help you decide where to go, and serve as a guide to planning, packing, and preparation.

A skein of migrating ducks, Palo Verde National Park

Guides can be hired through tour companies such as **Wild-land Adventures**; and most, like **Karla's Travel Experience**, have their own website.

Alternatively, you can let a tour company take care of all the planning by selecting a package deal.

Always choose a guide or tour company licensed by the **Costa Rica Tourism Board (ICT)**.

PLANNING YOUR TRIP

All national parks and many wildlife refuges are operated by the **National System of Conservation Areas (SINAC)**; other refuges and reserves are privately run. The relevant websites – and those of tour operators that specialize in wildlife viewing – are invaluable when planning your trip.

If you wish to visit several parks while in Costa Rica, invest in the **Amigos de los Parques Nacionales** (Friends of the National Parks) card, which allows entry to up to 12 national parks.

Most parks can be visited by car, although many can

BEST TIME TO GO

Costa Rica is a year-round destination, but ideal conditions for wildlife viewing vary from region to region. Guanacaste is best visited in the dry season (Dec–Apr), when animals gather at water holes and many trees shed their leaves, providing better viewing of arboreal creatures. This is also the best time for birding: many migrants flock in from colder climates and waterbirds fill the wetlands. Because this is peak season, the most popular parks can be overrun with visitors.

Wet season (May–Nov) sees high rainfall throughout the country, and the landscape turns green and lush. Many trails become muddy, and accessibility to some areas may be restricted. Wetlands such as Caño Negro Wildlife Refuge flood, granting greater accessibility by boat. During prolonged rains it is possible to enjoy quiet time at eco-lodges, which often have scopes for close-up viewing.

GUIDED AND INDEPENDENT TOURS

Independent travelers will no doubt chance upon many animals during their time in Costa Rica; however, in many habitats, the dense vegetation makes it hard to spot reclusive or well-camouflaged wildlife. Hiring a guide can make all the difference, as they are able to discern and point out creatures that you might otherwise miss, as well as impart information on local ecology.

A group of youngsters on a guided tour of Monteverde

be reached only with a 4x4, and others are accessible only by hiking or by boat, such as the Terraba-Sierpe International Humid Forest Reserve.

Bring wildlife identification books and charts and a pair of binoculars. Insect repellent, sunblock, sunglasses, and a flashlight are also essential.

WHAT TO WEAR

Loose-fitting, lightweight, and quick-drying clothes made of breathable nylon or natural fabrics are ideal. Closed hiking shoes and long sleeves and pants help keep insects at bay; a hat will protect you from the sun. Natural colors let you blend into the background and avoid alerting wildlife. A warm fleece jacket and a windbreaker are essential for mountainous areas, while a lightweight poncho offers protection against the rain.

CHOOSING AN ITINERARY

Early morning and late afternoon are the best times to see wildlife. Come dusk, many animals such as monkeys bed down, and a different cast of creatures steps onto the stage, including bats, kinkajous, and frogs. Cats are also most active after dark, though seeing one is rare. The nighttime exploration of lagoons and wetlands by boat reveals crocodiles and nocturnal birds such as owls and the boat-billed heron.

National parks close before dusk, but several private reserves with lodgings offer night tours. Nocturnal hikes can also be booked via many tour operators and guides.

Children witnessing the slow progress of a leatherback turtle on a beach

PHOTOGRAPHING WILDLIFE

An SLR camera is preferable to a point-and-shoot, and a lens with high magnification is essential for getting good-quality close-up images. A tripod or a lens with image stabilization will help reduce the risk of blurred images.

Be patient, still, and quiet. Creatures are often present but unseen, and they may show themselves after they get used to your presence. If you get too close, animals will flee, although at Manuel Antonio National Park, monkeys and raccoons are so used to humans they can often be photographed at close range.

SAFETY TIPS AND HEALTH ISSUES

Always keep a safe distance from all animals, which can become aggressive if startled or if they feel threatened.

Crocodiles are present in lowland rivers, so do not swim there. Be aware of snakes – look down while walking;

avoid feeling under rocks or in crevices; and never place your hand on a branch without looking, as many snakes are arboreal. If you're bitten, stay calm, move slowly, and seek medical assistance at once.

Never feed animals, as this makes them dependent on humans and creates the possibility of you being bitten.

Drink lots of water to prevent dehydration. Anti-malarial prophylactics are required only in the southern Caribbean region. Outbreaks of dengue also sometimes occur there.

Many eco-lodges provide access for disabled visitors and, often, specially adapted toilets and accommodations.

TAKING CHILDREN

Although most children are thrilled at the sight of wildlife, they may quickly become tired and irritable after hiking in the heat of the tropics. Most wilderness lodges welcome children, and many offer special family programs, as do some tour companies, such as Wildland Adventures.

DIRECTORY

GUIDED AND INDEPENDENT TOURS

Costa Rica Expeditions
Tel (506) 2257-0766.
www.costarica
expeditions.com

Costa Rica Tourism Board (ICT)
www.visitcostarica.com

Journey Latin America (UK)
Tel (020) 8747-8315.
www.journeylatin-
america.co.uk

Karla's Travel Experience
Tel (506) 8915-2386.
www.tortuguerovillage.
com/karlastravelexperience

National Geographic Expeditions (USA)
Tel (888) 966-8687.
www.national-
geographic
expeditions.com

Wildland Adventures (USA)
Tel (206) 365-0686.
www.wildland.com

PLANNING YOUR TRIP

Amigos de los Parques Nacionales
Tel (506) 2263-4162.
www.amigos
delosparques.org

National System of Conservation Areas
Tel (506) 2248-2451.
www.sinac.go.cr

Safaris, National Parks, and Wildlife Reserves

Costa Rica has almost 200 parks and reserves that, combined, protect every environmental habitat. The first-time visitor faces a daunting array of options, ranging from the dry deciduous forest of Santa Rosa National Park and riverine habitats of Palo Verde to the dense rainforest of the Osa Peninsula, in the southwest, and the high-mountain páramo of Chirripó National Park. This brief region-by-region overview of the country's top national parks and wildlife refuges, including private reserves, is provided to help narrow down the options.

THE CENTRAL HIGHLANDS

The nation's most visited park, **Poás Volcano National Park** lies 34 miles (54 km) northwest of San José. Most visitors drive up to the summit to view the active crater, but there are also four hiking trails offering a chance to spot the endemic Poás squirrel, sooty robins, and even the resplendent quetzal. Visit as early in the day as possible to avoid the clouds that typically set in by mid-morning.

The crater at **Irazú Volcano National Park** is also accessible by car. At 11,260 ft (3,432 m), it is at the limit of the tree line, and visitors can experience dwarf oak forest and páramo. The flora here has adapted to survive howling winds and bitter cold. The volcano junco, black-crowned antpitta, and yellow-eared toucanet are among the bird species most frequently seen. Both Poás and Irazú have trails accessible to disabled travelers.

A 4x4 is required to access **Turrialba Volcano National Park**, farther east. Trails lead around the crater rim and even into the caldera. The volcano began erupting in 2009 and has been periodically closed since. Since there is no ranger station, visitors are advised to stay at the only lodge in the area, the Volcán Turrialba Lodge, which offers guided

hikes and horseback riding. Quetzals, jaguarundis, and red-tailed hawks are frequently seen here.

At the base of Turrialba, **Guayabo National Monument** protects the country's main archeological grounds. The 539-acre (218-ha) site is surrounded by moist montane forest and is a premier birding site, especially for toucanets and oropendolas. Trails lead past fascinating pre-Columbian petroglyphs; buy the booklet at the ranger station for a self-guided tour.

The altitude of **Braulio Carrillo National Park** ranges from 9,534 ft (2,906 m) at the summit of Volcán Barva to 118 ft (36 m) in the northern lowlands. Smothered in cloud forest at high elevations and dense rain-forest below, it is often beset by clouds. Most of the nation's mammal species are here, plus more than 500 bird species. Rain gear is vital for exploring this park, as it is for **Tapantí-Macizo de la Muerte National Park**, on the northern slopes of the Talamanca massif and accessed via the Orosi Valley. Spanning 4,462 ft (1,360 m) in elevation range, it has trails for all abilities. February to April are the driest months here.

THE CENTRAL PACIFIC AND SOUTHERN NICOYA

Cabo Blanco Absolute Wildlife Reserve, at the southwest tip of Nicoya, was created in 1963 as the first protected area in Costa Rica. It takes its name ("White Cape") from

The crater of Irazú volcano, in the Central Highlands

the cliffs whitened by the guano of seabirds, including brown boobies. The public can access only one-third of this refuge, where the moist forest provides a home for large populations of monkeys, coatis, and carnivores.

Nearby, the private **Curú National Wildlife Refuge** is a major nesting ground for marine turtles, but its habitats also include mangrove and montane forest. Scarlet macaws and spider monkeys are bred here for release to the wild. Visitors can ride horses or take guided hikes.

In the Central Pacific, **Carara National Park** sits at the transition of the dry and moist zones. Despite its small size, it is rich in both Mesoamerican and South American flora and fauna. Trails are wide and level, offering excellent wildlife viewing. This is perhaps the best place in the country to see scarlet macaws, and crocodiles abound in the Tárcoles River.

Sightings of coatis, sloths, crab-eating raccoons, and white-faced monkeys are virtually guaranteed at **Manuel Antonio National Park**, and the steep Cathedral Point Trail is good for spotting agoutis. However, the park's proximity to dozens of hotels means it gets crowded; get there when the gates open. Licensed guides can be hired at the ranger station.

Spider monkeys relaxing on a tree branch

reserves, which also have visitors' centers, dormitory-style accommodations, and shops.

Hiking to the summit of the namesake volcano is a main reason many people visit **Rincón de la Vieja National Park**. Fumaroles and bubbling mud pools on the lower slopes are easily accessed by trails through scrub and dry forest that shelters coatis, monkeys, and some big cats.

Guanacaste National Park is one of Costa Rica's most rugged and remote parks, with only minimal facilities. Access requires a 4x4 vehicle and hiking. Attractions include pre-Columbian petroglyphs at the base of Volcán Cacao, which is topped by cloud forest.

In the extreme northwest, **Santa Rosa National Park** is centered on La Casona, the most hallowed historic site in Costa Rica. The dry forest and coastal wetlands support

Brown booby, often seen at Cabo Blanco

an unsurpassed list of animals. Surfers flock here to ride the waves. Santa Rosa has campsites, but in wet season access to the beaches is sometimes difficult; a 4x4 is obligatory.

Palo Verde National Park is one of the premier wetland habitats in Costa Rica, drawing huge flocks of migrant waterbirds. This is the nation's driest region, and the deciduous dry forests permit easy wildlife viewing. Animals to look out for here include roseate spoonbills, wood storks, and crocodiles.

To the west of Palo Verde, **Barra Honda National Park** centers on a limestone massif pitted with caves. Above ground, trails lead through scrub and dry forest. A local association offers guided hikes; a guide is obligatory for cave descents.

Leatherback Marine Turtle National Park is an important nesting site for the eponymous turtle. The nesting population has plummeted, but turtles can still be seen on the beaches between October and March.

GUANACASTE AND NORTHERN NICOYA

The golden toad that inspired the creation of **Monteverde Cloud Forest Biological Reserve** is now extinct, and the park has become synonymous with the quetzal. Laced with trails, it is home to an astonishing variety of reptiles, mammals, and birds, including the three-wattled bellbird and emerald toucanet. At a higher elevation, **Santa Elena Cloud Forest Reserve** boasts some creatures, such as the spider monkey, not found at nearby Monteverde. Guides are available at both

A canopy walk at Monteverde Cloud Forest Biological Reserve

THE NORTHERN ZONE

Residents of **Caño Negro Wildlife Refuge** include neotropic cormorants, roseate spoonbills, and Nicaraguan grackle. The dry season brings millions of migratory waterfowl. Caiman abound in the wet season, when the area floods. Guided exploration is by boat from several eco-lodges.

The extraordinary **Arenal Volcano National Park** is one of the most popular parks.

Centered on an active volcano, trails weave among the lava flows, and its forest is home to many creatures, from ocelots to opossums. There are many activities nearby.

Far less visited, **Tenorio Volcano National Park** is accessed from the village of Bijagua. The summit is off limits, but trails lead to teal-colored thermal pools, and tapirs are sometimes seen on the mid-elevation slopes.

La Selva Biological Station protects 3,707 acres (1,500 ha) of rainforest at the northern base of the Cordillera Central. Over 500 bird species and 120 mammal species have been recorded here. Reservations are required to visit and join its obligatory guided tours.

THE CARIBBEAN

Requiring a 4x4 vehicle, the lush rainforest of **Barbilla National Park** extends up the slopes of the Talamanca Mountains. The ranger station has minimal facilities, and visitors will need to be self-sufficient. Poison-dart frogs are abundant and easily spotted, and the park is also home to a large number of snakes.

The watery realm of **Tortuguero National Park** can be accessed only by plane or boat. Cormorants, river otters, caiman, and monkeys exhibit themselves as if in a gallery to visitors exploring on guided boat trips from the many eco-lodges lining Tortuguero Lagoon. The beach here is the Caribbean's prime nesting site for green turtles, and night-

A sandy beach in Cahuita National Park, in the Caribbean region

time tours are a specialty. A true treat would be to see a manatee or a green macaw.

A canal connects to **Barra del Colorado Wildlife Refuge**, where crocodiles bask on mud banks, and the many broad rivers and lagoons boil with tarpon and snook. Most visitors base themselves at the sportfishing lodges.

Cahuita National Park adjoins Cahuita village – visitors can hop out of bed and enter the park within a few minutes' stroll. The park is blessed with beautiful white-sand beaches, a coral reef, and rainforest and wetland habitats.

Nearby, rugged **Hitoy-Cerere National Park** lies at the eastern foot of the Talamanca massif. Visitors must come with raingear, but on clear days the pristine rainforest abounds with frogs, reptiles, birds, and mammals.

One of the most important marine turtle nesting sites in the region, **Gandoca-Manzanillo Wildlife Refuge** encompasses swamps, mangroves, rainforest,

and a coral reef. Freshwater dolphins and manatees are often seen on guided boat trips. Parrots and toucans are also numerous. Many visitors volunteer for extended stays on work projects meant to save the turtle populations.

THE SOUTHERN ZONE

A bastion of tropical lowland rainforest, remote **Corcovado National Park** ranges from sea level to an elevation of 2,444 ft (745 m). Several lodges and tent camps lie at its doorstep, and camping is also allowed at the four ranger stations. Look out for squirrel monkeys, scarlet macaws, and red-eyed tree frogs. This is also the best place for a lucky encounter with jaguars, tapirs, and harpy eagles.

Piedras Blancas National Park, across the Golfo Dulce, is a smaller version of Corcovado, but with a less developed trail system. Lacking a ranger station, it is administered through the Esquinas Rainforest Lodge.

Cocos Island National Park lies about 310 miles (500 km) southwest of Costa Rica and is primarily a marine park visited by experienced scuba divers. The waters around Cocos offer a rare chance to swim with whale sharks, manta rays, and hammerhead sharks. Booby birds, frigate-birds, and several other bird species endemic to the island are other attractions. A permit is needed to go ashore.

In **Chirripó National Park**, hikers ascend through cloud forest to treeless páramo to

Arenal volcano, one of the most active in the world

summit Costa Rica's highest peak. Quetzals inhabit the forest, and cougars are often spotted on the high alpine plains. February and March are the driest months here.

Chirripó abuts the vast and mostly unexplored **International Friendship Park (La Amistad)**, spanning many ecosystems and extending into Panama. Visitors can access only a tiny fraction of this park, which is a haven for jaguars, tapirs, and other endangered mammals.

North of the town of Dominical, **Hacienda Barú National Wildlife Refuge** combines several habitats, including mangrove and rainforest. Hawksbill and olive ridley turtles nest here, and trails offer a chance to spot anything from tamanduas to tayras. This private reserve has lodgings and offers the chance to go on dawn birding hikes, horseback rides, or to sleep on a treetop canopy.

Humpback whales are the main draw at the **Whale Marine National Park** (Dec–Mar and Jul–Oct). Dolphins can be seen year-round in the near-shore waters, where kayaking and snorkeling are popular activities.

The park merges south into **Terraba-Sierpe International Humid Forest Reserve**, a vast mangrove system that can be explored on guided boat trips.

A jaguar, one of the most elusive mammals in Costa Rica

DIRECTORY

THE CENTRAL HIGHLANDS

Braulio Carrillo National Park
Tel 2233-4533 or *2266-1883.*

Guayabo National Monument
Tel 2559-1220.

Irazú Volcano National Park
Tel 2200-5025.

Poás Volcano National Park
Tel 2482-1227.

Tapantí-Macizo de la Muerte National Park
Tel 2206-5615.

Turrialba Volcano National Park
Tel 2273-4335 (Volcán Turrialba Lodge) or *2248-2451* (SINAC, San José).

THE CENTRAL PACIFIC AND SOUTHERN NICOYA

Cabo Blanco Absolute Wildlife Reserve
Tel 2642-0093.

Carara National Park
Tel 2637-1080.

Curú National Wildlife Refuge
Tel 2641-0100.
www.curu.org

Manuel Antonio National Park
Tel 2777-5185.

GUANACASTE AND NORTHERN NICOYA

Barra Honda National Park
Tel 2659-1551

Guanacaste National Park
Tel 2666-7718 or *2666-5051.*

Leatherback Marine Turtle National Park
Tel 2653-0470.

Monteverde Cloud Forest Biological Reserve
Tel 2645-5122.
www.cct.or.cr

Palo Verde National Park
Tel 2200-0125.

Rincón de la Vieja National Park
Tel 2200-0269.

Santa Elena Cloud Forest Reserve
Tel 2645-5390. www. reservasantaelena.org

Santa Rosa National Park
Tel 2666-5051.

THE NORTHERN ZONE

Arenal Volcano National Park
Tel 2461-8499.

Caño Negro Wildlife Refuge
Tel 2471-1309.

La Selva Biological Station
Tel 2766-6565.
www.ots.ac.cr

Tenorio Volcano National Park
Tel 2200-0135.

THE CARIBBEAN

Barbilla National Park
Tel 8396-7611 or *2668-5341.*

Barra del Colorado Wildlife Refuge
Tel 2709-8086.

Cahuita National Park
Tel 2755-0461.

Gandoca-Manzanillo Wildlife Refuge
Tel 2759-9100.

Hitoy-Cerere National Park
Tel 2798-3170.

Tortuguero National Park
Tel 2709-8086.

THE SOUTHERN ZONE

Chirripó National Park
Tel 2742-5083.

Cocos Island National Park
Tel 2291-1215/16.

Corcovado National Park
Tel 2735-5036.

Hacienda Barú National Wildlife Refuge
Tel 2787-0003
www.haciendabaru.com

International Friendship Park (La Amistad)
Tel 2730-0846.

Piedras Blancas National Park
Tel 2741-8001 (Esquinas Rainforest Lodge).

Terraba-Sierpe International Humid Forest Reserve
Tel 2248-2451 (SINAC, San José).

Whale Marine National Park
Tel 2786-5392.

CONVERSATION

Costa Rica suffered severe deforestation and a rapid decline in the populations of many animal species in the 1900s. The disappearance of the *sapo dorado* (golden toad) and the plight of the great green macaw highlight the vulnerability of the country's wildlife. The rise of ecotourism and Costa Rica's efforts to protect its flora and fauna have led to the

Three-wattled bellbird

creation of a network of protected areas. Occupying about one-third of the country, this network includes 34 national parks, 56 wildlife refuges, 14 wetlands, and eight biological reserves. These conservation areas are administered by the National Conservation Areas System (SINAC) under the jurisdiction of the Ministry of the Environment and Energy (MINAE).

Deforestation is fueled by agricultural and real-estate development

HABITAT LOSS

The main environmental threat to Costa Rica comes from deforestation. Large swaths of the nation's lowlands have been cleared of rainforest rich in biodiversity to make room for large-scale cattle ranches and cash crops such as citrus, bananas, and pineapples. Peasant farmers also clear virgin mountain tracts for their own plots, and coastal forest has been felled at a quickening pace since the millennium as a result of a frenzied real-estate boom. More than 60 species of trees are now protected, and no tree may be felled without a government permit. However, compliance with the law is often tenuous.

Other threats to the local fauna and flora include pollution from fruit plantations, whose fertilizers and pesticides are blamed for killing off coral reefs at Cahuita; the trawl nets of shrimp boats, which result in the death of marine turtles;

and the potentially lethal danger posed by uninsulated electricity cables, which unsuspecting monkeys, sloths, and other arboreal mammals use to cross between trees.

HUNTING AND POACHING

Hunting is legal in Costa Rica except in national parks and reserves. Nonetheless, illegal hunting continues even within protected zones such as Corcovado, where there are not enough rangers to ensure the protection of jaguars,

A leatherback turtle hatchling

peccaries, and tapirs, which are prized as trophy kills.

Culling tapirs and other large mammals threatens the jaguar population by removing its food source. Peasants consider wild cats and other large carnivores to be pests and often shoot them on sight.

Poaching for the illegal pet trade has contributed to the severe decline of parrot and monkey populations; and marine turtle nests continue to be poached for eggs, which are reputed by some to have aphrodisiac qualities when consumed raw.

CITES

The Convention on International Trade in Endangered Species of Wild Fauna and Flora (CITES) is an agreement that aims to regulate the trade in products of plant and animal species – from live monkeys to marine turtle-shell products – and ensure that such trade does not threaten the species' survival. Signed in 1963, CITES protects more than 33,000 species of flora and fauna worldwide. Costa Rican species listed as threatened or endangered include 16 bird, 13 mammal, eight reptile, and two amphibian species, plus dozens of plants.

CITES requests that any trade in listed products be done only with a permit. Unfortunately, many species are trafficked illegally, including

Great green macaws at The Ara Project conservation center, Alajuela

parrots and macaws, which are stolen from their nests as hatchlings and can fetch more than $1,500 on the international market. Many endemic orchid species are also at risk due to illegal poaching by collectors and smugglers – rare specimens may sell for $2,000 or more. As a result, the guaria morada orchid, the national flower, is extremely rare in the wild.

ENDANGERED SPECIES

Costa Rican law protects 166 animal species from hunting, capture, or sale, as well as all orchid species. One of the most critically endangered animal species is the leatherback turtle, which faces threats from fishing, egg poaching, pollution, and rampant development near its main nesting beach, Playa Grande. Other species in danger of local extinction include the three-wattled bellbird and the great green macaw. Efforts to save the macaw populations are now finally bearing fruit.

ECOTOURISM

The popularity of ecotourism has done wonders for conservation efforts in Costa Rica. Not only does it generate direct revenue from entrance fees to parks and reserves, but it also creates employment, serves as a deterrent to hunters and poachers, and fosters a strong conservation ethic within local communities. The economic incentive to protect, rather than cull, local wildlife is particularly evident at Tortuguero, a coastal community that previously lived by poaching turtle eggs. Today, former poachers earn their income as guides. Many private landholders have also been inspired to turn existing woodland into private reserves as a source of income, leading to an increase in the percentage of land under forest. Greater ecological sensitivity has also seen Costa Ricans successfully lobby against proposed gold-mining and offshore oil-drilling projects.

MACAW-BREEDING PROGRAMS

With a large range throughout Central and South America, the scarlet macaw is considered a species of least concern. However, it has disappeared from many parts of Costa Rica, and the great green macaw is also listed as endangered. Several private initiatives have been set up to reverse the dramatic decline in population by breeding macaws for release into the wild as sustainable-size flocks, including in areas from which they have disappeared. The organizations leading these efforts include:
• The **Ara Project**, which breeds both green and scarlet macaws and is attempting to repopulate the southern Caribbean with green macaws;
• **ASOPROLAPA**, a program at Tambor that has freed more than 70 birds since 2007;
• **Zoo Ave**, which releases scarlet macaws into the wild, mainly from Piedras Blancas National Park.

DIRECTORY

SINAC/MINAE
Calle 25 & Avenidas 8/10, San José.
Tel 2248-2451.
www.sinac.go.cr

MACAW-BREEDING PROGRAMS

The Ara Project
Tel 8339-4329
or 8339-2407.
www.thearaproject.org

ASOPROLAPA
Tel 8980-0594.
www.delfines.com/costa-rica-photos/asoprolapa

Zoo Ave
Tel 2433-8989.
www.zooave.org

A sign in Corcovado National Park asking visitors not to feed the wildlife

FIELD GUIDE

Costa Rica's national parks and other protected areas harbor an astounding diversity of wildlife, from large predators such as the jaguar to monkeys, sloths, and other arboreal creatures. Yet these mammals represent a mere fraction of what this country has to offer. Bird enthusiasts can look forward to sighting an enormous range of winged creatures, and there are also almost 400 species of amphibians and reptiles. No one knows the accurate number of insects.

The following pages are an introduction to some of the many wild creatures that inhabit Costa Rica. Some, such as the inquisitive coati and the gregarious white-faced monkey, can be seen daily in a wide range of habitats throughout the country. Others – including the wild cats, the furtive kinkajou, and similar nocturnal hunters – are more elusive and at best glimpsed only as fleeting shadows. Many creatures – such as marine turtles, humpback whales, and migrant birds – are seasonal visitors that arrive and depart at predictable times of year. The tiny Manuel Antonio National Park, in particular, is one of the nation's most visited destinations, and it is host to many popular favorites, including all four species of monkeys. While the main focus of this field guide is mammals, a more generic overview of Costa Rica's

Toucan resting on a branch

varied cast of amphibians and reptiles is also provided, along with a few dozen of the more conspicuous and memorable bird species.

Despite the profligacy of wildlife in Costa Rica, much biodiversity has been lost during the centuries since the Spanish conquest, and many species are disappearing at an alarming rate. Jaguars, once numerous in many national parks nationwide, are now close to local extinction, and the spider monkey population in the wild today also hangs by a thread. Many endangered species can be seen at breeding facilities that work to save the most critically threatened creatures from a similar fate. Others are displayed at live exhibition centers and at rescue centers that work to rehabilitate injured and orphaned animals for return to the wild.

The stocky and powerful jaguar, found in protected areas of Costa Rican rainforest

◁ A colorful scarlet macaw in the luxuriant rainforest

Costa Rica's Wildlife Heritage

Until about three million years ago, North and South America were not connected. As the Central American isthmus rose from the sea, insects, reptiles, and rodents used the emerging islands as stepping stones between the continents. When the two land masses joined, North American mammals streamed south and South American marsupials moved north. Positioned at the juncture, Costa Rica became a hotspot of intermingling, leading to the evolution of new, distinctly tropical fauna. The country's diversity of climates, terrains, and habitats has fostered an astonishingly rich animal and plant life.

FIELD GUIDE ICONS

- Diurnal
- Nocturnal
- Dry deciduous forest
- Lowland rainforest
- Mangrove swamp
- Wetland
- Montane forest
- Cloud forest
- Páramo
- Marine environment

Wetland
The spectacled caiman is abundant in Caño Negro Wildlife Refuge. It enjoys basking in the sun atop logs or mud banks.

La Cruz

Los Chiles

Aguas Claras

Liberia

La Fortuna

Cañas

Ciu Ques

Santa Cruz

Las Juntas

Nicoya

Miramar

Carmona

Puntarenas

Sámara

Montezuma

Ja

Dry deciduous forest
Howler monkeys, the largest of Costa Rica's simians, are easy to spot in dry season, when trees shed their leaves.

Cloud forest
The resplendent quetzal is the quintessential symbol of the cloud forest.

Mangrove swamp
White ibis roost communally in trees overhanging the nutrient-rich waters of mangrove forests.

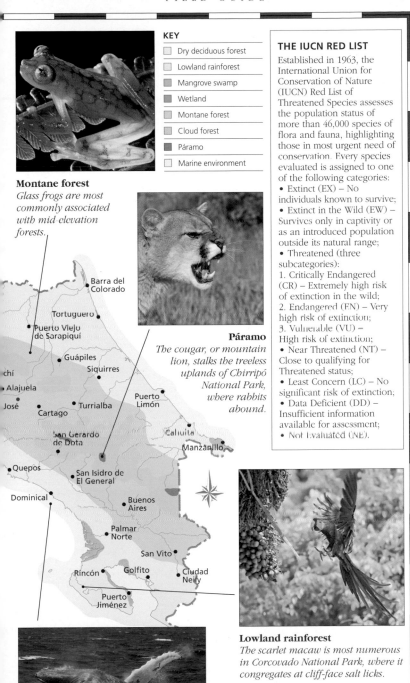

KEY

- Dry deciduous forest
- Lowland rainforest
- Mangrove swamp
- Wetland
- Montane forest
- Cloud forest
- Páramo
- Marine environment

THE IUCN RED LIST

Established in 1963, the International Union for Conservation of Nature (IUCN) Red List of Threatened Species assesses the population status of more than 46,000 species of flora and fauna, highlighting those in most urgent need of conservation. Every species evaluated is assigned to one of the following categories:
• Extinct (EX) – No individuals known to survive;
• Extinct in the Wild (EW) – Survives only in captivity or as an introduced population outside its natural range;
• Threatened (three subcategories):
1. Critically Endangered (CR) – Extremely high risk of extinction in the wild;
2. Endangered (EN) – Very high risk of extinction;
3. Vulnerable (VU) – High risk of extinction;
• Near Threatened (NT) – Close to qualifying for Threatened status;
• Least Concern (LC) – No significant risk of extinction;
• Data Deficient (DD) – Insufficient information available for assessment;
• Not Evaluated (NE).

Montane forest
Glass frogs are most commonly associated with mid-elevation forests.

Barra del Colorado

Tortuguero

Puerto Viejo de Sarapiquí

Guápiles

Siquirres

chí

Alajuela

José

Cartago

Turrialba

Puerto Limón

San Gerardo de Dota

Cahuita

Manzanillo

Quepos

San Isidro de El General

Dominical

Buenos Aires

Palmar Norte

San Vito

Rincón

Golfito

Ciudad Neily

Puerto Jiménez

Páramo
The cougar, or mountain lion, stalks the treeless uplands of Chirripó National Park, where rabbits abound.

Lowland rainforest
The scarlet macaw is most numerous in Corcovado National Park, where it congregates at cliff-face salt licks.

Marine environment
Humpback whales arrive from northern and southern waters to mate and birth off Costa Rica's Pacific southwest coast.

Cats

Elusive, solitary, and mainly nocturnal, cats belong to the Felidae family. Among the most difficult mammals to spot in the wild, these agile and stealthy killers are strictly carnivorous and feed on living creatures, from fish, rodents, and small birds to deer and tapirs. Each individual species varies in size and coloration, yet all cats are shaped like their domestic cousins, with round heads, keen eyes, and prominent canines; large paws with long, retractable claws; and sinuous bodies, plus long tails that aid balance. Most are well adapted to hunt both on the ground and in trees.

FAMILY

Costa Rica's six felid species are split into three genera: Leopardus, with small to medium-sized spotted cats; Puma, with two species, both with uniform coloration; and Panthera, with the jaguar representing big cats whose larynx modification permits them to roar.

OCELOT

(SPECIES: LEOPARDUS PARDALIS)

BEST SEEN: Cahuita National Park, Santa Rosa National Park

 LC

The largest of Costa Rica's spotted felids, this graceful yet secretive cat is widely distributed throughout lowland and mid-elevation habitats, from the dry savannas of Guanacaste to the rainforests of Corcovado. Called *manigordo* by the locals, the ocelot has a stocky body; it can grow to 39 in (100 cm) in length, and weigh up to 22 lb (10 kg). Its short, sleek, and golden or cream-colored fur is spotted with orange rosettes ringed by black and arranged in irregular chains along its back. Like its cousins, the margay and the oncilla, the ocelot has a black stripe on each cheek and twin black stripes running up its forehead, plus a black-banded tail. Adults are solitary and will often defend their territories – which they mark with pungent urine and feces – to the death. Like all cats, the ocelot has superb night vision, which it puts to good use when prowling dense forests in search of prey. More omnivorous than most cats, the ocelot will even feed on amphibians, fish, and small reptiles, although its main diet consists of small mammals, such as rabbits and rodents. Females typically give birth to a single cub – but, occasionally, two or even three kittens – every two years. Once hunted extensively for its fur and for the illegal pet trade (these cats are relatively docile in captivity), the ocelot is now considered of least concern on the IUCN list of endangered species and can be found in a wide area ranging from northern Mexico to the Tropic of Capricorn.

MARGAY
(SPECIES: LEOPARDUS WIEDII)

BEST SEEN: Corcovado, Tapantí-Macizo la Muerte

 NT

Less frequently seen than its larger cousin, the ocelot, to which it is superficially similar, the margay prefers a dense forest habitat, in which it is supremely adapted for life in the trees. This medium-sized cat has a longer tail and legs, and a smaller head with larger eyes, than the ocelot. An agile climber, it spends much of its time hunting birds and other creatures in the treetops, and it has evolved a special ankle structure that permits it to turn its feet 180 degrees. Capable of prodigious leaps, the margay can run headfirst down tree trunks and even hang from branches.

The margay, an agile climber adapted for life in the trees

ONCILLA
(SPECIES: LEOPARDUS TIGRINUS)

BEST SEEN: Braulio Carrillo, Monteverde

 VU

Almost entirely nocturnal and therefore rarely seen, this ground-loving forest dweller prefers higher elevations than its cousins, the ocelot and the margay. While at a glance it resembles the margay, the oncilla – or *tigrillo*, as the locals call it – is much smaller, growing to only 23 in (59 cm) in length. It also has a short, narrow jaw and is unmistakable thanks to its huge eyes. Heavily hunted for its fur, the oncilla is listed as vulnerable.

The forest-dwelling oncilla, a small nocturnal predator

A cougar, second in size only to the jaguar

COUGAR
(SPECIES: PUMA CONCOLOR)

BEST SEEN: Chirripó, Santa Rosa

LC

Known locally as *león*, the cougar is the most adaptable of the New World felids – in Costa Rica it is found in every habitat. This master of ambush stalks large prey such as deer but also eats rodents, reptiles, and even insects. Adult males average 8 ft (2.4 m) nose to tail. The cougar has the longest hind legs relative to body size of any New World felid, good for big leaps and short sprints of up to 35 mph (56 km/h). Its unicolored coat can range from silvery to tawny or chestnut, depending on its habitat.

JAGUARUNDI
(SPECIES: PUMA YAGOUAROUNDI)

BEST SEEN: Barra Honda, Rincón de la Vieja

 LC

Ranging from southern Texas to central Argentina, in Costa Rica this smaller relative of the puma is found in grassland, lowland scrub, and mid-elevation forest. It has a uniform coat, ranging from chestnut to dark chocolate, and an unusually long body with short legs, which have earned it the nickname "otter cat." Its ears are short and rounded, and its small face features piercing blue-green eyes. Although it purrs and hisses like a domestic cat, its vocalizations also include chirps and whistles. An agile hunter, the jaguarundi is diurnal, which makes it the most readily seen of Costa Rica's felids, often spotted darting across roads.

The jaguarundi, a versatile hunter

Key to Field Guide icons *see p60*

Jaguar

The largest land predator and the only Panthera species in Central America, the elusive jaguar resembles the African leopard, but it is stockier and more powerful. Although this cat can climb trees, it mostly prowls the dense forest floor. Adult jaguars require a vast range for hunting. Habitat fragmentation and illegal hunting have caused a decline in numbers, and today the jaguar is confined to a few protected areas in Costa Rica, notably in Corcovado, where fewer than 50 individuals remain. The "Path of the Panther" project aims to establish a migratory corridor along the jaguar's entire range.

Although adults *are mostly nocturnal and solitary, cubs spend much of their daylight hours playing and mock fighting with each other.*

FAMILY AND BREEDING

Like all New World cats, the jaguar is a loner. Each adult carves out a large territory for itself, marking it with scent trails. Females' home ranges (typically 8–15 sq miles/20–40 sq km) may overlap, though individuals avoid each other and chance meetings trigger an aggressive reaction. Males, whose territories cover 2–3 times the area of females, defend their turf against intrusions by other males, although actual fights between rivals are rare. Male and female adults generally meet only to mate, a brief and ill-tempered affair that can occur at any time of year. Pairs separate after mating, and females provide all the parenting. Cubs stay with their mother for up to two years before leaving to establish their own territory.

Females are fiercely protective of their cubs, *not just against external predators, but also against male jaguars, which often kill existing cubs when taking over a rival's territory.*

WHAT YOU MIGHT SEE

Sighting a jaguar in the wild is extremely rare. Nonetheless, fleeting chance encounters can occur, most notably on wide forest trails and on beaches when marine turtles are nesting, such as at Tortuguero and Corcovado National Parks. Exploring with an experienced guide may increase the odds of a sighting, but the movement of individual jaguars is highly unpredictable.

IUCN status NT: Near Threatened

Good swimmers*, jaguars stick close to water and like to cool off in lagoons and streams.*

A tawny coat *spotted with black rosettes offers excellent camouflage in the jungle.*

FEEDING

Jaguars are solitary nocturnal hunters who rely on stealth, not speed, to ambush prey. They eat a wide variety of animals, from agoutis to caimans, but prefer large ungulates such as tapirs and brocket deer. Jaguars that inhabit coastal terrain are also known to hunt marine turtles. Uniquely, they kill their prey with a bite to the skull using their huge canines. The jaguar's bite is the strongest of all felids – twice as powerful as that of a lion.

A jaguar's canines are strong enough to pierce even turtle shells

COMMUNICATION AND VOICE

Fearsome and furtive, adult jaguars rely on silence and guile to catch their prey and are thus not given to extensive articulation. When females come into estrus, they communicate their fertility by marking territory with urinary scents and by vocalizations, which range from purrs, mews, and grunts to the jaguar's characteristic hoarse, cough-like roar. Males typically emit a series of deeper roars, repeated several times, to advertise their presence to females and to warn rivals off their territories. Clashes between males elicit much snarling and hissing.

A fight between jaguars is punctuated by hisses and growls

KEY FACTS

Name: *Panthera onca*
Local names: *Tigre*

 Size Shoulder height: 26–30 in (65–75 cm); Weight: up to 350 lb (160 kg).

Lifespan 12–15 years in the wild.
Population in Costa Rica Unknown.
Conservation status NT.
Gestation period 90–105 days.
Reproduction Females reach sexual maturity at two years and give birth to litters of two to four cubs every 18–24 months.

 Habitat From dry deciduous forest to seasonally flooded wetlands and lowland rainforest.

A jaguar balancing on a tree branch

 Top places to see Corcovado, Santa Rosa, Talamancas, Tortuguero.

Sighting tips Look for the nesting sites of marine turtles and water holes, especially at dawn or dusk.

Friends and foes The jaguar's only foe is mankind. The main threats are deforestation, illegal hunting, and persecution by farmers.

 Facts and trivia A sacred animal for many pre-Columbian cultures, the jaguar featured prominently in tribal art. Believing it helped communication with the dead, ancient shamans would wear jaguar skins to summon the animal's power.

A black panther *is really a jaguar affected by melanism, or intense black pigmentation.*

A crepuscular creature, *the jaguar is most active around dawn and dusk, and it tends to sleep during the day.*

Adult males mark their territory *with urinary scents and scratch markings on trees.*

Other Carnivores

Costa Rica supports about two dozen species of non-felid carnivorous mammals, although most are omnivorous to various degrees. A few are easily observed, while others are highly elusive or rare – the olingo, for example, is a creature of the night and not likely to be readily seen. On the other hand, the raccoon and the coati are diurnal and often become quite bold in approaching lodges and tourists in the hope of being fed.

FAMILY

The gray fox and coyote belong to the Canidae family. The coati, raccoons, and olingo are members of the Procyonidae family, while the tayra and river otter are Mustelidae and are related to weasels.

The olingo has a dense, honey-colored coat

OLINGO
(SPECIES: BASSARICYON GABBII)

BEST SEEN: Carara, Corcovado, La Selva, Selva Verde

   LC

This bushy-tailed arboreal mammal, with short legs and small rounded ears, is strictly nocturnal. Lively and furtive, it lives in the upper forest canopy, where it feeds on insects, fruit, and small vertebrates. Its fur is cream on the belly and dark brown around the midriff, and its tail makes up more than half of its 35-in (90-cm) length. The olingo is a popular (but illegal) pet, which causes it to be poached from the wild.

WHITE-NOSED COATI
(SPECIES: NASUA NARICA)

BEST SEEN: Arenal, Cahuita, Manuel Antonio

   LC

The white-nosed coati (*pizote* to the locals) is a cousin of the raccoon and commonly seen in Costa Rica from sea level to an altitude of about 11,500 ft (3,500 m). Females and juveniles forage in bands of up to 30 individuals; males are solitary. The coati's chestnut body contrasts with its silvery chest and white nose, which is long and pointed. Ringed with black and white, the long tail is held aloft while walking, and it aids balance when climbing trees.

A white-nosed coati tucking into a banana tree

The tayra is as big as a medium-sized dog

TAYRA
(SPECIES: EIRA BARBARA)

BEST SEEN: Arenal, Braulio Carrillo, La Amistad

   LC

A forest-dwelling weasel, the tayra (*tolomuco*) averages 24–28 in (60–70 cm), plus tail. It is black except for a white throat, though its neck and head turn silver with age. Armed with large claws and powerful legs, this diurnal hunter is an expert climber capable of leaping between branches in pursuit of small monkeys, birds, and other prey. It also eats fruit, eggs, and honey.

NORTHERN RACCOON
(SPECIES: PROCYON LOTOR)

BEST SEEN: Cahuita, Santa Rosa, Tortuguero

   LC

Familiar to North Americans, the Northern raccoon (*mapache*) is found in most parts of Costa Rica. Mostly nocturnal, this omnivore also forages by day, using its dexterous front paws to manipulate objects. It can also rotate its paws backward to descend trees headfirst. It stands up to 12 in (30 cm) tall and has gray fur and a white face with trademark black mask.

Raccoons are highly intelligent and inquisitive

IUCN status DD: Data Deficient; LC: Least Concern

Crab-eating raccoons inhabit shoreline forests

CRAB-EATING RACCOON
(SPECIES: PROCYON CANCRIVORUS)

BEST SEEN: Manuel Antonio, Palo Verde, Terraba-Sierpe

 LC

Native to Central and South America, the crab-eating raccoon shares its Northern cousin's coloration, but its shorter fur gives it a smaller, leaner look. This coastal dweller favors shoreline forests, especially mangroves. Although it scavenges for birds' eggs, lizards, and fruits, its diet consists mainly of crabs and other crustaceans. Crab-eating raccoons are often seen begging or trying to steal tidbits from visitors at Manuel Antonio National Park.

The gray fox resembles a slender, long eared dog

GRAY FOX
(SPECIES: UROCYON CINEREOARGENTEUS)

BEST SEEN: Guanacaste, Rincón de la Vieja, Santa Rosa

 LC

The gray fox is easily recognized by its silvery coat, with white bib and rust-red underparts and neck; its large, alert ears; and its bushy, black-tipped tail. A stealthy, nocturnal predator, it hunts for small mammals and birds both on the ground and in trees, which it is able to climb thanks to the strong, curved claws on its hind paws. Although females expel males from the den after pups are born, the monogamous father continues to forage for food for his family. A territorial animal, the gray fox marks its turf with urine. The best time to see one is around dawn or dusk, and the best location is the lowlands of Guanacaste.

COYOTE
(SPECIES: CANIS LATRANS)

BEST SEEN: Palo Verde, Rincón de la Vieja, Santa Rosa

 LC

Opportunistic hunters, coyotes often pair up to kill rodents and ground-nesting birds. Their diet also includes snakes and large invertebrates. Closely resembling the gray fox, a coyote is more robust and stands up to 26 in (65 cm) tall at the shoulder, which is crossed by black-tipped guard hairs. A coyote's howl is often heard around dusk.

A coyote letting out its unmistakable drawn-out howl

NEOTROPICAL RIVER OTTER
(SPECIES: LONTRA LONGICAUDIS)

BEST SEEN: Cahuita, Gandoca-Manzanillo, Palo Verde, Tortuguero

DD

Known in Costa Rica as *nutria*, this sleek, robustly built aquatic mammal inhabits lowland riverine and swampy habitats, where it feeds on fish, amphibians, and crustaceans. The Neotropical river otter requires unpolluted waters and healthy riparian vegetation. It has short legs, a long body, thick neck, and a flat head with tiny ears and a broad, thickly whiskered muzzle. Its pelt is dense and sleek. Its heavily clawed, webbed feet and powerful tail provide propulsion in the water. You are most likely to see one at Tortuguero or Gandoca-Manzanillo Wildlife Refuge, where small groups are frequently spotted playing.

The Neotropical river otter has a short, dense coat

Key to Field Guide icons *see p60*

Primates

Costa Rica has four of the 53 species of New World primates, which are limited to a spectrum of tropical forest. They differ from their Old World counterparts in having flat noses with side-facing nostrils, plus (in many species) strong prehensile tails that can grasp branches and aid maneuvering through the treetops. The Costa Rican species are small to mid-sized, mostly herbivorous, and arboreal – only capuchin monkeys are adept at foraging on the forest floor. Intelligent and entertaining, primates also have a complex social structure.

MANTLED HOWLER MONKEY
(SPECIES: ALOUATTA PALLIATA)

BEST SEEN: Manuel Antonio, Santa Rosa, Tortuguero

 LC

Weighing up to 23 lb (10 kg), the mantled howler monkey, or *mono congo*, is the largest Costa Rican primate and the most widespread, present in most national parks and reserves. These monkeys are named for the male's extraordinarily loud and drawn-out throaty roar, emitted at dawn and dusk and to intimidate interlopers. The call is made by passing air through an enlarged hyoid bone to amplify the sound in the howler's balloon-like throat. The mantled howler is black, but adult males have a chestnut-colored mantle on their flanks and back. Its long, prehensile tail acts as an extra arm for gripping branches. The howler monkey eats mostly leaves, fruit, and flowers, and it spends much of the day snoozing to digest its low-energy food source. It lives in troops of up to 20 animals and is the most resilient of the monkey species to forest disturbance due to its small home range and low-energy lifestyle.

The male howler monkey emits a distinctive loud roar

A black-handed spider monkey swinging from a tree

SPIDER MONKEY
(SPECIES: ATELES GEOFFROYI)

BEST SEEN: Arenal, Braulio Carrillo, Corcovado, Palo Verde, Santa Elena

  EN

A gangly acrobat, the rust-colored spider monkey is named for its disproportionately long limbs, which are supremely adapted to life in the upper forest canopy. This monkey brachiates, or swings, beneath branches aided by its long prehensile tail, which is tipped by a palm-like pad and can support its entire weight. Its hands have long, hook-like fingers but only a vestigial thumb. One of several subspecies, Geoffroy's spider monkey has a black head and hands and a pale mask around the eyes and muzzle. Among the largest of New World monkeys, it can weigh up to 19 lb (9 kg). It lives in bands of up to 35 individuals but by day it forages for fruit and leaves in smaller groups. The spider monkey inhabits several forest habitats, from dry deciduous to montane cloud forest. It requires large tracts and is one of the first mammals to disappear due to habitat disturbance.

IUCN status EN: Endangered; LC: Least Concern; VU Vulnerable

WHITE-FACED MONKEY
(SPECIES: CEBUS CAPUCINUS)

BEST SEEN: Cabo Blanco, Cahuita, Manuel Antonio

 LC

This long-lived monkey is commonly called "capuchin" for its black cloak and cap and white chest, neck, and shoulders, which hint at the dress of the namesake Franciscan friars. Mischievous or malicious, depending on your point of view, this hyperactive and agile animal spends much of the day searching for food from ground to treetop, and it will snatch human belongings (such as bags left unattended on the beach) in its search for tidbits. An omnivore weighing 5.5–7.7 lb (2.5–3.5 kg), it eats everything from buds, fruits, and nuts to birds' eggs, insects, and small vertebrates. The white-faced monkey is the most intelligent of New World monkeys: it uses twigs to forage for insects, and stones to crack open crab shells; it even rubs itself with crushed millipedes to repel mosquitoes. Highly gregarious, this monkey lives in groups of ten to 35 members dominated by an alpha male and female. Territories tend to overlap, leading to hostile encounters that often result in infanticide by males that take over a group. The white-faced monkey is widely distributed throughout Costa Rica, where it lives in almost every kind of forest below 6,500 ft (2,000 m).

White-faced monkeys are easily identified by their coat

A squirrel monkey carrying a baby on its back

SQUIRREL MONKEY
(SPECIES: SAIMIRI OERSTEDII)

BEST SEEN: Corcovado, Golfito, Manuel Antonio

 VU

Handsome and tiny, the endearing squirrel monkey (called *mono tití* locally) is restricted in Costa Rica to the Central and Southern Pacific coastal forests, but it also extends into Panama. Unlike the other three local primates, its tail – which is far longer than its body – is not prehensile, and it is used purely for balance as the monkey scampers along branches on all fours. The most social of the species, the squirrel monkey lives in egalitarian groups of up to 100 members. Adult males share females, whose estrus is synchronized during a two-month mating season; rather than fighting, males engorge themselves to attract the females' attention. The squirrel monkey has short-cropped fur with an olive or orange body, white chest and face, and black mouth, hands, cap, and tail tip. Like the white-faced monkey, it is omnivorous but feasts primarily on fruit and insects. Being so small, it is preyed on by felids, raptors, and snakes. When predators are detected, male sentinels issue alarm calls, and the monkeys dive for cover. The species' population is recovering after a steep decline caused by deforestation.

Key to Field Guide icons *see p60*

Manatee

A large, lumbering marine mammal, the manatee is a placid aquatic herbivore and an exciting feather in the cap for nature lovers, who can encounter them in the backwaters of Tortuguero and Gandoca-Manzanillo. This distant relative of the elephant evolved from four-legged land mammals millions of years ago and today lives in warm brackish tropical and subtropical waters. Sometimes reaching lengths of more than 10 ft (3 m), manatees can remain underwater for long periods, surfacing for air at regular intervals.

A manatee calf can vocalize *within a few hours of being born, thereby establishing an immediate, strong link with its mother. Although fully weaned after about a year, a calf will stay with its mother for another year or so, to learn about feeding and resting grounds and travel routes.*

FAMILY AND BREEDING

Although generally solitary, manatees are sometimes spotted in groups. Females can come into estrus throughout the year, and about two years after giving birth. Like their cousin, the elephant, male manatees form ephemeral mating herds around estrus females and compete for their turn at copulation. Male–female bonds do not form. Females give birth to a single baby – or, rarely, twins – about 13 months after impregnation. The calf nurses from nipples located behind the mother's flippers. Mother and calf form a strong bond, remaining together for two years during weaning.

Gentle and slow-moving, *manatees face the greatest danger of injury and even death from fast-moving vessels. Every year, many of these plump marine mammals sustain nasty cuts from boat propellers and internal injuries from hull collisions. Boat traffic along the canals and lagoons of Tortuguero National Park scares them into the backwaters. Other threats to the manatee population include pesticides washing down from banana plantations.*

WHAT YOU MIGHT SEE

Visitors who explore the lagoons of Tortuguero and Gandoca-Manzanillo by canoe are often pleasantly surprised to encounter manatees, which sometimes emerge alongside the vessel for an eye-to-eye encounter. Manatees swim at a leisurely 3–5 mph (5–8 km/h) and often pause to float nonchalantly. However, they are also capable of swimming in much swifter bursts.

IUCN status VU: Vulnerable

The prehensile upper lip *is used to gather food and eat, much like an elephant's trunk.*

A manatee's paddle-shaped tail *is efficient at providing propulsion through water.*

FEEDING

A manatee's diet includes a wide range of plant species

Manatees are opportunistic browsers, with a varied diet consisting of more than 60 different aquatic plant species, including seagrasses, water hyacinths, and mangrove leaves. They spend the greater part of each day grazing and can eat up to 10 percent of their body weight daily. Lacking incisors and canine teeth, manatees rely on molars that, uniquely among mammals, are constantly replaced as they become worn down and fall out.

COMMUNICATION AND VOICE

Manatees use a varied repertoire of chirps, squeaks, and grunts to communicate with one another. Variations in pitch and tone have specific meanings – for example, short, harsh squeaks indicate anger or annoyance, while squeals reveal alarm or fear. Hungry calves squeak until allowed to nurse, while calves separated from their mum will cry until she answers – from as far away as 197 ft (60 m). Smell, taste, and touch are also used for communication: during mating season, male manatees caress females and utter excited squeals.

Manatees rely on a range of sounds to communicate among themselves

KEY FACTS

Name: *Trichechus manatus*
Local names: *Sea cow, manatí*

Size Length: up to 12 ft (3.6 m); Weight: up to 3,910 lb (1,775 kg).

Lifespan 55 years.
Population in Costa Rica 200+.
Conservation status VU.
Gestation period 13 months.
Reproduction Females first conceive at about five years of age, then give birth every 2–5 years until about 25.

Habitat Shallow, marshy coastal lagoons and rivers bordering the Caribbean Sea.

Resting at the bottom of a lagoon

Top places to see
Barra del Colorado, Gandoca-Manzanillo, Tortuguero.

Sighting tips
A trail of bubbles dribbling to the surface is a sure sign that a manatee is passing by below.

Friends and foes
Crocodiles may occasionally strike at manatee calves that stray too far from their mothers.

Facts and trivia
Manatees belong to the Sirenia order of animals, named for the beautiful sirens of Greek mythology. This is because the Spanish who first arrived in the New World thought these placid creatures were mermaids – that is, half-girl and half-fish.

Females in estrus *often beach themselves to avoid overly amorous male suitors.*

The manatee's thick gray skin *is covered with coarse hair and was prized by indigenous people for hides.*

Small, widely spaced eyes *are covered by a special transparent eyelid to aid underwater vision.*

Baird's Tapir

The largest Neotropical land mammal, Baird's tapir has a thick hide and huge bulk, which help protect it against its only predators – jaguars and crocodiles. Sadly, this shy, reclusive creature fares less well against illegal hunters. The remote heights of the Cordillera Talamanca are a rare sanctuary with a stable population, but elsewhere numbers are dropping: it is estimated that fewer than 5,500 individuals remain in the wild. Baird's tapir is therefore listed as endangered.

With a barrel-shaped body *and stocky legs, the tapir resembles the offspring of a horse and a pig. It has good hearing and a long, prehensile snout. Its keen sense of smell makes up for poor vision.*

FAMILY AND BREEDING

Adult tapirs mostly keep to themselves, although they are often seen with juveniles, and the bond between mother and calf is strong. Rival males fight to mate with a female. The excited winner initiates an elaborate courtship by spraying urine. The couple dances a quickening duet as they stand nose to tail, sniffing each other's genitals, before violent copulation in which each bites at the other. Females give birth to a single calf, weighing about 15 lb (7 kg). The calf is weaned for a year, then spends another year or two with the mother. Males do not contribute to raising their offspring.

The tapir has a thick, tough skin, *particularly on its hind quarters, and it is covered with short, bristly, tightly packed hairs. Individuals that live at higher elevations, such as the páramo of Chirripó National Park, grow thicker coats as protection from the cold.*

WHAT YOU MIGHT SEE

The water-loving tapir inhabits a wide range of habitats, from marshy grasslands and thick rainforest to high-mountain páramo. Chances of a sighting improve at marshy lagoons and high-mountain lakes, while tunnel-like tapir trails often lead to mud pools where tapirs come to wallow. If you encounter a tapir, keep your distance, as they alarm easily and can react aggressively.

IUCN status EN: Endangered

Tapirs enjoy cooling off *in lakes and pools. Only their head remains above water.*

Dark- or olive-brown, *tapirs have a cream-colored throat and white-tipped ears.*

FEEDING

A tapir feeding on leaves in the forest undergrowth

Baird's tapir is a grazer-browser that feeds primarily at twilight and by night, using its prehensile snout to forage for and pluck leaves and fruit. Its preferred diet consists of fruit and berries, plus tender shoots and young leaves supplemented by aquatic vegetation. Weighing up to 880 lb (400 kg), it can devour one-tenth of its own body weight in vegetative matter daily. The tapir's tendency to follow well-worn paths that meander through the thick forest undergrowth makes it relatively easy to find – for both hunters and wildlife enthusiasts.

COMMUNICATION AND VOICE

Solitary, unsociable, and territorial, tapirs mark their small home ranges with urine and dung. Except in breeding season, two tapirs that come into contact react aggressively by baring their teeth. If neither retreats, a fight can occur, with each trying to bite the other's hind legs – their sharp incisors can inflict serious wounds. Tapirs vocalize with shrills, snorts, squeaks, and whistles. These vary in pitch depending on meaning and are especially loud when the animal is sexually excited.

Baird's tapir using its sense of smell to read territorial markings

KEY FACTS

Name: *Tapirus bairdii*
Local names: *Danta*

Size Shoulder height: 3.9–5 ft (1–1.5 m); Weight: up to 880 lb (400 kg).

Lifespan 30 years.
Population in Costa Rica Less than 1,000.
Conservation status EN.
Gestation period 13 months.
Reproduction Females typically conceive after two years and give birth every two years.

Habitat Humid habitats from sea level to 11,400 ft (3,500 m).

A female tapir with her rust-colored calf

Top places to see Corcovado, La Amistad, La Selva, Rincón de la Vieja, Tenorio.

Sighting tips Tapirs mark well-tramped trails with urine and dung deposits. Their large, splayed toe tracks are unmistakable.

Friends and foes Tapirs are a tasty treat to jaguars, and large crocodiles can seize them at lagoons.

Facts and trivia Baird's tapir is named for the American naturalist Spencer Fullerton Baird, who studied them in the 1840s.

Calves are rust-colored, *with white spots and stripes serving as camouflage in the dappled forest.*

Active at dusk *and throughout the night, tapirs retire to shelter amid dense vegetation during the day.*

The tapir's hoofed toes *are splayed to allow for extra mobility in land marshes.*

Other Mammals

Costa Rica supports 212 mammal species. This figure includes approximately 100 species of bats. These are the only mammals in the world that have evolved for flight – their wings are really webbed forelimbs. Exclusively nocturnal, they navigate by emitting ultrasonic squeaks and track the echoes with special receptors. This is known as echolocation. Mammals that are active by day include rodents, ungulates, and the three-toed sloth, which is frequently seen.

FAMILY

Costa Rica's mammals are grouped in 11 orders, including the felids. Anteaters, sloths, and tamanduas are in the order Pilosa. Bats belong to the Chiroptera order, while peccaries and deers are even-toed ungulates – hoofed animals with more than 220 species worldwide.

THREE-TOED SLOTH
(SPECIES: BRADYPUS VARIEGATUS)

BEST SEEN: Braulio Carrillo, Cahuita, Manuel Antonio, Tortuguero

   LC

The three-toed sloth – more accurately called "three-fingered" sloth, since the two-toed sloth, confusingly, also has three toes – can be seen in every kind of forest in Costa Rica. It has a round face with a blunt nose, black eye mask, and prominent forehead, and it is able to rotate its neck by 360 degrees. Sloths spend virtually their entire lives suspended by their hook-like claws, or curled up asleep in the forks of branches. Active by day, they feed exclusively on the leaves of several tree species, notably the cecropia. The three-toed sloth's thick, long gray fur runs from its belly to its back to facilitate the drainage of rain while hanging upside down. Green algae grow on the fur, providing natural camouflage and food for a species of moth that lives in the fur and lays its eggs in sloth dung. The sloth grows to about 2 ft (60 cm) in length but weighs no more than 15 lb (7 kg). It requires sunshine to digest the cellulose in its leafy low-energy diet, and its slow metabolism and minimal muscle mass result in very slow movements. Females in estrus scream to attract males, which have an orange patch and a black stripe between their shoulders.

IUCN status VU: Vulnerable; LC: Least Concern

TWO-TOED SLOTH
(SPECIES: CHOLOEPUS HOFFMANNI)

BEST SEEN: Cahuita, Corcovado, Tapantí-Macizo

LC

Two-toed sloths are brown with pink noses

This nocturnal animal has many similarities to its smaller three-toed cousin, but it has only two claws on its fore-limbs, plus a more extensive diet that includes insects, fruit, and even birds' eggs. It has a cream-colored face and bulbous brown eyes. Although it crawls clumsily along the ground, it is a good swimmer. Females give birth to a single baby once a year and carry it clinging on their chests; if a baby falls, its calls are ignored and it is doomed – a meal for snakes, cats, or hawks.

NORTHERN TAMANDUA
(SPECIES: TAMANDUA MEXICANA)

BEST SEEN: Caño Negro, La Cruz, Santa Rosa

LC

This semi-arboreal mammal, a dedicated eater of ants and termites, supplements its diet with tiny beetles and other insects. The tamandua has a coarse cream coat with a shoulder band and black flanks. It grows up to 35 in (88 cm) in length and uses its strong forearms and huge claws to tear open ant nests. Its elongated snout tapers to a tiny mouth, through which an extremely long, narrow tongue darts to lick up insects. Lacking teeth, it has a powerful gizzard for grinding its food. A long prehensile tail aids when climbing trees in its preferred habitats – lowland forests.

The Northern tamandua is two-toned

GIANT ANTEATER
(SPECIES: MYRMECOPHAGA TRIDACTYLA)

BEST SEEN: Corcovado

VU

The unmistakable profile of the giant anteater

The largest of the three anteater species can exceed 7 ft (2.1 m) in length, half being its bushy tail and another 20 in (50 cm) its slender, curving snout, which provides a keen sense of smell. This gray, black, and white mammal shuffles along on its knuckles, like a chimpanzee. Its large front claws are perfect for ripping apart termite mounds, but also for defense – the anteater rears up on its hind legs to slash at attackers. This extremely rare animal has disappeared from most of its former range and is thought to be restricted to Corcovado.

SILKY ANTEATER
(SPECIES: CYCLOPES DIDACTYLUS)

BEST SEEN: Braulio Carrillo, Corcovado, Monteverde

LC

Also called the pygmy anteater for its relatively small size, which rarely exceeds 18 in (45 cm), this nocturnal animal is arboreal by nature. During the day, it sleeps curled up into a ball high up a tree, and by night, it hunts for ants, termites, and beetles. Resembling a teddy bear, it has soft, honey-colored fur, a short pink snout, and a long prehensile tail. The silky anteater forages in a variety of forest types and nests in tree hollows, where it gives birth to a single pup.

The tiny silky anteater

Key to Field Guide icons *see p60*

The agouti is quite relaxed in the presence of humans

AGOUTI
(SPECIES: DASYPROCTA PUNCTATA)

BEST SEEN: Corcovado, La Selva, Manuel Antonio, Monteverde

 LC

Known as *guatusa*, this large ground-dwelling rodent has grown so accustomed to humans that at many national parks it can be seen at close range, grooming or feeding. The agouti mostly eats palm nuts, which it buries for storage. Its chestnut-brown coat is glossy, and the male's rump hairs form a fan-shaped crest that is displayed during territorial disputes. Monogamous for life, the agouti breeds year-round. During courtship, the male sprays the female with urine.

PACA
(SPECIES: CUNICULUS PACA)

BEST SEEN: Braulio Carrillo, Corcovado, Tortuguero

 LC

A cousin of the agouti, the paca (called *tepezcuintle* in Costa Rica) is distinguished by its shiny dark-brown fur spotted with several parallel lines of white dots along its sides. If the agouti resembles a guinea pig, the paca is shaped like a giant tailless rat. A nocturnal animal, this herbivore enjoys a diet of seeds, roots, fruits, and flowers. A good climber and swimmer, where possible it flees to water to escape danger. It is illegally hunted for its tasty meat, and many *campesinos* (peasants) also raise pacas commercially.

The paca lives near mangrove swamps and river banks

The peccary bears a strong resemblance to the pig

COLLARED PECCARY
(SPECIES: PECARI TAJACU)

BEST SEEN: Braulio Carrillo, Corcovado, Santa Rosa

 LC

One of two peccary species in Costa Rica, this large mammal is only distantly related to the pig, which it resembles. Standing up to 24 in (60 cm) tall, it is covered in thick gray bristles; it has short legs and a massive head tapering to a tiny snout used for sniffing out fruits, nuts, and tubers. It roams many lowland environments, from savanna to rainforest. The collared peccary typically lives in groups of up to 20 individuals. Herds of the more aggressive white-lipped peccary can contain more than 100 animals.

CACOMISTLE
(SPECIES: BASSARISCUS SUMICHRASTI)

BEST SEEN: Braulio Carrillo, Carara, Corcovado

LC

Much smaller in size than its cousin, the raccoon, the cacomistle is also far rarer. Living in the upper levels of moist forests, it has been heavily impacted by deforestation – in Costa Rica it is listed as an endangered species. It has huge black eyes for vision while prowling at night for insects, small vertebrates, and fruit. With a narrow nose and extremely long, pointed ears, its face is catlike – indeed, cacomistle means "half-cat" in the Nahuatl language. At full stretch, it measures 3.3 ft (1 m) in length, equally divided between its body and its black-and-white hooped tail.

The cacomistle's tail makes up half of its body length

IUCN status DD: Data Deficient; LC: Least Concern

The Mexican tree porcupine has a bulbous snout

MEXICAN TREE PORCUPINE
(SPECIES: SPHIGGURUS MEXICANUS)

BEST SEEN: Rincón de la Vieja, Santa Rosa

 LC

Porcupines belong to the Erethizontidae family of rodents. As its name suggests, the Mexican tree porcupine is arboreal and mostly nocturnal, with a prehensile tail that aids in maneuvering around the treetops. It inhabits most forest types but prefers drier habitats and is rare in rainforest. Covered almost entirely in thick quills mixed with white-tipped black fur, this porcupine has a small round head and a fleshy snout. It eats leaves, fruits, and seeds. Normally silent, it wails during breeding season and can emit a disagreeable, garlicky odor.

The red brocket deer has a distinctive rust-brown coat

RED BROCKET DEER
(SPECIES: MAZAMA AMERICANA)

BEST SEEN: Arenal, Cahuita, Rincón de la Vieja

 DD

Endemic to Central America, this small deer inhabits thick forests, where its rust-brown fur is camouflaged by dark shade. The red brocket deer's lower legs are edged with black, while its throat and inner legs are whitish. Juveniles have two rows of white spots running along each flank. Adult males can be up to 31 in (80 cm) tall at the shoulder, and they grow small, spike-like antlers. The red brocket deer dines mostly on fruits, but it also browses on leaves. A shy creature, it is less commonly seen than the white-tailed deer.

KINKAJOU
(SPECIES: POTOS FLAVUS)

BEST SEEN: Corcovado, La Selva, Monteverde

 LC

An arboreal mammal related to the cacomistle, raccoon, and olingo, the kinkajou is distinct among them for its prehensile tail. It uses its dexterous forepaws to hold and eat figs and other fruits and insects, and its long, extrudable tongue to scoop up honey and nectar. Kinkajous are social animals and sometimes forage in groups. They are hunted for their short golden fur, as well as for the illegal pet trade. Your best chance of seeing this nocturnal mammal is on a night tour.

A prehensile tail helps the kinkajou navigate the treetops

WHITE-TAILED DEER
(SPECIES: ODOCOILEUS VIRGINIANUS)

BEST SEEN: Barra Honda, Caño Negro, Santa Rosa

 LC

Slightly bigger than the red brocket deer, the white-tailed deer prefers grassland, wetlands, and dry deciduous forest over dense ever-green forests, and it is particularly active around dawn and dusk. It is gray-brown to rust in coloration and displays the white underside of its tail when alarmed. Capable of huge leaps, it relies on speed and agility to outwit cougars, coyotes, jaguars, and human hunters. Groups of up to ten individuals are frequently seen foraging together. Males spar for dominance in breeding season, when they lose weight due to a singular focus on mating.

A white-tailed deer at a water hole

Key to Field Guide icons *see p60*

The armadillo, with its distinctive banded armor

NINE-BANDED ARMADILLO
(SPECIES: DASYPUS NOVEMCINCTUS)

BEST SEEN: Arenal, Caño Negro, Santa Rosa

   LC

Of South American origin, the armadillo is protected by a bony shell of interlinked scales. Armed with powerful claws that have evolved for burrowing, it thrives only in soft-soil environments. It usually emerges at dusk to dig frantically for termites, grubs, and tubers. Although it typically ambles, it can flee quickly from danger and – being capable of holding its breath for several minutes – it can easily run along riverbeds or even swim across. The nine-banded armadillo can reach 42 in (110 cm) in length, nose to tail.

The opossum is a semi-arboreal marsupial

COMMON OPOSSUM
(SPECIES: DIDELPHIS MARSUPIALIS)

BEST SEEN: Cahuita, Carara, La Selva

   LC

The opossum is the only marsupial in Costa Rica. A primitive yet adaptable creature, it inhabits a wide range of habitats below 6,600 ft (2,200 m), including urban environments. Active by night, it spends most of its time on the ground but can also climb trees in search of fruit and birds' eggs. Females give birth several times a year to tiny babies that emerge after only two weeks' gestation and climb into their mother's pouch to suckle.

IUCN status LC: Least Concern; NT: Near Threatened

STRIPED HOG-NOSED SKUNK
(SPECIES: CONEPATUS SEMISTRIATUS)

BEST SEEN: Cahuita, Poás, Santa Rosa

   LC

This widespread medium-sized mammal belongs to its own family, the Mephitidae. A solitary creature that lives in habitats from lowland grassland and scrub to moist mid-elevation forest, the *zorrillo* (as it is known locally) emerges at night to hunt for fruit and small invertebrates. Including its long bushy tail, this black-and-white striped animal grows up to 20 in (50 cm) long. The skunk wards off potential predators by spraying a foul-smelling sulphurous chemical from its anal scent gland.

The skunk defends itself by releasing an offensive odor

VARIEGATED SQUIRREL
(SPECIES: SCIURUS VARIEGATOIDES)

BEST SEEN: Carara, Monteverde, San Gerardo de Dota

LC

Related to the squirrels that are familiar to North Americans and Europeans, the variegated squirrel is endemic to Central America. This widespread rodent, the most frequently seen of five local squirrel species, has a copper-colored body with a black back and gray bushy tail, which typically curls along its back. It nests inside trees, and – unlike other squirrels – it feeds mostly on fruit. Bold by nature, it often scampers onto restaurant tables to steal patrons' fruit.

A variegated squirrel feeding on a coconut

The bulldog bat's wings can span 3.3 ft (1 m) across

GREATER BULLDOG BAT
(SPECIES: NOCTILIO LEPORINUS)

BEST SEEN: Drake Bay, Gandoca-Manzanillo, Tortuguero

LC

Visitors to Tortuguero are virtually guaranteed a sighting of the greater bulldog bat, also known as "fishing" bat, swooping low over the lagoons to snatch fish with its long claws. Its reddish fur is water-repellent, and its narrow wings act as oars to gain speed and take off if it falls in the water. The greater bulldog bat can be seen wherever there are large bodies of water, including sheltered coves on both the Caribbean and Pacific shores. Like all bats, it uses echolocation to find prey.

A colony of Jamaican fruit bats roosting in a cave

JAMAICAN FRUIT BAT
(SPECIES: ARTIBEUS JAMAICENSIS)

BEST SEEN: Arenal, Cahuita, Rincón de la Vieja

LC

One of the most important pollinators in the neotropics, this large bat has a huge wingspan – up to 16 in (40 cm) – although its body is usually no more than 4 in (10 cm) long. It has a short, broad snout topped by a nose leaf, and its gray-brown fur has a distinctive soapy smell. The bat snatches wild figs and other small fruits in flight and returns to its roost to eat the pulp. Like the Honduran white bat, it is one of 15 species that form a tent from large leaves; the Jamaican fruit bat prefers broad-leaf palms, but it also lives in hollow trees.

HONDURAN WHITE BAT
(SPECIES: ECTOPHYLLA ALBA)

BEST SEEN: Cahuita, Hitoy-Cerere, Tortuguero

NT

This tiny bat averages less than 2 in (5 cm) in length. It has snow-white fur and orange nose, ears, legs, and wings. Mostly a fruit eater, it lives only in the Caribbean lowland rainforest, where it roosts communally, shoulder to shoulder, inside "tents" made by chewing the veins of heliconia leaves until they fold. Usually the group comprises a single male with his harem. Sunlight filtering through the leaf makes the Honduran white bat's fur appear green, providing camouflage.

Honduran white bats roosting together in a leaf

COMMON VAMPIRE BAT
(SPECIES: DESMODUS ROTUNDUS)

BEST SEEN: Barra Honda, Caño Negro, Santa Rosa

LC

Costa Rica has three vampire bat species that feed on the blood of cattle and other mammals and birds, usually while they sleep. This manner of eating bears a little resemblance to the way the eponymous vampire in Bram Stoker's novel *Dracula* feeds. A vampire bat typically crawls toward its victim, whose fur it trims with clipper-like teeth, then pierces the skin with two sharp fangs. Its saliva contains an anticoagulant substance called draculin, which permits it to suck up free-flowing blood. After feeding, the bat uses its powerful pectoral muscles to leap into the air and take flight.

The vampire bat has straw-like grooves in its tongue

Key to Field Guide icons *see p60*

Marine Mammals and Fish

Costa Rica's large pelagic animals include rays, sharks, dolphins, humpback whales, and other cetaceans. Whale- and dolphin-watching trips are a great way to see these creatures – whales are frequently seen in Golfo Dulce, Golfo de Nicoya, and in the warm waters surrounding Isla Caño and Isla Cocos. Scuba divers can enjoy close-up encounters with groupers, hammerhead sharks, whale sharks, and other marine creatures.

FAMILY

Dolphins and whales are in the Cetacean order of air-breathing mammals that evolved for an aquatic life. Fish, on the other hand, belong to several dozen groups of loosely related marine vertebrates.

A short-finned pilot whale surfacing for air

PILOT WHALE
(SPECIES: GLOBICEPHALA MELAS)

BEST SEEN: Whale Marine National Park, Isla Caño

DD

An ocean nomad, this whale actually belongs to the dolphin family. It prefers deep waters, especially those at the edge of the continental shelf, where it feeds primarily on squid. Dark gray in color, the pilot whale is recognizable by its high, blunt forehead; sweeping dorsal fin set forward toward the rear of its head; and tiny tail flukes. It typically lives in groups of 10–30 individuals. Adult males can measure 16–20 ft (5–6 m), and females 11–17 ft (3.6–5.2 m).

HUMPBACK WHALE
(SPECIES: MEGAPTERA NOVAEANGLIAE)

BEST SEEN: Whale Marine National Park, Isla Caño, Drake Bay

LC

Twice a year (Dec–Mar and Jul–Oct), schools of humpback whales arrive in the waters off southwest Costa Rica to breed and give birth. These giants have long pectoral fins and a black-and-white tail fin; despite weighing up to 40 tons (36,000 kg), they perform spectacular leaps, or breaches. Males compose complex communal songs that are used in courtship.

A humpback whale performing an acrobatic breach

The bottlenose dolphin tracks its food by echolocation

BOTTLENOSE DOLPHIN
(SPECIES: TURSIOPS TRUNCATUS)

BEST SEEN: Gulf of Papagayo, Whale Marine National Park, Golfo Dulce

LC

This playful and extremely intelligent creature with a gray body and pale-pink belly can grow to 12 ft (3.7 m) long and weigh up to 1,400 lb (635 kg), although those found in Costa Rican waters tend to be smaller. It mostly eats fish and squid, which it pursues at speeds up to 20 mph (30 km/h). Highly social, it typically lives in groups of several hundred individuals.

SPINNER DOLPHIN
(SPECIES: STENELLA LONGIROSTRIS)

BEST SEEN: Drake Bay, Gulf of Nicoya, Isla Caño

DD

This long, dark-gray mammal is named for its acrobatic displays, performed either singly or alongside a pod of fellow dolphins. Unusually long fins help power the spinner dolphin, which can leap high enough in the air to spin many times before splashing down in belly or back flops. It can even somersault. Spinner dolphins communicate by slapping the water and by trailing bubbles from their blowhole.

The slender spinner dolphin has a pencil-thin beak

IUCN status DD: Data Deficient; EN: Endangered; LC: Least Concern; NE: Not Evaluated; VU: Vulnerable

Intimidatingly large, the whale shark has a gentle nature

WHALE SHARK
(SPECIES: RHINCODON TYPUS)

BEST SEEN: Gulf of Papagayo, Isla Caño, Isla Cocos

▢ ≋ VU

This gentle giant – the world's largest fish –
can grow to 40 ft (12 m), yet it is so docile
that it will let swimmers touch it. It scoops up
plankton and tiny sea creatures as it swims
slowly, with its vast mouth open. Its gray
upper body is marked with striped hoops
interspersed with rings of pale spots; three
ridges run along each flank. Whale sharks
exist in large numbers around the Bat Islands,
in the Gulf of Papagayo, and in the nutrient-
rich waters around Cocos Island.

The unmistakable scalloped hammerhead

HAMMERHEAD SHARK
(SPECIES: SPHYRNA LEWINI)

BEST SEEN: Gulf of Papagayo, Isla Caño, Isla Cocos

▢ ≋ EN

The scalloped hammerhead, one of nine shark
species named for a flattened cephalofoil
head structure, inhabits Costa Rica's Pacific
coastal waters and throngs around Isla Cocos.
Its hammer-shaped head, lined with super-
sensitive receptors for detecting prey, offers
360-degree binocular vision. Unlike most other
sharks, hammerheads swim in huge schools
that can number several hundred individuals.
At night the group disbands, and individuals
hunt solo for small fish. Females give birth to
live young. Unlike several other hammerhead
species, the scalloped hammerhead is not
considered dangerous or aggressive to humans.
Its population is threatened by fishing fleets,
which capture hammerheads in nets and on
lines, both inadvertently and deliberately,
for the Asian food and medicinal trade.

BLACK MARLIN
(SPECIES: MAKAIRA INDICA)

BEST SEEN: Gulf of Papagayo, Central Pacific waters

▢ ≋ NE

One of three marlin species in Costa Rican
waters (along with the blue and striped marlins),
the black marlin has a long, sharp upper jaw,
or bill, which it uses to slash at small tuna and
other prey. Its streamlined body is dark blue
above and silvery-white below, with faint blue
stripes. Capable of speeds up to 65 mph (100
km/h), it is the most highly prized game fish.
However, local sport fishers practice catch-
and-release, except for trophy-size specimens.

The black marlin, with its rapier-like upper jaw

SAILFISH
(SPECIES: ISTIOPHORUS PLATYPTERUS)

BEST SEEN: Gulf of Papagayo, Central Pacific waters

▢ ≋ NE

Unlike its cousins the marlin and the
swordfish, the sailfish has a huge dorsal fin
that forms a retractable sail. Taller than the
fish itself, this fin is laced with blood vessels
and thought to aid in cooling and heating
the fish as necessary. It is also useful when
herding prey – groups of sailfish are known
to corral schools of sardines and other fish.
The sail is folded down for swimming. Like
a chameleon, the sailfish can change body
color and even flash iridescent hues using
irregularly shaped cells containing crystals
that control the distribution and absorption
of pigment and light. Capable of incredible
leaps, the sailfish is even faster under water
than the black marlin.

The sailfish's dorsal fin runs the entire length of its back

Key to Field Guide icons *see p60*

Amphibians and Reptiles

Despite the fearsome reputation of toxic poison-dart frogs, venomous snakes with potentially lethal bites, and man-eating crocodiles, most of Costa Rica's amphibians and reptiles are perfectly harmless to humans. These cold-blooded creatures have variable body temperatures and depend on their surroundings for warmth, so they can frequently be spotted basking in the sun. Amphibians lay their eggs in fresh water, which they also need to stay moist. Prolific in warmer lowlands, they are relatively scarce at higher elevations.

FAMILY

Reptiles are arranged in four orders, including Crocodilia, Squamata (snakes and lizards), and Testudines (turtles and tortoises). Amphibians belong to three orders: Anura (frogs and toads), Caudata (newts and salamanders), and the worm-like Gymnophiona.

POISON-DART FROGS
(FAMILY: DENDROBATIDAE)

BEST SEEN: Barbilla, Braulio Carrillo, Corcovado, La Selva

         Most species: Variable

Small (0.6–2.4 in/1.5–6 cm) and brightly colored, these ground-dwelling frogs are named for their toxic skin secretions, which derive from their diet of ants and tiny beetles. The poison varies in potency, and only two species of poison-dart frog found in Panama and Colombia are strong enough to kill humans. Costa Rica has seven species, including the red-and-blue Dendrobates pumilio and the green-and-black Dendrobates auratus. By day, poison-dart frogs hop about the moist forest floor, safe from predators thanks to their gaudy coloration, which serves to advertise their toxicity. Females lay their eggs in moist places. Newly hatched tadpoles typically hitch a ride on their mother's back to be carried to water, where they can feed. Dendrobates pumilio even deposits unfertilized eggs into the water as food.

The gaudily colored strawberry poison-dart frog

The charismatic red-eyed tree frog is a master of camouflage

RED-EYED TREE FROG
(SPECIES: AGALYCHNIS CALLIDRYAS)

BEST SEEN: Cahuita, Corcovado, La Selva

        LC

This arboreal frog has a lime-green body, blue sides streaked with yellow, orange toes, and red eyes with narrow black pupils. It measures 1.5–2.75 in (4–7 cm), but more than twice that with its limbs extended. An excellent climber, it moves slowly and stealthily, feeding on moths and other flying insects, which it snares with its long, sticky tongue. When in danger, it flashes its bright body parts to startle the predator and facilitate escape. The red-eyed tree frog is a nocturnal hunter, and by day it sleeps folded on the underside of large leaves, using suction cups on its feet to hang upside down. During breeding season (Oct–Mar), the forests at night resound with the croaking of males calling for mates.

IUCN status LC: Least Concern; NE: Not Evaluated

The glass frog's abdominal skin is transparent

GLASS FROGS
(FAMILY: CENTROLENIDAE)
BEST SEEN: La Selva, Monteverde

                    Most species: Variable

Named for their transparent bodies, glass frogs are nocturnal, mostly arboreal, difficult to spot in the wild, and generally small, rarely exceeding 3 in (7.5 cm). Although the upper body is green and often spotted, the abdominal skin is translucent, exposing the frog's internal organs, such as its heart, intestines, and liver. Some species are entirely transparent. Denizens of the humid forests of Costa Rica at most elevations, glass frogs are particularly common and diverse in montane cloud forests.

An anole lizard displaying its orange dewlap

ANOLES
(FAMILY: POLYCHROTIDAE)
BEST SEEN: Manuel Antonio, Rincón de la Vieja, Selva Verde

Most species: Variable

Costa Rica has more than two dozen species of anoles, a common and diverse Neotropical lizard family that includes almost 400 species. They typically measure 3–8 in (8–20 cm) and have pointed snouts and long slender tails that they can break off to escape predators. Normally green or brown, anoles can change color depending on mood and temperature. Semi-arboreal and active by day, they stake out a territory around low-lying foliage. When an intruder is near, the male performs "push-ups" and displays the orange or red dewlap beneath its throat. If this does not scare away the intruder, a fight might ensue, in which the competitors bite at each other's necks.

BASILISK LIZARD
(SPECIES: BASILISCUS PLUMIFRONS)
BEST SEEN: Corcovado, Gandoca-Manzanillo, Tortuguero

                    NE

Ranging from bright green to olive, the basilisk lizard is also known as the Jesus Christ lizard because it can dart across water thanks to its long, slender webbed toes, which create air pockets above the water and prevent it from sinking. It lives in lowland rainforests and usually close to streams – it is an excellent swimmer. It grows to about 2 ft (60 cm) in length. Males have crests atop their heads and backs, which they use to court females.

A basilisk lizard walking across a body of water

GECKO
(SPECIES: HEMIDACTYLUS FRENATUS)
BEST SEEN: Barra Honda, Cahuita, Santa Rosa

   LC

Costa Rica has nine species of this adorable creature. The gecko is ubiquitous by night, its presence given away by its loud chirp, which is used by both sexes to attract mates and warn off competitors. One particular species, the house gecko, seems to find its way into every dwelling in Costa Rica. Measuring up to 6 in (15 cm), most geckos have velvety pinkish-gray skin with specks or stripes. They can scurry upside down across branches or ceilings thanks to their toe pads, which are covered with bristles, or setae, so fine they tap into electrical attraction at a molecular level. A devourer of mosquitoes, the gecko has such keen eyesight that it can detect color at night.

Geckos' toe bristles allow them to climb any surface

Key to Field Guide icons *see p60*

AMERICAN CROCODILE
(SPECIES: CROCODYLUS ACUTUS)

BEST SEEN: Barra del Colorado, Corcovado, Río Tárcoles, Tortuguero

 VU

One of the largest members of the crocodile family – it can attain a length of 23 ft (7 m) – the American crocodile inhabits brackish tidal estuaries and lowland rivers from southern Florida to Venezuela. In Costa Rica, it is most populous in the lagoons of Tortuguero, on the Caribbean; the Tempisque and Tárcoles rivers; and Corcovado National Park, on the Pacific. Its broad, massive, olive-green body tapers to a narrow, elongated head. The American crocodile can remain submerged for more than one hour and is capable of rapid bursts of speed on land, where it spends long hours in the sun to heat its body. It primarily feeds on fish, but occasionally seizes unwary mammals that come to the rivers to drink. Males defend their aquatic territories against rivals. Females lay eggs in sandy nests in the dry season. Crocodiles are felicitous parents, and both male and female will guard the nest and young hatchlings to protect them from predators. American crocodiles use the ocean to migrate between rivers, and very rarely they have been known to attack surfers and swimmers. In recent years, they have even been spotted in Lake Arenal – at about 1,640 ft (500 m) elevation. How they got there is a mystery.

The crocodile's back features several lateral rows of raised scales that act like the keel of a boat.

The nostrils are located atop the snout, so the crocodile can breathe while under water.

The American crocodile can live to 80 years of age

The green iguana uses its well-developed dewlap in courtship displays

GREEN IGUANA
(SPECIES: IGUANA IGUANA)

BEST SEEN: Corcovado, Manuel Antonio, Palo Verde, Santa Rosa

 LC

The green iguana is a scaly, dragon-like lizard that can grow up to 6.6 ft (2 m), with its tail taking up half its length. Mature green iguanas can range in color from gray-olive to dark brown, although all juveniles are lime green. During the mating season (Nov–Dec), males turn bright orange and advertise their prowess as potential lovers from the treetops. The green iguana inhabits various low- and mid-elevation ecosystems throughout Costa Rica, and it roams on ground level, which it prefers on cold days to forest canopy. An agile climber, it eats flowers, fruits, and leaves. A spiny crest extends along its back, and it has a regenerative tail that it can discard to escape predators, which it detects with the aid of a rudimentary third eye atop its head. Females lay 20–70 eggs in nests in the ground, but newborns are left to fend for themselves.

IUCN status LC: Least Concern; NT: Near Threatened; VU: Vulnerable

SPECTACLED CAIMAN
(SPECIES: CAIMAN CROCODILUS)

BEST SEEN: Caño Negro, Tortuguero, Gandoca-Manzanillo

 LC

Abundant throughout Costa Rica's Caribbean and Pacific lowland rivers and wetlands, this small olive-brown crocodilian is commonly seen basking in the sun along riverbanks. It grows up to 8 ft (2.5 m) in length and is easily identified by dark crossbands on its body and tail, and by a bony ridge resembling the bridge of a pair of spectacles between its eyes – hence its name. A nocturnal hunter, it eats mainly fish and amphibians. Caimans breed primarily in wet season. Females lay up to 40 eggs in nests scraped together from leaves, twigs, and sand; males help guard them. Raccoons prey on the nests, and baby caimans can be seized by herons and other birds of prey.

Spectacled caimans basking in the sun along a riverbank

The Mesoamerican slider turtle has an olive-green neck with yellow markings

SLIDER TURTLE
(SPECIES: TRACHEMYS SCRIPTA)

BEST SEEN: Caño Negro, Palo Verde, Tortuguero, Gandoca-Manzanillo

 NT

The slider turtle, the most common of the eight species of freshwater turtles found in Costa Rica, has two subspecies: the ornate slider and the Mesoamerican, or Nicaraguan, slider, limited to the extreme north of the country. This medium-sized turtle – it grows to 24 in (60 cm) – has dark-olive skin striped with yellow markings, yellow eyes, and a yellow underside to its carapace. They are usually seen in or close to large ponds and rivers, or sunning on partially submerged rocks or logs, often piled up one atop the other. Slider turtles are omnivores and eat anything from insects and fish to aquatic vegetation. They mate in spring and fall, when they sink to the bottom of the river- or lake bed to copulate. Females can store sperm for several months. The population is at risk from illegal poaching for the pet trade.

Key to Field Guide icons *see p60*

Marine Turtles

Five of the world's seven marine turtle species nest on Costa Rican beaches. Although they differ in shape and size, they all share the same lineage. Sea turtles begin life as hatchlings when they emerge from their sandy nests and crawl to the sea. The nest's ambient temperature determines the gender of the hatchlings, only a tiny fraction of which will survive to adulthood. Males will never return to land, while females come ashore to lay eggs. Turtle populations have seen a sharp decline, and two species are on the verge of extinction.

The leatherback turtle, with its teardrop-shaped body

LEATHERBACK TURTLE
(SPECIES: DERMOCHELYS CORIACEA)

BEST SEEN: Gandoca-Manzanillo, Playa Grande

             CR

The largest of the sea turtles, the leatherback can measure 6.5 ft (2 m) and weigh up to 1,200 lb (550 kg). It roams the world's oceans powered by massive front flippers. Its body is pewter-colored, pink underneath, covered with white blotches, and lined with seven ridges for hydrodynamic efficiency. Instead of a hard carapace, it has thick cartilaginous skin over-laying a matrix of small, polygonal bones and fatty flesh that permits it to resist the extreme

cold of Arctic waters and the pressure of deep ocean dives. Backward spines in its throat aid in eating slippery jellyfish, its main food source. Female leatherbacks nest at night on both the Caribbean (Feb–Jul) and Pacific (Oct–Mar) shores of Costa Rica and prefer soft-sand beaches facing deep water, such as Pacuaré and Playa Grande. The female lays 50–100 eggs in a deep nest dug with her rear flippers, before filling in the pit by flinging sand with her front flippers. The leatherback matures at about 10 years and can live to 40 years or more. These turtles are listed as critically endangered due to ocean pollution, incidental capture by long lines and drift nets, and the poaching of eggs by animals and humans.

Loggerhead turtles feeding on algae

LOGGERHEAD TURTLE
(SPECIES: CARETTA CARETTA)

BEST SEEN: Gandoca-Manzanillo, Tortuguero

             EN

With the exception of its copper-colored shell, the loggerhead turtle is similar in size and appearance to the green turtle. The males fight to copulate with the females, which mate with several partners and can store sperm until ovulation. Like all turtles, the female loggerhead lays as many as 50–100 eggs, principally nesting on the Caribbean shores of Costa Rica, and more infrequently on the Pacific side. As an omnivore, the loggerhead turtle has a varied diet, but it mostly feeds on bottom-dwelling invertebrates, which it crushes with its powerful jaws.

IUCN status CR: Critically Endangered; EN: Endangered; VU: Vulnerable

The hawksbill's beak-like mouth is an effective weapon

HAWKSBILL TURTLE
(SPECIES: ERETMOCHELYS IMBRICATA)

BEST SEEN: Gandoca-Manzanillo

 CR

This delicate-looking, mid-sized (up to 39 in/ 1 m in length) turtle is in fact extremely aggressive – it is named for its sharp beak-like mouth, which it uses to defend itself. It prefers shallow coastal waters and is frequently seen swimming around coral reefs. A solitary nester, the hawksbill turtle comes ashore in Costa Rica along both coasts; Atlantic and Pacific sub-species differ slightly in coloration. Adults eat all manner of sealife, including Portuguese man-of-war jellyfish, whose toxins make hawksbill meat unpalatable to humans. This turtle is targeted by hunters for its uniquely patterned, reddish-brown, and slightly iridescent carapace, which is used to make jewelry and trinkets. Artificial plastic with tortoise-shell patterns has only partially helped stem poaching, and today this beautiful creature is critically endangered. The hawksbill has large scales between its eyes, and the yellow-fringed scutes (plates) of its serrated, shield-shaped shell overlap.

GREEN TURTLE
(SPECIES: CHELONIA MYDAS)

BEST SEEN: Gandoca-Manzanillo, Pacuare, Tortuguero

 EN

The green turtle is the largest of the shelled species and can grow up to 5 ft (1.5 m) in length. Named for the green layer of fat under its shell, it has a small round head and a broad, heart-shaped carapace closely resembling that of the smaller hawksbill turtle, though the green turtle's shell ranges in color from olive green to chestnut or ocher. Uniquely, this turtle is a herbivore and grazes on shallow-water sea grasses. It has separate Atlantic and Pacific populations, and in Costa Rica it is primarily found at Tortuguero National Park, which, between June and November, is the species' main nesting site in the western hemisphere. In common with other shelled turtles, the male has a hook on each front flipper with which he grasps the female during copulation. Females mate every two to four years and lay 100–200 eggs. The green turtle's popula-tion appears to have stabilized after being decimated for the turtle-soup industry.

The herbivorous green turtle has a heart-shaped shell

OLIVE RIDLEY
(SPECIES: LEPIDOCHELYS OLIVACEA)

BEST SEEN: Camaronal, Ostional, Santa Rosa

VU

The smallest of Costa Rica's five turtle species, averaging 24–28 in (60–70 cm), the olive ridley is remarkable for nesting en masse at a few select locations worldwide. In Costa Rica, these include five or six beaches along the shores of Nicoya and Guanacaste, mainly at Ostional and Nancite. Each female nests up to three times per season. Synchronized arrivals take place as often as twice-monthly from July to December, peaking in August and September, when tens of thousands of female turtles arrive to lay eggs on the beach where they were born. The ridley's omnivorous diet includes algae, shrimp, and lobster.

Olive ridleys are thought to be the most abundant turtles

Key to Field Guide icons *see p60*

Snakes

Although snakes are present in most habitats in Costa Rica, seeing them is not easy as they are reclusive and mostly nocturnal. Most of the country's 135 recorded snake species are fairly harmless; 17 are venomous; and nine are classed as highly venomous. Pit vipers, for example, named for the heat-sensitive organs (pits) between their eye and nostril, can inflict lethal bites. It is wise to keep a safe distance regardless of the species.

A brown vine snake slithering among the trees

VINE SNAKES
(FAMILY: COLUBRIDAE; GENUS: OXYBELIS)

BEST SEEN: Caño Negro, Carara, Corcovado, Tortuguero

                                    LC

Costa Rica has two species of the mildly venomous vine snake. These extremely slender brown or bright-green reptiles have adapted for a life in the trees, where they feed primarily on birds. Measuring up to 6.6 ft (2 m) yet barely 0.8 in (2 cm) thick, they have pointed heads and large eyes. Vine snakes live in humid habitats at lower elevations.

BOAS
(FAMILY: BOIDAE)

BEST SEEN: Braulio Carrillo, Cahuita, Manuel Antonio, Santa Rosa

   LC

The thick-bodied boa constrictor is the largest snake in Costa Rica, growing to a length of 10 ft (3 m). Two smaller rainbow boa species also strangle their prey, and live only in moist areas. These wide-ranging snakes are semi-arboreal. All are patterned cream, gray, and brown, with darker saddles; they shine with a blue radiance when exposed to direct light.

A boa constrictor coiled around a tree branch

A young mussurana, recognizable by its bright-red skin

MUSSURANA
(SPECIES: CLELIA CLELIA)

BEST SEEN: Braulio Carrillo, Caño Negro, La Selva, Tortuguero

                                    LC

The mussurana is harmless to humans and remarkable for feeding on other snakes. People are known to keep one in the house as a measure against vipers, to whose venom it is resistant. Pink or bright red when young, mussuranas later turn dark gray with a cream belly, and can exceed 6.6 ft (2 m). They are found only in the Caribbean lowlands.

IUCN status LC: Least Concern

YELLOW-BELLIED SEA SNAKE
(SPECIES: PELAMIS PLATURUS)

BEST SEEN: Golfo de Papagayo, Isla Caño

LC

Often seen washed up on Pacific beaches, the yellow-bellied sea snake spends its entire life at sea, feeding on fish and eels, and propelling itself with its spatulate tail. Averaging 18–25 in (45–65 cm) in length, it is black above with a yellow belly. Although extremely venomous, this sea snake is docile and reluctant to strike.

The yellow-bellied sea snake swims in coastal waters

The Neotropical rattlesnake has thick brown scales

NEOTROPICAL RATTLESNAKE
(SPECIES: CROTALUS DURISSUS)

BEST SEEN: Barra Honda, Palo Verde, Rincón de la Vieja, Santa Rosa

 LC

The only rattlesnake in Costa Rica, the *cascabel*, as it is known locally, is found solely on the Northern Pacific slopes. It prefers low-elevation dry forest, savanna, and scrub, for which it is well camouflaged, with a blotchy beige-and-brown skin patterned with dark triangles and diamonds. Twin stripes run along the top of its neck. When threatened, this stout snake vibrates its rattle and lifts the front third of its body off the ground in preparation to strike. Its venom is one of the most toxic of all rattlesnake species.

Female fer-de-lances are much larger than the males

FER-DE-LANCE
(SPECIES: BOTHROPS ASPER)

BEST SEEN: Cahuita, Corcovado, La Selva, Tortuguero

 LC

This large, highly venomous pit viper, called *terciopelo* (meaning "velvet") locally, is the most feared snake in Costa Rica, accounting for half of all bites and most fatalities. Growing to 8 ft (2.5 m) and about as thick as a man's arm, the fer-de-lance inhabits a wide range of lowland habitats and is common along riverbanks. It is easily identified by its skin pattern of diamonds and diagonal stripes in various shades of brown and by its large, flat, sharply triangular head (fer-de-lance means "spearhead" in French), which is pale yellow on the underside. Mostly nocturnal, it rests in leaf litter by day. Unpredictable when disturbed, it is aggressive and fast-moving in defense. Females give birth to 20–100 live young, which are fully envenomed and potentially as deadly as their parents.

EYELASH VIPER
(SPECIES: BOTHRIECHIS SCHLEGELII)

BEST SEEN: Braulio Carrillo, Cahuita, Corcovado, Tortuguero

 LC

The sinister beauty and small size (22–32 in/ 55–80 cm) of this forest-dwelling pit viper belie its potentially lethal bite. Named for the large scales over its eyes, this nocturnal arboreal snake can be bright yellow, olive green, brown, and sometimes pink. It lives in moist forests up to 4,900 ft (1,500 m) and spends its days coiled up on branches; hikers should watch where they put their hands. Males compete for females by facing off with heads erect and attempting to push the other to the ground.

Eyelash vipers from the same litter can be of various colors

CORAL SNAKES
(FAMILY: ELAPIDAE; GENUS: MICRURUS)

BEST SEEN: Cahuita, Carara, Gandoca-Manzanillo, Tortuguero

 LC

Distinctive for their black, red, and yellow/ white banding, coral snakes possess the most potent venom of all New World snakes. Small – less than 3.3 ft (1 m) – and with tiny heads, they spend most of their time underground or in leaf litter, emerging to breed or hunt for frogs, lizards, rodents, and other prey. Unlike vipers, coral snakes have non-retractable teeth and hold on to a victim when biting. The rhyme "red on yellow, kill a fellow; red on black, friend of Jack," used to identify coral snakes in North America, does not apply in Costa Rica, where the order of the bands cannot be used as a gauge. Costa Rica has four species of coral snakes, across a range of lowland and mid-elevation habitats. Allen's coral snake is found only in the Caribbean lowlands.

A red-and-black coral snake in leaf litter

Key to Field Guide icons *see p60*

Birds

Boasting over 800 species grouped into 75 different families, Costa Rica's avifauna is exceptionally varied, exceeding that of the USA and Canada combined. More than 630 are resident species, although only six are endemic. Any part of the country is suited to successful birding, with many places offering the chance to see more than 100 species a day. Avian diversity peaks between October and April, when migrants flock in.

FAMILY

A growing body of genetic and fossil evidence suggests that birds are most properly placed with crocodiles as the only living members of the Archosauria family, a group that also includes the extinct dinosaurs.

The colorful scarlet macaw is spectacular in flight

SCARLET MACAW
(SPECIES: ARA MACAO)

RELATIVES: Green macaw

               LC

The smaller of Costa Rica's two macaw species, the scarlet macaw grows up to 36 in (90 cm) in length. It has a scarlet body and tail, turquoise rump, bright-yellow upper wings, and blue wing feathers. Today it occupies only a fraction of its former range throughout three-quarters of Costa Rica, being almost entirely restricted to Carara National Park and the Peninsula de Osa. Seasonally monogamous, the scarlet macaw emits loud, throaty squawks, especially when flying in pairs or flocking at clay licks. It nests in cavities in tall trees, where females lay one or two eggs (Dec–Apr).

KEEL-BILLED TOUCAN
(FAMILY: RAMPHASTOS SULFURATUS)

RELATIVES: Chestnut-mandibled toucan, collared aracari, emerald toucanet, fiery-billed aracari, yellow-eared toucanet

               LC

Costa Rica has six of the 42 toucan species, a Neotropical family of short-bodied birds with colorful, oversize beaks. The most recognizable is the keel-billed toucan, with a black body, yellow bib, red abdomen, and rainbow-hued bill. The chestnut-mandibled toucan has a brown and yellow bill; the two aracari species have red, yellow, and black bills; and the toucanets have smaller, green bodies. Toucans – whose main food is fleshy fruit, supplemented by small reptiles, hatchlings stolen from nests, and eggs – eat by throwing their head back and dropping the food into their throat.

The toucan's beak is lightweight and serrated like a saw

The great green macaw, found in the northern lowlands

GREAT GREEN MACAW
(SPECIES: ARA AMBIGUUS)

RELATIVES: Scarlet macaw

               CR

The second largest of the world's 17 macaw species, the great green, or Buffon's, macaw is known locally as *lapa verde* or *guacamayo*. It sports a bright-red fuzzy forehead, lime-green plumage that merges into teal-blue wings, and a blue-and-scarlet tail. Its massive hooked beak is designed to break open the nut of the *almendro* tree, its main food. As a result of deforestation and poaching for the illegal pet trade, only an estimated 300 great green macaws remain in the wild, including about 50 breeding pairs.

IUCN status CR: Critically Endangered; LC: Least Concern

The cattle egret's S-shaped neck gives it a hunched look

CATTLE EGRET
(SPECIES: BUBULCUS IBIS)

RELATIVES: Bare-throated tiger heron, great blue heron, green heron, snowy egret

 LC

This graceful, snow-white heron species is ubiquitous in open lowland habitats, mainly grassland, where it accompanies cattle and feeds on insects and small creatures such as frogs and lizards. It stands up to 22 in (56 cm) tall and has a short, stout neck, which it keeps drawn in an S-curve or tucked between its shoulders. Juveniles have black beaks that turn yellow as adults. In breeding season, its legs and bill turn red, and both sexes sprout orange plumes on the neck and back. Male egrets woo a different mate each season and display by raising their bills skyward and shaking twigs. It is common to see colonies roosting together in trees, usually beside rivers. The cattle egret is easily confused with the larger snowy egret, which has a black bill and legs.

BLUE-CROWNED MOTMOT
(SPECIES: MOMOTUS MOMOTA)

RELATIVES: Broad-billed motmot, keel-billed motmot, rufous motmot, tody motmot, turquoise-browed motmot

 LC

The most commonly seen member of the Momotidae family, the blue-crowned motmot is a low- and mid-elevation woodland species averaging 17 in (42 cm) beak to tail. It has a green body and wings, orange chest, and turquoise face with a black mask around its red eyes. Its long blue, bare-shafted tail with racket tips swings like a pendulum to warn predators. A heavy bill is good for skewering insects and lizards, but this bird also eats fruit and can even consume poison-dart frogs. Often living in colonies, the motmot makes its nest in a long tunnel that it carves from soil banks. Its call – "oot oot" – resembles that of an owl.

The blue-crowned motmot, with its distinctive tail

MONTEZUMA OROPENDOLA
(SPECIES: PSAROCOLIUS MONTEZUMA)

RELATIVES: Chestnut-headed oropendola

LC

A common resident of humid forests up to 3,300 ft (1,000 m), the oropendola is a deep-chestnut color, with a black head, turquoise cheeks, a pink wattle, an orange-tipped bill, and a bright-yellow tail. Averaging 20 in (50 cm), this bird lives in colonies of up to 60 individuals, choosing tall, free-standing trees in which females weave vines and twigs into pendulous nests that can be as long as 6.6 ft (2 m). When courting (Jan–May), the polygamous male makes rapid cooing calls and performs a complete somersault around a branch. A male will peck a female to ruffle her feathers prior to mating. The oropendola's diet consists of fruit, insects, and small vertebrates.

The Montezuma oropendola is a gregarious bird

Key to Field Guide icons *see p60*

Resplendent quetzal

Catching a glimpse of the resplendent quetzal – the largest and most striking member of the Trogon family and one of the most beautiful tropical birds – is the reason many people visit Costa Rica. The male, with its iridescent metallic-green feathers and arrestingly intense blood-red chest, bedazzles everyone who sees it in its mountainous cloud forest habitat, which ranges from southern Mexico to western Panama. It also features 24-in (60-cm) long tail feathers that it uses to impress females during mating displays. The female is less flamboyant.

The pit of the wild avocado fruit *is too big to pass through the quetzal's digestive tract, so the bird vomits it up after digesting the pulp.*

FEEDING

Although the quetzal's mixed diet includes caterpillars, insects, and even small frogs and lizards, this bird is primarily a frugivore that relies on wild avocados *(aguacatillos)* and other fruits of the laurel family. The quetzal is an altitudinal migrant, and its seasonal movements – between 3,280 ft and 9,840 ft (1,000 m and 3,000 m) – are dictated by the fruiting of various laurel species at different times of year. The quetzal swallows the fruit whole and eventually regurgitates the pit, in the process becoming an important propagator of the laurel tree. The quetzal is threatened by deforestation at lower altitudes, to which it descends during the non-breeding season.

FAMILY AND BREEDING

A solitary bird when not breeding, the resplendent quetzal is monogamous and territorial in the breeding season (Feb–Apr). The couple use their beaks to hollow out nests in soft, dead, or rotten trees. The cock and the hen take turns incubating the pale-blue eggs – the male by day and the female by night. Hatchlings typically emerge after 18 days, to be fed insects, larvae, and worms by both parents. Eventually, the female abandons the nest, leaving her young in the care of the male. Fledglings leave the nest after about one month.

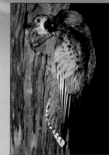

Young quetzals are fed larvae, insects, and worms

WHAT YOU MIGHT SEE

The quetzal initiates flight by dropping backward from its perch. Its flight is undulating, powered by intermittent and rapid wing beats. It feeds mid-flight, making an upward sally to pluck wild avocados. During breeding season, the male, which is highly territorial, will make spiraling flights to drive competitors away from its nest site, which is often an abandoned woodpecker nest.

The male looks after the eggs *by day and cares for the young when the female flees the nest.*

The quetzal's small, convex *wings are well adapted for flying through dense forests.*

IUCN status NT: Near Threatened

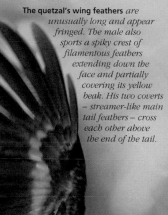

The quetzal's wing feathers *are unusually long and appear fringed. The male also sports a spiky crest of filamentous feathers extending down the face and partially covering its yellow beak. His two coverts – streamer-like main tail feathers – cross each other above the end of the tail.*

The Aztecs and the Mayas *worshiped the resplendent quetzal as a living depiction of Quetzalcoatl, the plumed serpent god. The male's tail feathers, used in ceremonies, were considered more precious than gold, and only nobles and priests were allowed to wear them. The bird's name derives from the Aztec word* quetzalli, *meaning "long plume."*

COMMUNICATION AND VOICE

The male quetzal is a true showman that attempts to impress a potential mate by flaunting its extraordinary tail feathers in spectacular mid-flight displays. Loose and slender, the feathers ripple gracefully behind it like the long ribbons of a rhythmic gymnast as the quetzal flies upward then swoops down in a graceful arc. Male quetzals also vocalize with at least six distinct calls, including a repetitive and slightly slurred "kwuee, kwuee, kwuee", shrill calls that resemble a cat's meow, and the striking of a high-pitched tuning fork.

The male quetzal has several very distinct calls

KEY FACTS

Name: *Pharomachrus mocinno*
Local names: *None*

Size Body length: 14–16 in (36–40 cm); Tail (male): 24 in (60 cm); Weight: 7–8 oz (200–225 g).

Lifespan 8–10 years.
Population in Costa Rica 2,800–4,800.
Conservation status NT.
Reproduction Females begin to reproduce in their second year and lay one or two eggs each season.

Habitat Humid subtropical forests and clearings above 3,300 ft (1,000 m).

Luscious subtropical forest in Chirripó

Top places to see
Chirripó, La Amistad, Monteverde, San Gerardo de Dota.

Sighting tips
The male's tail feathers are so long that they sometimes stick outside the nest.

Friends and foes
Adults are weak flyers, and they must keep a wary eye out for raptors. Olingos and other arboreal mammals raid nests.

Facts and trivia
The resplendent quetzal is difficult to keep in captivity due to its fragility. There is only one known case of it being successfully bred.

Males' tail feathers *begin to grow at three years, forming a train longer than its body.*

The quetzal's iridescent plumage *can vary from blue-violet to green-gold, depending on how sunlight hits it.*

Quetzals are sedate birds *and will perch motionless on branches for hours on end.*

BLACK VULTURE
(SPECIES: CORAGYPS ATRATUS)

RELATIVES: King vulture, turkey vulture, yellow-headed vulture

 LC

Known by Costa Ricans as *zopilote*, this black-feathered scavenger is present nation-wide below 6,600 ft (2,000 m). It stands 25.5 in (65 cm) tall and has a 5-ft (1.5-m) wing-span. The black vulture has a bald dark-gray head and a short hooked beak. It is frequently seen sunning with its wings outstretched, or hovering in the sky with its eye out for road kill and other carrion, its main food.

KING VULTURE
(SPECIES: SARCORAMPHUS PAPA)

RELATIVES: Black vulture, turkey vulture, yellow-headed vulture

 LC

A relative of the Andean condor, with a 6.6-ft (2-m) wingspan, the king vulture is a large lowland forest dweller. It has a white body and black wing and tail feathers; its bare neck, face, and beak are gaily colored in red, yellow, black, and purple. Mature birds also have a wrinkled fleshy swelling atop their beaks. The king vulture soars high in the sky; a sighting would be considered a feather in the cap for any birder.

HARPY EAGLE
(SPECIES: HARPIA HARPYJA)

RELATIVES: Black hawk-eagle, crested eagle, ornate hawk-eagle

 NT

By far the largest raptor in the Americas, this huge eagle is found in Costa Rica only in the Osa Peninsula and Talamancas. It is slate gray, with a white underside, black-and-white striped legs, and a pale-gray head crowned by an Elizabethan-style ruff. It hunts monkeys, sloths, and other prey in the rainforest canopy using its massive talons. The harpy builds a large nest high in a tree; females lay two eggs, but only the first is hatched.

NORTHERN CARACARA
(SPECIES: CARACARA CHERIWAY)

RELATIVES: Red-throated caracara, yellow-head caracara

 LC

One of the most common birds of prey in Costa Rica, the northern caracara is a lazy hunter that prefers to scavenge carrion. It is often seen stalking crabs and eels washed up on beaches, or perched roadside awaiting a chance kill. Standing up to 23 in (58 cm), it is brown except for a cream chest and head capped in black, plus yellow legs and a red cere at the base of its sharply hooked gray beak.

SLATY-TAILED TROGON
(SPECIES: TROGON MASSENA)

RELATIVES: Collared trogon, emerald trogon, violaceous trogon

 LC

Like all of Costa Rica's 11 trogon species, this cousin of the resplendent quetzal *(see pp92–3)* has an iridescent-green body, a short bill, and a long tail. Its abdomen is blood red. The slaty-tailed trogon likes humid lowland forest and can spend hours motion-less on a perch. It flies short distances on sallies to snatch insects and fruits on the wing, and it makes its home in rotten trees or termite nests.

FIERY-THROATED HUMMINGBIRD
(SPECIES: PANTERPE INSIGNIS)

RELATIVES: Green-crowned brilliant, rufous-tailed hummingbird

 LC

One of the most colorful of Costa Rica's 54 hummingbird species, this handsome bird is found only in the highlands. It grows to 4.5 in (11 cm) in length and has scintillating green and blue plumage, an orange throat, and a blue chest. It feeds on tiny insects and the nectar of bromeliads and epiphytes. Males aggressively defend their territories against competitors.

IUCN status LC: Least Concern; NT: Near Threatened; VU: Vulnerable

THREE-WATTLED BELLBIRD

(SPECIES: PROCNIAS TRICARUNCULATA)

RELATIVES: Bare-necked umbrella-bird, snowy cotinga

 VU

This elusive denizen of the cloud forest is famous for the male's distinctive three-part vocalization, which resembles the clang of a bell. Growing up to 12 in (30 cm) long, it has a copper-colored body, a white head, and three worm-like wattles dangling from atop its bill (hence its name). Its population is in rapid decline, but lucky birders might see one in Monteverde.

SUNBITTERN

(SPECIES: EURYPYGA HELIAS)

RELATIVES: Sungrebe

 LC

The sole member of the Eurypygidae family, this bird is similar to a heron but with a more horizontal posture and shorter legs. The sunbittern stalks small vertebrates and fish along streams and ponds in lowland forest. Its plumage – in multiple shades of gray, black, and brown – is broken up with linear patterns for camouflage in dappled sunlight. During courtship, or when threatened, it spreads its wings to display vivid red, yellow, and black eyespots.

GREAT CURASSOW

(SPECIES: CRAX RUBRA)

RELATIVES: Black guan

 VU

The great curassow is a large ground bird with dark-brown or black feathers and a black-and-white striped head topped by a prominent, forward-curling crest. The male's plumage has a lustrous blue sheen. Restricted to national parks as a result of hunting and deforestation, it lives in lowland humid forests, such as at La Selva Biological Station. The curassow runs rather than flies, and forages in the undergrowth for fruits, seeds, and insects.

BLUE DACNIS

(SPECIES: DACNIS CAYANA)

RELATIVES: Scarlet-thighed dacnis, yellow-throated euphonia

 LC

A characteristic passerine, this brightly colored member of the tanager family stands out for its azure plumage and turquoise cap, which contrast against its black wings and eye mask. The female is bright green, with blue head and shoulders. Common in the Pacific lowlands, the blue dacnis likes to hawk its insect prey at the forest edge, but it is also often seen feasting at banana feeders placed in hotel gardens to draw butterflies.

GREEN HONEYCREEPER

(SPECIES: CHLOROPHANES SPIZA)

RELATIVES: Gray-headed tanager, red-legged honeycreeper

 LC

Preferring the forest canopy and clearings, this 5.5-in (14-cm) long bird has a cyan body, teal wings, a black hood, and a yellow beak. The grass-green female has a straw-yellow throat but lacks the beautiful iridescence of the male. Its sleek profile, upright stance, and long, decurved bill give it a haughty posture. A fruit eater, it supplements its diet with nectar and insects, and it often feeds in flocks.

GREAT ANTSHRIKE

(SPECIES: TARABA MAJOR)

RELATIVES: Dusky antbird, russet antshrike, scaled antpitta

 LC

One of more than 30 related birds that specialize in feasting on ants and termites, the great antshrike is a striking two-tone bird with brilliant red eyes. The male is black with a white abdomen and white wing bars; the female is reddish. It typically hunts in pairs, using its sharp, heavy beak to pick at insects and skewer larger prey as it skulks about the dense forest undergrowth. It wags its tail feathers while it sings.

Key to Field Guide icons *see p60*

ANHINGA
(SPECIES: ANHINGA ANHINGA)

RELATIVES: Neotropic cormorant

 LC

Commonly seen swimming with only its neck above the water surface, this large freshwater bird has evolved for diving in search of fish and amphibians. It dries out its feathers by perching on branches and spreading its wings. Mostly black, with a brownish neck and a yellow beak, the anhinga has wings streaked with silver feathers. It has a long bill and a very long, S-shaped neck that explains its more common name: snakebird.

NORTHERN JACANA
(SPECIES: JACANA SPINOSA)

RELATIVES: Wattled jacana

 LC

Jacanas are medium-sized wetland birds with long legs and huge elongated toes that enable them to walk atop floating vegetation. Unusually among birds, the female is not monogamous, mating with up to four males, each of which builds and defends its own nest and raises the young alone. With its chestnut body, black head and neck, and yellow bill, the Northern jacana is a handsome sight tripping across the water lilies at Caño Negro Wildlife Refuge.

JABIRU STORK
(SPECIES: JABIRU MYCTERIA)

RELATIVES: Wood stork

LC

The huge Jabiru stork is unmistakable thanks to its massive and intimidating black bill, which is upturned at the tip. Standing up to 5 ft (1.5 m) tall, it is a common sight along rivers and wetlands such as Palo Verde National Park, where it lives in large groups that forage for fish and amphibians. It is conspicuous for its snow-white body and wings, which contrast with the red band around its neck and its soot-black head and legs.

WHITE IBIS
(SPECIES: EUDOCIMUS ALBUS)

RELATIVES: Glossy ibis, roseate spoonbill

 LC

The sight of white ibis flying with necks outstretched is a genuine thrill for birders. Colonial by instinct, the white ibis nests communally, often with hundreds of other individuals. Its preferred habitats are mangroves and brackish marshes. Its long, downcurved bill and gray-pink face mask turn flush during mating season. The black tips of its wings can be seen only in flight – the bird is all white when at rest.

ROSEATE SPOONBILL
(SPECIES: PLATALEA AJAJA)

RELATIVES: Green ibis, white-face ibis

 LC

Inhabiting shallow freshwater and brackish lagoons, this bird is named for its spatulate bill, which it sweeps from side to side in the water to sift aquatic beetles and vertebrates. This long-necked wader stands up to 31 in (80 cm) tall atop long legs. Its back, neck, and head are typically white, while its pink wing plumage derives from the shrimp in its diet. Like other members of the Threskiornithidae family, it lays eggs in a treetop stick nest.

BOAT-BILLED HERON
(SPECIES: COCHLEARIUS COCHLEARIUS)

RELATIVES: Bare-throated tiger heron, tri-colored heron

LC

One of the oddest-looking members of the heron family, the boat-billed heron has a big beak that is far broader than it is deep, looking like an upturned boat. Its huge black eyes hint at its nocturnal nature. Gray, fawn, and white, this handsome bird lives in mangroves and at the edge of freshwater habitats, where it hunts frogs, crabs, and fish. It will crouch for hours, awaiting prey.

BARE-THROATED TIGER HERON

(SPECIES: TIGRISOMA MEXICANUM)

RELATIVES: Great blue heron, green heron

 LC

This elegant upright wader is up to 3 ft (90 cm) tall, with a long, thick neck and gray-brown feathers striped with black streaks. Juveniles have more pronounced "tiger stripes" against their orange plumage. The most wide-spread of several beautiful heron species, it is often seen standing motionless beside watercourses and ponds, ready to skewer fish and frogs with its long yellow bill.

BLUE-WINGED TEAL

(SPECIES: ANAS DISCORS)

RELATIVES: Fulvous whistling duck, mallard

 LC

A seasonal migrant, this small duck flocks to Costa Rica in the winter months to escape the snows of North America and to breed; it is usually among the first migrants to arrive in the fall. Mottled brown with a gray-blue head and a black beak, it is named for its sky-blue wing patches. The mallard, well known in temperate countries for the iridescent-green head of the male, is another among 16 duck species in Costa Rica.

MUSCOVY DUCK

(SPECIES: CAIRINA MOSCHATA)

RELATIVES: American wigeon, Northern pintail

 LC

Despite its name, this large non-migratory duck is native to Central America – indeed, the male's hissing call is one of the distinctive sounds of the wetlands. Reaching up to 34 in (86 cm) in length, this bird has an iridescent black-green plumage with white wing patches, white neck, and a bright-red, heavily wrinkled eye patch. An avid insect eater, it helps keep down mosquito populations by gobbling their larvae.

BLUE-FOOTED BOOBY

(SPECIES: SULA NEBOUXII)

RELATIVES: Brown booby, masked booby

 LC

A delight to watch, either in flight or performing its court-ship dance, the blue-footed booby nests on rocky offshore islands from Nicoya to Isla del Coco. This long-winged seabird has fawn and white plumage and bright-blue feet, which the male displays – first one foot, then the other – to impress females while pointing its head and tail skyward. It feeds on fish and has nostrils sealed for diving.

BROWN PELICAN

(SPECIES: PELECANUS OCCIDENTALIS)

RELATIVES: White pelican

 LC

This large gray-brown seabird with a yellow head and crown nests in large groups on off-shore islands and is visible up and down both Costa Rican coasts. Brown pelicans are often seen flying overhead in long V formations or skimming the ocean in single file. Their huge wings, ideal for gliding, are tucked in for plunging dives into the ocean, while the lower half of their massive hooked bill has an expand-able pouch for scooping up vast quantities of fish.

FRIGATEBIRD

(SPECIES: FREGATA MAGNIFICENS)

RELATIVES: Great frigatebird

LC

An agile aerial pirate that feeds primarily by harassing other birds until they release or regurgitate fish, this huge iridescent-black seabird has a wingspan up to 85 in (215 cm) and the lightest weight-to-size ratio of any bird in the world. The frigatebird never lands on water, for which it is ill-suited. It has a forked tail, crooked wings, and a long, sinister beak. During court-ship, roosting males inflate a red sac on their throat while females fly overhead.

Key to Field Guide icons *see p60*

COSTA RICA
AREA BY AREA

Costa Rica at a Glance

Brimming with natural wonders, Costa Rica's incredibly diverse terrain offers lush rain- and cloud forests that host an array of colorful fauna, craggy mountains, smoke-spewing volcanoes, and stunning beaches in every shade, from gold to taupe to black. Wildlife and adventure activities abound, ranging from canopy tours and turtle-watching to scuba diving and whitewater rafting. It is best to concentrate on the national parks and other natural attractions; very few towns are of interest. This guide divides the country into seven regions; each area is color-coded as shown here.

Parque Nacional Santa Rosa *(see pp184–5)*

THE NORTHERN ZONE *(see pp194–209)*

GUANACASTE AND NORTHERN NICOYA *(see pp170–93)*

Parque Nacional Volcán Arenal (see p199) *features Costa Rica's most active volcano. It forms a dramatic backdrop for hiking, canopy tours, horseback riding, and soaks in thermal hot springs.*

THE CENTRAL PACIFIC AND SOUTHERN NICOYA *(see pp156–69)*

| 0 km | 50 |
| 0 miles | 50 |

Monteverde (see pp174–8) *is famous for its cloud forest reserves, which draw birders eager for a sighting of resplendent quetzals.*

ISLA DEL COCO

| 0 km | 2 |
| 0 miles | 2 |

Isla del Coco (see p241), *off the southwest coast, is remote and rugged. Hammerhead and whale sharks draw scuba divers.*

◁ Farmland in a valley in the province of Alajuela, in the Central Highlands

Parque Nacional Volcán Poás (see p140) *is popular with Costa Ricans, who drive to the rim to peer into the crater of this smoldering volcano. On clear days the views are magnificent.*

THE CARIBBEAN
(see pp210–21)

THE CENTRAL HIGHLANDS
(see pp130–55)

SAN JOSE
(see pp102–29)

Parque Nacional Tortuguero (see p217), *a pristine rainforest habitat, can be explored by boat along canals that offer excellent wildlife viewing. Green turtles nest on the seemingly endless beach.*

THE SOUTHERN ZONE
(see pp222–41)

Parque Nacional
Corcovado (see pp236–7)

Parque Nacional Manuel Antonio
(see pp168–9) *combines coral reefs, white-sand beaches, and lush forests full of wildlife that is easily spotted while hiking well-maintained trails.*

Teatro Nacional (see pp110–11) *is San José's major architectural draw. This bustling and amorphous city's attractions also include museums honoring pre-Columbian culture.*

SAN JOSE

Nestled amid craggy peaks, the capital city enjoys a splendid setting and idyllic weather. Its magnificent Teatro Nacional and outstanding museums add to San José's attractions. The city's strongest draw, however, is its location in the heart of Costa Rica, which is ideal for hub-and-spoke touring. For many visitors, San José is their first experience of the country, providing an intriguing introduction to the pleasures that await farther afield.

Affectionately called *chepe* (the local nickname for anyone named José) by its inhabitants, San José is perched at an elevation of 3,800 ft (1,150 m), with the Poás, Barva, and Irazú volcanoes rising gracefully over the city to the north, and the rugged Talamanca Mountains to the south. Temperatures are a springlike 25° C (76° F) year-round, and the air is crisp and clear thanks to near-constant breezes.

Founded in 1737, San José grew very slowly through its first 100 years. Its creation on the eve of the coffee boom in the heart of coffee country, however, was advantageous. By 1823, the town had grown to challenge Cartago – the then capital – for supremacy. Following a brief civil war, San José was named capital and quickly eclipsed other cities as prominent *cafetaleros* (coffee barons) imported skilled European artisans to beautify the city with fine structures.

Since the 1960s, high rise buildings and sprawling slum *barrios* (neighborhoods) have changed the profile of this city of one-third of a million people. Still, San José has its own charm. The main tourist sights, including the Teatro Nacional (National Theater), the gold and jade museums, and numerous plazas, are centered around the city core, within walking distance of one another. Everywhere, traffic squeezes tight at rush hour, when Costa Rican civility gives way to dog-eat-dog driving.

Varieties of fruit arranged temptingly in stalls at the Mercado Central

◁ Statue in the lavishly decorated foyer of San José's Teatro Nacional

Exploring San José

Downtown San José features the city's top places of interest. The dazzling Teatro Nacional on Avenida 2, graced by Baroque and Neoclassical architecture, is San José's most remarkable building. The nearby Museo del Oro Precolombino, as well as the Museo de Jade Fidel Tristán Castro and the Museo Nacional in the east – all of which display pre-Columbian artifacts – are also major attractions. Another must-see is the Centro Costarricense de Ciencias y Cultura, to the northwest, with its superb rotating art exhibitions. Busts of prominent historical figures dot Parque España and Parque Nacional. The main historic quarter, Barrio Amón, boasts fine colonial structures along Avenida 9, while the suburb of Escazú offers excellent dining and a lively nightlife.

A quiet, tree-lined street in a residential locality of San José

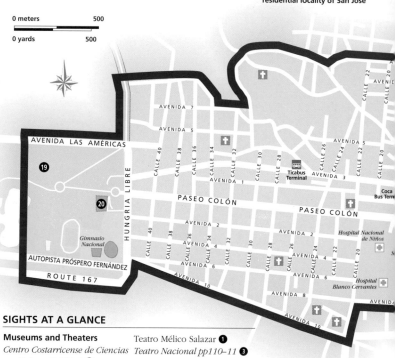

Getting ready for some angling at the man-made lake in Parque Sabana

GREATER SAN JOSE

Juan Santamaría International Airport

Tobias Bolaños Domestic Airport

Heredia
San Juan

San Pedro

SAN JOSE

Colón

Alajuelita

Desamparados

Aserri

0 km   5

0 miles   5

KEY

■ Area of the main map

SEE ALSO

• *Where to Stay* pp248–51

• *Where to Eat* pp272–4

ROUTE 108

ROUTE 108

BARRIO PASA DE LA VACA

BARRIO TOURNON

Río Torres

BARRIO AIZA

Bishop's Castle

PARQUE ZOOLÓGICA SIMÓN BOLÍVAR

BARRIO ARANJUEZ

Casa Verde

Hotel Don Carlos

Casa Amarilla

Legación de Mexico

Hospital Calderón Guardia

Mercado Borbón

Radiográfica Costarricense

Biblioteca Nacional

Banco Nacional de Costa Rica

Iglesia El Carmen

BARRIO MERCED

Banco Central

Tribunal Supremo de Elecciones

Iglesia La Merced

Ramón de Costa Rica

PLAZA DE LA CULTURA

Banco Central

PLAZA DE LA DEMOCRACIA

Gran Hotel

PARQUE CENTRAL

Teatro Variedades La Caja

BARRIO SOLEDAD

Iglesia La Soledad

KEY

■ Sight/place of interest

✈ International airport

✕ Domestic airport

🚌 Bus station

🚓 Police station

P Parking

✉ Post office

✚ Hospital

✝ Church

▬ Expressway

▬ Pedestrian street

GETTING AROUND

The main sights, concentrated in downtown San José, are best explored on foot. To explore farther afield, take a taxi – this is a good way of getting around the warren of narrow, congested, one-way streets. Alternatively, you can rent a car, but do be prepared for the aggressive driving style of Costa Ricans *(see p317)*. Jose Santamaría International Airport and Tobias Bolaños domestic airport are located 10 miles (17 km) northwest and 4 miles (6 km) west of downtown respectively. The international airport is well connected by airport taxis and buses to the city center; the domestic airport is served by taxis. For more details, see pages 310–11 and 316–17.

Street-by-Street: San José Center

Laid out in a grid of narrow, heavily trafficked one-way streets, San José's tightly condensed core contains the city's most significant sights. The main artery is the broad Avenida 2, which is thronged with honking taxis and buses threading past tree-shaded Parque Central. Running parallel to it and to the north is the Avenida Central, a pedestrian precinct lined with department stores, specialist shops, and places to eat. At the heart of this stroll-and-shop area lies the small concrete Plaza de la Cultura, which hums with activity all day – it is a popular meeting place for young people and is packed with hawkers as well as musicians and other entertainers.

Teatro Mélico Salazar
Dating from the 1920s, this theater has a Neoclassical façade and a simple interior ❶

Avenida 2
This bustling avenue is lined with important buildings, including banks, between Calles 1 and 3. Traffic flows eastward on this four lane-wide avenue, which slopes downhill east of Calle 3.

Parque Central
Laid out in 1885 and shaded by palms and guanacaste trees, the compact central plaza has an unusual bandstand, which is supported by arches. Beneath it is the children's library, Biblioteca Carmen Lyra.

Bronze statue of a street cleaner

Statue of Pope John Paul II, made from marble by Jiménez Deredia.

La Curia (The Archbishop's Palace)

★ Catedral Metropolitana
The blue-domed Metropolitan Cathedral, built in 1871 in a simple Greek Orthodox style, features an elaborate altar ❷

STAR SIGHTS

★ Catedral Metropolitana

★ Museo del Oro Precolombino

★ Teatro Nacional

Plaza de la Cultura
Created between 1975 and 1983, this is San José's main hub of social activity, despite its relatively austere layout.

★ Teatro Nacional
The capital's finest architectural gem, the National Theater is renowned for its ceiling, which depicts a coffee harvest, and for its lavish tri-level, 1,040-seat auditorium. The theater was built in the early 1890s ❸

The Gran Hotel, designed by architect Juan Joaquín Jiménez in 1930, is a city landmark *(see p248).*

Clock tower

★ Museo del Oro Precolombino
A subterranean modern structure, the Museum of Pre-Columbian Gold houses a superb collection of ancient gold adornments, as well as the National Coin Collection ❹

AVENIDA 1

AVENIDA

CENTRAL

CENTRAL

AVENIDA 2

CALLE 5

CALLE 3

CALLE 7

Teatro Variedades was founded in 1891. Today it functions as a cinema.

Parque Mora Fernández is a palm-shaded plaza, lively with *marimba* music.

AVENIDA 4

Statue of Juan Mora Fernández, Costa Rica's first president.

La Caja (Social Security Building)

0 meters	100
0 yards	100

KEY

- - - Suggested route

The horseshoe-shaped auditorium of Teatro Mélico Salazar

Teatro Mélico Salazar ❶

Map 1 C4. Calle Central and Ave 2.
Tel 2233-5424. 🚌 ◯ 8am–4pm
Mon–Fri. 📷 by appointment. 🖥
www.teatromelico.go.cr

One of the city's landmarks, this theater was built in 1928 as the Teatro Raventós, and was renamed in 1986 after Manuel "Mélico" Salazar Zúñiga (1887–1950), a celebrated Costa Rican tenor. Designed by architect José Fabio Garnier, it has a Neoclassical façade adorned with fluted Corinthian pilasters. To the left of the entrance is a larger-than-life bronze bust of Zúñiga. To the right is a bas-relief plaque honoring José Raventós Gual, who had the theater built.

The handsome lobby, in checkered green-and-black tile, leads into a triple-tiered, horseshoe-shaped auditorium, which hosts theatrical and musical events, as well as folk dance shows. The auditorium has a striking parquet wooden floor beneath a wood-paneled ceiling, which is decorated with a simple mural and a wrought-iron chandelier.

Catedral Metropolitana ❷

Map 1 C4. Calle Central and Aves 2/4. **Tel** 2221-3820. 🚌 ◯ 6am–noon & 3–6pm Mon–Sat, 6am–9pm Sun. 🚻 ♿

San José's pre-eminent church, the Metropolitan Cathedral was built in 1871 to replace the original cathedral, which

had been destroyed by an earthquake in 1820. Designed by Eusebio Rodríguez, the austere-looking structure combines Greek Orthodox, Neoclassical, and Baroque styles. Its linear façade is supported by an arcade of Doric columns and topped by a Neoclassical pediment with steeples on each side. Inside, a vaulted ceiling runs the length of the nave, supported by two rows of fluted columns. In a glass case to the left of the entrance is a life-size statue of Christ.

Fountain on Avenida Central

Although entirely lacking the ornate Baroque gilt of many other Latin American churches, the cathedral has many fine features, notably an exquisite Colonial-style tiled floor and beautiful stained-glass windows depicting biblical scenes. The main altar, beneath a cupola, comprises a simple wooden

Pillared façade of the austere Catedral Metropolitana

base atop a marble plinth and supports a wooden figure of Christ and cherubs.

To the left of the main altar is the Capilla del Santísimo (Chapel of the Holy Sacrament), which has walls and ceilings decorated with wooden quadrants painted with floral motifs. The short gallery that leads to the chapel contains a glass-and-gilt coffin with a naked statue of Christ draped with a sash in the colors of the Costa Rican flag.

To the south of the cathedral is **La Curía** (The Palace of the Archbishop), built in 1887. This two-story structure has been remodeled, and is closed to the public. A small garden in front features a life-size bronze statue of Monseñor Bernardo Augusto Thiel Hoffman (1850–1901), the German-born second archbishop of Costa Rica. Hoffman lies buried in the crypt of the cathedral, alongside former president Tomás Guardia (see p43).

On the cathedral's north side is a contemporary marble statue of Pope John Paul II by Jiménez Deredia.

Teatro Nacional ❸

See pp110–11.

Museo del Oro Precolombino ❹

See pp112–13.

Mercado Central ❺

Map 1 B3. Calles 6/8 and Aves Central/1. **Tel** 2295-6104. 🚌 ◯ 6am–8pm Mon–Sat. 🍴

An intriguing curiosity, San José's Central Market was built in 1881. The building, which takes up an entire block northwest of the Catedral Metropolitana, is itself rather uninspiring, but its warren of narrow alleyways, hemmed in by more than 200 stalls, immerse visitors in a slice of Costa Rican life. This quintessential Latin American market thrives as a chaotic emporium of the exotic, with every conceivable item for sale, from herbal remedies and fresh-cut flowers to snakeskin boots and saddles for *sabaneros* (cowboys).

Toward the center, *sodas* (food stalls) offer inexpensive cooked meals sold at the counter. The market extends one block north to **Mercado Borbón**, which has stalls of butchers, fishmongers, and fruit sellers, and buyers crowded in as thick as sardines. Next to the market's entrance on the southeast corner, there are plaques honoring important political figures.

Pickpockets operate within the tightly packed alleys of the market. Remember to leave your valuables in the hotel safe when you venture out. It is best to tuck your camera well out of sight when it is not in use.

Edificio Correos ⑥

Map 1 B3. Calle 2 and Aves 1/3. **Tel** 2223-6918. 🚌 ◯ 7:30am–6pm Mon–Fri, 7:30am–noon Sat. 🖥 ♿ **Museo Filatélico de Costa Rica Tel** 2223-9766 (ext. 205). ◯ 8am–5pm Mon–Fri. ● public hols. 🚫

The building housing the main post office, or Correo Central, was completed in 1917. Designed by Luis Llach in eclectic style, it has a pea-green reinforced concrete façade, which is embellished

The Edificio Correos, featuring a blend of architectural styles

with Corinthian pilasters. The arched centerpiece is topped by a shield and supported by angels bearing the national coat of arms. The post office is abuzz with the comings and goings of locals picking up their mail at *apartados* (post office boxes) that fill the ground floor of the two-storey atrium.

Philatelists can view rare stamps in the small **Museo Filatélico de Costa Rica** (Philatelic Museum of Costa Rica), which takes up three rooms on the second floor. The first room has a fine collection of old telephones and telegraphic equipment that goes back more than 100 years.

The collection of stamps occupies the other two rooms, which also have exhibits on the history of philately in Costa Rica. The nation's first stamp, from

1863, is displayed here. Other exhibits include important and rare stamps from abroad, including the English Penny Black. The museum hosts a stamp exchange on the first Saturday of every month. The Edificio Correos is fronted by a pedestrian plaza shaded by fig trees. Towering over the plaza is a statue of the first president of Costa Rica, Juan Mora Fernández, who was in power from 1824 to 1828. Nearby, to the southwest of the Edificio Correos is another square, **Plaza Los Presentes**, which is dominated by *Los Presentes*, a contemporary monument in bronze. Created in 1979 by the well-known sculptor Fernando Calvo, the monument consists of statues of a dozen Costa Rican *campesinos* (peasant farmers). Shoeshines can be seen at work in the leafy plaza.

Statue of Juan Mora Fernández opposite Edificio Correos

Los Presentes by Fernando Calvo, in Plaza Los Presentes, near Edificio Correos

Teatro Nacional ❸

Considered the finest historic building in San José, the National Theater was conceived in 1890, when Spanish-born prima donna Adelina Patti sidestepped Costa Rica while on a Central American tour due to the lack of a suitable venue. This spurred the ruling coffee barons to levy a tax on coffee exports to fund the building of a grand theater. Locals claim, disputably, that the structure was modeled on the Paris Opera House. Completed in 1897, it was inaugurated with a performance of *El Fausto de Gournod* by the Paris Opera. Declared a National Monument in 1965, the theater has a lavish Neo-Baroque interior, replete with statues, paintings, marble staircases, and parquet floors made of 10 species of hardwood.

Statue of Music

La Danza de Vignami, painted on the ceiling of the auditorium

Teatro Café
The coffee shop adjoining the lobby is decorated in black and white tile, and has marble-topped tables. The ceiling is painted with a triptych.

Allegorical statues of the Muses of Music, Dance, and Fame top the Neoclassical façade.

Statue of Calderón de la Barca, the 17th-century dramatist, by Italian artist Adriático Froli.

The small garden is formally patterned and features a life-size marble statue of a female flautist (1997) by Jorge Jiménez Deredia.

A statue of Ludwig van Beethoven, created in the 1890s by Adriático Froli, stands in an alcove.

Entrance Lobby
With its pink marble floor and bronze-tipped Corinthian marble columns, the lobby hints at the splendors to come. The doors are topped by gilt pediments adorned with lions' faces. The wooden ceiling has a simple floral motif.

STAR FEATURES

★ Auditorium

★ Coffee Mural

★ Foyer

★ **Coffee Mural**
Depicting a coffee harvest, the huge mural on the ceiling of the intermezzo, between the lobby and the auditorium, was painted in 1897 by Milanese artist Aleardo Villa. The scene is full of errors, with coffee being shown as a coastal crop instead of a highland one.

VISITORS' CHECKLIST

Map 1 C4. Calles 3/5 and Ave 2. **Tel** 2221-3756. 🚍 Cemeterio-Estadio. ◯ 9am–4pm Mon–Sat. 🎨 🎭 **Shows** Orquesta Sinfónia Nacional (National Symphony Orchestra) performances Mar–Dec: 8pm Thu and Fri; 10:30am Sun. 🎫 9am–5pm Mon–Sat. **www.**teatronacional.go.cr

The Palco Presidencial, or presidential balcony, has a ceiling mural, *Alegoria a la Patria y la Justícia*, painted in 1897 by Roberto Fontana.

The structure was built with a steel frame.

The exterior of the building is of sandstone.

★ **Auditorium**
Dominated by a rotunda ceiling with a mural of cherubs and deities, the red-and-gold auditorium has three floors, a horseshoe shape, and wrought-iron seats. The stage can be lowered and raised.

★ **Foyer**
A double staircase with gold-gilt banisters leads to the magnificent foyer, which features pink marble and a surfeit of crystals, gilt mirrors, and gold-leaf embellishments. Splendid murals show scenes of Costa Rican life.

Museo del Oro Precolombino ❹

Frog figurine in gold

Occupying the starkly modern subterranean space beneath the Plaza de la Cultura and managed by the Banco Central de Costa Rica, the Museum of Pre-Columbian Gold boasts a dazzling display of ancient gold items. The collection consists of more than 1,600 pieces of pre-Columbian gold dating back to AD 500. Most of the amulets, earrings, shamanic animal figures, and erotic statuettes exhibited here originated in southwest Costa Rica, attesting to the sophisticated art of the Diquis culture. The uses and crafting of these items are demonstrated with the help of models and other displays, which also depict the social and cultural evolution of pre-Columbian cultures.

★ Museo de Numismática
The National Coin Museum exhibits date back to 1502. The displays include coins, bank notes, and unofficial currency such as coffee tokens.

The First Coin
Costa Rica's first coin, called the Medio Escudo, was minted in 1825, when the country was part of the Federation of Central America (see p42).

Frog figurines, a traditional symbol of life for indigenous tribes, are among the gold displays.

Auditorium

★ El Guerrero
The most stunning piece is the life-size warrior adorned with gold ornaments, including a gold headband, chest disc (paten), amulets, and ankle rings. Gold objects were a symbol of authority.

Model of an Indian village

Third level

El Curandero (The Healer) is a life-size model of a "medicine man" performing a ritual healing using medicinal plants.

Gold Craftsmanship
This section explains how pre-Columbian cultures utilized repoussé, the technique of decorating metal surfaces by hammering from the back.

STAR FEATURES

★ El Guerrero

★ Museo de Numismática

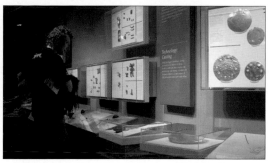

Golden treasures
The main exhibition space, situated on the third level, is packed with golden objects of all sizes, from large gold chest discs to small, intricate pieces of jewelry.

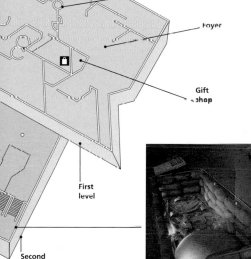

Entrance

Foyer

Gift shop

First level

Second level

GALLERY GUIDE

The museum occupies three floors below the plaza. Beyond the entrance, a broad foyer leads past a temporary exhibition space to the Museo de Numismática. Adjacent to this is a spiral staircase that descends to the second level. This floor offers an intro-duction to pre-Columbian culture and metallurgy, as well as temporary exhibitions that are changed every four months. The third level features an auditorium as well as the main gallery, which displays a permanent exhibi-tion of ancient gold items.

Finca 4 Site

This is a replica of a pre-Columbian grave unearthed in the 1950s. Discovered on a banana plantation in southeastern Costa Rica, the grave contained 88 gold objects.

Subterranean Vault
Accessed from Calle 5 by a broad staircase, the Gold Museum is housed in an underground space protected by steel doors.

LOST WAX TECHNIQUE

Pre-Columbian groups, notably the Chibchas and Diquis of the Pacific southwest, were masterful goldsmiths, skilled in the use of the "lost wax" technique. Here, the desired form is carved in wax, then molded with clay and baked. The wax melts, leaving a negative into which molten metal is poured to attain the required result. Most pre-Columbian pieces were alloys of gold and copper, with the alloy called *tumbaga* being the most commonly used.

Gold shaman figurine

The intriguing Edificio Metálico, constructed entirely of metal

Parque Morazán ❼

Map 2 D3 Calles 5/9 and Aves 3/5. 🚌

Laid out as Plaza González Víquez on the site of an open-air reservoir in 1930, this small park was later renamed after Francisco Morazán *(see p42)*. The Honduran-born Central American federalist served briefly as president of Costa Rica before being executed in 1842. Shaded by *tabebuia* (also called trumpet trees) that bloom in the dry season, the park is popular with office workers, schoolchildren, and lovers, although it is to be avoided at night when transvestites gather.

The park's four ornate iron gateways are topped by Roman urns. At its center is the domed Neoclassical **Templo de Música**, built in 1920. Busts honor Morazán and other luminaries such as South American liberator Simón Bolívar (1783–1830). To the park's southwest is a bronze statue of former president Julio García, seated in a chair. Facing the park on the northeast, is an 11-ft (3.5-m) tall statue of another former president, Daniel Quiros, by Costa Rican artist Olger Villegas.

Edificio Metálico ❽

Map 2 D3. Calle 9 and Aves 5/7. *Tel* 2222-0026. 🚌

Constructed entirely of pre-fabricated pieces of metal, this intriguing San José edifice, standing between Parque Morazán and Parque España, was designed by

French architect Charles Thirio. The metal pieces were cast in Belgium in 1892 and shipped to Costa Rica for welding and assembly in situ. Since then, it has functioned as an elementary school, the Escuela Buenaventura Corrales y Julia Lang. A small bust of Minerva, the Roman goddess of wisdom, sits on top of its imposing Neoclassical façade. Take in a bird's-eye view of its exterior from the lobby of the Museo de Jade Fidel Tristán Castro across the street.

Carved pillars at Casa Amarilla

Parque España ❾

Map 2 D3. Calles 9/11 and Aves 3/7. 🚌 **Casa Amarilla** *Tel* 2223-7555. ◯ *8am–4pm Mon–Fri.* 📷 *by appointment.*

Shaded by densely packed trees and bamboo groves, this leafy plaza is pleasantly full of birdsong. It was here,

The Colonial-style pavilion in Parque España

in 1903, that the Costa Rican national anthem, written by José María Zeledón Brenes (1877–1949) and Manuel María Gutiérrez (1829–87), was first performed.

On the northeast corner, a quaint Colonial-style *pabellón* (pavilion), erected in 1947, is inlaid with sepia-toned ceramic murals of the apparition of the Lady of Los Angeles, the church of Orosi, and the cathedral of Heredia. A patinated life-size statue of conquistador Juan Vásquez de Coronado *(see p40)* stands at the southwest corner of the park. Brick pathways wind past busts of important figures, including Queen Isabel II of Spain (1830–1904) and philanthropist Andrew Carnegie (1835–1919). Facing the northwest side of the park is the ocher-colored, stuccoed **Casa Amarilla** (Yellow House). Designed by architect Henry Wiffield in an ornate Spanish Baroque style, it was completed in 1916 to house the Pan-American Court of Justice. In later years it served as the Presidential Residence and the Asamblea Legislativa. Today, the Foreign Relations Ministry has its offices here.

The most striking element of Casa Amarilla is the grand ornamental lintel above the front door. The grounds behind the ministry contain a section of the Berlin Wall; this can be viewed at the corner of Calle 13 and Avenida 9.

The towering building west of the Casa Amarilla is the **Instituto Nacional de Seguro** (INS or the National Institute of Insurance). In its front courtyard, paying homage to the institution of the family, is *La Familia*, a huge sculpture by Francisco Zúñiga *(see p19)*.

The **Legación de Mexico**, 55 yd (50 m) east along Avenida 7, was built in 1924 and is a splendid example of Colonial-style architecture. The armistice of the 1948 War of Liberation was signed here.

◁ **The pedestrian plaza in front of the Edificio Correos**

Museo de Jade Fidel Tristán Castro ⑩

Map 2 D3. Calle 9 and Ave 7.
***Tel** 2287-6034.* 8:30am–3:30pm Mon–Fri, 9am–1pm Sat.
public hols.

Located on the first floor of the National Institute of Insurance (INS) building, the Fidel Tristán Castro Jade Museum contains the largest collection of pre-Columbian jade in the Americas. It was founded by Fidel Tristán Castro, the first president of the INS, in 1977. The collection consists of adzes, ceremonial heads, and decorative pieces from 500 BC to AD 800. There are also *metates* (grinding tables made of volcanic stone), ceramics, and gold ornaments. The Sala de Jade displays jade pendants in kaleidoscopic hues of green and blue, exquisitely backlit to demonstrate their translucent quality. The jade pieces that make up this collection did not come from archaeological sites – they were purchased from private collectors who had bought them from looters.

Barrio Amón ⑪

Map 1 C2. Calles Central/9 and Aves 7/13.

The richest architectural collection in San José is the complex of historic homes in this residential *barrio* (neighborhood), founded in the 1890s by French immigrant Amón Fasileau Duplantier. Once on the verge of decay, the area has now undergone restoration.

The most interesting homes are along Avenida 9; the stretch between Calles 3 and 7 is lined with beautiful ceramic murals by local artist Fernando Matamoros showing traditional Costa Rican scenes.

Begin at Calle 11, where No. 980 is a two-story colonial mansion boasting a life-size *campesino* (peasant) in pre-cast concrete gazing over the wrought-iron railing. At Calle 7, the **Hotel Don Carlos** *(see p248)* was

Detail of a ceramic mural showing a traditional scene, Barrio Amón

formerly the residence of President Tomás Guardia *(see p43)* and is a curious blend of Art Deco and Neoclassical styles. One block west, at the corner of Calle 5, is the **Casa Verde**, a clapboard building of New Orleans pine, dating to 1910 and notable for its soaring lounge spectacularly lit by a stained-glass atrium.

The most audacious building in this *barrio* is the **Bishop's Castle** at Avenida 11 and Calle 3. It was built in 1930 in ornate Moorish style with turrets, crenellations, keyhole windows, a central dome, and a façade decorated with glazed tiles showing scenes from *Don Quixote*.

Centro Nacional de la Cultura ⑫

Map 2 D3. Calles 11/15 and Aves 3/7.
***Tel** 2221-1022; Museo de Arte y Diseño Contemporáneo: 2257-9370.* 10:30am–5pm Tue–Sat. public hols. 10am–3pm Tue–Fri by appt. www.mcj.go.cr

Immediately east of Parque España, the rambling structure of the National Center of Culture takes up a block on the site of the former Fábrica

National de Licores (State Liquor Factory). In 1994, the defunct factory was converted into the multi-faceted Centro Nacional de la Cultura (CENAC), although traces of the old distillery can still be seen. The Ministry of Culture is located here, as are venues hosting the National Theater Company and the National Dance Company *(see p293)*. Most of the extant buildings date to 1856, as does the perimeter wall, whose stone west gate is topped by a triangular pediment. Note the *reloj de sol* (sun clock), carved into the perimeter wall to the right of the southeast *portalón* (gate) by architect Teodorico Quirós *(see p19)*.

The **Museo de Arte y Diseño Contemporáneo** (Museum of Contemporary Art and Design) occupies the southeast part of the complex and features permanent and rotating exhibitions of art, architecture, and ceramics in six rooms. *Evelia con baton*, a sculpture by Francisco Zúñiga, stands in the west courtyard.

Detail on the façade of the Centro Nacional de la Cultura

JADE CARVING

Jade carving was introduced to the region by cultures from the north around 500 BC and died out around AD 800, when it was replaced by gold. The indigenous people used saws made of fiber string, as well as drills and crude quartz-tipped chisels, to carve the semi-precious stone into necklaces, pendants, and religious figurines bearing replicas of animal motifs. No local source is known to have existed: jade was traded from Guatemala and neighboring regions.

Jade anthropomorphic figure

Street-by-Street: Around Parque Nacional

Commanding a bluff on the east side of downtown, Parque Nacional, one of the city's largest parks, is a bucolic tree-shaded retreat in the heart of San José. Surrounding the park on three sides are the country's most important government buildings, including the Legislative Assembly complex. Also in the vicinity are many of Costa Rica's significant cultural sights, such as the National Museum. The area makes for pleasant strolling, especially with the addition of a pedestrian precinct sloping south from Parque Nacional, which is a lovely place to sit and relax.

Biblioteca Nacional
This modern-looking structure was erected in 1969–71 to house the national library.

Centro Nacional de la Cultura
Occupying the site of the former State Liquor Factory, the National Center of Culture's attractions include the state-of-the-art Museum of Contemporary Art and Design **12**

A fish pond, stocked with koi, runs along the western side of the park.

Epítome del Vuelo statue

CALLE 17

AVENIDA 3

CALLE 15

AVENIDA 3

AVENIDA 1

CALLE 11

Plaza de la Libertad Electoral
This small, semi-circular plaza honors the nation's democracy. Neoclassical columns enclose a pink granite statue, Epítome del Vuelo (1996), created by sculptor José Sancho Benito.

The Tribunal Supremo de Elecciones building houses the government body that ensures the integrity of elections.

STAR SIGHTS

★ Asamblea Legislativa

★ Museo Nacional

★ Parque Nacional

| 0 meters | 100 |
| 0 yards | 100 |

KEY

– – – Suggested route

For hotels and restaurants in this region see pp248–51 and pp272–4

★ **Parque Nacional**
Centered on the impressive granite-and-bronze Monumento Nacional (1892), this fine park is thick with trees and dotted with busts of several Latin American heroes **⓯**

Bulevar Ricardo Jiménez
This stretch of Calle 17 running south of Parque Nacional is a handsome palm-lined, pedestrian-only causeway. It is also known as the Camino de la Corte.

Bust of José Martí, the Cuban patriot.

Statue of Juan Santamaría

★ **Asamblea Legislativa**
Costa Rica's Legislative Assembly is housed in three historic buildings dating back to 1914. Built in different styles, the structures contain several galleries **⓭**

Casa Rosada is occupied by congressional offices.

Castillo Azul, the oldest of the Asamblea Legislativa buildings, earlier served as the presidential palace.

Bulevar Ricardo Jiménez

Plaza de la Democracía was laid out in a series of concrete terraces in 1989 for the Hemispheric Summit. On the southwest corner stands a bronze statue of former president José '"Don Pepe" Figueres (see p45).

Bust of Don Andrés Bello, a Venezuelan intellectual.

★ **Museo Nacional**
Located in an early 19th-century fortress, Costa Rica's National Museum traces the history of the nation from pre-Columbian to contemporary times **⓮**

Asamblea Legislativa ⓭

Map 2 E3. Calles 15/17 & Ave Central. **Tel** 2243-2000. 🚍
🎫 compulsory; 9am; 2243-2547.
Legislative debates 3pm Mon–Thu; by appt. **www**.asamblea.go.cr

The country's seat of government is in an enclave of four buildings, covering an entire block. The main structure, **Edificio del Plenario**, built in 1958, serves as the congress building along with an adjoining edifice. A bronze statue of national hero Juan Santamaría (see p134), torch in hand, stands in the north courtyard. The pink **Casa Rosada**, to the northeast, houses the offices of various political parties.

The Mediterranean-style **Castillo Azul** to the southeast was built in 1911 for Máximo Fernández, then a presidential aspirant. It served as the Presidential Residence until 1927, after which it was briefly the US mission. Since 1989, it has been used for official functions and contains government offices. Its six salons, boasting beautiful hardwood floors and Italian marble, include the Sala Alfredo González Flores, which is used for cabinet meetings, and the Sala Próceres de la Libertad, with its gilt-framed portraits of Latin American liberators such as Simón Bolívar.

Visitors are admitted to the Edificio del Plenario to witness legislative debates. Note that sandals are not permitted for men, nor bare legs for either sex.

Part of the Asamblea Legislativa complex in San José

Pre-Columbian stone spheres in the Museo Nacional

Museo Nacional ⓮

Map 2 E4. Calle 17 & Aves Central/2. **Tel** 2257-1433. 🚍
🕒 8:30am–4:30pm Tue–Sat, 9am–4:30pm Sun. ⬤ public hols. 🈹 ♿
🖥 **www**.museocostarica.go.cr

Dramatic and imposing, the crenellated, ocher-colored Bellavista Fortress – opposite the Legislative Assembly – was built in 1917 and served as an army barracks. Its exterior walls, with towers at each corner, are pocked with bullet holes from the 1948 civil war. Following his victory, José "Don Pepe" Figueres (see pp44–5) disbanded the army, and the fortress became the venue for the National Museum, which had been founded in 1887.

The entrance, on the east side, opens on to a landscaped courtyard displaying pre-Columbian carretas (ox-carts), stone bolas (spheres), and colonial-era cannons. The museum, to the right of the entrance, is arranged thematically in a counter-clockwise direction. Rooms are dedicated to geological, colonial, archaeological, contemporary, and religious history. The displays start from the first arrival of humans in Costa Rica and go up to the formation of the nation and recent events: a key exhibit is the 1987 Nobel Peace Prize awarded to president Oscar Arias Sánchez (see p45). The museum has a particularly impressive pre-Columbian collection, notably of metates (grinding stones)

Bust of Don Andrés Bello in Parque Nacional

and ceramics, as well as spectacular gold ornaments displayed in the Sala de Oro, in the northeast tower. The Sala Colonial is laid out with rustic colonial furniture, and looks as a room would have looked in the 18th century.

Steps lead down from the courtyard to a large netted butterfly garden in the southwest corner. Beyond the butterfly garden lies **Plaza de la Democracia**, which was laid out in 1989 and received a much-needed facelift in 2009. The stepped plaza hosts a 1994 bronze statue of José Figueres; a crafts market occupies the western end.

Parque Nacional ⓯

Map 2 E3. Calles 15/19 and Aves 1/3. 🚍

The largest of San José's inner-city parks, laid out in 1895, this is also its most appealing, although it is to be avoided at night. The peaceful park is set on a gentle hill that rises eastward. Stone benches fringe the irregular paths that snake beneath flowering trees, swaying palms, and bamboo groves. The massive Monumento Nacional is under towering trees at the center. Cast in the Rodin studios in Paris and unveiled on September 15, 1892, it is dedicated to the heroic deeds of the War of 1856. Its granite pedestal has five bronze Amazons representing the Central American nations

Children playing by a fish pond in Parque Nacional

repelling the adventurer William Walker *(see p43)*. Costa Rica stands in the middle holding a flag in one hand and supporting a wounded Nicaragua with the other; El Salvador holds a sword, Guatemala an axe, and Honduras an arch and shield. Bronze bas-reliefs to each side depict scenes from the battles.

Busts dotted around the park honor such Latin American nationalists as the Mexican revolutionary and priest Miguel Hidalgo (1753–1811), the Venezuelan poet and intellectual Don Andrés Bello (1781–1865), and the Cuban patriot and poet José Martí (1853–95).

The park is surrounded by important buildings. The **Biblioteca Nacional** (National Library) is to the north, and to the south, the pedestrianized **Bulevar Ricardo Jiménez**, named for the three-time president, slopes downhill three blocks to the building of the Tribunal of Justice.

Antigua Estación Ferrocarril al Atlántico ⑯

Map 2 F3.
Calles 21/23 and Ave 3. 🚌

To the northeast of the Parque Nacional is the former Estación Ferrocarril al Atlántico (Atlantic Railroad Station). Built in 1908, this ornate building, which resembles a pagoda, later became the terminus for the famous "Jungle Train," discontinued in 1991 following a devastating earthquake that destroyed much of the railway line. The building once housed the Museo de Formas, Espacios y Sonidos (Museum of Form, Space & Sound), which closed in 2007, when the former station was earmarked as the entrance for a new presidential palace that is still awaiting construction. For the time being, rail buffs can appreciate the vintage rolling stock to the rear and east of the building. This includes Locomotora 59, a 1939 steam locomotive imported from Philadelphia for the Northern Railway Company.

A bust of Tomás Guardia *(see p43)*, under whom the railroad was established, stands in front of the building, next to an obelisk commemorating the abolition of capital punishment in 1877.

Display of butterflies at San José's Museo de Insectos

Universidad de Costa Rica ⑰

Calle Central, San Pedro. *Tel 2207-4000.* 🚌 **Museo de Insectos** *Tel 2207-5647.* ⭕ *1–5pm Mon–Fri.* 🔲 **Planetario** *Tel 2207-2580.* ⭕ *for shows: 8:30, 9:30 & 10:30am Mon–Fri; 10am, 11am, 2pm & 3pm Sat.* 🔲

The University of Costa Rica imbues the suburb of San Pedro with bohemian life. The campus entrance is on Calle Central (off Avenida Central), which throbs with student bars and cafés. The campus itself is not particularly appealing, although numerous busts and statues are sprinkled about the tree-shaded grounds. A botanical garden is located in the southwest corner.

The **Museo de Insectos**, in the basement of the Music Department in the northeast corner of the campus, boasts a large display of butterflies, beetles, spiders, wasps, and other insects. A planetarium hosts daily presentations in Spanish. Call ahead to request an English-language showing.

The ornate, pagoda-style exterior of the Antigua Estación Ferrocarril al Atlántico

Centro Costarricense de Ciencias y Cultura ⑱

Housed in a fortress-like building that served as the *penitenciario central* (central penitentiary) from 1910 to 1979, the Costa Rican Science and Cultural Center was inaugurated in 1994. The ocher façade, topped by salmon-colored crenellations, presents a dramatic sight at night, when it is illuminated. The center contains the Galería Nacional, whose airy exhibition halls feature paintings, sculptures, and other art forms by Costa Rica's leading exponents of avant-garde art. Also here is the Museo de los Niños, with dozens of thematic hands-on exhibits that provide children with an understanding of nature, science, technology, and culture. The center includes a youth center and auditorium. Scattered around the complex are models of various modes of transport.

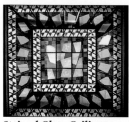

Stained-Glass Ceiling
A skylit vidriera *(stained-glass window) by Italian Claudio Dueñas lights the staircase to the Galería Nacional.*

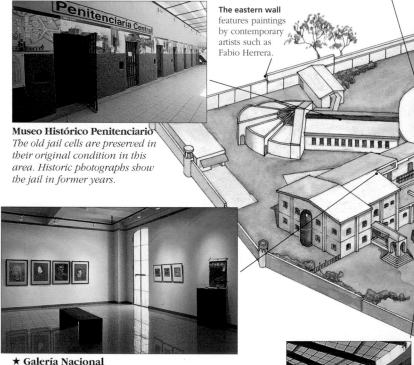

The eastern wall features paintings by contemporary artists such as Fabio Herrera.

Museo Histórico Penitenciario
The old jail cells are preserved in their original condition in this area. Historic photographs show the jail in former years.

★ **Galería Nacional**
Occupying 14 large rooms upstairs, the National Gallery showcases rotating exhibits of contemporary works by local artists in spotlit rooms converted from former jail cells.

STAR FEATURES

★ Galería Nacional

★ Museo de los Niños

Sala Kaopakome
Named for an indigenous Bribri word meaning "Hall of Meetings," this space is used for artistic performances and other events.

Genesis
This granite sculpture (1998) by Jorge Jiménez Deredia shows a woman evolving from an egg.

The Auditorio Nacional, the nation's premier auditorium, hosts performances of music and dance.

Imagen Cósmica (1998) by Jorge Jiménez Deredia is a bronze and marble sculpture.

The entrance is in the form of a medieval castle, with twin turrets.

★ **Museo de los Niños**
The Children's Museum, dedicated to interactive education, is spread throughout 39 separate rooms, with exhibits on the themes of astronomy, Earth, Costa Rica, ecology, science, human beings, and communications.

Escuela "El Grano de Oro" has exhibits on the coffee culture and the history of coffee in Costa Rica.

An electric train and carriages date from 1928–30, when the rail system was electrified.

Helicopter

Aircraft cockpit

Complejo Juvenil
Designed as a learning center for youth, the twin-level complex features a library, with books, audio cassettes, music CDs, interactive games, and an Internet café.

Parque Sabana ⑲

Calle 42/Sabana Oeste and Ave las Américas/Sabana Sur. 🚌 ♿

Officially named Parque Metropolitano La Sabana Padre Antonio Chapui, after the first priest of San José (1710–83), this park was the city's main airfield until 1955, when it was converted into a bucolic retreat and sports venue. The former airport buildings now house the Museo de Arte Costarricense. Looming over the park are the curving **ICE** (Costa Rican Institute of Electricity) tower to the north, and the strangely sloping **Controlaría de la República**, the government's administrative headquarters, to the south.

The park, which is accessed from downtown via the wide Paseo Colón, is popular with Costa Rican families, who picnic on weekends beneath the eucalyptus and pine groves. The park's facilities include jogging and cycling tracks, basketball, volleyball, and tennis courts, riding trails, a swimming pool, a gymnasium, soccer fields, and the National Stadium, completed in 2011. On the south side, a man-made lake is surrounded by modern sculptures. To the park's west, a cross honors Pope John Paul's visit to Costa Rica in 1983. It is best to avoid the park at night.

Flags for sale in downtown San José

Museo de Arte Costarricense ⑳

Calle 42 and Paseo Colón. **Tel** 2256-1281. 🚌 ⏺ 9am–4pm Tue–Sun. ⏺ public hols. 🎟 free on Sun. 🄯 🖉 www.musarco.go.cr

Costa Rica's leading museum of fine art, on the east side of Parque Sabana, is situated in the Colonial-style former airport terminal that closed in the 1950s. The Costa Rican Art Museum displays more than 3,200 important 20th-century works of art by Costa Rican sculptors and painters, as well as works by a smattering of foreign artists, including the Mexican Diego Rivera (1886–1957). Only a fraction of the museum's collection is on display, in rotating exhibitions that change yearly. Many of the works, most of which are privately owned, celebrate an archaic, pastoral way of life, best exemplified by *El Portón Rojo* (1945) by Teodorico Quirós Alvarado (*see p19*).

A highlight of the collection, and not to be missed, are Francisco Amighetti's wooden sculptures and woodcuts. On the second floor, the Salón Dorado has a bas-relief mural in bronze and stucco by French sculptor Louis Ferrón. Sweeping around all four walls, the panorama depicts an idealized version of Costa Rican history from pre-Columbian times to the

View of the Museo de Arte Costarricense, San José

1940s. On the north wall is a representation of Christopher Columbus with Indians kneeling before him.

The **Jardín de Esculturas** (Sculpture Garden) at the back of the museum, exhibits works by prominent sculptors, and also displays pre-Columbian *esferas* (spheres) and petroglyphs. Most intriguing are the *Tres Mujeres Caminando*, Francisco Zúñiga's sculpture of three women, and the granite *Danaide*, a female curled in the fetal position, by Max Jiménez Huete.

Museo de Ciencias Naturales "La Salle" ㉑

Sabana Sur. **Tel** 2232-5179. 🚌 ⏺ 7:30am–4pm Mon–Sat, 9am–5pm Sun. ⏺ public hols. 🎟 🄯 🖉

Located in the former premises of the Colegio La Salle school, the La Salle Museum of Natural Sciences was founded in 1960.

A spectacular bird diorama at Museo de Ciencias Naturales "La Salle"

For hotels and restaurants in this region see pp248–51 and pp272–4

Housing one of the most comprehensive collections of native and exotic flora and fauna in the world, it boasts more than 70,000 items, from molluscs to moths to manatees. A dinosaur exhibit in the central courtyard includes a replica skeleton of a Tyrannosaurus Rex made of resin. The fossil, shell, and butterfly displays are particularly noteworthy. Most exhibits are in dioramas that try to recreate natural environments. Snakes are poised to strike their prey. Fish swim suspended on invisible wire. The stuffed species are a bit moth-eaten, and their contrived contortions often comic. Despite this, the museum provides an interesting introduction to Costa Rica's natural world.

Victorian-style Casa de Las Tías hotel in San Rafael de Escazú

A traditional dance performance at Parque Diversiones

Parque Diversiones (Pueblo Antiguo) ㉒

1 mile (1.6 km) W of Hospital México, La Uruca. *Tel* 2242-9200. 9am–7pm Fri–Sun. www.parquediversiones.com/pueblo.htm

This splendid park, in Barrio La Uruca, 2 miles (3 km) west of downtown, draws local families not only for the roller coasters, water slides, and other pay-as-you-go rides, but also for the marvellous re-creations of typical early-20th-century Costa Rican settings in the adjoining Pueblo Antiguo (Old Village).

Pueblo Antiguo has three sections: the coast, the capital city, and the countryside. Buildings in traditional architectural style include a church, a market, a fire station, a bank, and a railway station. There are several original adobe structures, such as a coffee mill, a sugar mill, and a milking barn, which have been moved here from the countryside. A farmstead is stocked with live animals.

Horse-drawn carriages, oxcarts, and an electric train offer rides, and actors in period costume dramatize the past. Folkloric shows with music and dance bring the place to life on Friday and Saturday evenings. Parque Diversiones has several craft shops as well as a restaurant that serves traditional Costa Rican cuisine.

Escazú ㉓

2 miles (3 km) W of Parque Sabana. *Dia del Boyero (Mar).* **Barry Biesanz Woodworks** Barrio Bello Horizonte. *Tel* 2289-4337. 8am–5pm Mon–Fri, 9am–3pm Sat. www.biesanz.com

This upscale district lies west of Parque Sabana and is accessed by the Carretera Prospero Fernández. It exudes an appeal that it owes partly to its blend of antiquity and modernity, and partly to its salubrious position at the foot of Cerro Escazú mountain. The suburb, which derives its name from the indigenous word *itzkatzu* (resting place), sprawls uphill for several miles. It is divided into three main *barrios* – San Rafael de Escazú, San Miguel de Escazú, and San Antonio de Escazú.

Modernity is concentrated in congested San Rafael de Escazú, where an exquisite Colonial-style church, designed in the 1930s by architect Teodorico Quirós Alvarado, is encircled by high-rise condominiums and US-style malls. Half a mile (1 km) uphill, in San Miguel de Escazú, admire the colonial-era adobe houses, each painted with a strip of blue – many local residents still firmly believe that this will ward off witches.

San Antonio de Escazú, farther uphill, is a farming community. Time your visit here for the second Sunday of March, when flower-bedecked *carretas* (oxcarts) parade during Día del Boyero (Oxcart Drivers' Day), a festival honoring the men who drive the oxcarts. **Barry Biesanz Woodworks** is in the barrio of Bello Horizonte, in east Escazú. This is the workshop of Costa Rica's leading woodcarver and craftsman, who creates elegantly beautiful furniture, bowls, and boxes from Costa Rica's hardwoods. His works are available at the studio and at upscale San José stores.

Detail of church dome in San Miguel de Escazú

SAN JOSE STREET FINDER

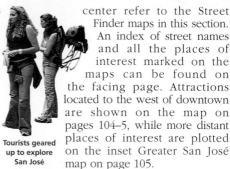

The map below shows the area covered by the map on pages 104–5, as well as the city center area shown on the Street Finder maps on pages 128–9. It also shows the main highways used for getting around the potentially confusing area that is greater San José.

All map references for places of interest, hotels, and restaurants in San José city

Tourists geared up to explore San José

center refer to the Street Finder maps in this section. An index of street names and all the places of interest marked on the maps can be found on the facing page. Attractions located to the west of downtown are shown on the map on pages 104–5, while more distant places of interest are plotted on the inset Greater San José map on page 105.

The busy Calle Central, which runs north–south through the center of downtown San José

SCALE OF MAPS 1–2

0 meters 500

0 yards 500

KEY TO STREET FINDER

- Major sight
- Place of interest
- Other building
- Bus station
- Visitor information office
- Hospital
- Police station
- Church
- Post office
- Pedestrian street

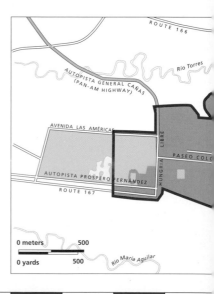

Street Finder Index

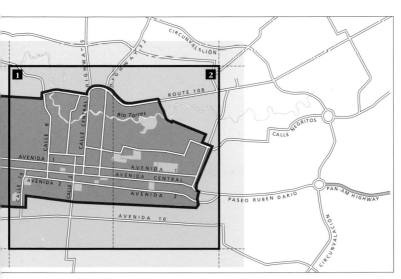

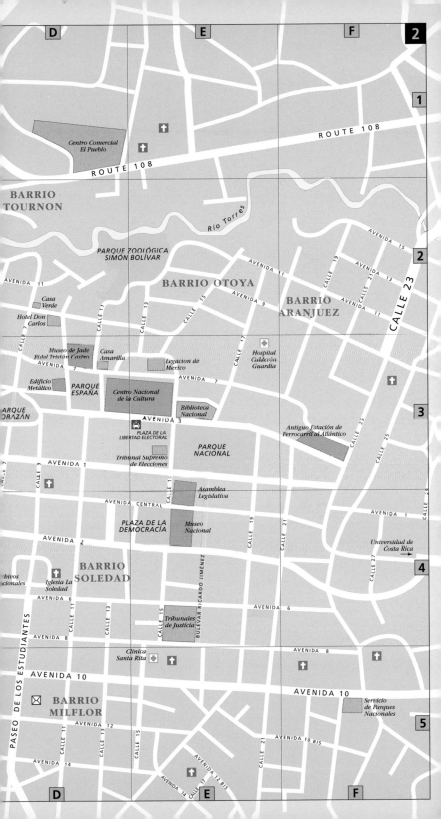

THE CENTRAL HIGHLANDS

*S*immering *volcanoes dominate the landscape of the Central Highlands as they tower over the country's central plateau – a broad valley at an altitude of around 3,300 ft (1,000 m). With steep slopes lushly covered by verdant forests and coffee bushes, the region offers glorious scenery. The climate is invigorating – one reason why two-thirds of the country's population live here today.*

The mild climate and fertile soils of the *meseta central* (central plateau) attracted early Spanish colonial settlers. Pre-Columbian peoples had already occupied the region for about 10,000 years, although their most evolved community – Guayabo – was mysteriously abandoned before the Spanish arrival and overgrown by tropical jungle until discovered 500 years later. Today, the indigenous communities are relegated to the remote margins of the Talamanca Mountains.

Agricultural communities evolved throughout the valley and, eventually, farther up the mountain slopes. During the period of Spanish rule, these humble adobe villages were relatively isolated, and even larger urban centers, such as Alajuela and Heredia, garnered few structures of importance. Earthquakes were responsible for the destruction of much colonial-era architecture, including some fine churches, and most of the surviving historically significant buildings are barely a century old.

The region has some stunning drives along roads that wind up the mountainsides through green coffee plantations, dairy pastures, and, higher up, cool forests of cedar and pine. Most of the mountain forests are now protected, and national parks and wildlife refuges provide excellent opportunities for hiking and wildlife viewing. Sights and activities ranging from butterfly farms and coffee *fincas* to canopy tours and world-class whitewater rafting make the area a thrilling microcosm of the country's tourist attractions.

The striking Iglesia de Sarchí, standing in Sarchí's main square

◁ Rafting on Río Pacuare, one of the world's finest whitewater rafting destinations

Exploring the Central Highlands

Mountains surround this temperate region. Bustling
Alajuela is a good base for exploring Volcán Poás,
where it is possible to drive to the summit. Nearby is
Heredia, a center of coffee production. To the northwest, the road to Sarchí and Zarcero makes a superb
drive. Two other lovely drives are La Ruta de los
Santos and the Orosi Valley. Costa Rica's main pre-
Columbian site, the Monumento Nacional Guayabo,
lies to the east of San José. For the more adventurous,
Reventazón and Pacuare rivers are ideal for rafting,
while the cloud-forested upper slopes of the Poás,
Barva, and Turrialba volcanoes offer great hiking
opportunities. Other options include coffee tours at
plantations such as Café Britt and the Doka Estate.

The decorated interior of Iglesia
de San José de Orosi

Orchid, Jardín Botánico
Lankester

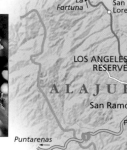

SIGHTS AT A GLANCE

KEY

▬▬	Pan-American Highway
▬▬	Major road
▬	Secondary road
▭▭▭	Minor road
▬	Scenic route
▬	Provincial border
△	Peak

Panoramic view from the slopes of Volcán Irazú

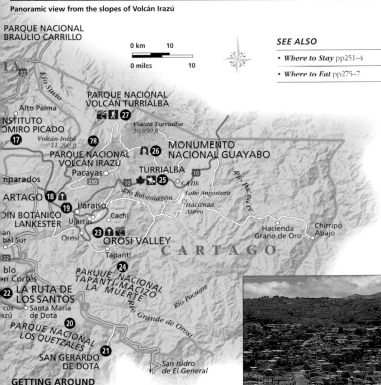

PARQUE NACIONAL
BRAULIO CARRILLO

0 km   10

0 miles   10

SEE ALSO

• *Where to Stay* pp251–4

• *Where to Eat* pp275–7

Río Sucio

Alto Palma

NSTITUTO
OMIRO PICADO **17**

Volcán Irazú
11,260 ft **28**

PARQUE NACIONAL
VOLCÁN TURRIALBA **27**

Volcán Turrialba
10,950 ft

26 MONUMENTO
NACIONAL GUAYABO

PARQUE NACIONAL
VOLCÁN IRAZÚ

Pacayas

TURRIALBA **25**

CAIIE

Río Pacuare

nparados

230

ARTAGO **18**

Paraíso **19**

Río Reventazón

Lake Angostura

Hacienda
Atirro

ÍN BOTÁNICO
LANKESTER

Cachí

23

Ujarrás

OROSI VALLEY

Hacienda
Grano de Oro

Chirripó
Abajo

an

bal Sur

Orosi

Tapantí

C A R T A G O

22

blo

n Cortés

24

PARQUE NACIONAL
TAPANTÍ-MACIZO
LA MUERTE

22 LA RUTA DE
LOS SANTOS

cos   Santa María
azú   de Dota

Río Pacuare

Río Grande de Orosi

PARQUE NACIONAL
LOS QUETZALES **20**

21

SAN GERARDO
DE DOTA

San Isidro
de El General

GETTING AROUND

Juan Santamaría International Airport is on the outskirts
of Alajuela, 1 mile (1.6 km) from the Pan-American Highway, which links the Central Highlands with the Pacific
coast. It's easiest to explore the region by car. However,
rótulos (directional signs) are few, and it's easy to get lost.
Avoid nighttime driving and beware of potholes, sharp
bends, and fog at higher elevations. Public buses run
between most towns and to places of interest, but service
can be erratic. Organized tours are available, and private
guides and transfers can be arranged from San José.

View of a small town near Grecia

Alajuela ❶

Road Map D3. 12 miles (19 km)
NW of San José. 🏘 45,000. 🚍 🚌
🏪 Sat. 🎭 Día de Juan Santamaría
(Apr 11); Festival de Mangos (Jul).

Sitting at the base of Volcán
Poás, this busy market town
is Costa Rica's third largest
city. The mango trees that
shade the main square, Plaza
del General Tomás Guardia,
are the source of Alajuela's
nickname, "City of Mangoes."
Centered on a triple-tiered
fountain with cherubs at
its base, the plaza has a
bandstand, and benches
with built-in chess sets. It is
dominated by the simple,
domed **Catedral de Alajuela**,
with a Classical façade. More
interesting is the
Baroque **Iglesia
Santo Cristo de
la Agonía**, five
blocks east, which
dates only from
1935. The interior
boasts intriguing
murals. The
former jail, one
block north of
the main plaza,
houses the
**Museo Cultural
y Histórico Juan
Santamaría**,
honoring the
local drummer-
boy who gave
up his life torching William
Walker's hideout in the War
of 1856 (see pp42–3). Call
ahead to arrange a screening
of a video about the event.
A bronze statue of Santamaría,
rushing forward with rifle
and flaming torch, stands in
tiny Parque Juan Santamaría,
which is two blocks south of
the main plaza.

Iglesia Santo
Cristo de la
Agonía

Environs
Southeast of Alajuela, **Finca
Hatched to Fly Free** is a
breeding center raising
green and scarlet macaws
for release into the wild.

🏛 **Museo Cultural y Histórico
Juan Santamaría**
Calles Central/2 and Ave 3.
Tel 2441-4775. ◯ 10am–5:30pm
Tue–Sun. 🎟 Tue–Fri. ♿
www.museojuansantamaria.go.cr

🦋 **Finca Hatched to Fly Free**
Río Segundo de Alajuela, 2 miles
(3 km) SE of Alajuela. **Tel** 8339-
4329. ◯ by appointment. 💲 by
donation. www.thearaproject.org

Zoo Ave Wildlife Conservation Park ❷

Road Map D3. Hwy 3, La Garita,
2 miles (3 km) E of Pan-Am Hwy.
Tel 2433-8989. 🚌 from San José
(Sat–Sun at 8am) & Alajuela.
◯ 9am–5pm daily. 🎟 ♿ 🍴 📷

With the largest collection
of tropical birds in Central
America, Costa Rica's foremost zoo covers 145 acres
(59 ha). The privately owned
zoo is one of only two in the
world to display resplendent
quetzals. More than 60 other
native bird species can be
seen in large flight cages.
Mammals are represented
by deer, peccaries, pumas,
tapirs, and the four native
monkey species. Crocodiles,
caimans, and snakes are
among the dozens of reptile
species found here.
Many of the animals and
birds were confiscated from
poachers, or rescued by the
National Wildlife Service.
Zoo Ave is also a breeding

An enclosure at Zoo Ave Wildlife
Conservation Park

center and has successfully
raised endangered species
such as green and scarlet
macaws. The breeding
center and wildlife rehabilitation are off limits.

La Guácima ❸

Road Map D3. 7.5 miles (12 km)
S of Alajuela. 🏘 15,500. 🚌

The sprawling community
of La Guácima is renowned
for **The Butterfly Farm**,
which supplies live pupae
to zoos all over the world.
Visitors can enjoy the splendid sight of some 60 native
butterfly species flitting
around a netted tropical
garden. Learn about lepidop-
teran ecology on an educational 2-hour tour. Sunny
mornings, when butterflies
are most active, are the best
times to visit.
Horse-lovers will find a visit
to **Rancho San Miguel**, on
the outskirts of La Guácima,
worthwhile. This stable and
stud farm raises Andalusian
horses and offers horseback
riding lessons, as well as a
dressage and horsemanship
show in the manner of the
Lipizzaners of the Spanish
Riding School at Vienna.

🦋 **The Butterfly Farm**
Guácima Abajo, 330 yd (300 m) SE
of Los Reyes Country Club. **Tel** 2438-
0400. ◯ 8:45am–4:30pm daily. 🎟
🦋 8:45am, 11am, 1pm, and 3pm.
♿ 📷 🍴 www.butterflyfarm.co.cr

🐴 **Rancho San Miguel**
2 miles (3 km) N of La Guácima.
Tel 2439-0003. ◯ 9am–5pm daily;
by reservation. 🐴 **Shows** 7:30pm
on Sat (Nov–Jul). 🍴 @ rancho
sanmiguel@gmail.com

Interior of Alajuela's Museo Cultural y Histórico Juan Santamaría

For hotels and restaurants in this region see pp251–4 and pp275–7

Costa Rica's Colorful Butterflies

A lepidopterist's dream, Costa Rica has more than 1,250 butterfly species. The butterfly population increases with the onset of the rain from May to July, when breeding activity peaks. Most species of butterfly feed on nectar, although some prefer rotting fruit, bird droppings, and even carrion. Butterflies discourage predators through a variety of means. Many, such as the Heliconiinae, which eat plants containing cyanide, taste acrid; they

A moth species of Costa Rica

advertise this to potential predators through distinct coloration – typically black striped with white, red, and/ or yellow – that other species mimic. Some are colored mottled brown and green to blend in with the background. Several butterfly species move seasonally between upland and lowland, while others migrate thousands of miles: the black-and-green Uranidae flits between Honduras and Colombia every year.

BUTTERFLY "FARMS"

These let visitors stroll through netted enclosures where dozens of species fly, forage, and reproduce. Some farms breed butterflies for export.

Caterpillars, *the larvae of moths and butterflies, start feeding the instant they emerge from the eggs. These voracious eaters sport impressive camouflage and defenses. Many have poisonous spikes; one species even resembles a snake.*

A chrysalid *is created when a caterpillar attaches itself to a leaf or twig and its body hardens to form an encasement. Some caterpillars spin cocoons of silk; others roll leaves into cylinders, tying them with silken threads. They then pupate and emerge as butterflies.*

TYPES OF BUTTERFLIES

With 10 percent of all known butterfly species in the world, Costa Rica has lepidopteria ranging from tiny glasswings with transparent wings, to the giants of the insect kingdom, such as teal-blue morphos.

Morphos *are dazzling, neon-bright butterflies whose iridescent upper wings flash with a fiery electric-blue sheen in flight. The wings are actually brown, not blue. The illusion is caused by the tiny, layered, glass-like scales on the upper wing. There are more than 50 species of this neotropical butterfly.*

Morpho's wing

Malachite butterflies change size and color between the wet and dry seasons.

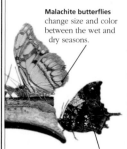

Swallowtails, found in open habitats and rainforest, have trailing hindwings.

Owl-eyes' *hindwings resemble the startling face of an owl, including two huge black, yellow-ringed "eyes."*

The postman *feeds on poisonous passion flower leaves as a caterpillar, making the butterfly bad-tasting to predators.*

Grecia's striking red-colored church, Iglesia de Grecia

Universidad de Paz ❹

Road Map D3. 8 miles (13 km) W of Escazú. 🚌 to Ciudad Colón, then by taxi. **Tel** 2205-9000. 🕐 8am–4:30pm Mon–Fri. 🎫 ♿ by appt. 🚹 Thu, Fri, Sat. **www**.upeace.org

A United Nations institution, the University of Peace (UPAZ) enjoys an idyllic setting on 750 acres (300 ha) donated by the owners of Hacienda Rodeo, a cattle estate and forest reserve on which the campus is located. Founded in 1980, the university is dedicated to research and education for the promotion of peace.

The botanical gardens within the campus contain busts of famed pacifists such as Mahatma Gandhi, Russian novelist Alexey Tolstoy, and Henry Dunant, founder of the Red Cross. Particularly moving is the life-size statue *Peace Pilgrim* by Fernando Calvo, dedicated to Mildred N. Ryder (1908–81), who, from age 44 until her death, walked for the cause of world peace.

Trails lead into the **Reserva Forestal el Rodeo**, a 4.6-sq-mile (12-sq-km) primary forest reserve sheltering deer, monkeys, wild cats, and more than 300 species of birds.

Grecia ❺

Road Map C3. 11 miles (18 km) NW of Alajuela. 🏛 14,000. 🚌

A peaceful market town founded in 1864 and recently voted the nation's cleanest town, Grecia's claim to fame is the **Iglesia de Grecia**, made of rust-red prefabricated steel

plates. Trimmed in white filigree, the church has twin spires and a wooden interior with an elaborate marble altar.

Close to Grecia, the open-air **World of Snakes** displays 300 snakes. Visitors are allowed to handle the non-venomous species.

Handmade stool, Fábrica de Carretas Joaquín Chaverrí

🐍 **World of Snakes**
0.5 mile (1 km) SE of Grecia.
Tel 2494-3700. 🕐 8am–5pm daily.
🎫 ♿ 🅿 📷
www.theworldofsnakes.com

Sarchí ❻

Road Map C3. 18 miles (29 km) NW of Alajuela. 🏛 11,000. 🚌 🚹 Plaza de la Artesanía, Sarchí Sur. 📷 Festival de las Carretas (Feb).

The country's foremost crafts center is set in the midst of coffee fields on the southern flank of Volcán Poás. The

Iglesia de Sarchí, which contains fine statuary by local artisans

town is famous for its wooden furniture, leather rocking chairs, and hand-painted oxcarts, decorated with signature floral motifs and geometric designs. The whitewashed buildings of Sarchí Norte, the town center, are graced by similar motifs. Don't miss the pink-and-turquoise **Iglesia de Sarchí** in the town plaza. One of its twin spires is topped by a trademark oxcart wheel.

Craft stores and *mueblerías* (furniture workshops) are concentrated in Sarchí Sur, 0.5 mile (1 km) east. A good place to buy souvenirs is **Fábrica de Carretas Joaquín Chaverrí** (*see p287*). Decorative oxcarts of various sizes are painted in *talleres* (workshops) at the rear. More fascinating is **Taller Eloy Alfaro**, the only remaining *taller* in the country that actually makes oxcarts. Sarchí is popular with tour groups – avoid visiting the town on weekends.

🏠 **Fábrica de Carretas Joaquín Chaverrí**
Sarchí Sur. **Tel** 2454-4411.
🕐 8am–6pm daily. 🎫 ♿ 🚹 🅿
http://sarchicostarica.net

🏠 **Taller Eloy Alfaro**
164 yd (150 m) N of Sarchí Norte.
Tel 2454-4131.
🕐 6am–6pm Mon–Fri. 🎫 ♿
www.fabricadecarretas.com

Los Angeles Cloud Forest Private Biological Reserve ❼

Road Map C3. 20 miles (32 km) NW of Sarchí. **Tel** 2461-3800. 🚌 to San Ramón, then by taxi. 🕐 8am–4pm daily. 🎫 🚹 🅿 🍴 ♿

Providing easy access to a cloud forest environment, this 3-sq-mile (9-sq-km) reserve reverberates with the calls of aricaris, bellbirds, and three species of monkeys. Wild cats prowl the mist-shrouded forests, which range from 2,300 ft to 5,900 ft (700–1,800 m) in elevation and are accessed by a comprehensive network of trails classified by

The impressive topiary archway on the central path of Parque Francisco Alvardo, Zarcero

length and degree of difficulty. The reserve has horseback rides, guided hikes, and a canopy tour *(see pp24–5)*.

El Silencio de Los Angeles Reserve is an extension of Cloud Forest Reserve. Clouds swirl around the colonial farmhouse here, which sits atop the Continental Divide and houses the Villablanca Cloud Forest Hotel & Spa *(see p252)*. Nearby, the tiny **La Mariana** chapel has a high ceiling covered with hand-painted tiles, each devoted to a different female saint. Outside, an effigy of the black saint San Martín de Porres welcomes visitors.

🏃 **El Silencio de los Angeles**
0.5 mile (1 km) NW of Los Angeles Cloud Forest Reserve. **Tel** 2461-0300. ⬜ *8am–5pm daily.* 📷 📱
www.villablanca-costarica.com

Zarcero ❽

Road Map C3. 14 miles (22 km) NW of Sarchí. 🏘 *3,800.* 🚌
🎭 *Feria Cívica (Feb).*

This quiet mountain town, at an elevation of 5,600 ft (1,700 m), has a spectacular setting, with lush pastures and forested mountains all around. It is renowned for its cheese, called *palmito*.

At the heart of the town, the main attraction is **Parque Francisco Alvardo**, a spacious park with well-tended gardens and topiary features. Since 1960, gardener Don Evangelisto Blanco has been transforming the park's cypress bushes into various fanciful forms: an ox and cart, an elephant with lightbulbs for eyes, a helicopter and airplane, a bullfight with matador and charging bull, and even a monkey riding a motorcycle. An Art Nouveau-style topiary archway frames the central pathway, which leads to a simple whitewashed church with a painted interior.

Bosque de Paz Rain/Cloud Forest Biological Reserve ❾

Road Map C2. 9 miles (14 km) E of Zarcero. **Tel** 2234-6676. 🚌 to Zarcero, then by taxi. ⬜ *7am–5pm daily; only by appointment.* 📷 📱 ♿
www.bosquedepaz.com

Set deep in the valley of the Río Toro on the northern slopes of Volcán Platanar, this 4-sq-mile (10-sq-km) reserve connects Parque Nacional Volcán Poás *(see p140)* with remote Parque Nacional Juan Castro Blanco. Some 14 miles (22 km) of trails lead through primary and secondary forest, which span rain-sodden montane growth to cloud forest at higher elevations The prodigious rainfall feeds the reserve's many waterfalls, as well as the streams that rush past a hummingbird and butterfly garden.

On clear days, *miradores* (viewpoints) offer fabulous vistas, as well as a chance to spot sloths, wild cats, and howler, capuchin, and spider monkeys. A favorite of bird-watchers, the reserve has more than 330 species of birds, including resplendent quetzals and three-wattled bellbirds.

Meals and accommodation are offered in a rustic log-and-riverstone lodge *(see p252)*.

TRADITIONAL OXCARTS

The quintessential symbol of Costa Rica, the traditional *carreta* (oxcart) was once a regular feature on farmsteads and for transporting coffee beans. The wheels, about 4 ft to 5 ft (1.2–1.5 m) in diameter and bound with a metal belt, are spokeless. In the mid-19th century, the carts began to be painted in bright colors enlivened with stylized floral and geometric starburst designs. Metal rings were added to strike the hubcab and create a chime unique to the cart when in motion. Though still made in the traditional manner, almost all of today's *carretas* are purely decorative; miniature versions serve as liquor cabinets. Full-size oxcarts can cost up to $5,000.

A hand-painted oxcart, Sarchí

A vast expanse of coffee plants on the Doka Estate

Doka Estate ⓾

Road Map D3. Sabanilla de Alajuela, 7 miles (11 km) N of Alajuela. 🚌 *from Alajuela.* **Tel** *2449-5152.* 🍽 🛍 *9am, 10am, 11am, 1:30pm, 2:30pm, and 3:30pm Mon–Fri; 9am, 10am, 11am, 1:30pm, and 2:30pm Sat & Sun; reservation recommended.* ♿ 🖥 🛍 www.dokaestate.com

Located on the lower slopes of Volcán Poás, this coffee *finca* was founded in 1929 by merchant Don Clorindo Vargas. Still owned by the Vargas family, the estate has some 6 sq miles (15 sq km) planted in coffee bushes and employs about 200 permanent employees; an additional 3,000 temporary workers are hired during the harvest season, which lasts October through January.

The Doka Estate, which still follows the time-honored tradition of drying coffee beans by laying them out in the sun, welcomes visitors eager to learn about coffee production and processing *(see pp28–9)*. A guided tour of the *beneficio*, which dates from 1893 and is a National Historic Landmark, starts on a delicious note with a coffee-tasting session. The tour demonstrates the various stages involved in coffee production and ends in the roasting room. The estate offers splendid views down the slopes and across the valley. There is a small hotel nearby *(see p253)*.

Parque Nacional Volcán Poás ⓫

Road Map D1. 23 miles (37 km) N of Alajuela. 🚌 *from Alajuela and San José.* 🛈 **Tel** *2482-2165.* ◯ *May–Nov: 8am–3:30pm daily.* ◐ *during phases of volcanic activity.* 🖼 ✔ ♿ 🖥 🛍 🍽

The nation's most visited national park was inaugurated on January 25, 1971. Covering 25 sq miles (65 sq km), the park encircles Volcán Poás (8,850 ft/2,700 m), a restless giant that formed more than one million years ago and is ephemerally volatile, with peak activity occurring in an approximately 40-year cycle. The volcano had a minor eruption in March 2006, and a 6.2 Richter earthquake on January 9, 2009 devastated much of the immediate region.

The gateway to the park is the mountain hamlet of **Poasito**. The summit of the volcano is reached by an immensely scenic drive, which winds along coffee fields, horticultural gardens, and dairy pastures, with spectacular views back down the valley. From the parking lot, a 5-minute walk along a paved path leads to the rim of one of the world's largest active craters. A viewing terrace grants visitors an awe-inspiring view down into the heart of the hissing and steaming

Toucans at Parque Nacional Volcán Poás

caldera (collapsed crater, *see p203*), which is 895 ft (300 m) deep and a mile (1.6 km) wide. It contains an acidic turquoise lake, sulfurous fumaroles, and a 245-ft (75-m) tall cone that began to form in the 1950s. On clear days, it is possible to get magnificent views of both the Caribbean Sea and the Pacific Ocean.

The dormant Botos crater, to the southeast, is filled by the jade-colored **Botos Lake**, accessed by a trail that leads through forests of stunted myrtle, magnolia, and laurel draped with bromeliads and mosses. Over 80 species of birds, such as fiery-throated hummingbirds, emerald toucanets and resplendent quetzals, have been identified in the forests. Mammal species include margays and the Poás squirrel, which is endemic to the volcano.

Facilities at the national park include an exhibition hall for audiovisual presentations, a shop and a café. Clouds typically form by midmorning, so it is best to arrive early. Bring warm clothing: the average temperature at the summit is 12° C (54° F), but cloudy days can be bitterly cold. If possible, visit midweek – locals wielding blaring radios crowd the park on weekends. Tour operators offer guided excursions to the park.

Botos Lake in a dormant volcano, Parque Nacional Volcán Poás

◁ **A view of the magnificent crater of Volcán Poás**

La Paz Waterfall Gardens ⑫

Road Map D2. Montaña Azul, 15 miles (24 km) N of Alajuela. *Tel* 2482-2720. ▣ from San José. ○ 8am–5:30pm; last admission: 4pm. 🖼🔌🍴🛍⊘ www.waterfallgardens.com

This multifaceted attraction's main draw is five thunderous waterfalls plummeting through deeply forested ravines on the northeast slopes of Volcán Poás. Paved pathways lead down-hill through pristine forest to the cascades, where spray blasts visitors standing on viewing platforms located above, below, and in front of the falls. Access to the falls involves negotiating metal staircases, but a shuttle runs visitors back uphill.

The landscaped grounds feature the **Hummingbird Garden**, which draws 26 species of hummers – about 40 percent of the nation's 57 species. As many as 4,000 butterflies flit about the **Butterfly Garden**; scores of macaws, toucans, and other birds can be seen in a walk-through aviary enclosed by a massive netted dome the length of a football field; and jaguars are a highlight of a wild cat exhibition. Other attractions include a walk-in ranarium displaying poison-dart and other frog species; a serpen tarium, with dozens of snake species; and a re-creation of a traditional farmstead

The Butterfly Garden in La Paz Waterfall Gardens

Water merging with sulfuric flow, Parque Nacional Braulio Carrillo

with staff in period costume. Renowned ornithologists lead birding tours.

The park's restaurant has a veranda with marvelous views over the valley and forest. Deluxe accommo-dations are available at the Peace Lodge (see p253).

Parque Nacional Braulio Carrillo ⑬

Road Map D2. Guápiles Hwy, 23 miles (37 km) N of San José. ▣ San José–Guápiles. 🏠 Puesto Quebrada ranger station, Hwy 32. *Tel* 2233-1533. ○ 8am–4pm Tue– Sun. 🖼⊘

Named for Costa Rica's third chief of state, this sprawling 185-sq-mile (480-sq-km) park ranges in elevation from 120 ft (36 m) at La Selva in the northern lowlands to 9,500 ft (2,900 m) at the top of Volcán Barva. The Parque Nacional Braulio Carrillo is bisected by the Guápiles Highway, which links San José with Puerto Limón; indeed, it was the construction of this highway that prompted the creation of the park in 1978 to protect the capital's major watershed. Despite its proximity to San José, the park is one of the nation's most rugged, with mountains, dense rainforest cover, and numerous waterfalls, plus it is subject to torrential rains. It protects

five life zones, including cloud forest at higher elevations. Wildlife is diverse, with 135 mammal species, 500 species of birds, and many species of snakes.

The main entrance to the park is the **Quebrada González** ranger station, located 8 miles (13 km) north of the Zurquí ranger station (closed to visitors), near the Rainforest Aerial Tram (see p209). The most rewarding hiking is around the summit of Volcán Barva, on the west side of the park and accessed by 4WD via the **Puesto Barva** ranger station above the village of Sacramento. From here, a trail leads through the spectacular cloud forest to the crater.

The dormant Barva has at least 13 eruptive cones, several of which are filled with lakes. Tapirs can be frequently seen around Danta and Barva Lakes.

Experienced hikers can tackle longer trails, taking several days, which descend the northern slopes

Margay at Parque Nacional Braulio Carrillo

via deep canyons. There are no facilities, and proper equipment is absolutely essential. Note that there have been instances of armed robberies and theft from cars parked near trailheads. Hikers must report to the ranger stations when setting out and returning. Tour operators in San José can arrange half-day or full-day tours.

Stained glass at La Parroquia de la Inmaculada Concepción, Heredia

Heredia **⓮**

Road Map D3. 7 miles (11 km) NW of San José. 👥 42,500. 🚌 🚗 by appointment. 🛍 Sat. 🎭 Easter Parade in San Joaquín de Flores (Mar/Apr).

A peaceful and orderly town founded in 1706, Heredia has a smattering of important colonial buildings at its heart and a bustling student life, owing to the presence of a branch of the University of Costa Rica (see p121). It is centered on Parque Nicolás Ulloa, popularly called Parque Central. Shaded by large mango trees, the park contains numerous busts and monuments. Dominating the park is the squat, weathered cathedral **La Parroquia de la Inmaculada Concepción**. Built in 1797, the cathedral has a triangular pediment, lovely stained-glass windows, and a two-tone checkerboard floor of marble.

On the north side of Parque Central, the forecourt of the municipality office features the *Monumento Nacional a la Madre*, an endearing bronze sculpture of a mother and child by Miguela Brenes. Adjoining the Municipalidad, to the west, the colonial-era **Casa de la Cultura** occupies the home of former president Alfredo González Flores (1877–1962). It is now an art gallery and a tiny museum. Nearby is **El Fortín**, an interesting circular fortress tower built in 1876.

Environs
A popular attraction in the lively town of Santa Barbara de Heredia, northwest of Heredia, is the **Ark Herb Farm**. Its orchards and gardens spread over 20 acres (8 ha). The farm exports medicinal herbs. North of Heredia, the

steep upper slopes of Volcán Barva are popular getaway spots for Josefinos for their crisp air and solitude. Tyrolean-style houses set amid cypress and pine forests can be rented at **Monte de la Cruz**, a reserve with trails. In July–August, **Hotel Chalet Tirol** (see p252) hosts the International Festival of Music. To the southeast of Heredia is the environmental park **INBioparque**, with exhibits relating to conservation and biodiversity, including various re-creations of natural habitats.

Label of a Café Britt product

🏛 Casa de la Cultura
Calle and Ave Central.
Tel 2260-4485. 🕐 9am–9pm daily.

🌿 Ark Herb Farm
Santa Barbara de Heredia, 3 miles (5 km) NW of Heredia. **Tel** 2239-2111. 🕐 8am–4pm Mon–Sat, by appt. 🚗 🛍 9:30am, by appt. 📷 www.arkherbfarm.com

🌿 INBioparque
3 miles (5 km) SE of Heredia.
Tel 2507-8107. 🕐 8:30am–2pm Tue–Fri, 9am–3:30pm Sat & Sun. 📷 🚻 🍴 🏪 📷 www.inbioparque.com

Visitors admiring tropical flowers at Ark Herb Farm, near Heredia

Café Britt **⓯**

Road Map D3. Santa Lucía, 0.5 mile (1 km) N of Heredia. **Tel** 2277-1600. 🚌 organized transfers from San José. 📷 🚗 mandatory; Dec 15–Apr 30: 9:30am, 11am, and 3pm; May 1–Dec 14: 9am and 3pm. **Concerts, lectures, films.** 🦽 🍴 📷 www.coffeetour.com

A mecca for coffee lovers and one of the country's most visited tourist attractions, this *beneficio* (processing mill) roasts and packs gourmet coffees. Entertaining guided tours are led by *campesinos*, played by professional actors in period costume. The guides' homespun repartee unfolds a spellbinding love story along with a fascinating educational narrative on the history and production cycle of coffee, from the plantation to the cup. Visitors are led through the 6-acre (2.5-ha) coffee estates before taking a hard-hat tour of the packing facility, where they breathe in the tantalizing aroma of roasting beans. The tour ends in the coffee bar and dining room, after a multimedia presentation that highlights coffee's role in cultivating Costa Rican democracy and molding a national identity.

Barva **⓰**

Road Map D3. 2 miles (3 km) N of Heredia. 👥 4,900. 🚌 from Heredia. 🎭 Festival de San Bartolomé (Aug 24).

One of the country's oldest settlements, this quaint town was founded in 1613, with the official name San Bartolomé de Barva. Located at the base of Volcán Barva, the town contains many simple 18th-century adobe houses with traditional red-tile roofs.

The flower-filled and palm-shaded town square, laid out in 1913, is graced by the pretty **Iglesia de San Bartolomé de Barva**, erected in 1867 on the site of an Indian burial ground. It replaced two earlier churches felled by earthquakes. On the northeast side is a grotto dedicated to the Virgin of Lourdes.

The **Museo de Cultura Popular**, on the outskirts of Barva, provides a portrait of late-19th-century life, with period pieces laid out in the fashion of the times. The building is a former home of ex-president Alfredo González Flores. A part of the dung-and-straw adobe masonry is exposed to view. The kitchen serves traditional meals.

🏛 **Museo de Cultura Popular**
Santa Lucía de Barva, just S of Barva. *Tel* 2260-1619. ◯ *8am–4pm Mon–Fri, by appt Sat & Sun.*

San Isidro de Coronado ⓱

Road Map D3. 6 miles (10 km) NE of San José. 🏠 *8,400.* 🚌 📷 *Festival de San Isidro Labrador (May 15).*

Clinging to the western slopes of Irazú volcano, San Isidro de Coronado is an agricultural center boasting the largest Gothic church in the country. The **Parroquia de San Isidro**, which soars over the town's tree-shaded plaza, was pre-fabricated in Germany in 1930 and erected in situ, being completed in 1934.

San Isidro is a gateway to Irazú Volcano National Park via an unbelievably scenic route through Rancho Redondo. The road snakes along the mountainsides, granting spectacular vistas over San José and the Central Highlands.

The Basílica de Nuestra Señora de los Angeles, Cartago

Cartago ⓲

Road Map D3. 13 miles (21 km) E of San José. 🏠 *120,000.* 🚌 📷 *Corpus Christi (May/Jun); Día de Nuestra Señora de la Virgen de los Angeles (Aug 2).*

Costa Rica's first city and original colonial capital was founded in 1563 by conquistador and Spanish governor Juan Vásquez de Coronado *(see p40)*. Named for the Spanish word for Carthage, it lost its capital status to San José at the Battle of Ochomogo in 1823. The city was destroyed when Volcán Irazú erupted in 1723. Most of the subsequent colonial structures were felled by violent earthquakes in 1841 and 1910.

Today the city, a renowned agro-industrial center, has limited appeal. How-

An orchid in Jardín Botánico Lankester

ever, Cartago remains the nation's religious capital, centered on the Byzantine-style **Basílica de Nuestra Señora de los Angeles** *(see pp144–5)*, dedicated to Costa Rica's patron saint, La Negrita.

Memories of the earthquake of April 13, 1910, remain in the ruins of the **Iglesia de la Parroquia**, originally built in 1575 and destroyed five times by earthquakes before its final demise. The mossy ruins now form the centerpiece of a small garden adjoining the stark central plaza. The **Museo Municipal de Cartago**, in the former army barracks, hosts revolving art exhibitions.

🏛 **Museo Municipal de Cartago**
Ave 6 and Calle 2. ◯ *9am–4pm Tue–Sat, 9am–3pm Sun.*

Jardín Botánico Lankester ⓳

Road Map D3. 4 miles (6 km) E of Cartago. *Tel* 2552-3247. 🚌 *from Cartago.* ◯ *8:30am–4:30pm daily.* 🖼 ♿ 🅿 www.jbl.ucr.ac.cr

Operated by the University of Costa Rica as a research center, these luxuriant botanical gardens were founded in 1917 by English horticulturalist and coffee-planter Charles Lankester West. Covering 27 acres (11 ha), they display almost 3,000 neotropical species in separate sections dedicated to specific plant families. The highlight is the orchid collection, spread throughout the garden. The 1,100 species are best seen in the dry season, especially from February to April. Pathways snake through a bamboo tunnel, a swathe of premontane forest, a medicinal plant garden, a cactus garden, a butterfly garden, and a Japanese garden. Visitors are given an orientation talk before setting out on a self-guided tour.

The weather-beaten ruins of Iglesia de la Parroquia, Cartago

Cartago: Basílica de Nuestra Señora de los Angeles

Detail on pillar

Named in honor of the country's patron saint, the Virgin of Los Angeles (also called La Negrita), Cartago's Cathedral of Our Lady of the Angels is Costa Rica's most important church. Legend has it that on August 2, 1635, a mulatto peasant girl called Juana Pereira found a small figurine of a dark-skinned Virgin Mary on a rock. The statue was put away in safe custody twice and mysteriously returned to the rock both times. The basilica was built to mark the spot. Destroyed in 1926 by a massive earthquake, it was rebuilt in 1929. The impressive Byzantine-style edifice features a stone exterior with a decorated façade and is topped by an octagonal cupola. A spring flowing beneath the basilica is considered to have curative powers.

Side Altars
The side altars contain a series of shrines to saints such as San Antonio de Padua, San Cayetano, San Vicente de Paul, and the black saint, San Benito de Palermo. There are also life-size statues of Jesus, Mary, and Joseph.

★ La Negrita Statue
The 8-inch (20-cm) high statue of Mary, the discovery of which supposedly led to the construction of the church, is installed in a shrine above the main altar. The shrine is encrusted with gold and precious stones.

Façade
The façade has Moorish-style arches and fluted pilasters capped by angels.

THE LA NEGRITA PILGRIMAGE

Every August 2, devout Costa Ricans join in the Día de Nuestra Señora de la Virgen de los Angeles procession. Thousands walk the 15 miles (24 km) from San José to Cartago – many crawl much of the way on their knees; others carry crosses. Devotees descend to the subterranean Cripta de la Piedra to touch the rock and collect holy water from the underground spring. The statue of La Negrita is paraded through the city before being replaced in its shrine.

Pilgrims and tourists outside the church

The Ceiling

The wooden ceiling is centered on an octagonal, wood-paneled dome ringed by windows through which sunlight pours in, illuminating the nave and producing a sense of religious exaltation.

VISITORS' CHECKLIST

Calle 14/16 and Aves 2/4, Cartago. *Tel* 2551-0465. from San José (Calle 5 and Aves 18/20). 6am–7pm daily. regular services throughout the day.

★ The Nave

The elaborate interior in the shape of a double cross is made entirely of hardwoods, painted with decorative floral patterns of white alabaster. Parabolic arches are supported atop clover-leaf-shaped wooden pillars.

The walls are made of galvanized steel stuccoed with cement.

The Cripta de la Piedra (Crypt of the Rock) is the subterranean shrine containing the rock where the La Negrita statue was supposedly found. Entered via a ramp to the rear of the basilica, it is filled with votive offerings.

Stained-Glass Window

The basilica boasts several fine vitrales (stained-glass panes) depicting biblical scenes. The finest are in the Sacristy, in the southeast corner, and depict Jesus with various saints.

STAR FEATURES

★ The Nave

★ La Negrita Statue

Cloud forest in the Parque Nacional Los Quetzales

Parque Nacional Los Quetzales ㉓

Road Map D3/D4. Pan-Am Hwy, 47 miles (76 km) SE of San José. 🚌 to Km 80, then hike. **Tel** 2200-5354. ◯ 8am–4pm daily. 🖳 www.sinac.go.cr

Bordering the Pan-American Highway is the Parque Nacional Los Quetzales, created in 2005 from the Los Santos Forest Reserve, the Biological Reserve of Cerro de las Vueltas, and various state properties. The park covers 12,355 acres (5,000 ha) of cloud forest, spread over the banks of the Rio Savegre. This is one of the most biologically diverse regions in Costa Rica, with 25 indigenous species, 116 species of mammals, mangroves, and lagoons of glacial origins. One of the highlights, however, are the quetzals for which the park is named. Other birds include sooty robins and hummingbirds.

Dantica Cloud Forest Lodge, which is just north of San Gerado de Dota, has trails running through primary cloud forest in which peccaries, deer, tapir, otters, ocelots, and pumas have all been sighted.

Dantica's three-room indigenous art gallery exhibits jewelry, textiles, ceramics, statues, and masks from such nations as Peru, Venezuela, and Colombia. There are also masks and natural-dye cotton bags produced by the

Boruca indigenous group from southern Costa Rica.

💥 Dantica Cloud Forest Lodge
Tel 2740-1067. ◯ 24 hrs. 🖳 🖳 🍽 🌐 www.dantica.com

San Gerardo de Dota ㉔

Road Map D4. 5.5 miles (9 km) W of Pan-Am Hwy at Km 80. 🚶 1,000. 🚌 to Km 80, then hike or arrange a transfer (call 8367-8141).

One of the best sites in Costa Rica for quetzal-watching, this small community is tucked into the bottom of a steep valley furrowed by Río Savegre. Go down a switchback from the Pan-Am Highway to reach the town, which was first settled in 1954 by Don Efraín Chacón and his family. Today, the Chacóns' **Savegre Mountain Hotel Biological Reserve** protects around 1,000 acres (400 ha) of cloud forest and houses the Quetzal Education Research Center (QERC). This study center for quetzal ecology is the tropical campus of the Southern Nazarene University of Oklahoma. April to May is nesting season, when quetzals are

most abundant. More than 170 other bird species are present seasonally.

Dramatic scenery, crisp air, and blissful solitude reward the few travelers who take the time to make the sharp descent into San Gerardo de Dota. Fruits grow in profusion in orchards surrounded by meadows and centenary oaks.

About 22 miles (35 km) of trails crisscross the forest. Activities include guided treks from the frigid heights of Cerro Frío (Cold Mountain) at 11,400 ft (3,450 m) to San Gerardo de Dota at 7,200 ft (2,200 m). Other trails lead along the banks of the gurgling river, which is stocked with rainbow trout.

💥 Savegre Mountain Hotel Biological Reserve
Tel 2740-1028. 🖳 🖳 🌐 www.savegre.co.cr

Savegre Mountain Hotel Biological Reserve, San Gerardo de Dota

La Ruta de los Santos ㉒

South of San José, the Cerro de Escazú rise steeply from Desamparados to the town of Aserrí. Twisting roads then pass through San Gabriel, San Pablo de León Cortés, San Marcos de Tarrazú, Santa María de Dota, and San Cristóbal Sur in the steep-sided coffee country known as Tarrazú. These off-the-beaten-track communities – named for saints Gabriel, Paul, Mark, Mary, and Christopher – give this fabulously scenic drive through verdant highlands and valleys its apt name, "Route of the Saints."

TIPS FOR DRIVERS

Tour length: *95 miles (153 km) round-trip.*
Stopping-off points: *Stop for a bite at the charming Vaca Flaca* (see p276) *or La Casona de Sara in Santa María* (see p277).
Information: *Beneficio Coopedota* ***Tel*** *2541-2828.* **www.**dotacoffee.com*; Beneficio Coopetarrazú.* ***Tel*** *2546-6098.* **www.**cafetarrazu.com

Desamparados ①
This town is dominated by its handsome church in Neoclassical style.

Aserrí ②
The mountainside above Aserrí offers superb vistas across the valley toward Barva, Irazú, and Turrialba Volcanoes.

San Cristóbal Sur ⑦
This is the setting for the mountain farm where Figueres *(see p45)* prepared to launch the 1948 revolution that resulted in civil war.

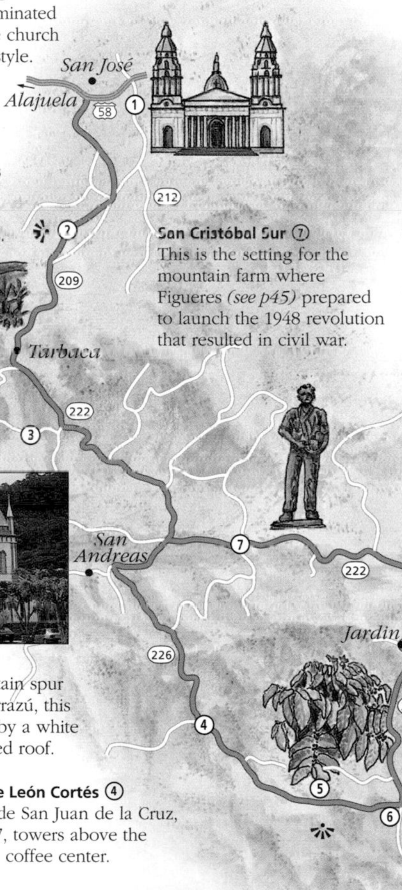

San José
Alajuela
58
212
209
Tarbaca
222
San Andreas
222
Empalme
Jardín
2
226
0 km 3
0 miles 3

Santa María de Dota ⑥
This tidy town's plaza has a granite monument commemorating those who died in the 1948 civil war. The Beneficio Coopedota accepts visitors – by reservation – for plantation tours.

San Gabriel ③
Occupying a mountain spur overlooking Río Tarrazú, this town is dominated by a white church with a domed roof.

San Pablo de León Cortés ④
The Iglesia de San Juan de la Cruz, built in 1997, towers above the plaza in this coffee center.

KEY

- Tour route
- Highway
- Other road
- Viewpoint

San Marcos de Tarrazú ⑤
Surrounded by coffee-covered slopes, the region's most important town boasts a fine church. Arrange a visit to Beneficio Coopetarrazú coffee mill in advance.

The Orosi Valley ㉓

South of Cartago, the land falls away steeply into the Orosi Valley, a large gorge hemmed to the south by the Talamanca Mountains. Río Reventazón drains the valley and joins Lago de Cachí, also fed by other streams and raging rivers tumbling out of hills enveloped by cloud forest. Shiny-leafed coffee bushes cover the valley, which was an important colonial center and has two of Costa Rica's oldest religious sites. The ruins of the 17th-century church in the village of Ujarrás, set at the edge of Lago de Cachí, are the highlight of a visit to the valley. Orosi village is home to the country's oldest extant church. The valley's social life centers on this tranquil hamlet. Looping around the Orosi Valley is Route 224, which passes the main points of interest and makes for a perfect half- or full-day tour.

View of the spillways of Cachí Dam on Lago de Cachí

Mirador de Orosi

Operated by ICT (Instituto Costarricense de Turismo), this mirador (viewpoint) offers stunning views over the valley and has picnic tables on lawns abuzz with hummingbirds.

Orosi

Surrounded by coffee plantations and peppered with waterfalls, the picturesque village of Orosi is known for the colonial-era Iglesia de San José de Orosi, which contains a small museum of religious art. Orosi has several thermal mineral springs called balnearios (see p150).

KEY

═══	Major road
═══	Other road
‑ ‑	Trail
☆	Viewpoint
⛵	Boating
▲	Campsite

VISITORS' CHECKLIST

Road Map D3. Cartago. 🏛
14,000. 🚌 *hourly from Cartago
to Orosi. Also to Cachí via Ujarrás.*
🛈 *2533-3640 (Orosi Tourism).*
🎭 *Romería Virgen de la Candelaria (3rd Sun of Apr), Orosi Colonial Tourist Fair (Sep).* **La Casona
de Cafetal** *Tel 2577-1414.*
⭕ *11am–6pm daily.* ♿ **Monte
Sky Mountain Retreat** *Tel
2228-0010.* ⭕ *8am–5pm daily.*

Ujarrás
*This village has all but vanished after being flooded in
1833. It is known for the ruins of the Iglesia de Nuestra
Señora de la Límpia Concepción, built in 1693* (see p150).

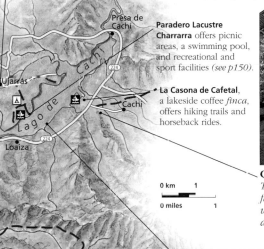

**Paradero Lacustre
Charrarra** offers picnic
areas, a swimming pool,
and recreational and
sport facilities *(see p150).*

La Casona de Cafetal,
a lakeside coffee *finca*,
offers hiking trails and
horseback rides.

0 km   1

0 miles   1

Casa el Soñador
*This is the home of the Quesada
family – famous woodcarvers
whose naive bas-relief art forms
adorn their property* (see p150).

Lago de Cachí
*Trout-fishing is popular in this lake,
created to generate hydroelectric power
by damming Río Reventazón* (see p150).

Monte Sky Mountain Retreat protects a 139-acre
(56-ha) area of cloud forest. Trails lead to waterfalls and offer a chance to spot quetzals. There
are also facilities for tent camping. A 4WD
vehicle is required to get here.

Exploring the Orosi Valley

Wood carving, Iglesia de San José de Orosi

The first colonists arrived in the valley of Río Reventazón in 1564 to convert the indigenous Cabécar people who were led by a *cacique* (chief) named Orosi. The valley soon became an important religious center. It is the colonial relics that draw visitors to the region, but the scenery is no less appealing. Route 224, which encircles the valley, brings in an ever-increasing number of tourists.

Iglesia de San José de Orosi's interior, dominated by wood and terra-cotta

Ujarrás

8 miles (13 km) SE of Cartago.

Located at the edge of Lake Cachí and surrounded by coffee bushes, the hamlet of Ujarrás features the ruins of the **Iglesia de Nuestra Señora de la Límpia Concepción**, completed in 1693. The ruins stand in a charming garden awash with tropical flowers.

The site previously housed the shrine La Parroquia de Ujarrás. According to legend, a converted Indian found a wooden box containing a statue of the Virgin Mary. He carried it to Ujarrás, where it suddenly became too heavy for even a team of men to lift. The local priest considered this a sign from God that a shrine should be built here. When pirates led by Henry Morgan attacked the region in 1666, local inhabitants prayed at the shrine for salvation. A defensive force led by Spanish governor, Juan Lopez de la Flor, routed the pirates and in gratitude built a church in honor of the Virgen del Rescate de Ujarrás (Virgin of Rescue). Damaged in a flood in 1833, the church was thereafter abandoned. Every third Sunday in April,

pilgrims walk to the shrine from Paraíso, which is 4 miles (6 km) to the west, in honor of the Virgin.

Orosi

5 miles (8 km) S of Paraíso. 🏠 8,862. **Balnearios Termales Orosi** *Tel* 2533-2156. ◯ 7:30am–4pm Wed–Mon. 🖼 🍴 **Museo de Arte Religioso** *Tel* 2533-3051. ◯ 1–5pm Tue–Fri, 9am–5pm Sat & Sun. 🖼 ♿ 🛍 🚫

Nestling neatly on the banks of Río Grande de Orosi, this small village is a coffee growing center. Mineral hot springs gush from the hillsides and can be enjoyed in orderly and well-maintained pools at **Balnearios Termales**

Ruins of Nuestra Señora de la Límpia Concepción, Ujarrás

Orosi. Orosi's pride is the beautifully preserved **Iglesia de San José de Orosi**, the oldest functioning church in Costa Rica. Built by Franciscans in 1743–66 and dominated by a solid bell tower, the white-washed church has withstood several earthquakes, despite its plain adobe construction. The interior features a beamed ceiling, terra-cotta floor, and simple gilt-adorned wooden altar. The Franciscan monastery adjoining the church is now the **Museo de Arte Religioso**, displaying period furniture and religious icons dating back three centuries. Most of the items – such as paintings, statuary, and altar pieces – come from Mexico and Guatemala.

🛶 Lago de Cachí

Paradero Lacustre Charrarra
1.6 mile (2 km) E of Ujarrás.
Tel 2574-7557. ◯ 8am–5pm daily.
🖼 ♿ 🍴
Casa el Soñador 5 miles (8 km) E of Orosi. ◯ 9am–6pm daily.

This massive lake was created between 1959 and 1963, when the ICE (Costa Rican Institute of Electricity) dammed Río Reventazón. The Presa de Cachí (Cachí Dam) funnels water down spillways to feed hydroelectricity turbines. Visitors can enjoy kayaking, canoeing, and boating on the lake, arranged by local tour operators. The national tourist board operates **Paradero Lacustre Charrarra**, a recreational complex offering boating from the north shore. Horseback riding is also on offer.

On the southern shore is **Casa el Soñador** (Dreamer's House), the pretty bamboo-and-wood studio of sculptor Macedonio Quesada Valerín (1932–94). Carved figures representing the town gossips lean out of the upper-story windows and a bas-relief of Leonardo da Vinci's *The Last Supper* adorns the exterior. Macedonio's sons carry on their father's tradition of carving walking sticks, religious figures, and ornaments from coffee plant roots. The studio serves as an art gallery for the works of other local artists.

A waterfall at Parque Nacional Tapantí-Macizo la Muerte

Parque Nacional Tapantí-Macizo la Muerte ㉔

Road Map D3. 5.5 miles (9 km) S of Orosi. **Tel** 2200-0090. ⬛ to Orosi, then by jeep-taxi. ◻ 8am–4pm daily. 🏞️ 🦆

South of the Orosi Valley, the vibrantly green Tapantí-Macizo National Park, created in 1982, protects 225 sq miles (583 sq km) of the Talamanca Mountains. Ranging in elevation from 3,950 ft to 8,350 ft (1,200–2,550 m). It features diverse flora, from lower montane rainforest to montane dwarf forest on the upper slopes. The national park is deluged with rains almost throughout the year, which feed the fast-flowing rivers rushing through it; February to April are the least rainy months, and the best time to visit.

Spectacularly rich in wildlife, the park has animals such as anteaters, jaguars, monkeys, tapirs, and even otters in streams. Tapantí is a birder's heaven – more than 260 bird species inhabit its thick forests. Resplendent quetzals frequent the thickets near the ranger station, which has a small nature display.

Well-marked trails lace the rugged terrain. A particularly pleasant and easy hike is **Sendero La Catarata**, which leads to a waterfall. Fishing in the park is permitted from April to October.

Turrialba ㉕

Road Map E3. 27 miles (44 km) E of Cartago. 🏠 32,000. ⬛

This pleasant regional center squats in a broad valley on the banks of Río Turrialba at 2,130 ft (650 m) above sea level, against the base of Volcán Turrialba (see p153). Once an important transportation hub midway between San José and the Caribbean, Turrialba had to forego that position with the opening of the Guápiles Highway in 1987, and cessation of rail service in 1991. Rusting railroad tracks serve as reminders of the days when the Atlantic Railroad thrived.

There is little of interest in the town; its importance lies in being a center for kayaking and rafting trips on Río Reventazón and Río Pacuare, and serving as a good base for exploring nearby attractions.

Wooden tortoise, Turrialba

Environs

The valley bottom southeast of Turrialba is filled by the 630-acre (255-ha) **Lake Angostura**, created by the building of a dam in 2000 to generate hydroelectricty. It lures several species of waterfowl and is a water sports center, although it is gradually being choked by water hyacinths. Río Reventazón (Exploding River) below the dam has Class III–IV rapids and is fabulously scenic, as is the nearby Río Pacuare, also favored by rafters

(see p152). **Hotel Casa Turire**, on the south shore of Lake Angostura, is a charming deluxe hotel offering biking, hiking, horseback riding, and many other activities (see p253).

East of Turrialba, the **Centro Agronómico Tropical de Investigación y Enseñanza (CATIE)**, or Center for Tropical Agriculture Investigation and Learning, has trails through 3 sq miles (9 sq km) of landscaped grounds, forests, and orchards, which grow exotic fruits, plus a botanical garden. A lake attracts waterfowl. Guided tours provide fascinating insights into ecology and animal husbandry.

Farther east is **Serpentario Viborana**, a serpentarium that exhibits several species of snakes, including boas, in a large walk-in cage. The guided tour includes a lecture on snake ecology.

Women in traditional dress can be seen at **Reserva Indígena Chirripó**, an incredibly scenic indigenous reserve in the Talamanca Mountains beyond Moravia del Chirripó, southeast of Turrialba.

🦋 **Centro Agronómico Tropical de Investigación y Enseñanza (CATIE)**
1.2 miles (2 km) E of Turrialba. **Tel** 2558-2000. 📷 7am–4pm daily (Jardín Botánico). 🦆 🍴
💻 🅵 www.catie.ac.cr

🦋 **Serpentario Viborana**
Pavones, 5.5 miles (9 km) E of Turrialba. **Tel** 2538-1510. ◻ 9am–5pm daily. 🏞️ 🦆 by appt. 🅱️

Casa Turire, a delightful hotel near Turrialba

Whitewater Rafting

Costa Rica boasts rivers that are perfect for whitewater rafting. The best of the runnable rivers flow down from the mountainous Central Highlands to the Caribbean, cascading through narrow canyons churned by rapids, and interspersed with calm sections. Small groups paddle downstream in large purpose-built rubber dinghies, led by experienced

Rafter in a life-jacket

guides. Trips can be anything from half a day to a week, catering to every level of experience: rivers are ranked from Class I (easy) to Class VI (extremely difficult). May, June, September, and October are the best months, when heavy rainfall gives rivers an extra boost. Rafting is organized by professional operators who provide gear, meals, and accommodations (see p301).

Costa Rica's whitewater rivers *offer an extraordinary combination of scenic beauty, wildlife sightings, and thrills. One of the finest rafting destinations, Río Reventazón (left) caters to enthusiasts of differing skill levels, with separate sections that have difficulty ratings ranging from Class II to V.*

Rafters should wear T-shirts, shorts, and sneakers or sandals, and carry spare clothes.

Guides steer and give commands from the rear.

Safety gear such as life-jackets and helmets are mandatory.

Calm stretches *provide ample scope for wildlife viewing – kingfishers, parrots, toucans, caimans, iguanas, and varieties of monkeys are among the easily seen fauna.*

RAFTING DOWN RIO PACUARE

Torrential Río Pacuare is ranked among the world's top five whitewater rivers. Rafting trips of varying duration take thrill-seekers on adrenaline-packed rides along thickly forested, wildlife-rich gorges, rushing currents, and amazing rapids.

Numerous waterfalls *pour down the sides of the river's gorges. Some fall hundreds of feet, showering rafters with cool water on hot days.*

Pounding rapids *are found all along the length of the Río Pacuare, and offer spectacular whitewater rides ranked Class III and IV in difficulty.*

Riverside stops *are arranged for hearty breakfasts and lunches. Overnight halts in wilderness lodges or tents on longer trips also offer opportunities for hiking and soaking in the scenery.*

Monumento Nacional Guayabo 26

See pp154–5.

Parque Nacional Volcán Turrialba 27

Road Map D3. 15 miles (24 km) NW of Turrialba. 🚍 to Santa Cruz, *then by jeep-taxi.* 🏨 2273-4335 *(Volcán Turrialba Lodge).* 🅿️ 🛶

The easternmost volcano in Costa Rica, the 10,950-ft (3,340-m) high Turrialba was dormant for more than a century following a period of violent activity in the 1860s. In January 2010, it became active again.

The volcano's name comes from the Huetar Indian words *turiri* and *abá*, which together mean "river of fire." Local legend says that a girl named Cira, lost while exploring, was found by a young man from a rival tribe, and they fell in love. When the girl's enraged father eventually found the two lovers and prepared to kill the young suitor, Turrialba spewed a tall column of smoke, signifying divine assent.

Established in 1955, the Turrialba Volcano National Park protects 5 sq miles (13 sq km) of land, much of which is covered in cloud forest. The upper forests contain gnarled and twisted oak and myrtle trees.

Dirt roads go to within a few miles of the summit, which is then accessible by trails. Stamina is required for the switchback hike to the top. From there, in clear weather, it is possible to see the Cordillera Central and the Caribbean coast. A trail also descends to the floor of the largest crater, where sulfurous gases hiss out of active fumaroles. Access is granted only during inactive phases.

There are no public facilities or transport within the park, but the privately run **Volcán Turrialba Lodge** *(see p254)*, on the western flank of the volcano at 9,200 ft (2,800 m), provides a base from which to explore the area.

Deep green lake in the largest crater of Parque Nacional Volcán Irazú

Parque Nacional Volcán Irazú 28

Road Map D3. 19 miles (30 km) N of Cartago. *Tel 2200-5025.* 🚍 *from Ave 2, Calles 1/3, San José, 8am daily.* ⏰ 8am–3:30pm daily. 🅿️

Encircling the upper slopes of Volcán Irazú, this 7-sq-mile (18-sq-km) park was established in 1955. At 11,260 ft (3,430 m), the cloud-covered Irazú is Costa Rica's highest volcano, and historically its most active – the first written reference to an eruption was in 1723. Several devastating explosions occurred between 1917 and 1921, and it famously erupted on March 13, 1963, when US President John F. Kennedy was in the country to attend the Summit of Central America Presidents.

The name Irazú is derived from the Indian word *istarú*, which means "mountain of thunder." Legend has it that Aquitaba, a local chief, sacrificed his daughter to the volcano gods. Later, in a battle with an enemy tribe, Aquitaba

Signage at Parque Nacional Volcán Irazú

called on the gods for their aid. The volcano erupted, spewing fire on the enemy, while a boiling river of mud swept away their village.

The road to the summit winds uphill past vegetable fields. A viewing platform lets visitors peer down into a 985-ft (300-m) deep, 0.5-mile (1-km) wide crater, containing a pea-green lake. Four other craters can be accessed, but there are active fumaroles, and the marked trails should be followed. Although the volcano is often covered by fog, the cloud line is frequently below the summit, which basks in bright sunshine. Arriving early increases the chances of clear weather and good views. The lunar landscape of the summit includes a great ash plain called **Playa Hermosa**. Hardy vegetation, such as myrtle and the large-leaved "poor man's umbrella," maintains a tenuous foothold against acidic emissions in the bitter cold. Wildlife is scarce, although it is possible to spot birds such as the sooty robin and endemic volcano junco.

Monumento Nacional Guayabo ㉖

Proclaimed a national monument in 1973, Guayabo, on the southern slope of Volcán Turrialba, is the nation's most important pre-Columbian site. Although minor in scale compared to the Mayan remains of Mexico, the 540-acre (218-ha) site, which is still shrouded in mystery, is considered to be of great cultural and religious significance. Believed to have been inhabited between 1500 BC and AD 1400, Guayabo is said to have supported a population as high as 10,000, before being abandoned for reasons unknown. The jungle quickly reclaimed the town, which was discovered in the late 18th century by naturalist Don Anastasio Alfaro. The peaceful site, most of which is yet to be excavated, has mounds, petroglyphs, walled aqueducts, and paved roads. Pottery, gold ornaments, flint tools, and other finds are displayed in San José's Museo Nacional *(see p120).*

Petroglyphs
The most noteworthy of the petroglyphs scattered around the site are along the Sendero de los Montículos. The Mono-litho Jaguar y Lagarto has a lizard on one side and, on the other, a spindly bodied jaguar with a round head.

Cisterns
Rectangular water tanks are situated in the western side of the settlement, and are spanned by a three-slab bridge.

Premontane rainforest
surrounding the site hosts hundreds of bird species, such as aracaris and oropendolas.

The stone aqueducts, forming a network of covered and uncovered channels, continue to feed water into stone-lined cisterns.

EXCAVATED SITE
Initiated in 1968, excavation of the site was led by archae-ologists from the University of Costa Rica. To date, only about 12 acres (5 ha) have been retrieved. Parts of the causeway and key structures have been rebuilt, and restoration work is ongoing.

Sendero de los Montículos
A 1-mile (1.6-km) self-guided trail leads from the entrance to a lookout, El Mirador Encuentro con Nuestros Origenes (The Encounter with Our Origins Lookout), before dropping down to the main archaeological site. Along the way, visitors can stop at 15 interpretive points that explain the social organization of the Guayabo tribe.

STAR SIGHTS

★ Calzada (Causeway)

★ Montículos (Stone Foundations)

VISITORS' CHECKLIST

Road Map E3. 12 miles (19 km) N of Turrialba. **Tel** 2559-1220. from Turrialba. 8am–3:30pm daily. www.sinac.go.cr

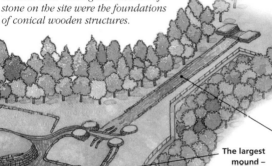

★ **Montículos (Stone Foundations)**
Believed to date from AD 300–700, the circular and rectangular mounds of stone on the site were the foundations of conical wooden structures.

The largest mound – measuring 98 ft (30 m) in diameter and 15 ft (4.5 m) in height – is thought to have been a base for the house of the local *cacique* (chief).

★ **Calzada (Causeway)**
The 21-ft (6.5-m) wide causeway is believed to have extended between 2.5 and 7.5 miles (4–12 km) from the main town. About 246 yd (225 m) have been reconstructed, including two rectangular stone structures thought to have been used as sentry posts.

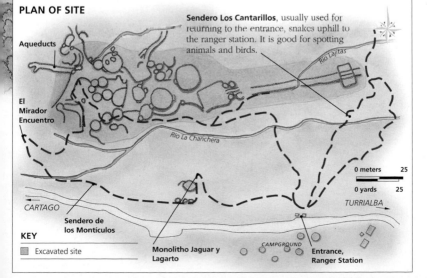

PLAN OF SITE

Sendero Los Cantarillos, usually used for returning to the entrance, snakes uphill to the ranger station. It is good for spotting animals and birds.

Aqueducts

Río Lajitas

El Mirador Encuentro

Río La Chanchera

0 meters 25
0 yards 25

CARTAGO

TURRIALBA

Sendero de los Montículos

Monolitho Jaguar y Lagarto

CAMPGROUND

Entrance, Ranger Station

KEY

Excavated site

THE CENTRAL PACIFIC AND SOUTHERN NICOYA

ine white beaches are scattered along the shores of Southern Nicoya, while the sun-drenched Central Pacific coastline is pummeled by non-stop surf and fringed with forest. The region acts as a transition between two ecosystems – the drier Meso-American to the north and the humid Andean to the south – with flora and fauna of both ecosystems. As a result, its wildlife reserves, such as Parque Nacional Manuel Antonio, are among the nation's best.

Mangroves line the shores of the Gulf of Nicoya, which is studded with islands that are important nesting sites for birds. Forest areas, notably in Southern Nicoya, were heavily denuded during the last century, but major conservation and reforestation efforts are now extending the protected areas.

Spanish conquistadors explored the region in the early 16th century and established short-lived settlements, which fell victim to tropical diseases and the ferocious resistance of indigenous tribes. However, the Indians were swiftly defeated. The principal city of the region, Puntarenas, was founded in the early 1800s. It flourished due to the 19th-century coffee trade, and developed into the nation's main port for coffee exports to Europe. In the early decades of the 20th century, bananas were planted along the narrow coastal plain farther south. They were replaced in the 1970s by African oil palms, which today dominate the economy and extend for miles between the shore and forested mountains. Jacó has now blossomed as a beach resort for surfers, while the town of Quepos retains its stature as a major sportfishing base.

Locals waiting for the bus in a small town in Southern Nicoya

◁ Yacht on the serene blue waters off Playa Blanca, on Costa Rica's Pacific coast

Exploring the Central Pacific and Southern Nicoya

Beaches and national parks, teeming with wildlife, are the highlights of this region. The main town is the fishing port of Puntarenas, from where it is possible to take a day-trip by ferry to Isla Tortuga with its fabulous beach. Other fine beaches in Southern Nicoya await at off-the-beaten-track Montezuma and Malpaís, which are popular with surfers and budget travelers. Nearby Cabo Blanco is the site of the nation's oldest wildlife refuge. Inland from the Central Pacific coast, nature lovers can enjoy a crocodile safari on Río Tárcoles and hikes in Parque Nacional Carara, where scarlet macaws, monkeys, and other wildlife can be easily spotted. Major attractions along this coast are the lively surfing town of Jacó and the sportfishing center of Quepos, which gives access to Parque Nacional Manuel Antonio, one of the country's most popular wildlife parks.

Reserva Natural Absoluta Cabo Blanco

SIGHTS AT A GLANCE

Towns and Villages
Jacó **9**
Malpaís **7**
Montezuma **5**
Puntarenas **1**
Quepos **12**
Tambor **4**

National Parks and Reserves
Parque Nacional Carara **8**
Parque Nacional Manuel Antonio pp168–9 **13**
Refugio Nacional de Vida Silvestre Curú **2**
Reserva Natural Absoluta Cabo Blanco **6**

Areas of Natural Beauty
Boca Damas **11**
Isla Tortuga **3**
Valle del Río Savegre **14**

Tour
Santa Juana Mountain Tour **10**

A riot of colors at the Tango Mar Resort in the fishing village of Tambor

Gleaming sportfishing boats lined up at Los Sueños Marina, near Jacó

An eye-catching sportfishing sign at Quepos docks

SEE ALSO

• **Where to Stay** pp254–6

• **Where to Eat** pp277–9

GETTING AROUND

Jacó and Quepos, in the Central Pacific region, and Southern Nicoya's Tambor are linked by daily scheduled flights to Juan Santamaría International Airport and San José's Tobias Bolaños domestic airport. Puntarenas, Jacó, and Quepos are served by bus from San José; several companies cater solely to tourists.

Puntarenas is the gateway for ferries to Southern Nicoya. A regular car and passenger ferry service links it with Paquera; from here, a bus service operates to Montezuma along badly deteriorated Highway 160. In the Central Pacific region, well-paved Highway 34 runs along the shore, linking all the major tourist sights. Away from the coastal highways, most roads are dirt tracks that can be treacherous during the wet season. A 4WD vehicle is essential if you plan to drive around.

KEY

━━ Pan-American Highway

━━ Major road

━ Secondary road

┅┅ Minor road

━━ Provincial border

Fishing and excursion boats moored at the Puntarenas docks

Puntarenas ❶

Road Map B3. 75' miles (120 km)
W of San José. 👥 *100,000.* 🚌 📷
*Carnaval (last week of Feb); Festival
de la Virgen del Mar (mid-Jul).*

Often seen as a provincial
backwater, the city of
Puntarenas (Sandy Point)
was once an important port.
First settled in 1522 by the
Spanish, Puntarenas later
became the main shipping
point for coffee beans,
brought from the highlands
in *carretas* (oxcarts). City
fortunes waned in 1890, once
the Atlantic Railroad was
built, and many of its wooden
structures are dilapidated.
Today this slightly down-at-
heel town exists on fishing,
as attested to by rows of
decrepit fishing boats moored
at the wharves. It remains the
main gateway for excursions
to Isla Tortuga and for ferries
to Paquera and Naranjo, on
the Peninsula de Nicoya.
   The town occupies a 3-mile
(5-km) long, thin peninsula
fringed on the south by a
beach offering good views
across the Gulf of Nicoya. A
broad estuary runs along the
north shore, where extensive
mangrove forests are home
to waterfowl such as roseate
spoonbills, storks, pelicans,
and frigate birds.
   Puntarenas is favored as a
balneario (bathing resort) by
Josefinos who flock to the
seafront boulevard, Paseo de
los Turistas. The main draw in
town is the **Museo Histórico
Marítimo**, situated in the
former 19th-century city jail.
The museum has displays on
indigenous cultures, maritime
history, and the coffee era.

Environs
The sweeping sands of **Playa
San Isidro**, 5 miles (8 km) east
of town, are very popular
with beachgoers from San
José. During the weekend it
can become crowded.

🏛 **Museo Histórico Marítimo**
Ave Central, Calles 5/7.
***Tel** 2661-0387.*
⏱ *10am–6pm Tue–Sun.*

Serene white beaches of Refugio
Nacional de Vida Silvestre Curú

Refugio Nacional de Vida Silvestre Curú ❷

Road Map B3. 2 miles (3 km)
S of Paquera. ***Tel** 2641-0100.*
🚌 *Paquera–Cobano.* ⏱ *7am–3pm
daily.* 📷 📸 *by appt.* 🍴 🐾 🏠
www.curu.org

Part of a much larger
privately owned hacienda,
the seldom-visited 210-acre
(85-ha) Curú National Wildlife
Refuge has been set up to
protect five distinct habitats
extending inland from
Golfo Curú.

The majority of the hilly
reserve is tropical deciduous
and semi-deciduous forest
populated by capuchin and
howler monkeys, anteaters,
agoutis, and sloths, as well as
several species of wild cats
and more than 220 species
of birds. Endangered spider
monkeys have also been
successfully reintroduced.
Since the number of visitors
is low, it is possible to spot
animals more easily than at
many other refuges. Marked
trails provide access.
   Three beautiful beaches –
Playa Colorada, Playa Curú,
and **Playa Quesera** – are tucked
inside the fold of green headlands and extend along 3 miles
(5 km) of coastline. Hawksbill
and olive ridley turtles crawl
ashore at night to nest in the
sand. Whales and dolphins can
sometimes be seen swimming
in the warm offshore waters,
while the mangrove swamps
and lagoons that extend
inland along Río Curú are
good for spotting caimans.

Isla Tortuga ❸

Road Map B3. 2 miles (3 km) SE
of Curú. 🚤 *organized excursions.*
🍴 📷

This sun-bleached island –
actually twin islets, Isla
Tolinga and unoccupied Isla
Alcatraz – offshore of Curú is
run as a privately owned 765-
acre (310-ha) nature reserve.
Isla Tolinga, which has no
overnight accommodation,
is very popular for day-visits.
   Isla Tortuga is rimmed by
white beaches that dissolve
into startlingly blue waters.
Coconut palms lean over the

Catamaran Manta Ray transporting
visitors to Isla Tortuga

Kayaking on offer at Isla Tortuga, along with other beach activities and water sports

beach. The hilly interior is covered by deciduous forest, accessed by a short but steep trail that leads to the highest point of the island (570 ft/ 175 m). Signs point out rare hardwoods, such as *indio desnudo* (naked Indian).

The preferred activity is to laze in a hammock while sipping the island cocktail *coco loco* (rum, coconut milk, and coconut liqueur) – served in a coconut shell. The warm waters are great for snorkeling. There are no jet skis to break the blissful silence, but visitors can choose from an array of other water sports.

Trips were pioneered in 1975 by **Calypso Cruises**, which operates a 70-ft (21-m) motorized, high-speed catamaran that departs from Puntarenas. Other companies offer similar excursions, which usually include hotel transfers, round-trip transportation, and buffet lunch. The 90-minute journey is its own reward – dolphins and whales are frequently spotted. A midweek visit is best, as weekends can get crowded.

Environs
Boobies, pelicans, frigate birds, and other sea birds nest on the scattered islands that comprise the **Reserva Biológica Isla Guayabo y Isla Negritos**, to the north of Isla Tortuga. Visitors are not allowed on shore. Excursion boats pass between the islets that make up the biological reserve.

> 🛥 **Calypso Cruises**
> *Tel* 2256-2727. 📷 🔢
> **www**.calypsocruises.com

Tambor 4

Road Map B3. 11 miles (18 km) SW of Paquera. 🚍

A small, laid-back fishing village with a wide silver-gray beach, Tambor lines the aptly named Bahía Ballena (Whale Bay), where whales gather in mid-winter. Palm-fringed sands extend from the bay north to mangrove swamps. The village itself is somewhat somnolent, but two upscale resorts just outside town attract a large number of foreign beachgoers and Josefinos, most of whom fly in to the local airstrip. Visitors can play a round of golf or a game of tennis for a fee at the **Tango Mar Resort** *(see p256)*, which has a 9-hole golf course, or at the **Los Delfines Golf and Country Club**, which has an 18-hole course. Scuba diving for all

abilities is on offer at the nearby **Playa Tambor Beach Resort and Casino**, which is affiliated to Barceló Los Delfines Club. The casino offers everything from slot machines and Caribbean poker to American roulette. Other activities popular in Tambor include sportfishing and horseback riding.

Environs
West of Tambor, **Hacienda La Esperanza** is a working farm offering horseback riding, mountain biking, and other activities.

> 🏌 **Los Delfines Golf and Country Club**
> 1 mile (1.6 km) E of Tambor.
> *Tel* 2683-0294. 📷 🔢 🍴 🔢 ⚓
> 🏇 **Hacienda La Esperanza**
> 12 miles (18 km) NW of Tambor.
> ⏰ 8am–5pm daily. **www**.
> hacienda-la-esperanza.com

The lush greens of the golf courses of Tambor

Bright signs adorning shop fronts in Montezuma village

Montezuma ❺

Road Map B3. 16 miles (26 km)
W of Paquera. 🚌 from Paquera.

A favorite with budget
travelers, this offbeat beach
community has a laidback
lifestyle, magnificent ocean
vistas and beaches, and
unpretentious yet hip bars.
The compact village is
tucked beneath precipitous
hills and opens onto a rocky
cove with fishing boats
bobbing at anchor. Two
superb beaches – Playa
Montezuma and Playa
Grande – unspool eastward,
shaded by tall palms and
backed by thickly forested
mountains. Swimmers
should watch out for
the riptides. Sliding
between treetops on
the **Montezuma Canopy
Tour** is a safe, fun, and
adrenaline-boosting
activity, while **Finca
Los Caballos** offers
invigorating horseback
rides in the hills abutting
the Reserva Absoluta
Nicolas Weissenburg.
The reserve, however,
has no public access.
Clambering up the
waterfalls to the west of
the village is unsafe; instead,
cool off in the pools at the
base of the waterfalls.

🧗 **Montezuma Canopy Tour**
1 mile (1.6 km) W of Montezuma.
Tel 2642-0808. ⬜ daily. 🅿 📷
8am, 10am, 1pm, and 3pm. www.
montezumatraveladventures.com

🌴 **Finca Los Caballos**
2 miles (3 km) NW of Montezuma.
📞 2642-0124. 📷 9am daily.
🛏 🔗 www.naturelodge.net

Reserva Natural Absoluta Cabo Blanco ❻

Road Map B4. 6 miles (10 km)
W of Montezuma. **Tel** 2642-0093.
🚌 Montezuma–Cabuya. Also taxis
from Montezuma. ⬜ 8am–4pm
Wed–Sun and public hols. 📷

Established in 1963 as the
nation's first protected area,
and elevated to the status of a
reserve in 1974, the 4-sq-mile
(10-sq-km) Cabo Blanco owes
its genesis to the tireless
campaign of the late Olof
Wessberg and his wife Karen
Morgenson; they also helped
set up the Costa Rican National
Park Service. Cabo Blanco
was initially an "absolute"
reserve, off-limits to all
visitors, but today there
is access to the eastern
part of the tropical for-
ests that cover the hilly
tip of the Nicoya Penin-
sula. About 85 percent
of the reserve is covered
by rejuvenated second-
ary forest and pockets
of lowland tropical
forest. There are
numerous monkeys,
as well as anteaters,
coatis, and deer. The 3-mile
(5-km) long Sendero Sueco
trail leads to the beautiful
Playa Cabo Blanco; other
beaches lie along the shore,
but exploring should not be
attempted when the tide is
rising.
Offshore, the sheer walls of
Isla Cabo Blanco are stained
white by guano deposited by
colonies of nesting seabirds,
including frigate birds and
brown boobies.

**Activities in
Montezuma**

Cabo Blanco is accessed from
the community of Cabuya, a
mile (1.6 km) along a rough
dirt road. It can also be
entered at Malpaís. Tour
operators nationwide offer
excursions to the reserve.

Malpaís ❼

Road Map B4. 6 miles (10 km)
NW of Montezuma. 🚌 from Cóbano,
4 miles (6 km) N of Montezuma.

Its name may mean "bad
land," but the Malpaís area's
Pacific shoreline is unsurpassed for its rugged beauty.
Until a few years ago, the
region was unknown; today
it is a famed surfers' paradise.
Named for their respective
gray-sand beaches, three
contiguous communities are
strung along the dirt road that
fringes the shore. Relaxed to
a fault, they are characterized
by colorful hotels, restaurants,
and bars. The main hamlet is
Carmen, from where the road
runs 2 miles (3 km) south,
through Santa Teresa, to the
fishing hamlet of Malpaís,
which gives the area its
popular name. Beyond
Malpaís, where vultures perch
on fishing boats, the beach
ends amid tidepools and
fantastically sculpted rocks
near the entrance to Cabo
Blanco. A 4WD is required.
The best surf beach is
Playa Santa Teresa, merging
in the north with *playas* that
are virtually uninhabited:
Los Suecos, Hermosa, and
Manzanillo. Santa Teresa
boasts the understatedly
deluxe Florblanca Resort *(see
p254)*, in stunning counter-
point to the budget options.

**Surfer and sun-lovers on Playa
Santa Teresa's Pacific shoreline**

Arachnids and Insects of Costa Rica

Costa Rica hosts more than 300,000 species of insects, including more than 1,250 species of butterflies *(see p135)*. No one knows the exact number of beetle species or ants, which are in their thousands. Bees, wasps, and myriad other flying creatures buzz about, while an astounding profusion of other types of insects creep, crawl, or leap. Many advertise their toxicity with gaudy coloration.

Stick insect on a branch

Others have adopted clever techniques of disguise to prey or avoid being preyed upon – swallowtail caterpillars, for example, camouflage themselves as bird droppings. Scorpions and other arachnids – from tiny jumping spiders to giant tarantulas – are ubiquitous too. Costa Rica celebrates its arachnid and insect diversity in butterfly gardens and insect museums around the country.

Army ants *are nomadic and swarm by day, capturing small prey. At night, they build a bivouac nest with their bodies.*

Golden orb spiders *spin giant webs with a sticky, golden-yellow thread that is five times stronger than steel and three times more resistant than Kevlar.*

Tarantulas *are large, hairy terrestrial spiders that live in silk-lined burrows. Some species grow up to 12 in (30 cm) – large enough to prey on lizards, mice, and small birds.*

Eight small eyes

Stinging hairs

Retractable claws

The praying mantis's *prayer-like stance and gentle rocking motion belie its predatory behavior. Its forelegs are spiked for grasping as it devours its prey. A female will often eat the male during mating.*

Rhinoceros beetles *are named for the males' horns, which are used for fighting in mating season. Primarily fruit eaters, they grow up to 3 in (8 cm) in length but are harmless to humans.*

A camouflaged praying mantis

CAMOUFLAGE TECHNIQUES

Many arachnid and insect species adopt camouflage or mimicry to hide from predators or to ambush prey. Praying mantises resemble bright green leaves; the dead-leaf katydid looks like a dried, curled-up leaf; while stick insects can appear like twigs. Several palatable butterfly species have evolved to look like toxic Heliconid species.

Hiking through a lower elevation forest at Parque Nacional Carara

Parque Nacional Carara ❽

Road Map C3. 31 miles (50 km) SE of Puntarenas. *Tel 2637-1054.* 🚌 *from San José and Jacó.* ⏰ *7am–4pm daily.* 🖼 ♿ **www**.sinac.go.cr

Occupying a climatological transition zone where dry northerly and humid southerly ecosystems meet, Carara National Park's forests are complex and varied. Despite its relatively small size – 20 sq miles (52 sq km) – the park offers some of the most diverse wildlife viewing in Costa Rica. Species from both the Meso-American and Amazonian environments are abundant, including the endangered spider monkey and the poison-dart frog. The birding is spectacular, with scarlet macaws being a major draw. They can be seen on their twice-daily migration between the forest and nearby coastal mangroves.

Carara's lower elevation forests have easy-to-walk trails that begin at the roadside visitor center; the longest is 5 miles (8 km) around. Guides can be hired to access pre-Columbian sites. Several tour operators in San José arrange day visits.

Environs
Carara is a Huetar Indian word for crocodile. The reptiles are easily seen from the highway as they bask on the banks of Río Tárcoles. Safaris are offered from **Tárcoles**, 2 miles (3 km) southwest of Carara. The

spectacular 600-ft (183-m) drop of **Catarata Manantial de Agua Viva** makes the waterfall popular with hikers who cool off in the pools at its base. Nearby, **Pura Vida Botanical Gardens** have walking trails through 30 lush acres (12 ha).

> 🏞 **Catarata Manantial de Agua Viva**
> Bijagual, 4 miles (6 km) E of Tárcoles. *Tel 8831-2980.*
> ⏰ *8am–3pm daily.* 🖼 🏞
>
> 🌺 **Pura Vida Botanical Gardens**
> Bijagual. *Tel 2645-1001.*
> ⏰ *7am–5pm daily.* 🖼 🏞 🍴
> 📷 🏞 **www**.puravidagarden.com

Jacó ❾

Road Map C4. 40 miles (65 km) S of Puntarenas. 🏘 *8,000.* ✈ 🚌 🎵 *International Festival of Music (Jul–Aug).*

Thriving on the surfer trade and that of Canadian "snowbirds" escaping the northern

winter, Jacó has evolved as the nation's largest and most party-oriented beach resort. Palms shade the 2-mile (3-km) long beach. Despite this, its gray sands are unremarkable, the sea is usually a murky brown from silt washed down by rivers, and riptides make swimming unsafe. There's no shortage of things to do, however – from crocodile safaris to horseback rides – and the nightlife is lively. Many of the nation's top surfers live here, although as a surf center, Jacó is best for beginners.

In town, **Pacific Bungee** offers the thrill of daredevil leaps, plus an adrenalin-charged catapult "ride". Outside town, the **Pacific Rainforest Aerial Tram** takes you on a 90-minute guided ride through the treetops on silent open-air gondolas. The modified ski lifts skim the forest floor, soar above giant trees, pass waterfalls, and give fabulous views along the Pacific coast. Guided tours such as the Poison-dart Frog Trail, are also offered along nature trails.

Environs
Sportfishing and excursion boats set out from Los Sueños Marina at **Playa Herradura**, a gray-sand beach tucked into a broad bay north of Jacó. The marina is part of the **Los Sueños Marriott Ocean & Golf Resort** (*see p256*), which boasts a championship golf course.

Perched on a headland just north of Playa Herradura,

The gray sands of palm-fringed Playa Jacó

Hotel Villa Caletas *(see p255)* is the remarkable creation of French designer Denis Roy. A long ridgetop driveway lined with Roman urns has dramatic vistas out to sea and also provides a striking entry to this deluxe restaurant and hotel. Musicians perform in a Greek-style amphitheater built into the hillside, a setting for the International Festival of Music. The Serenity Spa offers pampering treatments. A winding track leads down to **Playa Caletas**, a rocky beach with a bar and grill. South of Jacó, **Playa Hermosa** is served by dedicated surf hostels. Sand bars provide consistently good breaks swelling in from deep waters offshore.

A guided horseback ride, part of the Santa Juana Mountain Tour

🪂 **Pacific Bungee**
Ave Pastor Diaz and Calle Las Brisas.
Tel 2643-6682. ⏰ 9:30am–8:30pm daily. **www**.pacificbungee.com

🪂 **Pacific Rainforest Aerial Tram**
2 miles (3 km) E of Jacó.
Tel 2257-5961. ⏰ 9am–4pm Mon, 6am–4pm Tue–Sun. 🎫 🚻
📷 🅿️ **www**.rainforestram.com

Santa Juana Mountain Tour ⑩

Road Map D4. 8 miles (11 km) E of Hwy 34, 32 miles (50 km) S of Jacó. **Tel** 2777-0777.
🚐 organized transfers. 🎫 🚻 7:30am daily. 🍴 (lunch included.) **www**.sicomono.com/tours-activities

This educational tour takes visitors deep into the Fila Chonta Mountains inland of Quepos. The tour is centered on a remote rural community at the heart of an ecological project, the purpose of which is to engage individual local families in ecotourism while attempting to preserve traditional rural customs.

There are several hiking trails and a river walk, with waterfalls and pools for bathing and cooling off. Participants get to visit butterfly-breeding, animal-husbandry, and reforestation projects; learn about snakes at a serpentarium; and visit an authentic sugar mill powered by oxen. They

A small lizard resting on a leaf in the depths of the rainforest

can even help pick coffee and citrus, or fish for tilapia. A guided horseback ride is another option. A typical *campesino* (peasant) lunch is served at a restaurant offering sensational views.

Boca Damas ⑪

Road Map D4. 33 miles (53 km) S of Jacó. 🚐

Crisscrossed by countless sloughs and channels, this vast *manglare* (mangrove) complex extends along the shoreline between the towns of Parrita and Quepos, at the estuary of Río Damas. Coatis, pumas, white-faced monkeys, and several species of snakes inhabit the dense forests. Crocodiles and caimans lurk in the tannin-stained waters. Stilt-legged shorebirds and boat-billed herons, with their curious keel-shaped beaks, pick among the mudflats in search of molluscs.

Tour operators in Quepos offer kayaking excursions. Guides offer boat trips from the small dock at Damas.

CROCODILE SAFARI

Indiscriminate hunting during the past 400 years has resulted in a decimation of the American *cocodrilo* (crocodile) population. Since gaining protected status in 1981, however, crocodiles have managed to make a comeback. They can be seen in rivers throughout the Pacific lowlands, but are nowhere so numerous as near the mouth of Río Tárcoles, where populations of more than 200 crocodiles per mile have been counted. Boats depart from the village of Tárcoles, near the mouth of the river, for 2-hour crocodile-spotting safaris upriver. The reptiles, which grow up to 16 ft (5 m) in length, often approach to within a few feet. Keep your hands in the boat. You can also expect to see roseate spoonbills, scarlet macaws, and dozens of other Costa Rican bird species.

Crocodiles seen from a bridge over Río Tárcoles, Puntarenas

A relaxed cafeteria and ice-cream bar on a downtown Quepos street

Quepos ⓬

Road Map D4. 34 miles (55 km) S of Jacó. 🐾 15,000. ✈ 🚌 🎭 *Carnaval (Feb–Mar)*. **www**.quepolandia.com

Traditionally a game fishing base and center for the production of African palm oil, Quepos has blossomed as a tourist center and a gateway to Parque Nacional Manuel Antonio. The town buzzes both by day and at night, when its numerous bars and restaurants come alive.

On the north side of town, Boca Vieja village has wooden huts, which are linked by flimsy walkways that overhang the brown sands of **Playa Cocal**. In the hills to the south, quaint clapboard homes recall the 1930s, when the Standard Fruit Company established banana plantations. Panama disease killed them off, and today African oil palms dominate the coastal plains for miles around.

Environs
South of Quepos, a two-lane road winds over steep headlands to the hamlet of **Manuel Antonio**, fronted by **Playa Espadilla**, a wide scimitar of gray sand. At the north end of the beach is a lagoon with crocodiles. Restaurants, bars, and hotels line the route, including **El Avión**, a converted Fairchild C-123 transport plane, which was used by the CIA in the 1970s to run arms to the Nicaraguan Contras *(see p185)*.

Nearby, **Fincas Naturales Wildlife Refuge & Butterfly Garden** offers easy walks through 40 acres (16 ha) teeming with sloths, raccoon-like coatis, leafcutter ants, and phenomenal birdlife.

The **Río Naranjo Valley** extends east of Quepos into the Fila Nara Mountains. The ruins of a Spanish mission, established in 1570, still stand by the roadside. Whitewater rafting trips are a popular excursion from Quepos.

Farther up the valley, **Rancho Los Tucanes** offers guided horseback and 4WD tours of its vanilla and pepper plantations. Trails lead through montane rainforest to the 295-ft (90-m) high Los Tucanos waterfall.

> 🦋 **Fincas Naturales Wildlife Refuge & Butterfly Garden**
> 1 mile (1.6 km) S of Quepos.
> **Tel** 2777-0850. ⬜ 6am–8pm daily;
> butterfly garden: 8am–4pm daily.
> 🎟 📷 **www**.wildliferefugecr.com

> 🦜 **Rancho Los Tucanes**
> Londres, 7 miles (11 km)
> NE of Quepos. **Tel** 2777-0775.
> ⬜ 7am–3pm daily. 📷
> **www**.rancholostucanes.com

Parque Nacional Manuel Antonio ⓭

See pp168–9.

Valle del Río Savegre ⓮

Road Map D4. 15 miles (25 km) SE of Quepos. 🚌 *from Quepos.*

Cutting inland into the Fila San Bosco Mountains, the Río Savegre Valley is covered by plantations of African oil palms at its lower levels. Farther up the valley lies the rural community of El Silencio, where the local farmers' cooperative operates an ecotourist center called **Coopesilencio**. It offers horses for rides down rustic trails into a nature reserve, and has a wildlife rescue center with scarlet macaws, deer, and monkeys.

Modeled on a South African safari camp, **Rafiki Safari Lodge** *(see p256)* is set atop a ridge overlooking the Savegre. It makes a great base for hiking, birding, and horseback riding, as well as for exhilarating whitewater rafting and kayaking trips on Río Savegre. A 4WD vehicle is essential for negotiating the rugged track, which is often inundated in the wet season.

> 🦜 **Coopesilencio**
> 25 miles (40 km) SE of Quepos.
> **Tel** 2779-9554. ⬜ 9:30am–noon
> and 1–3:30pm daily. 🎟 📷 🍴 ⌨
> **www**.turismoruralcr.com

Plantations of African oil palms in the Valle del Río Savegre

Sportfishing on the Pacific Coast

The ultimate draw for the game-fishing enthusiast, Costa Rica's waters witness the setting of new International Game Fish Association records every year. More anglers have claimed "grand slams" – both species of marlin and one or more sailfish in a single day – on the country's Pacific coast than in any other place on earth. In the wet season (May–November), fishing is

Fishing lure

best off the Golfo de Papagayo. In the dry season (December–April), when high winds in the Golfo de Papagayo make the waters dangerous, the best fishing is found farther toward the south, out of the year-round marinas of Quepos, Bahía Drake, and Golfito. Angling on the Caribbean coast is different: inshore fishing using light tackle is the norm here *(see p299)*.

ORGANIZED FISHING TRIPS

Sportfishing vessels often journey 20 miles (32 km) or more from shore to find game fish. Hooking a fish is only the beginning. The real sport lies in the fight that ensues.

Charter shops *and fishing lodges abound in Costa Rica. Apart from hiring out boats, they can also arrange fishing licenses for visiting anglers.*

Anglers *strap themselves into the "fighting chair" to bring in larger species. Fights sometimes take hours and can tire the angler almost as much as the fish.*

A catch-and-release policy *is usually followed by sportfishing operators in Costa Rica. However, maritime laws designed to protect fish stocks from commercial over-exploitation are poorly enforced.*

DEEP SEA FISH

A wide variety of game fish await the keen angler on Costa Rica's Pacific coast. Angling is possible year-round, but there are prime areas and peak seasons for each species.

Yellowfin tuna *are extremely powerful, weighing up to 350 lb (160 kg). They are found in warm currents year-round, but June–October is best.*

Wahoo *are long, sleek, and explosively fast fish that are found in northern waters between May and August.*

Blue marlins *are considered the ultimate prize. The "Bull of the Ocean" puts up a fight like no other. Females weigh up to 1,000 lb (455 kg); males are smaller. August–December are generally the best months.*

Dorado *(also called dolphinfish or mahimahi) have scales that flash a wide range of colors. This dramatic fighter is found from May to October.*

Sailfish, *hard-fighting giants up to 7 ft (2 m) long, and known for their spectacular leaps when hooked, are plentiful from December to April.*

Parque Nacional Manuel Antonio ⑬

**Signage within
PN Manuel Antonio**

Named for a Spanish conquistador, and flanked by the ocean and forested hills, this beautiful park was inaugurated in 1972. Although it is the smallest in Costa Rica's park system, covering a land area of 6 sq miles (16 sq km), Manuel Antonio National Park has remarkable biodiversity, with abundant wildlife and magnificent beaches. Sightings of coatis, sloths, toucans, and scarlet macaws along the well-maintained trails are virtually guaranteed. This is one of the most visited parks in the nation: although there is a limit on the daily number of visitors, its wildlife is threatened by overuse, pollution, and unregulated hotel expansion.

Visitors queuing at the park entrance

TO QUEPOS

Playa Espadilla Sur
*A long swathe of coral-colored sand curling south
from Manuel Antonio village, this beach connects
with Playa Espadilla to the north.*

Punta Catedral
*This former island is
now connected to the
mainland by a tombolo
(natural land bridge).
The rocky promontory has
tidal pools at its base and
is encircled by a trail
that ascends to a
mirador (viewpoint).*

Manuel
Antonio

Playa
Espadilla
Norte

Playa
Espadilla
Sur

Playa
Manuel
Antonio

Punta
Catedral

Isla
Olocuita

PACIFI

Playa Manuel Antonio
*This scimitar-shaped beach
with soft white sands shelves
into calm jade waters
containing a small coral
reef. Snorkeling is splendid,
especially in the dry season.
Green and Pacific ridley
turtles sometimes nest here.*

Coral reefs form a
refuge for crabs, star-
fish, shrimp and color-
ful fish. Dolphins and
humpback whales are
often seen in this area.

THE MANCHINEEL TREE

Manchineel trees

Locally called *manzanillo*, or "beach apple," the manchineel tree is quite common on the beaches, causing problems for unwary visitors seeking its shade. This evergreen species *(Hippomane manicinella)*, identified by its short trunk and bright green elliptical leaves, is very toxic. The sap and bark inflame the skin, while the small yellow apple-like fruit is poisonous. Moreover, if its wood is burnt, the smoke is an irritant to the lungs.

VISITORS' CHECKLIST

Road Map D4. 100 miles (160 km) S of San José and 5 miles (8 km) S of Quepos. **Tel** 2777-5185. 🚌 from San José and Quepos. ⬜ 8am–4pm Tue–Sun. Limited to 600 visitors a day. 📷 🗓 🖥

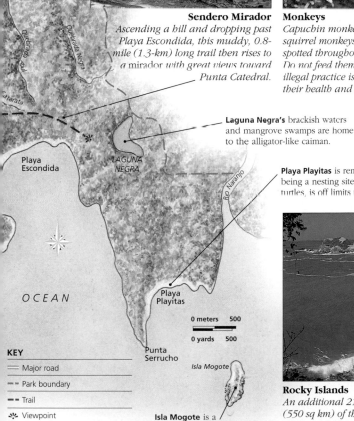

Sendero Mirador
Ascending a hill and dropping past Playa Escondida, this muddy, 0.8-mile (1.3-km) long trail then rises to a mirador with great views toward Punta Catedral.

Monkeys
Capuchin monkeys and tiny squirrel monkeys are easily spotted throughout the park. Do not feed them – the illegal practice is a threat to their health and behavior.

Laguna Negra's brackish waters and mangrove swamps are home to the alligator-like caiman.

Playa Playitas is remote and, being a nesting site for marine turtles, is off limits to visitors.

Quebrada Azul

Quebrada Negra

Catarata

Playa Escondida

LAGUNA NEGRA

Río Naranjo

OCEAN

Playa Playitas

0 meters 500
0 yards 500

Punta Serrucho

Isla Mogote

Isla Mogote is a sacred site for the Quepoa Indians.

Rocky Islands
An additional 212 sq miles (550 sq km) of the park protects 12 islands that host large colonies of seabirds.

KEY

═ Major road

▬ ▬ Park boundary

▬ ▬ Trail

☀ Viewpoint

ℹ Visitor information

GUANACASTE AND NORTHERN NICOYA

W*ith its arid plains, men on horseback, rodeos, and bullfights, the province of Guanacaste is steeped in the hacienda heritage. The region stretches from the cloud-tipped volcanoes of the Cordillera de Guanacaste to the marshes of the Río Tempisque basin and the magnificent surf-washed beaches of Northern Nicoya – paradise for marine turtles and surfers.*

A chain of volcanoes and mountains runs across this vast region, framing it to the east. To the northwest, the rugged Pacific shore, which is serrated by deep bays, has many of the nation's best beaches. Between mountain and coast lies a broad trough whose wetlands harbor crocodiles and waterfowl. To the southwest, the Nicoya Peninsula enfolds the mangrove-fringed Gulf of Nicoya. Although the plains can be searingly hot, the mountains offer cool, beautiful retreats, while refreshing breezes caress the beaches.

In spring, the sparsely foliated deciduous forests of the plains explode in a riot of color while offering the advantage of relatively easy wildlife spotting. Thick evergreen cloud forests on the upper slopes of the mountains provide a splendid study in contrasts.

The Chorotega culture was one of the region's most developed at the time of the Spanish arrival, and was quickly assimilated. While no great pre-Columbian architecture has been discovered, a tradition of superb pottery continues in the Guaitíl area. The predominant culture now is that of the *sabanero* (cowboy), tracing a lineage back to colonial days, when great haciendas were constructed. Raising or tending cattle is still the dominant occupation here, although many inhabitants cling to a way of life established in pre-Columbian times, earning their livelihood from fishing.

Sabaneros (cowboys) herding cattle at a ranch in Liberia

◁ An *espavé* tree *(Anacardium excelsum)* entwined by a strangler fig, Parque Nacional Rincón de la Vieja

Exploring Guanacaste and Northern Nicoya

The driest of Costa Rica's regions offers possibilities ranging from the spectacular cloud forests of Monteverde to the volcano parks of Rincón de la Vieja, Miravalles, and Guanacaste, and the beach-fringed Parque Nacional Santa Rosa. Birding is superb at Palo Verde, Lomas Barbudal, and near Cañas. To the north is Liberia, with its colonial buildings. Laid-back Playas del Coco to the west is a base for scuba diving, while Playa Flamingo is a sportfishing destination. Farther south is the surf center of Tamarindo, and Playa Grande and Ostional draw marine turtles. Guaitíl is famed for its traditional pottery, while Barra Honda attracts cavers.

Liberia's main plaza, flanked by trees

SIGHTS AT A GLANCE

Towns and Villages

Cañas **3**
Guaitíl **22**
Islita **19**
Liberia **7**
Nicoya **20**
Nosara **17**
Sámara **18**
Santa Cruz **21**
Tamarindo **15**
Tilarán **2**

National Parks and Reserves

Monteverde and Santa Elena pp174–8 **1**
Parque Nacional Barra Honda **23**
Parque Nacional Guanacaste **9**
Parque Nacional Palo Verde **4**
Parque Nacional Rincón de la Vieja **8**
Parque Nacional Santa Rosa pp184–5 **11**
Refugio Nacional de Vida Silvestre Ostional **16**
Reserva Biológica Lomas Barbudal **5**
Zona Protectora Volcán Miravalles **6**

Areas of Natural Beauty

Bahía Culebra **12**
Bahía Salinas **10**

Beaches

Playa Flamingo **14**
Playas del Coco **13**

A mask at Rancho
Armadillo, Playas
del Coco

Peñas
Blancas

N

BAHÍA
SALINAS **10** La Cruz

*Refugio Nacional
de Vida Silvestre
Isla Bolaños*

Volcán Orosi
4,900 ft

Santa Rita

Playa Blanca Cuajiniquil

PARQUE NACIONAL
SANTA ROSA

Volcán
5,4

*Islas
Murciélagos* **11** La Casona

PARQUE
NACIONAL
GUANACASTE **9**

Potrerillo

*Playa
Nancite*

*Playa
Naranjo*

Cañas
Dulce:

Curu

Hacienda
Culebra

Daniel Oduber
International Airport

BAHÍA CULEBRA **12**

Playa Hermosa

PLAYAS DEL COCO **13**

Playa Ocotal

Guardia

LI

*Isla
Catalina*

Filadelfia

PLAYA FLAMINGO **14** Tempate

Playa Conchal

GUA N

TAMARINDO **15**

Playa Grande

*Parque Nacional
Marino Las Baulas*

Río Cañas

Bernabela

SANTA
CRUZ
21 GUA

San Juan

Playa Negra

Florida

NICOYA **2**

Vista al Mar

Hojanc

REFUGIO NACIONAL
DE VIDA SILVESTRE
OSTIONAL **16**

Pilas
Blancas

17

Río Nosara

NOSARA

Sant
Mari

Playa Guiones

SÁMARA **18**

*Playa
Carillo* Car

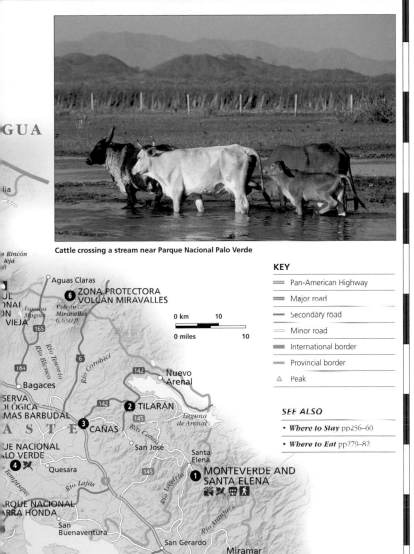

Cattle crossing a stream near Parque Nacional Palo Verde

KEY

▬▬	Pan-American Highway
▬▬	Major road
—	Secondary road
═══	Minor road
▬▬	International border
▬▬	Provincial border
△	Peak

SEE ALSO

- **Where to Stay** pp256–60
- **Where to Eat** pp279–82

GETTING AROUND

The Pan-American Highway runs the length of the region, connecting with the Nicaraguan border. Dirt roads connect the highway with Monteverde and other sights. Highway 21 links Liberia to Northern Nicoya, with feeder roads extending west to the principal beach resorts.

An efficient bus service connects towns along the Pan-American Highway, as well as several beach resorts, with San José, but bus travel between resorts requires time-consuming connections. Cars can be rented at Liberia and Tamarindo. Liberia has an international airport, while Tamarindo, Nosara, Tambor, and Sámara are served by domestic airports.

Monteverde and Santa Elena ●

Monteverde logo

Known worldwide for its unique cloud forest reserve that helped promote Costa Rica's reputation for ecotourism, Monteverde boasts a pastoral alpine setting at an elevation of 4,600 ft (1,400 m), in the heart of the Cordillera de Tilarán. To the northwest is Santa Elena, which is the main commercial center. Several other reserves, incorporated within the Zona Protectora Arenal-Monteverde, are found in the area. Monteverde's fame has spawned all manner of attractions, including a variety of tours that permit visitors a monkey's-eye view of the forest canopy. However, even in the face of these ever-increasing services and attractions, Monteverde retains a bucolic charm.

Canopy Tours
Four canopy tours permit visitors to explore the canopy along a zipline or by rappeling.

Reserva Bosque Nuboso Santa Elena
Offering similar wildlife species to the Monteverde Cloud Forest Biological Reserve, the Santa Elena reserve is, however, less crowded (see p178).

Monteverde Orchid Garden
displays one-third of Costa Rica's orchid species (see p176).

Las Juntas

Sky Walk/ SkyTrek

Reserva Bosque Nuboso Santa Elena Selvatura Park and Monteverde Trainforest

SANTA ELENA

Original Canopy To

Original Canopy Tour Office

CERRO PLANC

Frog pond of Monteverde

Skywalk/Sky Trek Office

SAN JOSÉ

Finca Ecológico
has four trails through montane tropical forest.

Quebrada Maquine

Serpentario
This boasts close-up encounters with snakes that inhabit the local forests, as well as various other amphibians and reptiles (see p176).

Bajo del Tigre Trail
is a self-guided interpretative trail. Three-wattled bellbirds and quetzals are frequently seen.

Bat Jungle has a bat flyw

KEY

══ Major road

══ Other road

▪▪ Trail

▪▪ Park boundary

ℹ Visitor information

Monteverde Butterfly Garden
Dozens of butterfly species flit about inside netted gardens at this educational center, which has displays spanning the insect world (see p176).

Santa Elena
Located downhill of Monteverde, with the locality known as Cerro Plano lying in between, this is the area's main village, with a bank, bus stop, and other services.

La Lechería
Started by immigrant Quakers from the United States, the "Cheese Factory" is the foundation of the local economy. It offers visitors an insider's view of cheese-making (see p176).

Pastures
Monteverde's lush rolling hills are fertile pastures for the cattle that are the source of the area's famous cheeses.

0 meters   500

0 yards   500

migos Trail

Sarah Dodwell
Watercolor Gallery

MONTEVERDE

La Lechería

Río Guacimal

Friend's
Meeting House

SAN
LUIS

● Sloth Sanctuary
of Monteverde

**RESERVA
BIOLÓGICA
BOSQUE
NUBOSO
MONTEVERDE**

Reserve Entrance

Monteverde is actually the name of the Quaker community of American extract, whose members live in scattered homes in the forests below the Monteverde reserve.

The Friend's Meeting House is the venue for meetings of Monteverde's Quaker community (see p176).

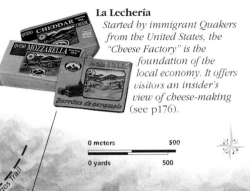

**Reserva Biológica
Bosque Nuboso Monteverde**
The world-famous Monteverde Cloud Forest Biological Reserve is the nation's foremost locale for viewing resplendent quetzals – one among more than 400 species of birds found here (see p177).

Exploring Monteverde and Santa Elena

Monteverde Reserve sign

Cool and verdant Monteverde has its fair share of interesting sights, many of which are spread out along the winding dirt road that slopes gently upward from Santa Elena to the Monteverde Cloud Forest Biological Reserve. Other sights are tucked away off side roads, some of which are quite rugged and steep. Walking is a pleasurable option, but the heavily trafficked roads can be muddy or dusty, depending on the weather. It is always a wise idea to take along an umbrella. Dozens of hotels and restaurants line the route. A steeper dirt road leads northeast from Santa Elena to Santa Elena Cloud Forest Reserve, passing several key attractions along the route.

🐾 Frog Pond of Monteverde

330 yd (300 m) SW of Santa Elena.
Tel 2645-6320. ◯ 9am–8:30pm daily. 🖼 🎟 ♿ 🛗
www.frogpondmonteverde.com

The Frog Pond of Monteverde displays about 28 species of frogs and other amphibians, as well as snakes, salamanders, and lizards in large glass cases that attempt to replicate their natural environments. Several of Costa Rica's most intriguing *ranas* and *sapos* (frogs and toads) can be seen here, including poison-dart frogs, the endearing red-eyed tree frogs, transparent frogs, and huge marine toads. The best time to visit the Frog Pond is evening or night, when the frogs are most active and visitors can hear their distinctive calls.

🐾 Serpentario

550 yd (500 m) S of Santa Elena.
Tel 2645-6002. ◯ 8am–8pm daily.
🖼 🎟 ♿ www.snaketour.com

Among more than 20 snakes shown behind glass in this snake house are the fearsome *terciopelo* (fer-de-lance, or *Bothrops asper*) and its nemesis, the *terciopelo-eating musarana* (*Clelia clelia*). Most species displayed here can be encountered in local forests. Also exhibited are turtles, iguanas, basilisk lizards, chameleons, and frogs. Although the educational labels are only in Spanish, English-speaking guides are available.

Delicate orchids grown at the Monteverde Orchid Garden

🐾 Monteverde Orchid Garden

0.8 mile (1.3 km) E of Santa Elena.
Tel 2645-5308. ◯ 8am–5pm daily.
🖼 🎟 www.monteverde orchidgarden.com

A great place to learn about orchids (*see p183*), the Monteverde Orchid Garden has more than 500 local species. They are arranged in 22 groups along a winding self-guided trail labeled with educational signs. Visitors are each handed a magnifying glass to help them appreciate such diminutives as the liverwort orchid (*Platystele jungermannioides*), the world's smallest flower.

🐾 Monteverde Butterfly Garden

1.2 miles (1.8 km) S of Santa Elena.
Tel 2645-5512. ◯ 9:30am–4pm daily. 🖼 🎟 🛗 www.monteverde butterflygarden.com

With educational exhibits as well as butterfly arenas representing three distinct habitats, this nature center is an ideal locale for learning about the life cycle of the butterfly. The fascinating displays also include tarantulas, stick insects, giant rhinoceros beetles, and 5-in (13-cm) long caterpillars.

Educational videos are shown, and a video "bug cam" gives visitors a larger-than-life real-time view of leafcutter ants inside a nest. The highlight of the hour-long guided tour is a large netted flyway where more than 40 species of colorful butterflies flit about amid dense foliage. Go midmorning, when the butterflies become active.

🐾 Bat Jungle

1.75 miles (2.5 km) SE of Santa Elena. *Tel* 2645-7701. ◯ 9am–7pm daily. 🖼 🎟 www.batjungle.com

Costa Rica boasts 109 species of bats (Monteverde alone has 65 of them), and you can learn all about these fascinating creatures at this exhibit. The highlight is a glass-walled flyway that is a habitat for eight bat species. Documentaries are shown, and you can don giant ears to gain a sense of a bat's phenomenal acoustic abilities.

THE QUAKERS

The original settlers of Monteverde were 44 members of the pacifist Protestant religious group called Quakers. Hailing from Alabama, USA, where they had been jailed for refusing to be drafted, they arrived in Costa Rica in 1951, drawn by the fact that the country had abolished its army following the 1948 Civil War. They settled in the Cordillera de Tilarán, raising dairy cattle to produce the cheese that is now famous throughout the nation. The Quakers have been at the forefront of local conservation efforts in Monteverde.

Painting of a Quaker in traditional attire

THE GOLDEN TOAD

In 1964 scientists discovered a new species of toad *(Bufo periglenes)* in the cloud forest above Monteverde. They named the brilliant orange creature *sapo dorado* (golden toad). In fact, only the male, which is 1 in (3 cm) long, is bright orange; the female is larger and speckled in patches of black, red, and yellow. Although abundant as recently as 1986, *sapo dorado* has not been seen since 1988 and is now considered extinct.

Golden toads, now extinct

🏠 La Lechería

2 miles (3 km) SE of Santa Elena.
Tel 2645-5436. ⏰ 7:30am–5pm
daily (to 12:30pm Sun). 📷 🎫 9am
and 2pm. **www**.monteverde.net

Founded by the original Quaker settlers of Monteverde in 1953, the "Cheese Factory" today produces 14 types of pasteurized cheese, including parmesan, Gouda, and the bestselling Monte Rico. Guided tours show visitors the manufacturing process, resulting in the production of more than 2,200 lb (1,000 kg) of cheese daily. Visitors can buy *cajeta*, a butterscotch spread, and cheeses on-site.

🦋 Reserva Biológica Bosque Nuboso Monteverde

4 miles (6 km) SE of Santa Elena.
Tel 2645 5122. ⏰ 7am–4pm daily.
📷 🎫 by reservation. 🏠 🚻 ♿
www.cct.or.cr

The dirt road that winds uphill from Santa Elena ends at the 40-sq-mile (105 sq km) Monteverde Cloud Forest Biological Reserve, the jewel in the crown of the vast Arenal-Monteverde Protection Zone. Owned and operated by the Tropical Science Center of Costa Rica, the reserve straddles the Continental Divide and comprises six distinct ecological zones extending down the Pacific and Caribbean slopes. The upper elevation forests of the reserve are smothered by near-constant mists fed by sodden trade winds sweeping in off the Atlantic. On the more exposed ridges, trees are reduced to stunted dwarfs by the battering of the wind.

Wildlife abounds here. There are more than 150 species of amphibians and reptiles, and over 500 species of butterflies. More than 100 species of mammals include five wild cats – jaguars, jaguarundis, pumas, margays, and ocelots. The umbrella bird and the endangered three-wattled bellbird are among the 400 species of birds. Quetzals are easily seen, the best viewing time being the April–May mating season, when they are especially active after dawn. Also easily spotted are hummingbirds, which gather at feeders outside the visitor center; the reserve counts more than 30 species. Most wildlife, however, is elusive and difficult to detect. The reserve is crossed by 75 miles (120 km) of trails. A self-guided booklet corresponds to educational posts along the most popular trails, which are covered with wooden boardwalks and are linked together to form what is colloquially called "the triangle." Sendero Chomogo is a steep trail leading to a *mirador* (viewpoint) atop the Continental Divide. From here, on rare days when the mists clear, visitors can see both the Pacific and the Caribbean. More challenging trails extend down the Caribbean slopes to the lowlands; these involve a full day's hike, with mud oozing underfoot. Rubber boots can be rented, along with binoculars. The driest months are between December and April. Hotels organize transport, and both taxis and buses operate from Santa Elena.

Iguana at Reserva Biológica Bosque Nuboso Monteverde

A hike through Reserva Biológica Bosque Nuboso Monteverde

⚄ Reserva Bosque Nuboso Santa Elena

4 miles (6 km) NE of Santa Elena. **Tel** 2645-5390. ◯ 7am–4pm daily. 🎦 📷 7:30am, 11:30am, and 7pm, by appointment. ☐ 📷 www.reservasantaelena.org

Funded and run by the community of Santa Elena, the 2-sq-mile (5-sq-km) Santa Elena Cloud Forest Reserve is dedicated to conservation and education. The students of the local high school play a vital role in its development.

Set at a higher elevation than the more famous and crowded Reserva Biológica Bosque Nuboso Monteverde (see p177), this magical green world is cloudier and wetter. Spider and howler monkeys are easily seen, as are resplendent quetzals, orange-bellied trogons, squirrels, and agoutis. More elusive are the tapirs, jaguars, ocelots, pumas, and tayras, which belong to the same family as otters and weasels. On clear days, there are fabulous views toward Volcán Arenal in the northeast. A self-guided booklet is available for the 7 miles (11 km) of hiking trails.

⚄ Sky Walk/SkyTrek

3 miles (5 km) NE of Santa Elena. **Tel** 2645-5238. ◯ 7am–4pm daily. 🎦 📷 8am, 10am, and 1pm (Sky Walk); 7:30am, 9:30am, 11:30am, and 1:30pm (SkyTrek). ♿ 🖥 📷 www.skywalk.co.cr; www.skytrek.com

With high walkways, ziplines, and suspension bridges, this project on the edge of Reserva Bosque Nuboso Santa Elena

A visitor trying the Sky Walk along the cloud forest canopy

offers a variety of ways in which to explore the cloud forest canopy. Thrillseekers can try the 2-hour SkyTrek. Securely harnessed, visitors slide between treetop platforms along ziplines that total a mile (1.6 km) in length. Two observatory towers offer panoramic views of the Guanacaste and Puntarenas lowlands. The more sedate Sky Walk is just as good for wildlife viewing, with 3,300 ft (1,000 m) of aerial pathways, including five suspension bridges hung between treetop platforms.

⚄ Selvatura Park

4 miles (6 km) NE of Santa Elena. **Tel** 2645-5929. ◯ 7am–5pm daily. 🎦 🖥 ♿ 🍴 📷 www.selvatura.com

Selvatura Park boasts 2 miles (3 km) of treetop walkways with eight suspension bridges

that meander through the cloud forest canopy. Visitors can also take part in a 14-platform zipline canopy tour, one of the longest in the whole of Costa Rica, for a monkey's-eye view of the upper elevation forest.

A highlight of Selvatura Park is the **Jewels of the Rainforest Bio-Art Exhibition**, which features a superb display of the world's largest private insect collection, put together by entomologist Dr. Richard Whitten. Beautifully laid out in a riot of colors, thousands of stick insects, butterflies, spiders, wasps, beetles, moths, and other insects are exhibited in educational panels arranged according to geographic regions and themes. Other exhibits in the Jewels collection include giant crustaceans and skulls of prehistoric creatures, such as the saber-toothed tiger. There are also human skulls, ranging from Australopithecus to Homo sapiens. Fascinating videos about insect life are shown in an auditorium. Visitors can also watch scientists at work in the Selvatura laboratory via a real-time video link.

Selvatura Park's other attractions include a hummingbird garden with more than 14 species of hummingbirds, a climbing wall, guided nature walks, and a domed, climate-controlled butterfly garden with over 20 species of butterflies, including the shimmering blue morphos.

The entrance to Reserva Bosque Nuboso Santa Elena

For hotels and restaurants in this region see pp256–60 and pp279–82

Cloud Forests of Costa Rica

Clear-wing butterfly

Named for the ephemeral mists that always envelop them, Costa Rica's cloud forests are typically found at elevations above 3,500 ft (1,050 m). More properly called montane tropical rainforests, they show extreme local variations in flora. On wind-swept, exposed ridges, trees and shrubs grow close to the ground as a form of protection, forming elfin forest with a primeval quality. More protected areas have taller vegetation typical of rainforests, with several levels *(see pp22–3)*. However, the lush canopies rarely reach 100 ft (30 m), although massive trees occasionally break through. Epiphytic plants such as orchids and bromeliads cling to branches, which also drip with lichen, fungi, mosses, and liverworts.

Pipers, *found in moist areas, can have large leaves up to 20 inches (50 cm) in size. Costa Rica has 94 species of pipers.*

Swirling mists are created by humid Caribbean trade winds that condense as they sweep up to the Continental Divide.

Mosses *breathe and draw water directly from the air through roots that hang from branches like an old man's beard.*

FLORA AND FAUNA

The constant interplay of sunshine, clouds, and rainfall in cloud forests produces flora of astounding diversity. Fauna is correspondingly abundant, although the mists and thick foliage hamper sightings.

Trees include guarumo, wild fig, and the huge zapote, with branches often weighed down by epiphytic plants.

Collared peccaries *forage in large groups and are highly social. They use their long canines to defend themselves.*

Prong-billed barbets *have a telltale yodel but are reclusive and rarely seen. At night they sleep huddled together.*

Howler monkeys *are arboreal leaf- and fruit-eaters. Males are known for their intimidating, booming roars.*

Tilarán ❷

Road Map B2. 14 miles (22 km) E of Cañas. 👥 *7,700.* 🚌 🎉 *Feria del Día Cívica (Apr–Jun).*

This neat little town, at an elevation of 1,800 ft (550 m) on the Continental Divide, has crisp air and a pretty plaza shaded by pines and cypress trees. It makes a delightful stop en route to and from Lake Arenal, although the only sight of note is the 1960s modern-looking, arch-roofed cathedral, decorated with marquetry. An agricultural town surrounded by undulating fields, Tilarán is known for its annual livestock show and rodeo.

Tower, Tilarán cathedral

Cañas ❸

Road Map B2. 48 miles (77 km) N of Puntarenas. 👥 *19,000.* 🚌 🎉 *Feria Domingo de Resurrección (Mar/Apr).*

This dusty cowboy town set dramatically in the lee of the Cordillera de Guanacaste is also known as Ciudad de la Amistad (City of Friendship). Surrounded by cattle haciendas in the searingly hot Tempisque basin, Cañas is most appealing for its *sabaneros* (cowboys). It sits astride the Pan-Am Highway, and serves as the gateway to Parque Nacional Palo Verde and Lake Arenal.

Environs

To the north, the **Centro de Rescate Las Pumas** (Puma Rescue Shelter) is a private facility for rescued wild cats. Some of the cats – which include jaguars, pumas, ocelots, margays, jaguarundis, and oncillas – are quite tame, having been raised by the late founder, Lilly Bodmer de Hagnauer. No guard rails prevent visitors from going up to the cages – caution is needed. Nearby, Río Corobicí is popular for rafting trips offered by **Safaris Corobicí**; small rapids add touches of excitement.

Bird-watching from canopied boats at Parque Nacional Palo Verde

Centro de Rescate Las Pumas
Pan-Am Hwy, 3 miles (5 km) N of Cañas. ***Tel*** *2669-6044.* 🕐 *8am–5pm daily.* 🎫 **http**://laspumas.org

Safaris Corobicí
Pan-Am Hwy, 3 miles (5 km) N of Cañas. ***Tel*** *2669-6091.*

Parque Nacional Palo Verde ❹

Road Map B2. 26 miles (42 km) W of Cañas. ***Tel*** *2200-0125.* 🚌 *to Puerto Humo, then boat to trailhead leading to park HQ; to Bagaces (14 miles/22 km N of Cañas), then by jeep-taxi.* 🕐 *8am–4pm daily.* 🎫 [K] 🍴 🛍 [A] **www**.acarenaltempisque.org

Palo Verde spreads over 50 sq miles (130 sq km), protecting a mosaic of habitats that includes mangrove swamps, marshes, savanna, and tropical dry forest at the mouth of Río Tempisque. Much of the vegetation consists of such drought-tolerant species as ironwood and sandbox, as well as evergreen *paloverde* (green stick) trees, which give the park its name.

Fauna is diverse and abundant. During the dry season (Dec–Apr), the trees burst into vibrant bloom. The ripening fruits draw monkeys, coatis, white-tailed deer, peccaries (wild hogs), pumas, and other mammals. In the wet season, much of the area floods and draws flocks of waterfowl to join herons, jabiru storks, ibis, roseate spoonbills and other stilt-legged waders. Palo Verde has more than 300 species of birds, including a large population of scarlet macaws and curassows. **Isla de Pájaros**, in the middle of Río Tempisque, is a major nesting site.

Wildlife viewing is best in the dry season, when the deciduous trees lose their leaves and animals collect near waterholes. Well-maintained trails lead to lookout points.

Several private wildlife refuges border the park to the west. **El Viejo Wildland Refuge & Wetlands** offers guided tours of Palo Verde's fringe forests and wetlands using amphibious all-terrain vehicles. The refuge includes a sugarcane estate and a traditional sugar-processing mill.

El Viejo Wildland Refuge & Wetlands
10 miles (17 km) SE of Filadelfia. ***Tel*** *2665-7759.* [K] *9am, 11am, 1:30pm, and 3:30pm daily.* 🎫 **www**.elviejowetlands.com

Reserva Biológica Lomas Barbudal ❺

Road Map A2. 4 miles (6 km) SW of Pan-Am Hwy, 12 miles (19 km) NW of Bagaces. ***Tel*** *2200-0125.* 🚌 *to Bagaces, then by jeep-taxi.* 🕐 *8am–4pm daily (subject to change).* 🎫 *by donation.* [A]

Famous for its plentiful insect population, not least the 250 species of bees, the

Rare dry forests of Reserva Biológica Lomas Barbudal

seldom-visited Reserva Biológica Lomas Barbudal (Bearded Hills Biological Reserve) protects rare tropical dry forest. Established in 1986, the hilly, densely forested terrain hosts a similar array of wildlife to Parque Nacional Palo Verde. The reserve also has plant species not usually found in dry forests – its waterways are lined with evergreens such as guapinol and fruit-bearing *níspero*.

Trails span the 9-sq-mile (23-sq-km) reserve from the Casa de Patrimonio visitor center on the banks of Río Cabuyo, which has pools that are good for swimming. The best time to visit is during February and March, when the park's trees bloom in spectacular profusion.

Fumaroles near Las Hornillas, Zona Protectora Volcán Miravalles

Zona Protectora Volcán Miravalles ➏

Road Map B2. 16 miles (26 km) N of Bagaces. 🚌 *from Bagaces.*

This active volcano rises 6,650 ft (2,030 m) above the Guanacaste plains. Few visitors hike the trails that lace the 42-sq-mile (109-sq-km) Miravalles Forest Reserve on the upper slopes. Tapirs are drawn to lakes near the summit, and there are several other species of fauna.

The main draw is **Las Hornillas** (Little Ovens), an area of steam vents and mud pools bubbling and hissing on the western slopes. The Institute of Electricity (ICE) produces power from the super-heated water vapor

at **Proyecto Geotérmico Miravalles**. The fumaroles and mud pools are best viewed at **Las Hornillas Volcanic Activity Center**, where a short trail leads into an active crater. You can even wallow in warm, therapeutic mud before diving into a swimming pool. There are also horseback rides and a thrilling thermal waterslide that plunges you into a pool with magnificent volcano views.

> 🔥 **Proyecto Geotérmico Miravalles**
> 17 miles (27 km) NE of Bagaces. *Tel* 2673-1111, ext 232. 🕒 *by appt.* 🅿
>
> 🔥 **Las Hornillas Volcanic Activity Center**
> 1 mile (1.6 km) SE of Proyecto Geotérmico Miravalles. *Tel* 8839-9769. 🕒 *8am–5pm daily.* 🅿 📷
> 🍴 www.hornillas.com

Liberia ➐

Road Map A2. 16 miles (26 km) N of Bagaces. 🏘 *42,000.* 🚌 🚕
📅 *Día de la Anexión de Guanacaste (Jul 25).*

Guanacaste's charming, historic capital, founded in 1769, is known as the White City for its whitewashed adobe houses with terracotta tile roofs. The loveliest houses are on Calle Real (Calle Central). The city is also known for its *puertas del sol* – double doors, one on each side of a corner, to catch both morning and afternoon sun. Liberia's cowboy tradition is celebrated at the **Monumento Sabanero**, on the main boulevard, and at **Hacienda**

Interior of a colonial-era house on Calle Real, Liberia

Liberia's Monumento Sabanero

La Chácara, a ranch that hosts various horse-related activities. The main plaza has the modern **Iglesia Inmaculada Concepción de María**. Next door, the *ayuntamiento* (town hall) flies Guanacaste's flag, the only provincial flag in the country. Each July, locals celebrate Guanacaste's separation from Nicaragua in 1824. The Iglesia de la Ermita de la Resurección, familiarly known as **Iglesia de la Agonía**, is an engaging 1825 adobe colonial church, which features a small museum of religious art. Liberia is the main gateway to Parque Nacional Rincón de la Vieja *(see p182)* and the beaches of Northern Nicoya.

> 🐎 **Hacienda La Chácara**
> 1.5 miles (2.5 km) W of Liberia. *Tel* 8350-1527. www.haciendalachacara.com
>
> ⛪ **Iglesia de la Agonía**
> Calle 9 and Ave Central. *Tel* 2666-0107. 🕒 *2:30–3:30pm daily.*

COWBOY CULTURE

A majority of Guanacastecos make their living as *sabaneros* (cowboys), also called *bramaderos* after the hardy Brahma cattle. Proud, folkloric figures, the *sabaneros* ride straight-backed in their elaborately decorated saddles, leading their horses in a high-stepping gait. The most important days of the year in Guanacasteco culture revolve around *topes* (horse shows) and *recorridos de toros* (bullfights). Bulls are ridden and baited, but never killed.

Sabanero on a working ranch

The impressive Volcán Rincón de la Vieja

Parque Nacional Rincón de la Vieja ❽

Road Map B1. 19 miles (30 km) NE of Liberia. **Tel** 2200-0296. 🚐 *to Liberia, then by jeep-taxi.* 🕒 *7am–5pm daily; last admission: 3pm.* 🗺 🚻 ⚠ **www**.acguanacaste.ac.cr

The dramatically beautiful Rincón de la Vieja volcano is studded with nine craters, of which only Rincón de la Vieja crater (5,900 ft/1,800 m) is active. The highest is Santa María (6,250 ft/1,900 m), while Von Seebach crater is filled with an acidic turquoise lake.

The park protects an area of 55 sq miles (140 sq km). The eastern slopes of the volcano are rain-soaked all year round; the western side has a distinct dry season, and ranges from deciduous forest at lower elevations to cloud forest below the stark moonscape summit.

Visitors can spot capuchin, howler, and spider monkeys, anteaters, sloths, kinkajous, and more than 300 species of birds, including quetzals and three-wattled bellbirds. Pea-green **Lago Los Jilgueros** is visited by tapirs.

The park offers superb hiking. Trails start at the park headquarters, the 19th-century **Hacienda Santa María**, and at **Las Pailas** ranger station. They lead past mud pools, hot sulfur springs, waterfalls, and fumaroles. The challenging 11-mile (18-km) summit trail requires a pre-dawn departure. The summit offers fabulous views as far as Lake Nicaragua.

Hikers must report to the ranger stations when setting out and returning. Both

ranger stations can be reached from Liberia by jeep-taxis, and they are linked by a trail. The dry season from December to April is the best time to visit.

Environs

Several nature lodges on the western slopes of the volcano also operate as activity centers. On its southwestern flanks, **Hacienda Lodge Guachipelín** *(see p259)*, accessed from Liberia via Curubandé, is a working cattle ranch, specializing in horseback rides. Nearby, **Rincón de la Vieja Lodge** *(see p259)* has a 900-acre (364-ha) private forest reserve. Both lodges offer canopy tours. From Liberia, a road leads via Cañas Dulces to **Buena Vista Mountain Lodge & Adventure Center** *(see p259)* on the northwestern slopes. It offers horseback rides, a canopy tour, and a 1,300-ft (400-m) long water slide. **Hotel Borinquen**

Careta la Cangreja waterfall in the Parque Rincón de la Vieja

Mountain Resort Thermae & Spa nearby has bubbling mud pools and spa treatments.

> 🏨 **Hotel Borinquen Mountain Resort Thermae & Spa**
> 19 miles (30 km) NE of Liberia via Cañas Dulces. **Tel** 2690-1900. 🗺 🚻 🚭 **www**.borinquenresort.com

Parque Nacional Guanacaste ❾

Road Map A1. 22 miles (35 km) N of Liberia. **Tel** 2666-5051. 🚐 *to Liberia, then by jeep-taxi.* 🕒 *8am–5pm daily with advance notice.* 🗺 🚭 *by reservation.* ⚠ **www**.acguanacaste.ac.cr

This remote national park encompasses more than 325 sq miles (840 sq km) of reforested woodland and pasture extending to the top of Volcán Cacao (5,400 ft/1,650 m) and Volcán Orosi (4,900 ft/1,500 m). Facilities are few, but the rewards are immense, with a variety of habitats and superb wildlife viewing. Biological stations **Cacao**, **Pitilla**, and **Maritza** have spartan accommodations; Cacao and Maritza can be accessed only on foot or horseback.

Pre-Columbian petroglyphs can be seen at **Llano de los Indios**, on the lower western flanks of Volcán Orosi.

Bahía Salinas ❿

Road Map A1. 38 miles (62 km) NW of Liberia. 🚐 *to La Cruz, then by jeep-taxi.*

Framed by cliffs to the north, salt pans to the east, and mangrove-fringed beaches to the south, this flask-shaped bay is swept by breezes from December to April. Fishing hamlets line its shores. Hotels at La Coyotera and Playa Copal serve as surfing centers. The Costa Rican Tourism Board visitor center in La Cruz has great views.

Frigate birds use the drafts around **Refugio Nacional de Vida Silvestre Isla Bolaños** to take off. A protected nesting site for pelicans and American oystercatchers, this island is off limits to visitors.

Costa Rica's Dry Forests

Dry deciduous forests once swathed the lowlands of the Pacific littoral from Mexico to Panama, covering most of today's Guanacaste and Nicoya. After the arrival of Columbus, the Spanish cleared vast areas of these forests to raise cattle, which still dominate the economy of the Pacific northwest. Today, only about 2 percent of the original cover remains, notably in the Tempisque basin, and Santa Rosa, Rincón de la Vieja, and Guanacaste National Parks. Recent conservation efforts, spearheaded by the US biologist Dr. Daniel Janzen, are returning large areas of savanna and ranchland to their original state. The intent is to link the existing patchwork and regenerate dry forest ecosystems.

The orange bloom of the *poró*

The understory consists of short trees; above are stout-trunked, flat-crowned trees.

Grass and thorn scrub dominate at ground level.

Trees typically grow no higher than 40 ft (12 m) and are widely spaced.

The forest is relatively sparsely vegetated, with fewer species of flora

The dry season *sees the forest exploding in an outburst of color. Pink poui blooms first, followed by bright orange poró, rose-colored Tabebuia rosea, vermilion malinche, and purple jacaranda.*

Parque Nacional Santa Rosa (see pp184–5) *protects the most important remnant of dry tropical forest in all Central America.*

Guanacaste trees *spread their wide-reaching branches close to the ground, providing precious shade in the searing midday heat. Such dry forest species have evolved to withstand the long seasonal drought by shedding their leaves.*

Indio desnudo, *or naked Indian, is named for its distinct copper-red bark, which readily peels to reveal an olive-colored trunk. Naked Indian is also called the gumbo-limbo.*

White-tailed deer *blend in well with the dun-colored grasses and dry forest. The best times to see them are dawn and dusk, when they emerge to search for food.*

Thorny scrub, *such as acacia, have long spikes to prevent birds and animals from eating their leaves and seeds.*

Parque Nacional Santa Rosa ⑪

The country's first national park, inaugurated in 1971, Santa Rosa National Park covers 190 sq miles (492 sq km) of the Santa Elena Peninsula and adjoining land. It is divided into two sectors. To the north is the little-visited Murciélago Sector, with hidden beaches – notably Playa Blanca – accessed along a rugged dirt track. To the south, the much larger Santa Rosa Sector was the site of battles in 1856 and 1955, and boasts most of the sights of interest. The park protects the nation's largest stretch of tropical dry forest, as well as nine other distinct habitats. With 115 mammal species, including 20 types of bats, and 250 species of birds, the park is a superb wildlife-viewing area, especially in the dry season, when the deciduous trees shed their leaves.

Islas Murciélagos
The waters around these islands offer splendid scuba diving (see p300). Manta rays, grouper, and other large species are common.

Playa Nancite
This is one of three sites in Costa Rica where olive ridley turtles nest en masse in synchronized arribadas (see p191), *especially in September–October. Protected as a research site, it is off-limits to visitors except by permit.*

Playa Tule

Estacion Biológia Nancite

Playa Nancite

Estero Real

Bahía Naranjo

Peña Bruja

Playa Naranjo

Río Calera

Río Nispera

SAN

PACIFIC OCEAN

Crocodiles
The mangroves at the northern and southern ends of Playa Naranjo harbor crocodiles.

Witch's Rock, off Playa Naranjo, is renowned among surfers for the powerful, tubular waves that rise here and pump ashore.

Playa Naranjo
A gorgeous white-sand surfing beach, Playa Naranjo has campsites with basic facilities. It is reached by an arduous dirt road that often gets washed out in wet season – check with rangers before setting out for the beach.

KEY

Murciélago Sector

Santa Rosa Sector

VISITORS' CHECKLIST

Road Map A1. 22 miles (35 km) N of Liberia. **Tel** 2666-5051. Santa Rosa Sector: from Liberia; Murciélago Sector: from Santa Rosa park entrance, via Cuajiniquil. tours to Playa Naranjo from Playa Tamarindo and Playas del Coco. 8am–4pm daily for vehicles; 24 hrs for hikers. by reservation. by reservation. www.acguanacaste.ac.cr

Tanquetas (armored vehicles) lie half-buried in the undergrowth as rusting relics of an ill-fated attack launched by Nicaraguan dictator Anastasio Somoza against Costa Rica in 1955.

Sendero Indio Desnudo
Named for indio desnudo *(naked Indian) or gumbo-limbo trees, this short trail features a monument to the Costa Ricans who fought in the battles of 1856 and 1955.*

Centro de Investigaciones is the main center for tropical dry forest research in Costa Rica.

Sendero Los Patos leads to waterholes, which provide excellent opportunities for viewing peccaries and other mammals in the dry season.

La Casona
Also called Hacienda Santa Rosa, this important monument is a replica built in 2001 after the 1663 original was destroyed by arsonists. The battle of 1856 against William Walker (see p43) was fought outside the hacienda, which now functions as a historical museum.

0 km 2

0 miles 2

KEY

Pan-Am Highway

Other road

Trail

Park boundary

Visitor information

Camping

Viewpoint

THE CONTRA CONNECTION

Col. Oliver North

During the 1980s, the remote Murciélago Sector was utilized as a secret training ground for the CIA-backed Nicaraguan Contras in their battle to topple the Sandinista government *(see p44)*. An airstrip was illegally established here under the orders of Colonel Oliver North, a key player in the Iran-Contra scandal that shook the US in 1983–8. The road to the park entrance runs alongside the airstrip, which occupies land confiscated from Nicaraguan strongman Anastasio Somoza.

Visitors soaking up the sun on the wide gray-sand beaches of Tamarindo

Bahía Culebra ⑫

Road Map A2. 12 miles (19 km)
W of Liberia.

Ringed by dramatic cliffs and fringed by beaches of varying hues, Bahía Culebra (Snake Bay) is the setting for Proyecto Papagayo, a controversial tourism project that has restricted access to the bay's sparkling waters. Spilling down the cliffs are big hotels, including the **Four Seasons Resort at Papagayo Peninsula** *(see p256)*. Pre-Columbian settlements on the bay await excavation. **Witch's Rock Canopy Tour** has ziplines and a walkway through the dry forest canopy.

> 🚡 **Witch's Rock Canopy Tour**
> 23 miles (37 km) W of Liberia. **Tel** 2666-7101. ◯ 8am–5pm daily. 📷
> **http**://witchsrockcanopytour.com

Playas del Coco ⑬

Road Map A2. 22 miles (35 km)
SW of Liberia. 👥 2,000. 🚌
📷 *Fiesta Civica (Jan); Festival de la Virgen del Mar (mid-Jul).*

This wide beach combines the allure of a traditional fishing community with a no-frills resort. Although the pelican-patrolled beach is not particularly attractive, it is a favorite with Costa Rican families, and has a lively nightlife. Local outfitters offer sportfishing and scuba tours to Islas Murciélagos *(see p184)* and Isla Catalina, where schools of rays can be seen.

Environs
Secluded Playa Ocotal, west of Playas del Coco, has the region's best dive site. It is

also a premier sportfishing destination. Playas Hermosa and Panamá, north of Coco, have exquisite settings, with Isla Catalina silhouetted dramatically at sunset.

Playa Flamingo ⑭

Road Map A2. 38 miles (62 km) SW of Liberia. 👥 2,000. 🚌

With gently curving white sands cusped by rugged headlands, the gorgeous Playa Flamingo justifies its official yet less common name, Playa Blanca (White Beach). The large marina is a sportfishing base, but it is temporarily closed. Deluxe villas dot the rocky headlands. Most of the hotels are upscale timeshare resorts and, despite its fine beach, Flamingo is shunned by the offbeat and party crowd.

Surfers heading for the water

Environs
North of Playa Flamingo, the estuary of Río Salinas opens out at modestly appealing Playa Penca, where roseate spoonbills, egrets, and a rich variety of other birdlife can be spotted in the mangroves.

Southwest of Flamingo is **Playa Conchal** (Shell Beach), with its shining sands; the diamond-like sparkle of the sands is caused by crushed seashells. The beach slopes gently into turquoise waters, which are ideal for snorkeling and other water sports. For a fee, visitors can access **Westin Playa Conchal Beach & Spa** *(see p258)*, which boasts a championship golf course.

Tamarindo ⑮

Road Map A2. 11 miles (18 km)
S of Flamingo. 👥 5,000. ✈ 🚌
📷 *International Festival of Music (Jul–Aug).*

Formerly a sleepy fishing village, Tamarindo has rapidly developed into the region's premier resort. This hip surfers' haven is also a center for sportfishing, diving, and snorkeling. Tamarindo is popular with backpackers, but also boasts a cosmopolitan selection of restaurants and boutique hotels.

The area lies within **Parque Nacional Marino Las Baulas** (Leatherback Turtle Marine National Park), inaugurated in 1990. It protects 85 sq miles (220 sq km) of ocean and 1,100 acres (445 ha) of beach – **Playa Grande** – a prime nesting site of leatherback turtles. Between October and April, as many as 100 leatherbacks can be seen on the beach. Pacific ridley, green, and hawksbill turtles occasionally nest here. During the nesting season, nobody is permitted on the beach after sundown, except guided groups by reservation.

The park also incorporates Playa Langosta, south of Tamarindo, and 990 acres (400 ha) of mangroves, which can be explored on boats.

> 🚩 **Parque Nacional Marino Las Baulas**
> **Tel** 2653-0470.
> ◯ 6am–6pm daily. 📷
> 📷 compulsory on the beach; Oct–Feb: 6pm–6am daily.

Surfing Beaches of Northern Nicoya

Acclaimed as the "Hawaii of Latin America," Costa Rica offers world-class surfing and warm waters year-round. The greatest concentration of surfing beaches is in Northern Nicoya, where Pacific breakers pump ashore all year. Conditions are ideal between December and March, when the Papagayo winds kick up high waves. Dozens of beaches guarantee that surfers will find a fairly challenging ride on any day, while extremely varied tidal conditions provide breaks for every level of experience. Be warned, however: riptides are common and many surfers lose their lives every year; few beaches have lifeguards. Numerous villages and resorts have become surfers' havens and are heavily reliant on the waveboard trade, with scores of surf camps and surf shops.

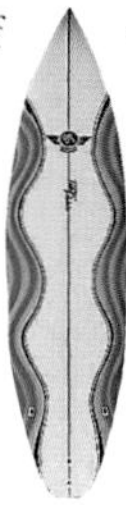

Surfing board

Playa Naranjo ①
This remote beach in the Golfo de Papagayo boasts a superb beach break, called Witch's Rock. Naranjo is accessed by 4WD or by boat from the resorts of Northern Nicoya.

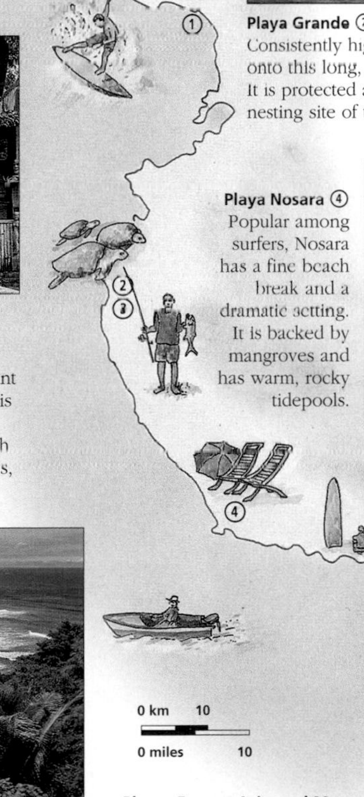

Playa Grande ②
Consistently high waves pump ashore onto this long, easily accessible beach. It is protected as part of a prime nesting site of the leatherback turtle.

Tamarindo ③
The surf capital of Northern Nicoya, Tamarindo offers a rivermouth break, rocky point break, and beach breaks. It is also the gateway to nearby isolated surfing beaches such as Playas Langosta, Avellanas, and Negra.

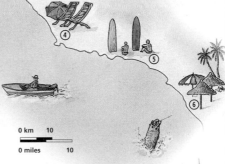

Playa Nosara ④
Popular among surfers, Nosara has a fine beach break and a dramatic setting. It is backed by mangroves and has warm, rocky tidepools.

Playas Bejuco and San Miguel ⑤
Long slivers of silvery sand are washed by good surf. These remote beaches are oriented to budget travelers.

Playas Bongo, Arío, and Manzanillo ⑥
All three are as off-the-beaten-track as possible in Costa Rica. Just getting there is half the fun. Cracking waves, combined with the solitude, guarantee surfer bliss. Facilities are virtually nonexistent.

Refugio Nacional de Vida Silvestre Ostional ⑯

Road Map A3. 34 miles (55 km) S of Tamarindo. *Tel 2682-0470.* 🚌 *from Santa Cruz and Nicoya via Nosara.* ◯ *24 hrs daily.* 📷 *compulsory for the beach.*

The setting for one of the most remarkable occurrences in nature, Ostional National Wildlife Refuge protects 4 sq miles (10 sq km) of land and sea around Playa Ostional. The beach is one of only a dozen worldwide where Pacific ridley turtles nest in synchronized *arribadas*. The best time to view them is during August and September. Green and leatherback turtles also nest here in smaller numbers. Ostional is the only place in Costa Rica where residents are legally allowed, under strict guidelines, to harvest eggs during the first 36 hours of an *arribada*.

Ostional is accessed by dirt roads that require 4WD during the wet season. The remote setting and the surrounding forests have shielded the area from development, though now there are a few hotels. Personal contact with turtles is forbidden, as are flashlights and flash photography.

Vultures, Nosara

Nosara ⑰

Road Map A3. 3 miles (5 km) S of Ostional. 🏠 *3,000.* ✈ 🚌

This isolated community on the Nicoya coast comprises twin villages. **Bocas de Nosara**, 3 miles (5 km) inland, on the banks of Río Nosara, is a peasant hamlet where ox-carts still creak along dusty lanes. **Beaches of Nosara**, to the south, is a predominantly foreign settlement, with contemporary homes amid forests near the shore. The maze of roads comprising Beaches of Nosara backs onto the stunning **Playa Guiones**, a long, calm stretch of white sand and sun-warmed

A participant in a surfing competition at Playa Guiones, Nosara

tidepools in which monkeys can sometimes be seen enjoying a good soak. Strong tides rule out swimming, but the breakers are perfect for surfing. To the north, small **Playa Pelada** is encircled by steep cliffs. Nearby, **Reserva Biológica Nosara** protects 125 acres (50 ha) of tropical forest along the Río Nosara estuary. Over 250 bird species nest here, including wood storks, white-fronted parrots, and frigate birds. Crocodiles can be seen in the estuary.

> 🦋 **Reserva Biológica Nosara**
> Bocas de Nosara. *Tel 2682-0035.*
> 📷 📷 *by appointment.* 🍴 🖥 📷
> 🖫 www.lagarta.com

Sámara ⑱

Road Map A3. 16 miles (26 km) S of Nosara. 🏠 *2,700.* ✈ *at Carrillo.* 🚌

Popular with backpackers, surfers, and middle-class Costa Ricans, Sámara is the most southerly of the beach resorts developed for tourism. At the southern end of Playa Sámara, at Matapalo, villagers eke out a living from the sea. There are few other sights of interest, and life revolves around lazing on the gray sands, or going surfing and riding. **Playa Carrillo**, 2 miles (3 km) south of Sámara, is a sportfishing center, while to

Beach sign, Sámara

the north, the **Flying Crocodile Lodge and Flying Center** offers flights by ultralight plane.

> **Flying Crocodile Lodge and Flying Center**
> Esterones, 3 miles (5 km) N of Sámara. *Tel 2656-8048.*
> ◯ *7am–3pm daily.* 📷 🍴 📷 🖫
> www.flying-crocodile.com

Islita ⑲

Road Map B3. 9 miles (14 km) S of Sámara. 🏠 *1,000.* ✈ 🚌 *to Sámara, then by jeep-taxi.*

Set in the lee of the soaring Punta Islita, this charming village is known for the **Hotel Punta Islita** *(see p257)*, a hilltop resort that houses the **Galería de Arte Contemporáneo Mary Anne Zürcher**. Artworks in varied media by established and local artists are available here. The hotel also fosters the **Museo de Arte Contemporáneo al Aire Libre** (Open Air Museum of Contemporary Art), spread around the village – houses, individual trees, and even the soccer field have been decorated by residents and hotel staff with murals and other spontaneous aesthetic expressions. Several rivers have to be forded along the rough dirt road linking Islita to Sámara. During the wet season, long detours via San Pedro to the east are often necessary, which is why many people choose to fly here.

Arribadas of Olive Ridley Turtles

The synchronized mass nestings called *arribadas* (arrivals), which are unique to the ridley turtle, are known to occur regularly at only a dozen or so beaches worldwide. Of these, three are in Costa Rica – Playa Nancite, Playa Ostional, and Playa Camaronal. *Arribadas* take place between April and December, peaking in August and September. Lasting between three and eight days, they happen at two- to four-week intervals, usually during the last quarter of the moon's cycle. On any one night, as many as 20,000 turtles congregate just beyond the breakers. Then, wave after wave of turtles storm ashore, even climbing over one another in a single-minded effort to find a nesting spot on the crowded sands. Millions of eggs are laid during each *arribada*, believed to be an evolutionary adaptation to ensure survival in the face of heavy predation.

Mosaic turtle

Ridley turtles *come ashore in groups numbering up to 100,000 turtles during a single* arribada. *Ridleys nest every year, sometimes as often as three times a season.*

Hatchlings *emerge together at night for the dangerous run to the sea and the safety it offers. Only about 1 percent survive to adulthood.*

Flippers scatter sand on the nest to disguise it.

Females lay an average of 100 eggs each during an *arribada*.

THE NESTING PROCESS

Turtles seek sandy sites above the high-water mark in which to nest. Incubation typically takes around 50 days. The temperature of the nest affects the gender of the hatchling – cooler nests produce males, while warmer ones produce females.

Nests are scooped out to a depth of about 3 ft (1 m) using rear flippers.

Scientists *tag ridley turtles during an* arribada *at Santa Rosa's Playa Nancite in an effort to track and study them.*

Coatis, *as well as raccoons and vultures, dig up turtle nests to feast on the eggs; less than 10 percent of turtle eggs hatch.*

Commercial harvesting *of eggs is legally done only by villagers of Ostional.*

Nicoya ⑳

Road Map A3. 44 miles (71 km) SW of Liberia. 🏘 *21,000.* 🚌 🎫 *Fiesta de la Yegüita (Dec 12).*

Emanating sleepy colonial charm, Nicoya dates back to the mid-1600s, and is named after the Chorotega *cacique* (chief) who greeted the Spanish conquistador Gil González Davila in 1523. An advanced Chorotega settlement existed here in pre-Columbian times. Today, the town serves as the administrative center for the Nicoya Peninsula and bustles with the comings and goings of *campesinos* (peasants) and cowboys. Nicoya is also the gateway for Sámara and the Pacific beaches of the south-central Nicoya Peninsula.

Life centers around the old plaza, **Parque Central**. Built in 1644, the intimate, wood-beamed **Iglesia Parroquia San Blas**, located in the northeast corner of the plaza, has a simple façade inset with bells. Inside, a small museum has a display of historical artifacts and religious memorabilia.

The simple exterior of the Iglesia Parroquia San Blas in Nicoya

Environs

Nature lovers can head about 17 miles (27 km) northeast to **Puerto Humo**, a riverside port town from where boats depart for Parque Nacional Palo Verde *(see p180).* Buses operate from Nicoya. Nearby, **Tempisque Safari Ecological Adventure** is a rescue and breeding center for animals such as tapirs, crocodiles, and wild cats.

🐾 Tempisque Safari Ecological Adventure
4 miles (6 km) NW of Puerto Humo. **Tel** 2698-1069. ◯ 10am–5pm daily. 🌐 🚗 🍴
www.tempisquesafaricr.com

Santa Cruz ㉑

Road Map A2. 14 miles (22 km) N of Nicoya. 🏘 *17,500.* 🚌 🎫 *Fiesta Patronal de Santo Cristo (mid-Jan); Fiesta de Santiago (Jul 25).*

Steeped in local tradition, Santa Cruz is Costa Rica's official La Ciudad Folklórica (National Folkloric City). Connected by Highway 160 to Tamarindo and the beaches of the north-central Nicoya Peninsula, this center

Ruined bell tower, Plaza Bernabela Ramos, Santa Cruz

was founded in 1760. Many of the wooden colonial edifices that once graced its historic core were destroyed in a fire, but the overall ambience is still charming. **Plaza de los Mangos** serves as a focal point for the city's festivals, which draw visitors from miles around to enjoy traditional *marimba* music and dance. *Topes* (horse shows) and *recorridos de toros* (bull-fights) also take place here.

The architectural highlight of Santa Cruz is the landscaped **Plaza Bernabela Ramos**. On its east side is a modern church with fine stained-glass windows. Next to it is the ruined bell tower of a Colonial-style church, which was destroyed by an earthquake in 1950. The plaza is a pleasant spot to relax and admire the statues, including that of Chorotega *cacique* Diría in the southwest corner, and a *montador* (bull-rider) on a bucking bull in the northeast.

Statue of a bull-rider, Plaza Bernabela Ramos, Santa Cruz

FIESTA DE LA YEGÜITA

The Virgin of Guadalupe by Miguel Cabrera

Also known as the Festival of the Virgin of Guadalupe, this fiesta blends Chorotega and Catholic traditions. According to legend, twin brothers were battling to death for the love of an Indian princess when a *yegüita* (little mare) intervened to stop the fight. The festival takes place every December and features traditional Costa Rican food, bullfights, rodeos, street processions, fireworks, music and dance, and ancient Indian rituals.

Guaitíl ❷

Road Map A2. 7 miles (11 km) E of
Santa Cruz. 🏠 *1,500.* 🚌

This small village offers the
most authentic display of
traditional culture *(see pp30–
31)* in Costa Rica, with virtually the entire community
deriving its income by making
ceramics in pre-Columbian
style. Guaitíl sits on the cusp
between cultures – even the
contemporary pieces draw
inspiration from traditional
Chorotega designs.

Headed by the matriarch of
the family, most households
have a traditional wood-fired,
dome-shaped *horno* (oven) for
firing pots and other ceramic
objects. Visitors are welcome
in the yards to watch artisans
work the red clay dug from
nearby riverbanks. The dusty
lanes are lined with thatched
stores and open-air shacks
where the pottery is displayed.

A regeneration of Chorotega
culture is now spilling over into
the nearby villages as well. In
San Vicente, the tiny **Ecomuseo
de la Cerámica Chorotega**
offers a historical and cultural
profile on the ceramic tradition.

🏛 **Ecomuseo de la Cerámica
Chorotega**
1 mile (1.6 km) E of Guaitíl. *Tel
2681-1563.* ☐ *8am–4pm Mon–Fri.*
🖥 www.ecomuseosanvicente.org

Parque Nacional
Barra Honda ❸

Road Map B3. 11 miles (18 km) E of
Nicoya. *Tel 2659-1551.* 🚌 *Nicoya–
Santa Ana village (0.5 mile/1 km from
park entrance), then by jeep-taxi.*
☐ *8am–4pm daily; last admission:
noon; caving: 7:30am–1pm daily
(Dec–Apr: to 2pm).* 🎥 📷 🍴 🛍 🅰

One of the best spots for
caving, this national park
was established in 1974, and
spreads over 9 sq miles (23 sq
km). A tropical dry forest area,
Barra Honda was used for
raising cattle, but is now in the
process of being reforested.

The park has excellent
hiking. Trails lead to lookout
points atop Cerro Barra Honda
(1450 ft/442 m), a massif lifted

CHOROTEGA POTTERY

Guaitíl artisans use the same simple tools as their ancestors
did to craft pottery in the age-old manner, perpetuating their
native traditions. The decorative bowls, pots, and
clay figures are polished with *zukias* (ancient
grinding stones), and blessed by shamans,
after which totemic animal motifs in black,
red, and white are painted on ocher backgrounds. The quintessential Guaitíl piece is
a three-legged vase in the form of a cow.
Although most pieces are traditional, some
artisans work in a creative synthesis that blurs
the line between the old and the new.

**Clay figure
from Guaitíl**

---

up by powerful tectonic forces.
Cerro Barra Honda is riddled
with limestone caverns formed
by the action of water over
millions of years. Of the 40
caves discovered so far, 20
have been explored. **Santa
Ana**, the largest cave, soars
to a height of 790 ft (240 m).
Inside **Cueva Terciopelo**, a
dripstone formation called El
Órgano (The Organ) produces
musical tones when struck.
El Pozo Hediondo (Stinking
Well) is named for the droppings of the bats roosting
here. Some caves have blind
salamanders and blind fish,
and most boast dramatic
stalactites and stalagmites.
Indigenous artifacts have
been found in some caves.

Cave descents into Cueva
Terciopelo are permitted; a
licensed guide is compulsory.
Guides are also compulsory
for the Las Cascadas trail,
which leads to waterfalls.
Spelunkers enter Terciopelo
via a 100-ft (30-m) ladder.
Access to the other caves
requires prior permission.
Spelunking equipment and

**Puente de Amistad con Taiwan
across Río Tempisque on Hwy 18**

guides can be hired. Hikers
must report to the ranger
station. A 4WD is needed
to reach the park entrance.
Jeep-taxis run from Nicoya.

Environs
The **Puente de Amistad
con Taiwan** (Friendship with
Taiwan Bridge) is a dramatic
suspension bridge over Río
Tempisque. It links Nicoya
to the Pan-Am Highway.

A spelunker at Cueva Terciopelo, Parque Nacional Barra Honda

THE NORTHERN ZONE

he northern provinces are Costa Rica's flatlands – a gentle landscape quilted in pastures, fruit plantations, and humid rainforest. This wide-open canvas is framed by a dramatic escarpment of mountains. The extreme north of this perennially wet region is a world of seasonally flooded lagoons and migratory water-fowl, while the mountains in the south are cloaked in dense forests, which are protected in a series of national parks and wildlife reserves.

The rolling *llanuras* (plains) form a triangle, narrow to the west and broadening eastward, which extends north from the base of the *cordilleras* (mountain ranges) to Río San Juan, on the Nicaraguan border. The scenery is nowhere more splendid than around Lake Arenal, located on a depression between the Guanacaste and Tilarán Mountains. Volcán Arenal looms ethereally over the waters. Its near-constant eruptions and other local attractions have given a boost to the nearby town of La Fortuna, now a base for various adventure activities.

At the time of the Spanish arrival, the Corobicí peoples occupied the lower flanks of the mountains and were at war with their Nicaraguan neighbors. During the colonial era, settlements were restricted to the main river courses, and were subject to constant plundering by pirates.

The region remained aloof from the rest of the country until the early 19th century, when a trade route was laid linking highland towns to a wharfside settlement – today's Puerto Viejo – which gave access to the Caribbean. Founded around that time, Ciudad Quesada grew to become the region's administrative center. The settlement campaign initiated in the 1950s led to the decimation of huge tracts of forest to make room for cattle farms as well as banana and citrus plantations. More settlements have since sprung up throughout the region.

Cloud-wreathed Volcán Arenal, the country's most active volcano

◁ Crossing one of the Arenal Hanging Bridges

Exploring the Northern Zone

The main gateway to the northern lowlands is Ciudad Quesada, a dairy town on the mountain flanks that fringe the region's southern border. La Fortuna, to the west, is a center for outdoor activities, from caving to horseback riding. The region's major attraction is Volcán Arenal, great for hiking and for soaking in the thermal waters of Tabacón. Nearby Lake Arenal offers fine fishing and world-class windsurfing. To the east of Ciudad Quesada are several private reserves – one of which includes the Rainforest Aerial Tram. Boats depart the nondescript town of Puerto Viejo de Sarapiquí for nature cruises along Río Sarapiquí. Caño Negro Wildlife Refuge, in the far north, is a superb birding and angling destination.

Stone figurine, Centro Neotrópico SarapiquíS

SIGHTS AT A GLANCE

Towns and Cities

Ciudad Quesada (San Carlos) 🔟
La Fortuna 1️⃣
Puerto Viejo de Sarapiquí 1️⃣2️⃣

National Parks and Reserves

Parque Nacional Volcán Arenal 3️⃣
Parque Nacional Volcán Tenorio 9️⃣
Refugio Nacional de Vida Silvestre Caño Negro 8️⃣
Refugio Nacional de Vida Silvestre Corredor Fronterizo 1️⃣4️⃣

Areas of Natural Beauty

Arenal Hanging Bridges 5️⃣
Arenal Rainforest Reserve and Aerial Tram 6️⃣
Cavernas de Venado 7️⃣
Heliconia Island 1️⃣6️⃣
La Selva Biological Station 1️⃣5️⃣
Laguna de Arenal pp200–2 4️⃣
Rainforest Aerial Tram 1️⃣8️⃣
Rara Avis 1️⃣7️⃣
Selva Verde 1️⃣3️⃣
Tabacón Hot Springs Resort and Spa 2️⃣

Indigenous Site

Centro Neotrópico SarapiquíS 1️⃣1️⃣

A cowboy at Selva Verde

cán Arenal shrouded in mist

SEE ALSO

- *Where to Stay* pp260–62
- *Where to Eat* pp282–3

The hot springs at Tabacón, near Volcán Arenal

REFUGIO NACIONAL DE VIDA SILVESTRE CORREDOR FRONTERIZO ⑭

Concho

Boca San Carlos

Coopevega

Rio San Juan

Laguna Canacas

Trinidad

Rio San Carlos Boca Tapada

San Marcos

Pangola

Las Medias

uenos Aires

H E R E D I A

PUERTO VIEJO DE SARAPIQUÍ

SELVA VERDE

Pital

La Virgen de Sarapiquí

SARAPIQUÍ HELICONIA ISLAND

LA SELVA BIOLOGICAL STATION

Las Horquetas

CIUDAD QUESADA (SAN CARLOS) ⑩

CENTRO NEOTRÓPICO SARAPIQUÍS

⑰ RARA AVIS

Alajuela

Guápiles

RAINFOREST AERIAL TRAM ⑱

Y

| Major road |
| Secondary road |
| Minor road |
| Track |
| International border |
| Provincial border |
| Peak |

GETTING AROUND

The towns of Upala and Los Chiles are access points for the Caño Negro Wildlife Refuge, which is reached by rough roads. Sansa and Nature Air offer flights to La Fortuna, which is linked by tourist buses with San José and key resorts beyond the region. Organized tours can be booked through tour operators and hotels. However, the best way of getting around is to rent a car. A 4WD is essential to reach Caño Negro and other sights away from the main roads. Many roads are prone to landslides, especially along the north shore of Lake Arenal and those that link La Fortuna and Upala.

La Fortuna ❶

Road Map C2. 81 miles (131 km)
NW of San José. 🏠 9,750. 🚌

Volcán Arenal towers over this agricultural community and tourist hub, officially known as La Fortuna de San Carlos. Situated on a gentle slope, the picturesque town is laid out on a grid around a broad, landscaped plaza, which has a sculpture of an erupting volcano. A modern church stands on the plaza, its tall bell tower contrasting with Arenal behind. Numerous restaurants and hotels cater to the tourists who come here in search of adventure. Several agencies offer horseback rides, caving, fishing, biking, and rafting. A popular horseback trip is to Monteverde (see pp174–8), but the ride is very demanding on the horses, so ensure you choose a well-kept animal.

Horseback riding in La Fortuna

Environs
The **Ecocentro Danaus Butterfly Farm and Tropical Garden** provides an educational introduction to the local fauna. It has a netted butterfly garden, a snake zoo, a frog garden, and a small lagoon stocked with waterfowl and caimans. **Arenal Natura** opened in 2010 with the best live frog, snake, and crocodile exhibits in the area. **Arenal Mundo Aventura** is a 2-sq-mile (5-sq-km) wildlife refuge and ecotour center with trails, rappeling, and canopy tours. Nearby, a steep, muddy trail leads to the base of **Catarata Río Fortuna**, a refreshingly cool, ribbon-like 210-ft (70-m) high waterfall. Swimming in the pools at its base is unsafe after heavy rains. Instead, visitors can soak in thermal waters at **Baldi Termae Spa**, which has landscaped outdoor pools and a swim-up bar and restaurant. Southeast of La Fortuna on Highway 142, **Hotel Bosques de Chachagua** (see p260) is a working cattle ranch with a 320-acre (130-ha) private forest

One of the many buses that run from La Fortuna to various sights

reserve at the base of soaring mountains. The reserve, which also welcomes day visitors, offers horseback rides into the forest and has hiking trails too.

🦋 **Ecocentro Danaus Butterfly Farm and Tropical Garden**
2 miles (3 km) E of La Fortuna.
Tel 2479-7019. 🕙 8am–4pm daily.
🖼 🎫 www.ecocentrodanaus.com

🦋 **Arenal Natura**
4 miles (6.5 km) W of La Fortuna.
Tel 2479-1616. 🕙 8am–7:30pm daily. 🖼 🎫 www.arenalnatura.com

🦋 **Arenal Mundo Aventura**
1 mile (1.6 km) S of La Fortuna.
Tel 2479-9762. 🕙 8am–5pm daily.
🖼 🎫 🖥 www.arenalmundoaventura.com

🏞 **Catarata Río Fortuna**
3 miles (5 km) SW of La Fortuna.
Tel 2479-8078. 🕙 8am–5pm daily.
🖼 🖥 www.arenaladifort.com

💧 **Baldi Termae Spa**
3 miles (5 km) W of La Fortuna.
Tel 2479-2190. 🕙 10am–10pm daily. 🖼 🖥 🍴 🖥
www.baldihotsprings.cr

Tabacón Hot Springs Resort and Spa ❷

Road Map C2. 8 miles (13 km)
W of La Fortuna. **Tel** 2519-1999.
🚌 from La Fortuna and Nuevo Arenal. 🕙 10am–10pm daily. 🖼 🏢 ♿
🍴 🖥 ♻ www.tabacon.com

Steaming-hot waters pour out from the base of Volcán Arenal and cascade through this lush, landscaped *balneario* (bathing resort). Río Tabacón feeds a series of therapeutic mineral pools with temperatures that range from 27° to 39° C (80°–102° F). Spa treatments are available. The main pool has a swim-up bar, and there is a splendid restaurant with views (see p283). The *balneario's* Grand Spa is one of the country's most sumptuous and offers treatments in the lush outdoors.

The town of Tabacón is in the path of the main lava flow and, along with Pueblo Nuevo, it was decimated in 1968 when Arenal erupted. Nonetheless, the resort is usually crowded on weekends and throughout the high season.

Environs
Arenal Waterfall Gardens offers landscaped thermal pools and cascades, plus a wild cat rescue center and an activity center.

🦋 **Arenal Waterfall Gardens**
6 miles (10 km) W of La Fortuna.
Tel 2401-3313. 🕙 8am–midnight daily. 🖼 🍴 www.thesprings costarica.com

The landscaped pools of the *balneario* at Tabacón

A panoramic view of Volcán Arenal and the San Carlos Plains

Parque Nacional Volcán Arenal ❸

Road Map C2. 11 miles (18 km) W of La Fortuna. **Tel** 2461-8499. 🚌 to La Fortuna, then by jeep-taxi. ☐ 8am–4pm daily; last entrance: 3pm. 🏷 🥾

Encircling the country's most active volcano, Arenal Volcano National Park spreads over 45 sq miles (120 sq km). Rising from the San Carlos Plains, the majestic Arenal is one of Costa Rica's most rewarding sights. Pre-Columbian tribes considered it the sacred "Home of the Fire God." Arenal ceased activity between the 13th and 16th centuries, and stayed inactive until July 29, 1968, when an earthquake re-awakened it. The perfectly conical 5,400-ft (1,650-m) high volcano now smolders incessantly and minor eruptions occur almost daily. At night it can look like a firecracker as it spews out red-hot lava, which pours down its northwestern flank. Witnessing an eruption is a matter of luck, as clouds often conceal the upper reaches; the dry season is the best for viewing. Ask to be woken if there is a nocturnal eruption.

Trails cross a moonscape of smoking lava scree on Arenal's lower western slopes. Hikers should note that access to some areas is restricted, and should observe the posted "no entry" zones. The volcano has already claimed several lives. The ranger station at the park entrance sells maps and has restrooms. Tour companies and hotels in La Fortuna offer guided tours.

The park also includes the dormant 3,800-ft (1,150-m) high Volcán Chato to the east. **Arenal Observatory Lodge** *(see p261)*, midway up the western flank of Chato, has stunning views of Arenal and Lake Arenal. A museum provides an understanding of volcanology, and the restaurant offers grandstand views when Arenal erupts. Trails from the observatory lead through thick forests to Chato's summit, where a jade-colored lake shimmers in the crater. Canoes can be hired here.

Sign at Arenal Observatory Lodge

Laguna de Arenal ❹

See pp200–1.

Arenal Hanging Bridges ❺

Road Map C2. 12 miles (19 km) W of La Fortuna. **Tel** 2290-0469. 🚌 to La Fortuna, then by jeep-taxi. ☐ 8am–4:30pm daily. 🏷 🎫 ♿ 🖥 **www**.hangingbridges.com

A self-guided trail meanders through 620 pristine acres (250 ha) of primary forest and is punctuated by a series of 14 bridges suspended over ravines. The relatively easy, 2-mile (3-km) trail clings to the mountainside and offers close-up views of every level of the moist tropical forest, from ground to canopy. Guided walks include dawn birding and a night tour.

Arenal Rainforest Reserve and Aerial Tram ❻

Road Map C2. El Castillo, 14 miles (22 km) W of La Fortuna. **Tel** 2479-9944. ☐ 7:30am–5pm daily. 🚌 to La Fortuna, then by jeep-taxi. 🏷 🎫 7:30am and 3:30pm. ♿ 🍴 📷 **www**.arenalreserve.com

Aerial trams *(teleféricos)* whisk visitors up the northern slopes of the Cordillera de Tilarán at this private facility on the southern shore of Lake Arenal. The open-air carriages climb steeply through rainforest to a lookout point at 4,250 ft (1,300 m) from where visitors can enjoy fabulous views of the lake and the volcano. From the *mirador*, 2 miles (3 km) of ziplines connect treetop canopies and offer exhilarating rides across broad ravines.

Environs

The **Butterfly Conservancy** has a small, fascinating display of insects, scorpions, and snakes, as well as a butterfly garden and a medicinal herb garden.

🦋 **Butterfly Conservancy**
El Castillo, 14 miles (22 km) W of La Fortuna.
Tel 2479-1149. ☐ 8am–5pm daily.
🌐 **www**.butterflyconservancy.org

Open-air *teleféricos* **at the Arenal Rainforest Reserve & Aerial Tram**

Laguna de Arenal ❹

Butterfly at Laguna de Arenal

Ringed by hills, with Volcán Arenal standing tall to the east, Lake Arenal has a breathtaking setting at an elevation of 1,800 ft (540 m). The 48-sq-mile (124-sq-km) lake fills a tectonic depression forming a gap between Tilarán and the Cordillera de Guanacaste, and was created in 1973 when the Instituto Costarricense de Electricidad (ICE) dammed the eastern end of the valley. The sole town is Nuevo Arenal, on the lake's north side. The easternmost shores are forest-clad, while huge swathes of verdant pasture lie to the south and west. The lake is swept by near-constant winds, providing windsurfers with world-class conditions. Archaeologists have identified pre-Columbian settlements beneath the waters.

Lucky Bug Gallery
This small shop attached to Restaurante Willy's Caballo Negro (see p283) sells an eclectic range of quality artwork and crafts.

Lago de Coter
The small lake features an activity center offering kayaking, swimming, and birding (see p202).

Hotel Tilawa has a brewpub with lake views.

Wind turbines line ridges of the Continental Divide on the exposed western side of the lake, supplying electricity to the national grid *(see p202).*

Tilawa Viento Surf Center *(see p202)*

0 km 3

0 miles 3

KEY

═══ Major road

═══ Other road

▬ ▬ Parque Nacional Volcán Arenal boundary

The magnificent setting of Laguna de Arenal

For hotels and restaurants in this region see pp260–62 and pp282–3

Arenal Hanging Bridges
A series of suspension bridges are part of a 2-mile (3-km) self-guided interpretive trail through rainforest. The trail offers superb views of Volcán Arenal 5

VISITORS' CHECKLIST

Road Map B2.
11 miles (18 km) from La Fortuna along Hwy 142.
from La Fortuna.
Hotel Tilawa *Tel 2695-5050.*
www.hotel-tilawa.com

Presa Sangregado, the 288-ft (88-m) long, 184-ft (56-m) high earthen dam that created the lake, generates a large portion of the nation's hydroelectric power.

Arenal Rainforest Reserve and Aerial Tram
The Arenal Rainforest Reserve's "sky tram" consists of open-air carriages, which ascend forest-covered mountain slopes. Fabulous views of the lake and volcano can be seen 6

VENADO

nión

Mata de Cana

Arenal Hanging Bridges

Presa Sangregado

LA FORTUNA

A R E N A L

Volcán Arenal

Arenal Rainforest Reserve

El Castillo

Rancho Margot

El Castillo
This community is a starting point for horseback rides to Monteverde via the Cordillera Tilarán. Other attractions include Jardín de Mariposas, which has a small museum displaying insects and reptiles, and a butterfly garden (see p199).

Rancho Margot is a self-sufficient organic farm that also has a wildlife breeding center and trails into a rainforest reserve. Also on offer are kayaking and more extreme activities (see p202).

Exploring Laguna de Arenal

Lake Arenal is encircled to the west and north by the winding Route 142, which links Tilarán with La Fortuna. East of Nuevo Arenal, the road deteriorates and is frequently blocked by landslides. A dirt road along the southeastern shore is impassable from the west at all times. The hotels and restaurants lining the northern shore make a pleasant break from driving. The greatest attractions of the area are the picture-postcard vistas, which can be best appreciated from Arenal's southwest shore. The lake is also a favored spot for sportfishing, windsurfing, and other water sports.

Tilawa Viento Surf Center on Lake Arenal

Nuevo Arenal

24 miles (39 km) W of La Fortuna.
🏠 2,200.

Replacing the old village, which was flooded in 1973 by the formation of the lake, this orderly town is a service center for the lake region. It has the only fuel station in the area, as well as several good restaurants. A dirt road, leading north through the Río Quequer Valley, links Nuevo Arenal with San Rafael on Highway 4.

A view of Lake Arenal

🍴 Rancho Margot

2 miles (3 km) W of El Castillo. *Tel 8302-7318.* 🚌 to La Fortuna, then by jeep-taxi. ⬜ 8am–5pm daily. 🎫 🎫 🚻 www.ranchomargot.org
The dirt road along the southeastern shore of Lake Arenal leads past Parque Nacional Volcán Arenal to Rancho Margot, a self-sustainable farm, hotel, and activity center beside the Río Caño Negro. Educational tours of the eco-oriented farm give fascinating insights, and visitors can also enjoy the wildlife rescue,

rehabilitation, and breeding center. Many sporting enthusiasts come here for activities such as kayaking, horseback riding, waterfall rappeling, and hiking in Rancho Margot's 375-acre (152-ha) forest reserve. There are also yoga and Spanish classes. Meals are served in a colonial farmstead.

Tilawa Viento Surf Center

11 miles (18 km) SW of Nuevo Arenal. *Tel 22695-5050.*
http://windsurfcostarica.com
Swept by steady, strong northeasterly winds between November and March, Lake Arenal is rated as one of the finest windsurfing sites in the world. The Tilawa Viento Surf Center, located on the lake's western shore, caters to all levels of windsurfers. In addition to hiring out sailboards, it offers multiday packages and beginners' and advanced lessons.
The **Tico Windsurf Center** (tel 2692-2002; www.ticowind. com), 9 miles (15 km) southwest of Nuevo Arenal, offers a similar range of services between the months of November and April.

🛥 Rain Goddess

Tel 8321-6189.
www.arenalhouseboattours.com
This 65-ft (20-m) private houseboat is furnished with deluxe accommodations in wood-paneled cabins. It can be rented for tailor-made itineraries that include fishing for *guapote* (rainbow bass) and other light-tackle game fish – Lake Arenal is considered a premier angling spot. The boat also has kayaks.

🦜 Lago de Coter

4 miles (6 km) NW of Nuevo Arenal.
North of Lake Arenal, Lago de Coter occupies a basin in the Fila Vieja Dormida Mountains. The **Lake Coter Eco-Lodge** *(see p261)* is a center for activities such as canoeing, kayaking, horseback riding, and mountain biking. It also offers appealing accommodations. More than 350 species of birds have been recorded in the surrounding forests. A 3-sq-mile (9-sq-km) forest reserve nearby offers guided hiking and birding tours, as well as a zipline canopy tour.

WIND TURBINES

Rising over emerald pastures on the western shores of Lake Arenal, two parallel ridge crests are dotted with over 100 wind turbines, each 120-ft (35-m) high. Situated near the village of Tejona, which has some of the highest average wind speeds in the world, this wind farm

Electricity-generating wind turbines on Lake Arenal's shores

is the largest in Central America, with a projected annual production of up to 70 MW. Electricity is sold to the state-owned ICE (Instituto Costarricense de Electricidad).

Volcanoes in Costa Rica

Located in one of the world's most volcanic zones, Costa Rica has seven active volcanoes, and at least 60 that are either dormant or extinct. Volcanoes are created by plate tectonics – that is, the movement of the interlocking plates making up the earth's crust that ride on the magma (molten rock) in the mantle. Most volcanoes occur at the boundaries where plates meet or

"Poor man's umbrella," found on volcanic soil

move apart, with magma bursting through cracks in the plate. Lying between 100 and 150 miles (160–240 km) inland of the subduction zone of the Cocos and the Caribbean plates, Costa Rica's volcanoes are concentrated in the northwestern and central regions. Most are steep-sided cones formed by silica-rich magma, and are highly explosive, with Arenal being the most active.

THE FORMATION OF COSTA RICA'S VOLCANOES

Costa Rica's landmass sits on the Caribbean plate, beneath which the east-moving Cocos plate is being forced to form a subduction zone. The intense pressure melts the rocks – this viscous magma wells up to create volcanoes.

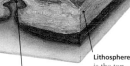

Cocos plate

Dormant volcanoes can have vents blocked by "plugs" of hardened lava.

The subduction zone is the region where a plate starts sinking below another.

The Caribbean plate is the thicker continental plate.

The magma chamber feeds the volcano.

Lithosphere is the topmost part of the mantle.

Volcanic eruptions *can be viewed at Arenal, which erupts every few hours during its active phases, oozing hot lava down its slopes. Lava blasted laterally from volcanoes appears as* nuées ardentes (glowing clouds) – *superheated avalanches of gas, ash, and rock that move downhill at astonishing speeds.*

Smoke and ash *are often steadily emitted by active volcanoes such as Volcán Arenal (see p199). Smoking cinder blocks can sometimes be seen rolling down the slopes.*

Bubbling mud pools *and fumaroles (vents of steam), formed from rainwater superheated from below, are still features of volcanoes such as Miravalles (see p181).*

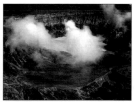

Calderas *are formed when the craters of volcanoes collapse, creating huge circular depressions. This caldera on 8,850-ft (2,700-m) high Volcán Poás is a mile (1.6 km) wide, still emits smoke, and contains a mineral lake (see p140).*

The wetlands of Refugio Nacional de Vida Silvestre Caño Negro

Cavernas de Venado ●

Road Map C2. 1 mile (1.6 km) W of Venado, 24 miles (39 km) NW of La Fortuna. **Tel** 2478-9081. ▦ from Ciudad Quesada. ◯ 9am–4pm daily. ▦ ✔ ▤

Bioluminescent fungi help light the way for visitors scrambling through the underground passageways of these limestone caverns. Ten chambers, extending almost 2 miles (3 km), have been explored. Exquisite stalagmites, stalactites, and other subterranean formations fill the labyrinthine and narrow chambers, many of which contain marine fossils. **Cascada de La Muerte** is an underground waterfall that gushes during the wet season from May to November and after heavy rain. Bats flit about, blind fish swim in the underground streams, and small transparent frogs hop around in the ooze.

Guides lead 2-hour long explorations. Wilbert Solis, who owns the land on which the caves are located, supplies safety helmets, flashlights, and rubber boots. Come prepared to get covered in mud, and bring a change of clothes.

Agencies in La Fortuna offer tours. Venado is also accessible by a dirt road that begins at Hotel La Mansion Inn *(see p261)*, on the north shore of Lake Arenal. The village offers basic accommodation.

Refugio Nacional de Vida Silvestre Caño Negro ●

Road Map C1. 65 miles (105 km) NW of La Fortuna. **Tel** 2471-1309. ▦ from Upala. ⛴ from Los Chiles. ◯ 8am–4pm daily. ▦ ✎

One of Costa Rica's main wetland conservation areas, Caño Negro Wildlife Refuge protects over 38 sq miles (98 sq km) of marshlands, lagoons, and *yolillo* palm forest. Most visitors come to fish for snook and tarpon, which thrive in Río Frío and other watercourses that feed Lago Caño Negro, a 3-sq-mile (9-sq-km) seasonal lake. Rare ancient garfish also inhabit the tannin-stained waters. The short dry season (Dec–Apr) is best for viewing crocodiles, caimans, and the large mammals that gather near permanent bodies of water. Monkeys and tapirs are numerous, while jaguars and other cats are more elusive. Lucky visitors may also see large flocks of migratory birds and waterfowl, including jabiru storks, Nicaraguan grackles, roseate spoonbills, and the largest colony of neotropic cormorants in Costa Rica.

Caño Negro village, on the west bank of Lago Caño Negro, is the only community within the reserve. The park headquarters are located here, as are several lodges that arrange guided tours

Neotropic cormorant

and fishing licenses. Boats can be rented in nearby Los Chiles, and agencies in San José offer tours, especially during the fishing season (Jul–Mar). Much of the area floods in the wet season, and access along the dirt roads can be a challenge.

Parque Nacional Volcán Tenorio ●

Road Map B2. 7 miles (11 km) E of Bijagua. **Tel** 2200-0135. ▦ from Upala, then by jeep-taxi. ◯ 8am–4pm daily. ▦ ✔

Several nature lodges offer easy access to this 71-sq-mile (184-sq-km) park. Trails lead through montane rainforest to thermal springs and the **Pozo Azul**, a teal-blue pool at the base of the volcano. Local guides lead hikes in search of tapirs and other wildlife, but the summit trail is closed to all but scientists.

Ciudad Quesada (San Carlos) ●

Road Map C2. 59 miles (95 km) NW of San José. ⛪ 36,350. ▦ ℹ ICT, 75 yards N of Universidad Católica, 2461-9102. ⛪ Sat. ⚑ Feria del Ganado (Apr).

An important market center serving the local dairy and cattle industries, Ciudad Quesada is set amid pastures atop the mountain scarp of the Cordillera de Tilarán, at an elevation of 2,130 ft (650 m).

Mineral spring pools at Termales del Bosque, Ciudad Quesada

The town, known locally as San Carlos, is the administrative center for the region, and is famous for its annual cattle fair and *tope* (horse show). The town plaza and numerous *talabarterías* (saddle-makers' workshops) justify a visit here.

Environs
Highway 140 slopes east, passing **Termales del Bosque**, where visitors can soak in thermal mineral springs and have mud baths. Hiking trails lace botanical gardens, and horseback rides and a zipline canopy tour are also on offer.

Nearby, **La Marina Zoológica** is a private, non-profit zoo that takes in orphaned and rescued animals. Its numerous inhabitants include jaguars, agoutis, monkeys, peccaries, and snakes, as well as macaws, toucans, and many other bird species. Tapirs are bred for release into the wild.

Termales del Bosque
4 miles (6 km) E of Ciudad Quesada. *Tel* 2460-4740.
7am–10pm daily.
www.termalesdelbosque.com

La Marina Zoológica
6 miles (10 km) E of Ciudad Quesada. *Tel* 2474-2202.
8am–4pm daily.

Shaman healing table and stones, Museo de Cultura Indígena

Centro Neotrópico SarapiquíS ⑪

Road Map D2. La Virgen de Sarapiquí, 29 miles (47 km) N of Alajuela. *Tel* 2761-1004. San José–Puerto Viejo de Sarapiquí.
9am–5pm daily.
www.sarapiquis.org

This broad-ranging ecological center on the banks of Río Sarapiquí offers an enriching insight into indigenous cultures (see pp30–31).

Parque Arqueológico Alma Alta at the Centro Neotrópico SarapiquíS

The state-of-the-art **Museo de Cultura Indígena** is dedicated to Costa Rica's living indigenous communities and the preservation of their artifacts. Its impressive exhibits include a large collection of masks, bark cloth paintings, and other decorative, domestic, and ritual objects, including shamanic healing sticks. An air-conditioned theater shows a 15 minute documentary.

The **Parque Arqueológico Alma Alta**, set in an orange orchard, is centered around four indigenous tombs, dating from the 15th century, and a representation of a pre-Columbian village. Indian guides offer tours of **Chester's Field Botanical Gardens**. Named for the naturalist Chester Czepulos (1916–92), the gardens have about 500 native species of plants renowned since pre-Columbian times for their medicinal use. The center also has a quality restaurant, hotel, library, and conference center.

Environs
The center adjoins the **Tirimbina Rainforest Reserve**, which protects 750 acres (300 ha) of mid-elevation premontane forest. It can be reached from Centro Neotrópico SarapiquíS by a 855-ft (260-m) long suspension bridge across Río Sarapiquí. A 325-ft (100-m) canopy walkway features among Tirimbina's 5 miles (8 km) of trails. Guided tours include a special "World of Bats" night walk. The reserve's Education Center, which is on Tirimbina Island in the middle of the river, is used for scientific

investigation and has a library on tropical ecology.

Hacienda Pozo Azul is a working cattle ranch that offers whitewater rafting trips and canopy tours. Accommodation is available at Magsasay Lodge, adjoining Parque Nacional Braulio Carrillo (see p141). The nearby **Snake Garden** allows visitors to get nose-to-nose with 70 snake species.

Tirimbina Rainforest Reserve
Tel 2761-0333.
7am–5pm daily.
www.tirimbina.org

Hacienda Pozo Azul
La Virgen de Sarapiquí.
Tel 2438-2616.
9am–6:30pm daily.
www.haciendapozoazul.com

Snake Garden
La Virgen de Sarapiquí.
Tel 2761-1059.
9am–5pm daily.
snakegarden@costarricense.co.cr

Horseback riding at Hacienda Pozo Azul, a working ranch

Puerto Viejo de Sarapiquí ⓬

Road Map D2. 52 miles (84 km)
N of San José. 🏠 *16,300*. 🚌 🚢

Positioned at the base of the Cordillera Central, on the banks of Río Sarapiquí, Puerto Viejo has functioned as an important river port since colonial days. Before the opening of the Atlantic Railroad in 1890, the town was the main gateway between San José and the Caribbean Sea. While the port trade has reduced, *pangas* (water-taxis) still connect the town to Parque Nacional Tortuguero *(see p217)* and Barra del Colorado via Río San Juan. Boats also set out on nature excursions.

Banana trees cover most of the Llanura de San Carlos flatlands around Puerto Viejo. **Bananero La Colonia**, a processing factory in the middle of banana fields, welcomes visitors.

Bananero La Colonia
3 miles (5 km) SE of Puerto Viejo.
Tel 2768-8683. 🎥 🎥 by appt. 🛈
www.bananatourcostarica.com

Water-taxis on Río San Juan at Puerto Viejo de Sarapiquí

A verdant trail in the rainforests of Selva Verde

Selva Verde ⓭

Road Map D2. 5 miles (8 km) W of Puerto Viejo de Sarapiquí. **Tel** 2766-6800. 🚌 *San José–Puerto Viejo via Vara Blanca.* 🕐 *7am–3pm daily.* 🎥
🎥 🍴 🛈 ⌖ www.selvaverde.com

One of the country's best private reserves, the 470-acre (190-ha) Selva Verde (Green Forest) reserve adjoins Parque Nacional Braulio Carrillo *(see p141)*. A prime destination for birders, the virgin low-elevation rainforest is home to over 420 bird species, including eight species of parrots. Ocelots, sloths, capuchin monkeys, and mantled howler monkeys are among the 120 species of mammals to be seen. Poison-dart frogs are numerous, as are snakes, although these are difficult to spot. Several of Selva Verde's 500 species of butterflies can be seen in a netted butterfly garden.

Guided canoe trips are offered on Río Sarapiquí, which runs through Selva Verde. Naturalist guides can be hired, and maps are provided for the well-maintained trails. The reserve also has a lodge with comfortable rooms.

Refugio Nacional de Vida Silvestre Corredor Fronterizo ⓮

Road Map C1. Bahía Salinas to Punta Castillo. **Tel** 2471-2191 *(Los Chiles)*.
@ refugio.fronterizo@sinac.go.cr

Intended as a biological corridor, the 230-sq-mile (590-sq-km) Frontier Corridor National Wildlife Refuge protects a wide strip of Costa Rican territory along the border with Nicaragua, from Bahía Salinas on the west coast to Punta Castillo on the east. The eastern part of the refuge runs along Río San Juan. Lined with virgin rainforest, this broad river flows 120 miles (195 km) east from Lake Nicaragua to Punta Castillo, and has long been disputed by the two nations.

Pangas link Puerto Viejo de Sarapiquí to Trinidad village, at the confluence of Ríos Sarapiquí and San Juan. The river trip through the reserve is splendid for spotting sloths, crocodiles, and myriad birds, including oropendolas and rare chestnut-bellied herons.

Environs
Boca San Carlos, 24 miles (39 km) upstream of Trinidad on Río San Juan, has an airstrip and can also be reached by a dirt road. It is a gateway for river journeys into Nicaragua. Nearby, **Laguna del Lagarto** is a private reserve protecting 2 sq miles (5 sq km) of virgin rainforest and swamps. Elusive manatees inhabit the lagoons, and a nature lodge offers a good base for wildlife viewing. The restored, 17th-century, mossy hilltop fort of **Fortaleza de la Inmaculada Concepción**, near the Nicaraguan hamlet of El Castillo, 25 miles (40 km) upstream of Boca San Carlos, is worth a visit. Its small museum recalls the days when Spanish defenders fought back pirates and an English invasion fleet led by Lord Nelson.

🚶 **Laguna del Lagarto**
10 miles (16 km) S of Boca San Carlos. **Tel** 2289-8163. 🎥 🍴 ⌖
http://lagarto-lodge-costa-rica.com

FRESHWATER SHARKS

The presence of sharks in freshwater Lake Nicaragua has been a puzzle for centuries. In the 1970s, scientists tagged individual sharks with electronic monitors and found that they migrate along Río San Juan between the Caribbean Sea and the lake, a distance of 106 miles (169 km). These euryhaline sharks, capable of living in both fresh- and saltwater, are even able to navigate rapids.

Bull shark in the waters of Lake Nicaragua

Leaf-Cutter Ants

Present in most lowland and mid-elevation environments in Costa Rica, leaf-cutter ants are fascinating insects. They farm their own food, gathering leaves, petals, and other plant parts, and transport them to vast underground nests. They then compost the vegetation to farm a fungus whose spores feed the entire colony, which can number up to 10 million individuals.

Leaf-cutter ant nest

Ant societies are incredibly complex. Communities are divided into different-size castes, each with its own specialized task. Mature colonies produce reproductive ants, who mate with peers from other colonies. Virgin queens carry with them some fungus culture. Males die after mating, leaving fertilized females to start their own nests using the fungus culture.

Medium-sized ants, *or medaie, cut the leaves and carry them back to the nest along trails that can exceed 656 ft (200 m). Each leaf shard may weigh three times more than the ant. Smaller siblings, or minors, hitch rides atop the shards and act as sentinels to ward off phorid flies.*

Medaie carry leaves

Minors stand guard

Trees are often defoliated completely, *in as little as 24 hours, by leaf-cutter ants. Scouts carry samples of trees, bushes, and flowers to foragers, who may reject them as unsuitable.*

THE PHORID FLY

Tiny phorid flies (1–6mm) are the natural enemies of ants and can devastate whole communities. After mating, each female phorid fly seeks out an ant and swiftly deposits an egg in a fleshy crevice in the ant's thorax. The larva hatches inside the ant and eats it. Attacks can trigger panic in ant colonies.

The spongy fungal garden *is cultivated by minims, the smallest ant caste. They mulch leaves into compost and smear the garden with antibiotic secretions to keep it free from the virulent Escovopsis mold.*

The major's powerful jaws *are used to defend the colony from invaders and to carry away debris that is too large for smaller castes. Pre-Columbian people used the jaws as sutures to stitch together deep cuts.*

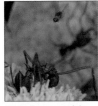

Phorid fly, enemy of the leaf-cutter ant

Broad-billed motmot, La Selva Biological Station

La Selva Biological Station ⓯

Road Map D2. 2 miles (3 km) S of Puerto Viejo. **Tel** 2766-6565. OTS shuttles from Puerto Viejo & San José. 8am–5pm by appt. 5:30am, 8am, and 1:30pm. www.ots.ac.cr

Created by the scientist Dr. Leslie Holdridge in 1954, La Selva Biological Station has been run as a private research facility by the Organization of Tropical Studies (OTS) since 1968. Scientific research at this 6-sq-mile (15-sq-km) reserve spans physiological ecology, soil science, and forestry, with over 1,000 tree species in the Holdridge Arboretum.

The predominant habitat is a vast swathe of lowland and premontane rainforest at the base of Parque Nacional Braulio Carrillo (see p141). Snakes, although profuse, are rarely seen. More noticeable are poison-dart frogs, enameled in gaudy colors, and more than 500 species of butterflies, including neon blue morphos. Elusive jaguars

and other big cats prowl the forests, preying on monkeys, coatis, and deer, which are among La Selva's 120 mammal species. Leaf-cutter ants are underfoot everywhere, carrying their scissored cargos. About half of Costa Rica's bird species have been sighted here; the annual 24-hour La Selva Christmas Bird Count has become a pilgrimage for ornithologists from around the world. A basic bird-watching course is offered on Saturday mornings.

Access to the reserve is restricted to 65 people at any given time, and although it is open to the public by reservation, scientists and students get priority. Over 31 miles (50 km) of boardwalk trails crisscross La Selva, but precipitation can exceed 157 in (400 cm) in a year, and many trails are muddy. The gift shop has self-guiding booklets. OTS offers guided excursions from San José that include transport. Dormitory lodging is offered on a space-available basis.

Heliconia Island ⓰

Road Map D2. 5 miles (8 km) S of Puerto Viejo. **Tel** 2761-5220. San José–Puerto Viejo de Sarapiquí via PN Braulio Carrillo. 8am–5pm daily. by appointment. www.heliconiaisland.com

This beautifully laid-out garden on the banks of Río Puerto Viejo was created in 1992 by the American naturalist Tim Ryan and is now run by Dutch owners. Hundreds of tropical plant species grow amid the lush 5-acre (2-ha) lawns. The garden specializes in heliconias, of which it has more than 80 species from around the world. Various species of gingers thrive here, and also a superb collection of bamboos and orchids. Equally impressive are the palms, which include the traveler's palm, native to Madagascar. It is so named because in an emergency, travelers can drink the water that is stored in its stalk.

Tropical heliconia

Hummingbirds hover as they sip nectar. Violaceous trogons and orange-chinned parakeets are among the more than 200 species of birds drawn to the exotic flora. Rare green macaws nest in *almendro* (almond) trees and are frequently sighted.

Guided tours impart fascinating trivia on tropical plant ecology. The torchlit nighttime tours are especially rewarding. The river has calm stretches safe for swimming, and the island has a restaurant, plus B&B hotel rooms.

POISON-DART FROGS

The rainforests of Central and South America are inhabited by poison-dart frogs, so named because Indians use their poison to tip their arrows and blow-darts. About 65 separate species exist, although only three species are deadly to humans (none are found in Costa Rica). The frogs, which are no more than an inch (3 cm) long, produce the bitter toxin in their mucous glands and advertise this with flamboyant colors – mostly vivid reds, greens, and blues – to avoid being eaten by predators. Thus, unusually for frogs, they are active by day among the moist leaf litter. Several species of non-toxic frogs mimic their coloration. In captivity, poison-dart frogs tend to lose their toxicity, which they derive from their principal diet of ants and termites.

A colorful poison-dart frog

Rara Avis ⑰

Road Map D2. 17 miles (27 km)
S of Puerto Viejo. **Tel** 2764-1111.
San José–Las Horquetas.
www.rara-avis.com

This world-famous rainforest
reserve was among the first
private reserves in Costa Rica.
Adjoining Parque Nacional
Braulio Carrillo and La Selva,
the 4-sq-mile (10-sq-km)
Rara Avis is perched on the
remote northeast slopes of
Volcán Chato at an elevation
of 2,300 ft (700 m).

The brainchild of entre-
preneur Amos Bien, who
created it in 1983, Rara Avis
pioneered the notion of
generating income through
ecologically sustainable
ventures in protected primary
forests. Its selective farming
projects include a butterfly
farm and philodendron and
orchid cultivation.

Trails wander through
pristine mid-elevation
rainforest. The biodiversity is
impressive, from anteaters,
spider monkeys, and
porcupines to boa
constrictors, coral
snakes, red-eyed
tree frogs,
elusive jaguars
and pumas, and
almost 400 species
of birds, including
the umbrella bird,
sunbitterns, and the endangered great green macaw.
A rappeling system lets you
get eye-to-eye with canopy
dwellers such as toucans and
capuchin monkeys. The park
has several waterfalls, but
caution is required when
swimming in the pools that
form at their base.

Rara Avis is accessed by a
daunting track that is often
knee-deep in mud. Transfers
from Las Horquetas, on
Highway 4, are by tractor-
drawn canopied trailer, a
bumpy 9-mile (14-km)
journey that takes an hour.
Come prepared for heavy
rainfall, which averages more
than 200 inches (500 cm)
per year. Rubber boots are
provided for hikers. Two-
night minimum stays are
required; accommodation is
in a choice of rustic lodges.

**Porcupine in
Rara Avis**

**Ripening fruit at a
banana plantation**

BANANAS

Costa Rica is the world's seventh
largest banana producer and its
second largest exporter. Plantations
cover 195 sq miles (500 sq km) of
the nation. Massive tracts of protected rainforest are felled each year to
plant bananas, and many chemicals
are used to maintain output. When
washed out to sea, these chemicals
kill fish, poison the waters, and
foster the growth of plants that
choke estuaries and corals. As a
result of environmental campaigns,
the banana industry now follows
more ecologically sensitive practices.

Rainforest Aerial Tram ⑱

Road Map D3. Hwy 32, 25 miles
(40 km) NE of San José. **Tel** 2257-
5961. San José–Guápiles.
9am–4pm Mon; 6:30am–4pm
Tue, Sun.
www.rainforesttram.com

Offering an alternative view
of the forest canopy, this
automated explora-
tion system was
conceived by the
American
naturalist Dr.
Donald Perry
while he was
involved in scientific
investigation at Rara
Avis. Inaugurated in
1994, the Rainforest Aerial
Tram, also called "El Teleféri-
co," is the highlight of a 875-
acre (355-ha) private nature
reserve on the eastern edge
of Parque Nacional Braulio
Carrillo. Visitors ride in open

gondolas that silently skim
the floor of the rainforest and
then soar above the trees on
a 2-mile (3-km) circuit. The
90-minute tour is preceded by
a video, which describes the
construction of the $2 million
system, and the flora and
fauna to be seen. A naturalist
guide accompanies each
gondola to assist visitors in
spotting and identifying wildlife. Howler and white-faced
monkeys are occasionally
seen at close quarters, as are
iguanas, sloths, and snakes.
Early morning and late afternoon are the best times to spot
wildlife, but visitors should
keep in mind that the main
aim of the journey is to learn
about rainforest ecology.

Trails lead to Río Corinto,
and guided birding trips
are offered, along with
frog, snake, and butterfly
exhibits. Accommodations
are in the form of cabins.
Tour agencies nationwide
offer package excursions.

Rainforest Aerial Tram gondola at the start of its tour

THE CARIBBEAN

*U*nique within the country for its Afro-Caribbean culture, this region is steeped in traditions brought by Jamaican forebears, which lend a colorful, laid-back charm to the ramshackle villages that sprinkle the coast. One of Costa Rica's wettest regions, it extends along 125 miles (200 km) of the Caribbean coastline between the Nicaraguan and Panamanian borders. Stunning beaches line the shore, and primordial rainforest merges with swampy lagoons in the north and rises into the rugged Talamanca Mountains in the south.

After the closure of the port of Puerto Limón to trade in 1665 *(see p41)*, the Spanish made little attempt to settle the region. This drew pirates and smugglers, who induced slaves to cut precious hardwoods for illicit trade. In the late 19th century, Jamaican laborers and their families arrived to build the Atlantic Railroad and work on banana plantations. Succeeding generations adopted a subsistence life of farming and fishing, which continues in today's Creole culture. Inland, descendants of the original indigenous tribes live in relative isolation in designated reserves in the Talamanca foothills, clinging to shamanism and other traditional practices.

The region's only significant town is Puerto Limón, located midway down the coast. Northward, flatlands extend to the Nicaraguan border. The coastal strip is backed by swampy jungles and freshwater lagoons that culminate in Tortuguero National Park and Barra del Colorado National Wildlife Refuge. A network of canals, created in the 1960s to link Puerto Limón with Barra, opened up this otherwise virtually inaccessible region. South of Puerto Limón, the shore is lined with stupendous beaches. The communities of Cahuita and Puerto Viejo are popular with surfers and a predominantly young crowd seeking offbeat adventure.

Brightly colored wooden house in the village of Cahuita

◁ Palms lining the surfing beach Playa Chiquita, near Puerto Viejo de Talamanca

Exploring the Caribbean

With several national parks and wildlife refuges, the humid Caribbean has as its jewel Parque Nacional Tortuguero, with its dense rainforests, raffia palm swamps, and exotic range of fauna. Farther north, rain-sodden Barra del Colorado attracts anglers. The port town of Puerto Limón is a gateway to the villages of Cahuita and Puerto Viejo de Talamanca, vibrant centers of indigenous Afro-Caribbean culture. Parque Nacional Cahuita, which adjoins Cahuita village, also protects a small coral reef. Fine beaches extend south to Gandoca-Manzanillo, a coastal wetland harboring manatees and also an important nesting site for marine turtles. Several horticultural venues along Highway 32 exhibit tropical flora.

Entrance to a house in Puerto Limón

SEE ALSO

- **Where to Stay** pp262–4
- **Where to Eat** pp283–4

KEY

━━ Major road

━ Secondary road

═══ Minor road

━━ International border

━ Provincial border

-- Canal

SIGHTS AT A GLANCE

Towns and Villages
Cahuita **10**
Puerto Limón **3**
Puerto Viejo de Talamanca **12**

National Parks and Reserves
Aviarios del Caribe Sloth Sanctuary **8**
Parque Nacional Cahuita **11**
Parque Nacional Tortuguero **5**
Refugio Nacional de Fauna Silvestre
    Barra del Colorado **6**
Refugio Nacional de Vida Silvestre
    Gandoca-Manzanillo **13**
Reserva Biológica Hitoy-Cerere **9**
Veragua Rainforest Research and
    Adventure Park **7**

Areas of Natural Beauty
EARTH **2**
Las Cusingas **1**

Tour
Canal de Tortuguero Tour p216 **4**

Indigenous Sites
Indigenous Reserves **14**

For additional map symbols *see back flap*

Beach at Puerto Viejo de Talamanca

A picker cushioning a large bunch of bananas, Cahuita

④ CANAL DE TORTUGUERO TOUR

atina   Punta de Riel

Estrada
VERAGUA   **PUERTO**
RAINFOREST Moín **LIMÓN**
RESEARCH &   **③**
ADVENTURE ⑦   *Isla Uvita*
PARK
Petróleo   Irebol
Aquas Zarcas

Finca Banaga   **AVARIOS SLOTH**
Reserva Selva   **SANCTUARY**
Bananito   **⑧** Penshurst
ó   *Río Banano*   *Playa Negra*
Finca 7   **⑪ PARQUE NACIONAL**
Vesta   **CAHUITA ⑩**   **CAHUITA**
Cuen **⑨**
RESERVA BIOLÓGICA **PUERTO VIEJO DE**   *Playa*
HITOY-CERERE   **TALAMANCA ⑫** *Cocles*
Ó N   *Río Telire* Bribri   **REFUGIO NACIONAL**
Teliré   Shiroles   Manzanillo **DE VIDA SILVESTRE**
INDIGENOUS   Gandoca **GANDOCA-MANZANILLO**
RESERVES ⑭   Bratsi
San José   *Río Coén*
Cabécar   Sixaola

PANAMA

Purisqui

0 km   20
0 miles   20

GETTING AROUND

Highway 32, linking San José to Puerto Limón, is heavily trafficked, particularly along the mountainous sections. A bus service provides easy access to Cahuita and Puerto Viejo de Talamanca. No roads penetrate to Tortuguero and Barra del Colorado, but both villages have airstrips serviced by daily scheduled flights from San José. Another popular option is to journey by canal – tour operators can make arrangements. An infrequent bus service connects the indigenous reserves along rough dirt roads – an uncomfortable, albeit cheap, ride.

Green honeycreeper, one of the species of birds found in Las Cusingas

Las Cusingas ❶

Road Map D3. 2 miles (3 km) S of Hwy 32, 37 miles (59 km) E of San José. 🚌 San José–Guápiles, then by jeep-taxi or hiking. 📞 2382-5805. 🕐 8:30am–4:30pm daily. 🅿️ 🚻 🍴 🛍

This botanical garden, spread over 35 acres (14 ha) near the less-than-appealing town of Guápiles, undertakes scientific investigation into tropical flora, fruits, and more than 80 species of medicinal plants. Hummingbirds, parrots, and scores of other birds flock to feed on the nectar and seeds. There are two short forest trails, one of which leads to Río Santa Clara and 10 sq miles (26 sq km) of protected forest. The visitor center, which includes a library, offers an introduction to reforestation, conservation, tropical ecology, and the use of medicinal plants.

Guided tours are offered, each about 2 hours long. A rustic family-size cabin with a wood-fired oven can be rented, and visitors can dine with the friendly Tico owners.

Environs
Acclaimed American-born artist Patricia Erickson welcomes visitors to her studio **Gallery at Home**, which displays her vibrant paintings inspired by scenes of Caribbean family life. To get there, turn south at Río Blanco; the studio is a short way down, on the left. Across the street, her husband Brian's **Muebles de Bamboo** offers a chance to watch bamboo furniture being made, using 32 different species grown in a bamboo garden.

Located on the borders of Parque Nacional Tortuguero and Refugio Nacional de Fauna Silvestre Barra del Colorado (see p217), **Finca La Suerte** offers superb opportunities for wildlife-viewing in a variety of habitats, including rainforests and marshes. Poison-dart frogs (see p208) and monkeys are abundant. This private research center specializes in residential workshops in tropical ecology, and offers overnight accommodation. It can be accessed from Guápiles by buses via the community of Cariari.

🏛 **Gallery at Home**
330 yd (300 m) S of Hwy 32, 4 miles (6 km) W of Guápiles. **Tel** 2711-0823. 🕐 by appointment.

🏛 **Muebles de Bamboo**
Tel 2710-1958. 🕐 8am–5pm Mon–Fri, by appt. **www.**brieri.com

🦋 **Finca La Suerte**
La Primavera, 27 miles (43 km) NE of Guápiles. **Tel** 2710-8005. 🕐 9am–5pm daily. 🅿️ 🚻 🍴 🍴 🌐 **www.**lasuerte.org

EARTH ❷

Road Map D2. 1 mile (1.6 km) E of Guácimo. **Tel** 2713-0000. 🚌 San José–Puerto Limón. 🕐 9am–4pm daily. 🅿️ 🚻 🛍 🌐 **www.**earth.ac.cr

One of the world's leading tropical research centers, the Escuela de Agricultura de la Región Tropical Húmeda (Agricultural College of the Humid Tropical Region) focuses on ecologically sustainable practices. EARTH operates its own experimental banana plantation, banana processing plant, and paper-making plant that uses banana skins. There are guided tours and nature trails through the rainforest; horses can also be hired.

Environs
More than 600 species of tropical flowers, including several varieties of heliconia, color the landscape at **Costa Flores**, the world's largest commercial farm for tropical flowers. Hummingbirds zoom around the landscaped gardens, which are open only to cruise-ship groups. Every Sunday, at the **Centro Turístico Las Tilapias**, local resident Chito swims in a lagoon to wrestle and perform tricks with Poncho, the one-eyed crocodile he rescued after the animal was shot by a farmer.

Heliconia, Costa Flores

🌸 **Costa Flores**
9 miles (14 km) E of Guápiles. **Tel** 2716-6430. 🕐 8am–4pm Mon–Fri, by appt Sat & Sun. 🅿️ 🚻 🛗

🦋 **Centro Turístico Las Tilapias**
3 miles (5 km) N of Siquirres. **Tel** 8398-1517. 🕐 4pm Sun. 🅿️ **www.**chitotarzantico.com

Sign for EARTH, a center for tropical research

Bust of Don Balvanero Vargas in Puerto Limón's Parque Vargas

Puerto Limón ❸

Road Map F3. 100 miles (160 km) E of San José. 🚶 65,000. ✈ ⛴ 🎭 🎵 Black Culture Festival (Sep); Día de las Culturas (Oct 12).

Located in the bay where Christopher Columbus and his son Fernando anchored in 1502, the port town of Puerto Limón had its origins in early colonial days. Used by pirates and smugglers for trading mahogany and other tropical hardwoods, the settlement thrived on this illicit traffic under the nose of the Spanish authorities. The town has a large Chinese population, whose forebears arrived during the 1880s as indentured laborers for the construction of the Atlantic Railroad. A small Chinese cemetery at the entrance to the town honors this Asian heritage. Today, the port handles most of the nation's sea trade; the main highway into town is crowded with container trucks throughout the day. The maritime facilities have been expanded to serve cruise ships plying the Caribbean coast.

Columbus supposedly landed at **Isla Uvita**, half a mile (1 km) offshore. His landfall is commemorated by a bronze bust, which was unveiled in 1992, in time for the 500th anniversary of his arrival in the Americas. The bust faces **Parque Vargas**, a tiny tree-shaded park named after Don Balvanero Vargas, a former governor of Limón

province. The park, which features a bust of Don Vargas, is at the east end of the pedestrian-only Avenida 2 (also known as El Bulevar). Nearby, a beautiful mural by artist Guadalupe Alvarez depicts local history since pre-Columbian days.

Puerto Limón has some intriguing architecture, with pretty filigreed iron balconies in the style of New Orleans. To the west of Parque Vargas, the cream-colored stucco Belle Epoque **Alcaldía** (Town Hall) is a fine example. Other structures are classics of the Caribbean vernacular style, made of wood and painted in lively tropical pastels, with broad balconies on stilts beneath which locals gather to play dominoes. Visit the lively **Mercado Central**, to the north of the museum, for everything from pigs' heads to freshly caught fish.

Detail of mural by Guadalupe Alvarez near Parque Vargas

Shoppers outside Mercado Central in Puerto Limón

A dramatic post-modernist concrete cathedral, La Catedral del Sagrado Corazón rises over the center of town with its crystal-shaped 154-ft (47-m) spire.

Environs
Local surfers find their fun off **Playa Bonita**, 2 miles (3 km) north of town. This golden-sand beach gets crowded on week-ends with Limonenses, as the town's inhabitants are known. Swimming in the south end of the bay is dangerous. A mile (1.6 km) to the north of Playa Bonita, **Moín** is where Costa Rica's crude oil is processed and bananas loaded for shipment to Europe and North America. Boats leave from here for Tortuguero (see p216).

🏛 **Mercado Central**
Calles 3/4 and Avés Central/2.
🕐 6am–6pm daily.

CARNAVAL

In the second week of October, Puerto Limón erupts into kaleidoscopic color for Carnaval (see p35), a week-long Caribbean Mardi Gras celebration culminating on Día de las Culturas (Columbus Day). Special buses bring revelers from San José, and the city packs in as many as 100,000 visitors. Live reggae, salsa, and calypso get everyone dancing. Other amusements include beauty contests, bull-running, desfiles (parades), street fairs, and firework displays. The highlight is the Grand Desfile, a grand parade of flamboyant costumes and floats held on the Saturday before October 12. Most events take place on the docks.

Extravagantly dressed dancers at Carnaval

Canal de Tortuguero Tour ❹

Kingfisher

Travel along the Caribbean seaboard became possible with the building of the Tortuguero canal system in 1966–74. Four canals make up this 65-mile (105-km) long aquatic highway, which connects the port of Moín to Barra del Colorado village, and is lined with rainforest. Narrow in places, when the looming forest seems to close in on the water, the canal offers the chance of fascinating boating trips, with sightings of caimans and river turtles, and birds such as aracaris and kingfishers.

A tourist boat moving through the Tortuguero Canal

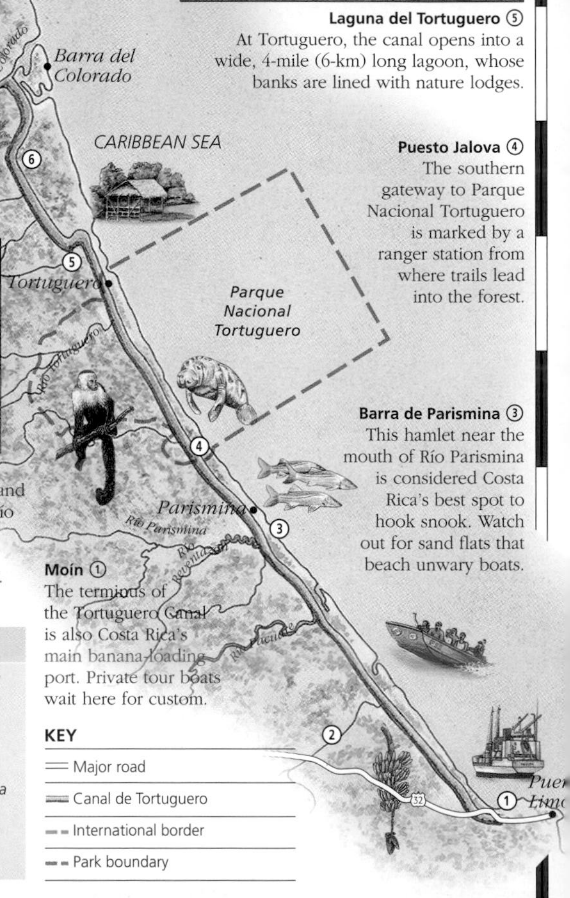

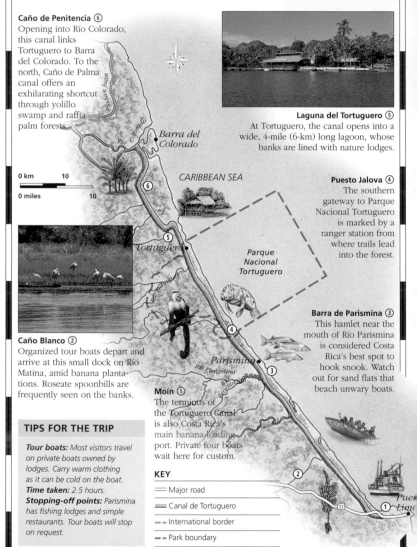

Caño de Penitencia (6)
Opening into Río Colorado, this canal links Tortuguero to Barra del Colorado. To the north, Caño de Palma canal offers an exhilarating shortcut through yolillo swamp and raffia palm forests.

Laguna del Tortuguero (5)
At Tortuguero, the canal opens into a wide, 4-mile (6-km) long lagoon, whose banks are lined with nature lodges.

Puesto Jalova (4)
The southern gateway to Parque Nacional Tortuguero is marked by a ranger station from where trails lead into the forest.

Caño Blanco (2)
Organized tour boats depart and arrive at this small dock on Río Matina, amid banana plantations. Roseate spoonbills are frequently seen on the banks.

Barra de Parismina (3)
This hamlet near the mouth of Río Parismina is considered Costa Rica's best spot to hook snook. Watch out for sand flats that beach unwary boats.

Moín (1)
The terminus of the Tortuguero Canal is also Costa Rica's main banana-loading port. Private tour boats wait here for custom.

TIPS FOR THE TRIP

Tour boats: *Most visitors travel on private boats owned by lodges. Carry warm clothing as it can be cold on the boat.*
Time taken: *2.5 hours.*
Stopping-off points: *Parismina has fishing lodges and simple restaurants. Tour boats will stop on request.*

KEY

- Major road
- Canal de Tortuguero
- International border
- Park boundary

A guide escorting a tour group through Parque Nacional Tortuguero

a new ethic as conservationists. The **John H. Phipps Biological Station and Natural History Visitor's Center** has excellent displays on local ecology, especially marine turtles.

> **✕ John H. Phipps Biological Station and Natural History Visitor's Center**
> 550 yd (500 m) N of Tortuguero village. **Tel** 2709-8125.
> ☐ 10am–noon and 2–5pm Mon–Sat; 2–5pm Sun. ⚲

Refugio Nacional de Fauna Silvestre Barra del Colorado ❻

Road Map E2. 21 miles (34 km) N of Tortuguero. **Tel** 2709-8086. ⛴ from Tortuguero, Puerto Viejo de Sarapiquí, and Pavona. ☐ 8am–4pm daily. ⚲ included with PN Tortuguero.

Connected to Parque Nacional Tortuguero by Caño de Penitencia, this 350-sq-mile (910-sq-km) refuge extends north to the border with Nicaragua. The flooded marshes, teeming rainforest, and vast raffia palm forests are home to an abundant wildlife, but despite this the refuge is virtually untapped as a wilderness destination. Crocodiles as well as birds such as jabiru storks and endangered great green macaws can be spotted, while tapirs, jaguars, and manatees inhabit the deep forests and swamps. The refuge's many rivers have populations of tarpon, snook, and garfish, and lodges catering to fishing enthusiasts are centered around Barra del Colorado at the mouth of Río Colorado.

Parque Nacional Tortuguero ❺

Road Map E2. 32 miles (52 km) N of Puerto Limón. **Tel** 2709-8086. ⛴ from Pavona, Moín, and Caño Blanco. ☐ 6am–6pm daily; last admission: 5pm. ⚲ ⛴

Created to protect the most important nesting site of the green turtle in the Western Hemisphere, the 73-sq-mile (190-sq-km) Tortuguero National Park extends along 14 miles (22 km) of shoreline and 19 miles (30 km) out to sea. The Canal de Tortuguero runs through the park, connecting a labyrinth of deltas, canals, and lagoons.

With 11 distinct life zones ranging from raffia palm forest to herbaceous swamps, the park offers one of the most rewarding nature experiences in the country. Although trails start from the ranger stations at the northern and southern ends of the park, this watery world is best seen by boat: the wide canals allow grandstand wildlife viewing, and silent approaches on the water permit unusually close contact with the fauna. River otters, caimans, and howler, spider, and white-faced monkeys are easily sighted, as are birds such as oropendolas, toucans, and jacamars and other waterfowl. A guide is strongly recommended to avoid getting lost in the waterways and to identify wildlife that might otherwise be missed.

For most visitors, the star attraction is the green turtle, which nests between June and November. Three other species of marine turtles also come ashore throughout the year, although in lesser numbers. Entry to the beach is strictly regulated at night – only two tour groups are allowed each night, escorted by guides from the local cooperative.

Note that there are no roads to the park; access is by boat or small planes that land at Tortuguero village. Local lodges organize guided tours, and Tortuga Lodge (see p264) offers sportfishing.

Environs
The villagers of **Tortuguero**, to the north of the park at the junction of Laguna del Tortuguero and the Canal de Tortuguero, traditionally made their living by lumbering or by culling turtles. Today, tourism is the major source of employment, and locals have learned

MANATEES

The endangered West Indian manatee (Trichechus manatus), or sea cow (see pp70–71), is found in lagoons and coastal habitats. With front flippers and a paddle-like tail, this hairless gray-brown mammal resembles a tuskless walrus. It feeds primarily on aquatic vegetation such as water hyacinths. Spending most of its time submerged, it is rarely seen. However, increasing encounters with manatees in Tortuguero and Barra del Colorado suggest that the population may be increasing.

West Indian manatee (Trichechus manatus)

Jesus Christ lizard, Veragua Rainforest Research & Adventure Park

Veragua Rainforest Research & Adventure Park ❼

Road Map F3. 18 miles (28 km) SW of Puerto Limón. **Tel** 2296-5056. 🚌 *Puerto Limón–Liverpool, then by jeep-taxi.* ⬤ *9am–3pm daily.* 📷 ✔ 🍴 **www**.veraguarainforest.com

This 3,200-acre (1,300-ha) reserve is used for ecological research by INBio, whose laboratory is open to visitors. You can walk through butterfly and frog gardens, view snake and insect exhibits, and hop aboard an aerial tram for a ride downhill to riverside trails, where poison-dart frogs hop about underfoot. Try out the canopy zipline tour or visit the restaurant. The entrance fee includes a guided tour. Visitors driving themselves to the park may need a four-wheel-drive vehicle.

Poison-dart frog, Veragua Rainforest Research & Adventure Park

Aviarios del Caribe Sloth Sanctuary ❽

Road Map F3. 5 miles (8 km) N of Cahuita. **Tel** 2750-0775. 🚌 *from Puerto Limón to Cahuita and taxi from Cahuita.* ⬤ *7am–2:30pm daily.* 📷 ✔ **www**.slothrescue.org

This is the world's only center devoted to sloth research and rescue. The facility began in 1992 with the adoption of an orphaned three-fingered sloth. Many more sloths soon followed and since then, Aviarios Sloth Sanctuary has become a leading research center on sloth ecology. Injured sloths, including those electrocuted while crawling along power lines, are treated at a "slothpital". Many are released into the wild, while others can be seen in enclosures. Visitors are led on guided tours that include an educational learning center, a sloth nursery, and the rehabilitation facilities where two- and three-toed sloths are cared for, alongside agoutis, coatis, monkeys, toucans, and other rescued animals. Trails lead into the 185 acre (75 ha) wildlife refuge composed of rainforest and marshland where caiman, river otter, and other aquatic creatures can be spotted.

Reserva Biológica Hitoy-Cerere ❾

Road Map F3. 28 miles (45 km) S of Puerto Limón and 12 miles (20 km) SW of Hwy 36 at Penshurst. **Tel** 2798-3170. 🚌 *from Puerto Limón to Finca 12, further by jeep-taxi.* ⬤ *8am–5pm daily.* 📷 **www**.sinac.go.cr

Lying near the head of the Río Estrella valley and extending up the western flanks of the Talamanca Mountains, the 38-sq-mile (100-sq-km) Hitoy-Cerere Biological Reserve appeals to hardy hikers and nature lovers. It offers pristine rainforest habitats fed by heavy rainfall. July, August, November, and December are the wettest months, when rivers thunder down the steep slopes. Large mammals thrive amid the dense forests, including all six of Costa Rica's cat species *(see pp62–5).* Lucky visitors might even spot the extremely rare harpy eagle. Note that this isolated refuge offers minimal infrastructure.

Environs
Reserva Selva Bananito, bordering Parque Internacional de La Amistad *(see p227),* protects 5 sq miles (13 sq km) of ecologically sustainable farmland and rainforest at the foothills of the Talamanca Mountains. It offers guided hikes and horseback rides, plus more adrenalin-charged activities, such as waterfall rappeling and a zipline ride to a 30-meter-tall (100-foot) canopy observation platform. A 4WD vehicle is required to get here. Overnight stays in the Caribbean-style lodge are recommended. **Piedmont** is a local organic tropical fruit farm. Botanist Pierre Dubois offers guided tours that let visitors cut banana stems and sample homemade chocolate.

🍽 **Reserva Selva Bananito**
22 miles (35 km) SW of Puerto Limón. **Tel** 2253-8118. 📷 ✔ 🍴 ✔ **www**.selvabananito.com

🏕 **Piedmont**
Penshurst, 22 miles (31 km) S of Puerto Limón. **Tel** 2750-0789. ⬤ *9am–3pm daily.* 📷 ✔ ♿ 🍴 ⛺

Cahuita ❿

Road Map F3. 27 miles (43 km) S of Puerto Limón. 🚶 *5,300.* 🚌 📷 *Festival de la Cultura y el Ambiente Walter Furgerson (Jul); Carnavalito Cahuita (early Dec).*

With its rich Afro-Caribbean heritage, Cahuita (meaning "mahogany point") is Costa Rica's most colorful village. Its inhabitants – a mix of folks with Jamaican and other

One of Parque Nacional Cahuita's many beaches

Afro-Caribbean heritage – live in brightly-painted wooden houses and shacks, some of which stand on stilts over the sandy streets. Unlike many other beach-focused villages, such as neighboring Puerto Viejo, Cahuita has been skipped by the tourist boom and stays true to its laid-back Caribbean island roots. North of the village are the black sands of palm fringed Playa Negra, extending north to the estuary of the Río Estrella and perfect for tidepooling and horseback rides. The Festival de la Cultura y el Ambiente Walter Ferguson, in July, celebrates Cahuita's musical and cultural traditions.

Environs
Tree of Life Wildlife Rescue Center & Botanical Gardens, located toward the north end of Playa Negra, aims to promote conservation. The center

cares for wild creatures that have suffered due to loss of habitat, been injured, or even confiscated as illegal pets. Animals being rehabilitated for release back in to the wild cannot be viewed but others, including howler monkeys, peccaries, and white tailed deer, are on show to the public. There are 12 acres (5 ha) of botanical gardens, with a range of palms and diverse tropical plants.

One of Parque Nacional Cahuita's snakes

🦋 **Tree of Life Wildlife Rescue Center & Botanical Gardens**
2 miles (3 km) N of Cahuita.
Tel 2755-0427. ◯ 9am–3pm Tue–Sun. ◯ mid Apr–May, Sep–Oct. 🈺
www.treeoflifecostarica.com

Parque Nacional Cahuita ⓫

Road Map F3. 27 miles (43 km) S of Puerto Limón. *Tel* 2755-0461. 🚌 *Puerto Limón–Cahuita.* ◯ 6am–5pm daily (Kelly Creek); 8am–4pm Mon–Fri, 7am–5pm Sun (Puerto Vargas). 🈺 at Puerto Vargas ranger station; by donation at Kelly Creek station.

Situated immediately south of Cahuita is this 4-sq-mile (10-sq-km) park. Wildlife abounds, including armadillos, rodent-like agoutis, and anteaters, as well as toucans and green macaws. Crocodile-like caimans can be seen in freshwater rivers, while parrot fish, lobsters, and green turtles swim around a depleted coral reef off Playa Blanca. Swimming off Playa Vargas, farther to the south, is not advisable; waves pummel the long beach where marine turtles nest. A 4-mile (6-km) trail connects Cahuita village's Kelly Creek ranger station to the one at Puerto Vargas. Riptides may be present so check with rangers before swimming. A guide is obligatory for snorkeling.

CARIBBEAN CULTURE

Rastafarian culture is widespread in Cahuita

Distinct in many ways from the Hispanic culture found elsewhere in Costa Rica, the culture of the Caribbean coast has close affinities with the English-speaking Caribbean islands. About one-third of the population trace their bloodline back to black Jamaicans whose own ancestors were

African. They first arrived in Costa Rica's Caribbean lowlands in the late 19th century to work on the Atlantic Railroad and banana plantations. Many people still speak a lilting English-based creole dialect, with parochial phrases familiar to the West Indies. The Latin music of the highlands here is replaced by the mellow riffs of Bob Marley, the Jamaican reggae superstar whose image adorns a lot of buildings in Cahuita. Many young males sport Rafastarian dreadlocks and smoke ganja (marijuana). The spicy local cuisine *(see p270)* is also distinct, not least for its use of chilies and tongue-searing peppers. Jerk (spiced and smoked) chicken, rondon ("rundown") of mackerel cooked in coconut milk, and fried sponge dumplings called johnnycakes all hark back to Caribbean island culture. *What Happen: A Folk History of Costa Rica's Talamanca Coast* and *Wa'apin Man*, both by Paula Palmer, provide fascinating accounts of the lives of early Afro-Caribbean settlers.

Puerto Viejo de Talamanca ⑫

Road Map F3. 8 miles (13 km) S of Cahuita. 🏠 *5,000.* 🚌 ℹ️ *2750-0398 (Talamanca Association for Ecotourism & Conservation/ATEC).* www.ateccr.org

One of the Caribbean coast's best surfing areas, Puerto Viejo de Talamanca is also a must-visit destination for offbeat travelers in Central America. Little more than a collection of stilt-legged shacks a decade ago, it has since expanded rapidly. Although electricity arrived in 1996, followed by a paved road in 2001, the village retains an earthy, laid-back quality.

Surfers come here between December and March to test their skills against the reef break La Salsa Brava, which can attain heights of up to 21 ft (6.5 m). The palm-fringed black sands of **Playa Negra** curl north from town. North of the beach, **Finca La Isla Botanical Garden** is an excellent place to explore the coastal rainforest along well-kept trails. Bromeliads are a specialty of this 12-acre (5-ha) garden, which also grows exotic fruits and ornamental plants. A self-guided booklet is available.

Puerto Viejo has some of the best budget accommodation in Costa Rica, as well as numerous outstanding eateries. Open-air bars and discos

Detail of a statue at a lodge in Puerto Viejo

come alive at night, with revelers spilling onto the sands.

Environs
A string of surfing beaches – **Playa Cocles**, **Playa Uva**, and **Playa Chiquita** – runs south from Puerto Viejo to the hamlet of Manzanillo. A paved road lined with hotels and *cabinas (see p245)* lies along the shore, with forested hills rising inland. **Crazy Monkey Canopy Ride** whisks you between treetops on a zipline. The **Mariposario** butterfly garden sits on a ridge overlooking Playa Uva. Public transport in these areas is limited, but bicycles, scooters, and cars can be rented in Puerto Viejo.

🦋 Finca La Isla Botanical Garden
0.5 mile (1 km) NW of Puerto Viejo. **Tel** *2750-0046.* ⏰ *10am–4pm Fri–Mon.* 💶 ✅ www.costaricacaribbean.com

Crazy Monkey Canopy Ride
8 miles (13 km) S of Puerto Viejo. **Tel** *2271-3000.* 💶 ✅ *8am & 2pm daily.* www.almondsandcorals.com

TUCUXI DOLPHIN
The rare *tucuxí* dolphin *(Sotalia fluviatilis)* – pronounced "too koo shee" – lives in the freshwater rivers and lagoons of Gandoca-Manzanillo and similar environments. This small species grows to 6 ft (2 m) in length and is blue-gray with a pink belly and long snout. It is shy and generally avoids boats, but is known to interact with its larger sea-going cousin, the bottle-nosed dolphin.

Tucuxí dolphin

🦋 Mariposario
4 miles (6 km) S of Puerto Viejo. **Tel** *2750-0086.* ⏰ *8am–4pm daily.* 💶 ✅

Refugio Nacional de Vida Silvestre Gandoca-Manzanillo ⑬

Road Map F4. 8 miles (13 km) S of Puerto Viejo. 🚌 *from Puerto Viejo de Talamanca.* ⏰ *8am–4pm daily.* 💶 🍴 ♻️ 🅿️

Enclosing a mosaic of habitats, Gandoca-Manzanillo Wildlife Refuge is a mixed-use park occupied by settlements whose inhabitants live in harmony with the environment. Created in 1985, this 32-sq-mile (83-sq-km) reserve extends out to sea, protecting a coral reef and 17 sq miles (44 sq km) of marine habitat where several species of turtles breed. The Costa Rican conservation society **Asociación ANAI** runs a volunteer program for those who are keen to assist with research and protection of

The beach at Refugio Nacional de Vida Silvestre Gandoca-Manzanillo

turtles. On land, the refuge has mangrove swamp, rare *yolillo* palm swamp and *cativo* forest, and tropical rainforest, all swarming with wildlife. Manatees and *tucuxi* inhabit the lagoons and estuaries. The waters are also important breeding grounds for sharks, game fish, and lobsters.

A coastal trail and several inland ones – often overgrown and muddy – afford unparalleled opportunities for spotting mammals and an astounding diversity of birds, amphibians, and reptiles. The coast trail leads to Punta Mona (Monkey Point) and **Punta Mona Center**, an educational institution and organic farm.

Environs

Aquamor offers scuba diving and snorkeling, plus kayaking and a dolphin-spotting trip into Gandoca-Manzanillo Wildlife Refuge. A local cooperative, **Guias MANT**, also offers guided trips into the reserve, plus fishing and snorkeling. **Finca Lomas**, run by ANAI, is an experimental farm inside the refuge.

Inside a house in the Reserva Indígena KeköLdi

Asociación ANAI
Manzanillo. *Tel 2224-3570.*
www.anaicr.org

🍴 **Punta Mona Center**
3 miles (5 km) SE of Manzanillo.
Tel 2614-5735. ⬜ *8am–5pm daily.*
📷 🚲 🚹 http://puntamona.org

Aquamor
Manzanillo. *Tel 2759-9012.*
⬜ *7am–6pm daily.* **www**.
greencoast.com/aquamor.htm

Guias MANT
Manzanillo. *Tel 2759-9064.*
⬜ *8am–5pm daily.*

Indigenous Reserves ⑭

Road Map F4. 🚌 to Bribri, then by jeep-taxi. 🛈 ATEC: 2750-0398; **www**.ateccr.org; Red Talamanca Ecoturismo Comunitario: **www**.sitiviajes.com/red_talamana.html

The indigenous Bribri and Cabécar peoples inhabit a series of fragmented reserves on the Caribbean slopes of

Green iguanas raised on Reserva Indígena KeköLdi

the Talamanca Mountains, surviving primarily through subsistence agriculture. These two related groups have managed to retain much of their culture, native languages, animistic dances, and shamanistic practices *(see pp30–31)*.

The most accessible reserve is the **Reserva Indígena KeköLdi**, spread across 14 sq miles (36 sq km) in the hills southwest of Puerto Viejo. The reserve's local conservation projects include a farm where green iguanas are bred. The farm is located off the main road near Hone Creek, a 30-minute walk from Puerto Viejo. Farther south, beyond the regional administrative center of Bribri, is the **Reserva Indígena Talamanca-Bribri**. Centered on Shiroles, 11 miles (18 km) southwest of Bribri, this reserve encompasses the Valle de Talamanca, a broad basin carpeted by plantations of bananas. Trips to communities within the reserve are offered by

Albergue Finca Educativa Indígena, an educational center and tourist lodge in Shiroles.

From Bambú, 6 miles (10 km) west of Bribri, a trip by dug-out canoe down Río Yorkín leads to **Reserva Indígena Yorkín**, where visitors housed in traditional lodgings gain an appreciation of indigenous culture.

Another reserve worth visiting in this area is the **Reserva Indígena Talamanca-Cabécar**, reached from Shiroles along rugged dirt roads that push up the valley of Río Coén. This remote settlement of the San José Cabécar is considered the most important center of shamanism and Indian culture. Guided hikes and overnight visits to the reserves are arranged by the Talamanca Association for Ecotourism and Conservation (ATEC) in Puerto Viejo de Talamanca, or by Red Talamanca Ecoturismo Comunitario. Note that the only place where a permit to visit is not required is the iguana farm in the Reserva Indígena KeköLdi.

SHAMANISM

The Bribri and Cabécar have a spirit-filled, animist vision of the world in which the shaman-healer – called *awá* by the Bribri and *jawá* by the Cabécar – is the central authority in the community. Shamanic tools include magic stones, *seteé* (medicine collars), *uLú* (healing canes), and a whole pharmacy of medicinal herbs. These are used along with ritual song and dance to cure a person who is ill, or to restore harmony within the community.

Instrument used in ritual music

A Bribri shaman feather

THE SOUTHERN ZONE

rom world-class surfing and sportfishing to hardy mountain hikes and scuba diving with hammerhead sharks, Costa Rica's remote south is a setting for splendid adventures. Pre-Columbian relics lie smothered in jungles that offer some of the finest wildlife viewing in the nation. The country's largest indigenous communities live in isolated mountain retreats in this region.

Spanish conquistadors marched into the region to conquer the nomadic Chibchas and Diquis tribes, and to search in vain, as it turned out, for gold. The coastal area remained isolated and neglected throughout the colonial period and beyond. In 1938, the United Fruit Company arrived, and planted bananas across the valleys of the Sierpe and Coto-Colorado Rivers; banana plantations are still the economic mainstay of the region. To the north, the shore is hemmed by the thickly forested Fila Costanera Mountains, while waves crash upon gray-sand beaches. Farther south, the Peninsula de Osa is deluged with rains that feed a huge swathe of emerald green rainforest. The peninsula hooks around Golfo Dulce – a calm bay attracting dolphins and whales, as well as sportfishing boats from the town of Golfito. Isla del Caño floats on the horizon. Considered sacred by pre-Columbian tribes, it contains ancient burial sites. To the southwest, uninhabited Isla del Coco is surrounded by teeming sealife.

The Talamancas, in the northeast of the region, rise to 12,530 ft (3,820 m) at the top of Cerro Chirripó. Here, the Boruca and Guaymí peoples struggle to maintain their cultures in remote communities threatened by logging and other commercial interests. Thick forests carpet the rugged peaks, forming a virginal environment where jaguars, tapirs, and other endangered species thrive. Between the two mountain ranges, the fertile Valle de El General is a breadbasket of agricultural produce.

A hiker surveying the vast expanse of Parque Nacional Chirripó

◁ A school of jackfish circling round in the waters off Isla del Coco

Exploring the Southern Zone

The jungled shore of the Southern Zone is peppered with some of the country's finest beaches, including those at Bahía Drake, Zancudo, and Parque Nacional Marino Ballena. Surfers flock to Dominical and Pavones, while Golfito is a base for sportfishing. Whales and dolphins cavort in offshore waters, especially around Isla del Caño, while experienced divers can swim with hammerhead and whale sharks at remote Isla del Coco. Along the coast lie the rainforests of Parque Nacional Corcovado (on the Peninsula de Osa) and lesser-known sites such as the forest reserves Terraba-Sierpe and Barú. To the north, Chirripó offers an exciting hike to the summit.

Kayaking in Reserva Forestal del Humedad Nacional Terraba-Sierpe

KEY

▬▬	Pan-American Highway
▬▬	Major road
▬▬	Secondary road
▭▭	Minor road
▬▬	International border
▬▬	Provincial border
△	Peak

SIGHTS AT A GLANCE

Lush vegetation fringing aquamarine waters at Bahía Drake

Colorful blooms outside a house near Parque Nacional Chirripó

GETTING AROUND

Palmar, Puerto Jiménez, Golfito, and Ciudad Neily have domestic airports, while charter planes serve smaller airstrips. Major tourist sights can be reached from San José by long-distance bus. Local buses are the main form of transportation in this region, although more remote sights are accessible only by jeep-taxi or cheap but uncomfortable *colectivos* (pickup trucks).

Highway 2 (the Pan-American Highway) is paved, as is Highway 16 through the Valle de Coto Brus, but most connecting routes are potholed dirt roads that are covered with mud after rains. Many nature lodges on the Osa Peninsula and the Golfo Dulce shores can be reached only by water-taxi.

Winding road in the valley of Cerro de la Muerte

Cerro de la Muerte ❶

Road Map D4. 31 miles (50 km) S of Cartago. 🚌 *San José–San Isidro.*

Cerro Buenavista is popularly called Cerro de la Muerte (Mountain of Death), in remembrance of the people who died of exposure while taking their produce to San José before the Pan-Am Highway was built across it.

The highway, connecting San José with the Valle de El General, passes below the actual summit (11,500 ft/ 3,500 m), which is buffeted by high winds. The vegetation is Andean *páramo* (grassland), with species that have adapted to the cold, boggy conditions. When the clouds part, there are superlative views.

The **Príncipe de la Paz**, a 10-m (30-ft) high statue of Christ, stands overlooking the road just after the descent from Cerro de la Muerte, about 4 miles (6 km) from San Isidro. Designed by the Costa Rican sculptor Francisco Ulloa, the statue was built as a symbol of peace in 1979, during the Nicaraguan civil war. Avoid this stretch of the Pan-Am Highway at night.

The **Mirador Vista del Valle** has a mountainside zipline tour with seven platforms.

🎿 **Mirador Vista del Valle**
Km 119, 5 miles (8 km) N of San Isidro. ℹ 2200-5465. ◷ 8am–5pm daily. 🖼 **www.**valledelgeneral.com

San Isidro de El General ❷

Road Map E4. 51 miles (82 km) S of Cartago. 🚶 *41,200.* 🚌 ℹ *Selva Mar, Calle 1 and Aves 2/4, 2771-4582.* 🎎 *Día de San Isidro Labrador (May 15).* **www.** exploringcostarica.com

The peaceful market town of San Isidro de El General sits at the base of Cerro de la Muerte and is the administrative center for Valle de El General. For tourists, it serves mainly as a refueling stop and as a convenient base for exploring Chirripó and Parque Internacional La Amistad. The only sight of interest in town is the modern, concrete cathedral. Built in 1967 on the east side of the plaza, the cathedral has stained-glass windows and a simple altar, which is dominated by a mural of San Isidro Labrador, patron saint of San Isidro.

Environs
Bird-lovers are in for a treat at **Los Cusingos Neotropical Bird Sanctuary**. Administered by the Tropical Science Center of Costa Rica, this 350-acre (142-ha) refuge for birds was founded by the eminent American ornithologist Dr. Alexander Skutch (1904–2004), co-author of the authoritative volume *Birds of Costa Rica*. More than 300 bird species have been noted in this sanctuary. Also of note are the Indian petroglyphs and Skutch's former home, maintained as if he still lived there.

The striking modern cathedral of San Isidro de El General

🦜 **Los Cusingos Neotropical Bird Sanctuary**
Quizarrá de Pérez Zeledón, 9 miles (14 km) SE of San Isidro. ℹ *2253- 3267 (Tropical Science Center).* ◷ *7am–4pm daily (to 1pm Sun), by appt.* 🖼 🎥 🌐 **www.**cct.or.cr

Works of art at the Museo el Pelicano, Valle del Río Chirripó

Valle del Río Chirripó ❸

Road Map E4. 6 miles (10 km) E of San Isidro. 🚌 *from San Isidro.*

This valley is scythed from the Talamanca Mountains by the turbulent Río Chirripó. Trout swim in the river's waters, and rapids provide kayaking thrills. A great place to stop in the valley is the fruit-and-coffee *finca* **Rancho La Botija** (*see p267*), a popular destination for locals on weekends. Its attractions include an antique sugarcane mill, restaurant, and accommodation. Nearby, the roadside **Piedra de los Indios** (Rock of the Indians) bears pre-Columbian petroglyphs as well as some modern graffiti.

The scenery grows more dramatic and the climate more alpine as the road climbs into the mountains to reach **San Gerardo de Rivas**. Perching over the river gorge, this hamlet is the gateway to Parque Nacional Chirripó. Close by, **Museo el Pelicano** is a curiosity for its inspired stone and timber art by coffee farmer Rafael Elizondo Basulta. Nearby, **Aguas Termales** has natural thermal pools popular with local families seeking to counter the chilly mountain

Variety of flora at the Chirripó Cloudbridge Reserve

air. A steep track, strewn with boulders, leads past the trailhead to the summit of Cerro Chirripó and ends at the **Chirripó Cloudbridge Reserve**. The locally endemic parrot mountain snake can be seen at this private reserve; there are also some good hiking trails.

🏛 **Museo el Pelicano**
Canaan, 10 miles (16 km) E of San Isidro. *Tel* 2742-5050.
◯ *8am–8pm daily.* ⏸

🔥 **Aguas Termales**
0.5 mile (0.8 km) NW of San Gerardo. *Tel* 2742-5210.
◯ *7am–6pm daily.* 🌄

✹ **Chirripó Cloudbridge Reserve**
San Gerardo de Rivas, 12 miles (20 km) E of San Isidro. ◯ *8am–4pm daily.* 🌄 📷 www.cloudbridge.org

Parque Nacional Chirripó ❹

See pp228–9.

Parque Internacional La Amistad ❺

Road Map F4. 🚌 to Guácimo, 66 miles (107 km) SE of San Isidro, then by jeep-taxi. 🛈 Estación Altamira HQ, 31 miles (50 km) SE of Buenos Aires, 2730-9846.
◯ *8am–4pm daily.* 🌄 📷 ♿ 🅰

Extending into Panama, the International Friendship Park is contiguous with other protected areas that form the Reserva de la Biosfera La Amistad (Amistad Biosphere Reserve). It sprawls over

675 sq miles (1,750 sq km) of the rugged Talamanca Mountains, and ranges from elevations of 490 ft (150 m) to 11,650 ft (3,550 m) atop Cerro Kamuk. This enormous park spans eight "life zones," from low montane rainforest to swampy high-altitude grassland. The diverse wildlife includes five cat species and the endangered harpy eagle.

With permits and a guide, experienced hikers can cross the Talamancas on a trail that starts from the town of Buenos Aires, 38 miles (61 km) southeast of San Isidro, and leads to Reserva Indígena Talamanca Cabécar *(see p221)*.

The main ranger station, a hostel, and an ecology exhibition are at **Estación Altamira**, the recommended entry point. All the official access points require 4WD.

Environs
East of Buenos Aires, **Reserva Biológica Durika**, a 3-sq-mile (9-sq-km) forest reserve, is a self-sufficient holistic community offering guided hikes, vegetarian meals, and rustic

Ferns, Las Cruces Biological Station

accommodation. At **Finca Coffea Diversa**, below Estación Altamira, visitors can wander among rows of flowering shrubs and more than 200 coffee bush species. The rural communities of Biolley, Carmén, and Altamira are enlivened with ceramic murals.

✹ **Reserva Biológica Durika**
11 miles (18 km) N of Buenos Aires. *Tel* 2730-0657. 📷 ⏸ ♿
www.durika.org

🌸 **Finca Coffea Diversa**
Altamira, 0.5 miles (1 km) W of Estación Altamira. ◯ *8am–5pm daily.* 🌄 www.coffeadiversa.net

Las Cruces Biological Station ❻

Road Map F5. 4 miles (6 km) S of San Vito. *Tel* 2773-4004. 🚌 San Vito–Ciudad Neily. ◯ *8am–5pm daily.* 🌄 📷 ⏸ 🅰 ♿ www.ots.ac.cr

One of the world's leading tropical research and educational centers, Las Cruces is run by the Organization of Tropical Studies (OTS). The center is surrounded by a 580-acre (235-ha) mid-elevation forest, in which an incredible diversity of birds and mammals can be seen along 6 miles (10 km) of trails. Clouds envelop the reserve, nourishing the many ferns, palms, bromeliads, and orchids laid out in the 25 acre (10-ha) **Wilson Botanical Gardens**, designed by distinguished Brazilian landscaper Roberto Burle-Marx. A riot of color in even the rainiest of weather, the collection extends to greenhouses, where varieties of tropical plants are propagated.

PRE-COLUMBIAN PETROGLYPHS

Costa Rica's pre-Columbian peoples left their legacy etched on boulders. Significant finds include Guayabo National Monument *(see pp154–5)*, where jaguars, snakes, frogs, and birds of prey symbolize creation, wealth, and power. Piedra de Los Indios and Rancho La Bojita, both in the Valle del Río Chirripó *(see p226)*, have interesting petroglyphs, including a crude map of the Talamanca region.

Petroglyph

Parque Nacional Chirripó ❹

Red-tailed hawk

Costa Rica's highest mountain, Cerro Chirripó (12,530 ft/3,820 m) is enfolded in the 194-sq-mile (502-sq-km) Chirripó National Park. Part of the Amistad Biosphere Reserve, the park protects three distinct "life zones" in rugged, virgin territory where wildlife flourishes with minimal interference from humans. As many as 60 percent of all wildlife species in Costa Rica are found here, including all six types of wild cats *(see pp62–5)* and many endemic species of flora and fauna. Glacial activity some 35,000 years ago carved small U-shaped valleys and deposited moraines, still visible today. Spring is the best time for hiking, although weather is always unpredictable, with frequent fog and rain.

COSTA RICA

The Southern Zone

PACIFIC OCEAN

KEY

☐ Parque Nacional Chirripó

▨ Area of park illustrated

CORDILLERA DE TALAMANCA

Cerro Ura
10,900

Río Urán

Río Chirripó Pacífico

Río Blanco

●Herradura

San Gerardo de Rivas

Río Bo

Río Chirripó

Refugio
Llano Bonito

SAN ISIDRO
DE EL GENERAL

Cloud Forest
Almost constantly shrouded in mist, the forests above 8,200 ft (2,500 m) are typified by dwarf blueberry trees festooned with epiphytes and mosses. Monkeys and quetzals are found in plenty.

The ranger station in San Gerardo de Rivas has a trail map. Visitors must report here before setting out on the hike to the summit.

Sendero Termometro, leading into cloud forest, is one of the steepest stretches of the trail.

HIKING IN THE PARK

Most visitors hike to the summit along a well-marked trail that ascends 8,200 ft (2,500 m) from the trailhead, near San Gerardo de Rivas. The 20-mile (32-km) hike to the top and back normally takes two days, with an overnight stay near the summit. Hire guide-porters in San Gerardo. An alternative route is from Herradura via Cerro Uran.

Hikers in Parque Nacional Chirripó

KEY

═══ Minor road

▬ ▬ Park boundary

▬ ▬ Trail

🔆 Viewpoint

ℹ️ Visitor information

△ Peak

Serene Lago San Juan, Parque Nacional Chirripó

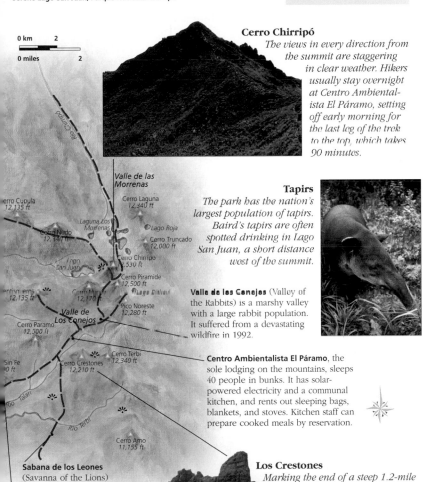

Cerro Chirripó
The views in every direction from the summit are staggering in clear weather. Hikers usually stay overnight at Centro Ambientalista El Páramo, setting off early morning for the last leg of the trek to the top, which takes 90 minutes.

Tapirs
The park has the nation's largest population of tapirs. Baird's tapirs are often spotted drinking in Lago San Juan, a short distance west of the summit.

Valle de los Conejos (Valley of the Rabbits) is a marshy valley with a large rabbit population. It suffered from a devastating wildfire in 1992.

Centro Ambientalista El Páramo, the sole lodging on the mountains, sleeps 40 people in bunks. It has solar-powered electricity and a communal kitchen, and rents out sleeping bags, blankets, and stoves. Kitchen staff can prepare cooked meals by reservation.

Sabana de los Leones (Savanna of the Lions) is named for the pumas frequently seen on the southern slopes.

Monte Sin Fe (Faithless Mountain) is reached by a steep uphill section called La Cuesta del Agua.

Los Crestones
Marking the end of a steep 1.2-mile (2-km) long climb called La Cuesta de los Arrepentidos (Repentants' Hill), these dramatic vertical rock formations were considered a sacred site by pre-Columbian Indians.

Valle de las Morrenas

Cerro Cupula
12,135 ft

Cerro Laguna
12,340 ft

Cerro Nudo
12,340 ft

Laguna Los Morrenas

Lago Roja

Cerro Truncado
12,080 ft

Cerro Chirripó
12,530 ft

Rio Chirripó

Lago San Juan

Cerro Piramide
12,500 ft

Lago Ditkevi

Pico Noreste
12,280 ft

Valle de Los Conejos

Fantismierro
12,135 ft

Cerro Hturin
12,170 ft

Cerro Paramo
12,500 ft

Cerro Terbi
12,340 ft

Sin Fe
ft

Cerro Crestones
12,210 ft

Rio Talari

Rio Terbi

Cerro Amo
11,155 ft

0 km 2

0 miles 2

Zipline tour in Refugio Nacional de Vida Silvestre Barú

Refugio Nacional de Vida Silvestre Barú ❼

Road Map D4. 2 miles (3 km) N of Dominical. **Tel** 2787-0003. 🚌 Dominical–Quepos. ⏱ 7am– 5:30pm daily. 📷 🎫 ♿ 🍴 🏠 ☕ www.haciendabaru.com

A former cattle ranch and cocoa plantation, the 815-acre (330-ha) Hacienda Barú has varied habitats, including 2 miles (3 km) of beach that draw nesting hawksbill and olive ridley turtles. Turtle eggs are collected and incubated in a nursery for release. Barú has more than 310 bird species and several mammal species, such as jaguarundis and the arboreal kinkajous. There are butterfly and orchid gardens. Guided tree-climbing, canopy tours, kayak trips through the mangroves, hikes, horseback rides, and overnight stays in treetop tents are also on offer.

Dominical ❽

Road Map D4. 18 miles (29 km) SW of San Isidro de El General. 🏛 1,400. 🚌

The ultimate surfer's destination, this village thrives on the backpacker trade: the community consists mostly of foreign surfers who settled here. Its long beach extends south from the mouth of Río Barú to the fishing hamlet of Dominicalito. Experienced surfers are drawn by the beach, reef, and rivermouth breaks, but non-surfers should beware of the riptides.

Environs
The thickly forested mountains south of Dominical, the Fila Costanera, are also called **Escaleras** (Staircase). Tour companies in Dominical offer hikes, plus all-terrain-vehicle and horseback trips into the mountains, where each Friday night (Dec–Apr), US expat Harley "Toby" Toberman shows movies at **Cinema Escaleras**, his private villa. Highway 243 winds through the Río Barú valley, connecting Dominical to San Isidro. Tour companies offer trips to **Don Lulo's Nauyaca Waterfalls**, a dramatic, two-tiered waterfall that is a 4-mile (6-km) horseback ride away from the highway. Nearby, **Parque Reptilandia** exhibits dozens of snakes and other reptile species, includ- ing a komodo dragon from Indo- nesia. Guided tours offer an insight into reptilian behavior.

Signage for RNVS Rancho Merced

🎬 **Cinema Escaleras**
1.5 miles (2.5 km) NE of Escaleras. **Tel** 2787-8065. ⏱ from 5pm Fri.

🎬 **Don Lulo's Nauyaca Waterfalls**
Platanillo, 6 miles (10 km) E of Dominical. **Tel** 2787-0541. 📷 🎫 8am and 2pm.

🦎 **Parque Reptilandia**
Platanillo. **Tel** 2787-8007. ⏱ 9am–9:30pm daily. 📷 🎫

Parque Nacional Marino Ballena ❾

Road Map D4. 11 miles (18 km) S of Dominical. **Tel** 2786-5392. 🚌 from Dominical. ⏱ 6am–6pm daily. 📷 🍴 🅰 www.sinac.go.cr

Created to protect the nation's largest coral reef, Whale Marine National Park stretches for 8 miles (13 km) along the shore of Bahía de Coronado, and extends 9 miles (14 km) out to sea. It is named after the humpback whales that gather in the warm waters to breed in the dry season between December and April.

The park incorporates **Las Tres Hermanas** and **Isla Ballena**, which are important nesting sites for frigate birds, brown boobies, and pelicans. Hawksbill and olive ridley turtles nest on the palm- fringed beaches. Kayaking and scuba diving trips can be arranged.

Environs
To the north, **Refugio Nacional de Vida Silvestre Rancho Merced** offers city- slickers a chance to play cowhand; it also functions as a wildlife refuge. Nearby, **Reserva Biológica Oro Verde**, a family-run farm in the Fila Tinamaste Mountains, is known for its birding. Inland, the twin hamlets of **Tortuga Abajo** and **Ojochal** make a good base for exploring the area; Ojochal has two outstanding restaurants. Sustainably oper- ated, **La Cusinga Lodge** offers great wildlife on its trails.

🐴 **Refugio Nacional de Vida Silvestre Rancho Merced**
Uvita, 11 miles (18 km) S of Dominical. **Tel** 8861-5147. 🎫 ☕ www.ranchomerced.com

🐴 **Reserva Biológica Oro Verde**
2 miles (3 km) NE of Uvita. **Tel** 2743-8072. 🎫 🍴 ☕ www.uvita. info/uvita/oro-verde-nature-reserve

🏨 **La Cusinga Lodge**
3 miles (5 km) S of the Uvita bridge, between Km 166 and Km 167. **Tel** 2770-2549. 🎫 🍴 ☕ www.lacusingalodge.com

Surfers wading into the sea at the beach at Dominical

For hotels and restaurants in this region see pp264–7 and pp284–5

Costa Rica's Tropical Flowers

A luxuriant hothouse of biodiversity, Costa Rica nurtures over 15,000 known plant species, including 800 types of ferns. Varieties of tropical flowers such as cannas, plumerias, and begonias flourish in the warm and humid regions, as do bromeliads and other epiphytes, which draw moisture and oxygen from the air. Cacti are found on the parched lowlands, while stunted dwarf forests and vivid clusters of pink, white, and lilac impatiens grow at higher elevations. Flowering trees color the tropical forests: the poinciana flames with vermilion blossoms, and the jacaranda drops its violet-blue, bell-shaped blooms to form spectacular carpets in spring.

Orchid bloom

Heliconias *are known for their unusual bracts. The lobster-claw heltconia (right) has a yellow-tipped red bract. Costa Rica's 30 native species of heliconia thrive in areas with plenty of moisture.*

Bracts are flowerheads atop huge stems that can grow up to 25 ft (8 m).

Large leaves are typical of heliconias, of which the banana plant is a member.

Passion flowers *emanate a foul smell to attract pollinators, especially Heliconiinae butterflies.*

The Aristolochia, *or "Dutchman's pipe," gives off a fetid odor resembling that of rotting flesh. This draws flies, its principal pollinators.*

Anthuriums *have a distinctive heart-shaped spathe – usually red, white, or greenish – from which the flower spike protrudes.*

Ginger lilies *have large, hyacinth-like flowers rich in nectar. Introduced from Asia, these shoulder-high plants are common in landscaped gardens.*

Bromeliads *collect water in their tightly wrapped, thick, waxy leaves. Falling leaf matter decays inside this whorl, providing nutrients for the plant and creating a self-contained ecosystem.*

The bird of paradise *flowers from a dramatic spathe with bright orange sepals and vivid blue petals. Set at right angles to the stem, the spathe looks like a bird's head.*

ORCHIDS

More than 1,400 species of orchids grow in Costa Rica, from sea level to the heights of Chirripó *(see pp228–9).* The greatest numbers are found below 6,000 ft (1,830 m). Orchids range from the 0.03-inch (1-mm) wide liverwort orchid *(Platystele jungermannioides),* the world's smallest flower, to others with pendulous 3-ft (1-m) long petals. All orchids have three petals and three sepals. Some have evolved unique features to attract specific pollinators: for example, the markings on certain orchids are visible only to insects that can see in the ultraviolet spectrum.

Detail of a mural showing various orchids

Reserva Indígena Boruca ⑩

Road Map E5. 22 miles (35 km) SW of Buenos Aires. ⊞ *from Buenos Aires*. 🎭 *Fiesta de los Diablitos (Dec 31–Jan 2).*

This is just one of several indigenous reserves – inhabited by the Boruca and Bribri – in the mountains hemming the Valle de El General. Located in the Fila Sinancra Mountains, the reserve is known for its Fiesta de los Diablitos, as well as its carved *jícaras* (gourds) and balsawood *máscaras* (masks). The women use traditional backstrap looms to weave cotton purses and shawls. The ridgetop drive to the hamlet of **Boruca** offers great views of the Río Terraba gorge. Local culture is showcased in the **Museo Comunitario Boruca**.

Reserva Indígena Térraba and **Reserva Indígena Curré** flank the Boruca reserve. **Reserva Indígena Cabagra**, home to the Bribri, can be accessed from the town of Brujo, 7 miles (11 km) southeast of Buenos Aires. With visitors demonstrating a growing interest in indigenous cultures, these remote communities are gradually opening up to tourism.

🏛 **Museo Comunitario Boruca**
Boruca, 25 miles (40 km) SW of Buenos Aires. *Tel 2730-1673.* ◯ *9am–4pm daily.* 🖼

Palmar ⑪

Road Map E5. 78 miles (125 km) SE of San Isidro de El General. 🏃 *9,900.* ✈ ⊞

Sitting at the foot of the Río Terraba valley, at the intersection of Costanera Sur and the Pan-Am Highway, Palmar is the service center for the region. The town straddles Río Terraba, which flows west through the wide Valle de Diquis. Pre-Columbian *esferas de piedra* (stone spheres) and a centenarian steam locomotive are displayed in the plaza of Palmar Sur. Palmar Norte is the town's modern quarter.

Reserva Forestal del Humedad Nacional Terraba-Sierpe

Reserva Forestal del Humedad Nacional Terraba-Sierpe ⑫

Road Map E5. 11 miles (18 km) W of Palmar. 🚤 ℹ *2788-1212 (Tours Gaviota de Osa).* www.uvita. info/uvita/oro-verde-nature-reserve

Created to protect the nation's largest stretch of mangrove forest and swamp, the Terraba-Sierpe National Humid Forest Reserve covers an area of 85 sq miles (220 sq km) between the deltas of the Sierpe and Terraba rivers. Countless channels criss-cross this vitally important ecosystem, which fringes 25 miles (40 km) of coastline.

Visitors kayaking in these quiet channels can see a variety of wildlife, including basilisk lizards, iguanas, crocodiles, and caimans, as well as monkeys, coatis and crab-eating raccoons. The birding opportunities are also excellent. Guided boat and

kayak tours are offered from Sierpe, 9 miles (14 km) south of Palmar.

Reserva Biológica Isla del Caño ⑬

Road Map D5. 12 miles (19 km) W of Bahía Drake. ℹ *2735-5036 (PN Corcovado).* 🚤 *tours from Bahia Drake, Manuel Antonio & Dominical.* ◯ *8am–4pm daily.* 🖼 www.sinac.go.cr

Thrust from the sea by tectonic forces, the 805-acre (325-ha) uninhabited Isla del Caño was named a protected reserve in 1976, along with 10 sq miles (26 sq km) of surrounding waters. Today, it is administered as part of Parque Nacional Corcovado *(see p239)*. In the past, the island was considered to be sacred by the pre-Columbian Diquis peoples.

The coral-colored beaches are great for sunbathing. In the shallows, coral reefs teem with lobsters and fish, while dolphins, whales, and manta rays swim in the warm waters farther out. Diving is permitted in designated zones *(see p300)*. Terrestrial wildlife is relatively limited, although the lucky hiker might come across four-eyed foxes, brown boobies, and ospreys.

Mossy pre-Columbian tombs and granite *esferas* (spheres) are scattered along a trail running from the beachfront ranger hut to a lookout point. The trail winds past milk trees *(Brosimum utile)*, named for their drinkable milky latex.

Overnight stays are not permitted. Lodges in the Bahía Drake area *(see p238)* offer day trips and diving.

FIESTA DE LOS DIABLITOS

At midnight on December 31, the Boruca gather to reenact the war between their ancestors and the Spanish conquis-

Borúcas in devil masks

tadors. At the sound of a conch shell, men dressed in burlap sacking and devil masks pursue a fellow tribesman dressed as a bull. The *diablitos* (devils) drink *chicha* (corn beer) and perform theatrical skits recalling tribal events. After three days, the bull is symbolically killed, metaphorically freeing the tribe from colonial repression.

The Mangroves of Coastal Costa Rica

Costa Rica's shores contain five of the world's 65 species of mangroves – black, buttonwood, red, tea, and white. Mangroves are woody halophytes – plants able to withstand immersion in saltwater – and form swampy forests in areas inundated by tides. These communities are of vital importance to the maritime ecosystem, fostering a wealth of

Crab found in mangroves

wildlife. The tangled roots buffer the action of waves, preventing coastal erosion. They also filter out the silt washed down by turbulent rivers: the accumulated mud extends the land out to sea. Threatened by the country's coastal development, this fragile ecosystem is now legally protected, with the Terraba-Sierpe reserve being the largest tract.

THE MANGROVE ECOSYSTEM

Mangroves grow in mud so dense that there is little oxygen, and nutrients supplied by decomposing leaf litter lie close to the surface. Hence, most plants develop interlocking stilt roots that rise above the water to draw in oxygen and food.

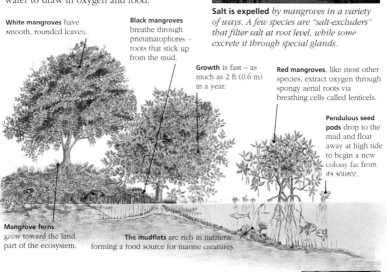

Salt is expelled *by mangroves in a variety of ways. A few species are "salt-excluders" that filter salt at root level, while some excrete it through special glands.*

White mangroves have smooth, rounded leaves.

Black mangroves breathe through pneumatophores – roots that stick up from the mud.

Growth is fast – as much as 2 ft (0.6 m) in a year.

Red mangroves, like most other species, extract oxygen through spongy aerial roots via breathing cells called lenticels.

Pendulous seed pods drop to the mud and float away at high tide to begin a new colony far from its source.

Mangrove ferns grow toward the land part of the ecosystem.

The mudflats are rich in nutrients, forming a food source for marine creatures.

THE RICH FAUNA OF THE MANGROVES

The microorganisms that grow in the nutrient-rich muds foster the growth of larger creatures such as shrimps and other crustaceans, which in turn attract various species of mammals, reptiles, and birds.

Aquatic nurseries *for oysters, sponges, and numerous fish species, including sharks and stingrays, thrive in the tannin-stained waters. The roots protect baby caimans and crocodiles from predators.*

Larger species, *such as raccoons, coyotes, snakes, and wading birds forage for small lizards and crabs.*

Birds, *such as frigate birds and pelicans, and endemic species such as the yellow mangrove warbler roost atop mangroves.*

Peninsula de Osa ⑭

Scarlet macaw

Washed by warm Pacific waters on three sides, the isolated Osa Peninsula curls around the Golfo Dulce. The peninsula was a center for the pre-Columbian Diquis culture, whose skill as goldsmiths sent Spanish conquistadors on a futile search for fabled gold mines. Deluged by year-round rains, much of this rugged area remains uninhabited and trackless, and is covered with virgin rainforest. About half of Osa is protected within Parque Nacional Corcovado, the largest of the parks and reserves that make up the Corcovado Conservation Area. Those with a taste for adventure are richly rewarded with majestic wilderness and some of the most spectacular wildlife-viewing in the nation.

Bahía Drake
With a beautiful setting, Drake Bay is great for scuba diving and sportfishing centered on the small village of Aguijitas (see p238).

Playa San Josecito
Backed by rainforest, this is a beautiful golden-sand beach with accommodations. Access is by boat or hiking trail.

Refugio Nacional de Vida Silvestre Punta Río Claro, located inland of Punta Marenco, protects more than 400 bird species, four monkey species, and prime rainforest habitat adjoining Corcovado *(see p239).*

0 km   5
0 miles   5

Parque Nacional Corcovado
Sprawling Corcovado National Park protects one of the last original tracts of the Pacific coast's tropical rainforest in Meso-America. La Leona (left) is one of its four ranger stations. Crocodiles, tapirs, jaguars, and scarlet macaws are found in the park in large numbers (see p239).

◁ A flock of brown pelicans at Parque Nacional Corcovado

LOGGING

The peninsula's large stands of precious hardwoods, such as mahogany, have suffered from excessive logging. Although restrictions have been placed on the activities of lumber companies, the cutting of protected tree species continues unabated.

Logging truck

VISITORS' CHECKLIST

Road Map E5. SW Costa Rica.
🏘 12,000. ✕ at Puerto Jiménez;
airstrips at Carate, PN Corcovado,
and Bahía Drake. 🚌 to Puerto
Jiménez or La Palma, then take
a jeep-taxi to the park or hike
(from La Palma to Los Patos). 🚢
to Bahía Drake, then take another
boat to the park or hike (caution
is required to wade the Río Claro).

Dolphins

Dolphins and humpback whales are frequently seen playing in the Golfo Dulce (Sweet Gulf).

KEY

══	Main road
══	Minor road
▬ ▬	Trail
▬ ▬	Park boundary
✕	Airstrip
▲	Camping
ℹ	Visitor information

Puerto Jiménez

The only town of significance on the Osa Peninsula, this is the starting point for visits to Corcovado, and a center for hiking, surfing, and similar activities, including kayaking through nearby mangroves (see p238).

Pan-American Highway

cón

erto
dido

La Palma

Barrigones

Golfo Dulce

Agujas

Sandalo

Lalitas

Dos Brazos

Puerto Jiménez

Playa Preciosa
Playa Platanares

RNVS PRECIOSA PLATANARES

DE OSA

rro Rincón
2,450 ft

HUMEDAL LACUSTRINO LAGUNA PEJEPERRITO

eona
er Station

Carate

RESERVA FORESTAL GOLFO DULCE

RNVS PEJEPERRO

Cerro Osa
1,050 ft

Playa Sombrero

Playa Platanares

Playa Platanares
A vital nesting site for marine turtles, the beach is fringed by wildlife-rich forest. A coral reef offshore is good for snorkeling.

Cabo Matapalo

Carate, the gateway to Corcovado, is accessed by chartered planes and a rugged dirt track.

Laguna Pejeperrito is inhabited by caimans, crocodiles, and waterfowl.

Dos Brazos, a former gold mining center, welcomes visitors for gold-panning trips with community members.

Cabo Matapalo is popular with surfers.

For hotels and restaurants in this region see pp264–7 and pp284–5

Exploring Peninsula de Osa

Ranger station, Parque Nacional Corcovado

The lush rainforests of Corcovado lie at the heart of the Osa Peninsula. Although tourism to the region is booming, travel into the interior is still a challenge. Highway 245 follows the eastern shore and a rugged dirt road links Rincón to Bahía Drake, but the only guaranteed access to the western shores is by boat or by small plane. Wilderness lodges line the coast.

Along the shore of sweeping Bahía Drake

Bahía Drake

Rocky cliffs and forested hills provide a compelling setting for the scalloped Drake Bay. Sir Francis Drake is said to have anchored the *Golden Hind* here in March 1579.

This is one of the most inaccessible areas in Costa Rica. In 2003, a dirt road was cut from Rincón, on Golfo Dulce, to Bahía Drake (pronounced "DRA-cay"), but the route is often impassable in wet weather, even for 4WD vehicles. Most visitors still arrive by boat from Sierpe *(see p232)*. The small village of **Agujitas**, toward the bay's southern end, survives largely on subsistence farming and fishing.

Popular attractions include dolphin- and whale-watching trips on the bay. Snorkeling is another fun activity, especially in the southern bay, where the canyon of Río Agujitas can be explored by kayak. There are several budget accommodation options, as well as more expensive lodges that offer scuba diving and sportfishing. One such is **Aguila de Osa** *(see p264)*, which features snorkeling along with scuba diving and deep-sea angling.

Among its other attractions are zipline tours and a treetop observation walkway. You can also whiz between treetops with **Corcovado Canopy Tour**, which has 11 ziplines.

From Agujitas, a coastal trail leads south for 8 miles (13 km), via **Playas Cocalito**, **Caletas**, and **San Josecito**, to Parque Nacional Corcovado, passing by the **Refugio Nacional de Vida Silvestre Punta Río Claro**. This 2-sq-mile (5-sq-km) nature reserve adjoins Corcovado, and is home to much the same species of wildlife as can be seen in Corcovado. Guided hikes can be booked at Punta Marenco Lodge, which is nearby. Tapirs and crocodiles are frequently sighted while canoeing on **Laguna Chocuaco**, to the east of Agujitas; the local community cooperative offers trips.

✗ Corcovado Canopy Tour
Los Planos, 8 miles (14 km) SE of Agujitas. **Tel** 2775-0459. **www**.corcovadocanopytour.com

✗ Refugio Nacional de Vida Silvestre Punta Río Claro
Playa Caletas, 4 miles (6 km) S of Agujitas. ☎ 8877-3535. ☐ 8am–5pm daily. **www**.puntamarenco.com

Puerto Jiménez
⛯ 6,200.

The only settlement of significance on the peninsula, this dusty village is popular with backpackers. In the 1980s, Puerto Jiménez briefly blossomed on income from local gold and had a reputation as a "Wild West" frontier town, where carrying a gun was considered a good idea and prostitutes were paid with gold nuggets. Today, the town thrives on tourist money.

Various adventure activities are offered by local operators. Kayakers flock to the mangroves extending east along the shore of the Golfo Dulce to the estuary of Río Platanares. Home to crocodiles, caimans, freshwater turtles, and river otters, this ecosystem is protected within the 555-acre (225-ha) **Refugio Nacional de Vida Silvestre Preciosa Platanares**. The refuge lies along the shores of the lovely **Playa Platanares**, which has a small coral reef good for snorkeling. The beach is a nesting site for five species of marine turtles, best sighted from May to December. A small *vivero* (nursery) raises hatchlings for release into the jade-green waters.

The shore south of Puerto Jiménez is lined with beaches. **Cabo Matapalo**, at the tip of the peninsula, and **Playa Sombrero** offer great surfing.

✗ Refugio Nacional de Vida Silvestre Preciosa Platanares
2 miles (3 km) E of Puerto Jiménez. ☑ by donation.

Locals on the main street of Puerto Jiménez

A lounging area on the beach at Parque Nacional Corcovado

Parque Nacional Corcovado

25 miles (40 km) SW of Puerto Jiménez. **Tel** 2735-5036.
⬜ 8am–4pm daily. 🏞️ 🍴 ♿ 🅰️
www.sinac.go.cr

Considered the crown jewel among the protected regions of the humid tropics, this 165-sq-mile (425-sq-km) park was created in 1975 to preserve the largest Pacific coast rainforest in the Americas, as well as 20 sq miles (52 sq km) of marine habitat. Corcovado (meaning "hunchback") has eight distinct zones, including herbaceous swamps, flooded swamp forest, and montane forest. The area receives up to 158 inches (400 cm) of rainfall per year, with torrential rains from April to December.

Wildlife viewing is splendid and among the most diverse in Costa Rica. The park has over 400 species of birds, including the endangered harpy eagle, and the largest population of scarlet macaws in Central America; birdwatchers are guaranteed sightings. Jaguars are spotted more frequently here than at any other park in the nation,

as are tapirs. Both species are often seen on the beaches, especially around dusk. Corcovado is known for its large packs of peccaries – menacing wild hogs that should be avoided. The endangered *tití* (squirrel monkey) is also found here. There are over 115 species of amphibians and reptiles. Poison-dart frogs (*see p208*) are easily seen in their gaudy livery, but the elusive lime-green red-eyed tree frog and Fleischmann's transparent frog are harder to spot. The fortunate might witness green, hawksbill, leatherback, or Pacific ridley turtles crawling ashore to nest. However, the park is understaffed and the wildlife is under threat by poachers.

Although there are hotels and organized tours close by, the park is best suited to self-sufficient hikers who enjoy rugged adventures. There are four official entry points and ranger stations. **San Pedrillo**, to the west, is linked by a trail

Small biplane used for transport within Osa

from Bahía Drake. **Los Patos**, to the east, can be reached from La Palma, 12 miles (19 km) northwest of Puerto Jiménez. **La Leona**, to the south, is 1 mile (1.6 km) west of the airstrip at Carate, a hamlet 25 miles (40 km) west of Puerto Jiménez; visitors must then hike or ride a horse from Carate. **Sirena**, the main ranger station, is 10 miles (16 km) northwest of La Leona and 16 miles (26 km) southeast of San Pedrillo. Poorly marked trails connect the stations; it is wise to hire a guide.

The coastal San Pedrillo–La Leona trail passes the dramatic 100-ft (30-m) high **Cascada La Llorona**. Be prepared to ford rivers inhabited by crocodiles on this two-day hike. The trail's northern section is open only from December to April. The San Pedrillo–Los Patos trail allows access to **Laguna Corcovado**, where tapirs and jaguars are often sighted.

There is no scheduled air service to the airstrips near the park, but air-taxis are offered by charter companies.

Interesting attractions close to Parque Nacional Corcovado include the 105-acre (43-ha) wetlands **Humedal Lacustrino Laguna Pejeperrito**, 2 miles (3 km) east of Carate, and the 865-acre (350-ha) **Refugio Nacional de Vida Silvestre Pejeperro**, 2.5 miles (4 km) farther east. They are little visited, but offer good opportunities for spotting birds, as well as crocodiles.

GOLD MINING

Oreros (gold panners) had sifted for gold in the rivers of the Osa Peninsula since pre-Columbian days. When the United Fruit Company (*see p39*) pulled out of the region in 1985, unemployed workers flooded the peninsula, leading to a latter-day gold rush. This short-lived gold rush caused major damage: trees were felled, river banks dynamited, and exposed soils sluiced. After violent clashes with the authorities, the *oreros* were ousted in 1986. Some still work the outer margins of Corcovado, while others earn their income leading gold hunts for tourists.

Nuggets of gold

Parque Nacional Piedras Blancas ⑮

Road Map E5. 28 miles (46 km)
SE of Palmar. **Tel** 2741-8001
(Esquinas Rainforest Lodge).
🚌 from Golfito. 🕐 8am–4pm daily.

Split off from Parque Nacional
Corcovado in 1991, this 55-sq-
mile (140-sq-km) park protects
the forested mountains to the
northeast of Golfo Dulce. In
the village of La Gamba, a
cooperative runs the **Esquinas
Rainforest Lodge** (see p266),
which breeds the rodent-like
tepezcuintles and offers hikes.

The emerald forests spill
over the beaches – Playa
Cativo and Playa San Josecito,
which has the botanical garden
Casa de Orquídeas, known for
its large collection of orchids
and ornamentals. Lining the
shores are wilderness lodges.
Boat trips, including water-taxi
rides, from Puerto Jiménez
and Golfito to the two beaches
make for pleasant excursions.

> 🌺 **Casa de Orquídeas**
> Playa San Josecito, 6 miles (10 km)
> N of Puerto Jiménez. **Tel** 8829-
> 1247. 🕐 8am–5pm Sat–Thu by
> appointment. 🖼️ 📷

**Sign of the colorful botanical
garden, Casa de Orquídeas**

Golfito ⑯

Road Map F5. 48 miles (77 km)
SE of Palmar. 🚶 10,900. ✈️ 🚌

A sportfishing base, port, and
administrative center for the
southern region, dilapidated
Golfito (Small Gulf) unfurls
along 4 miles (6 km) of
shoreline. Established by the
United Fruit Company in
1938, the town's reign as the
nation's main banana shipping
port ended when the company
pulled out of the region in
1985. The legacy of "Big
Fruit" can be seen in the
intriguing architecture of Zona
Americana, the north end of

**Stilt-legged house in Zona
Americana, Golfito**

town, which has stilt-legged
wooden houses. The small
plaza in Pueblo Civíl, the
town center, abuts a busy
water-taxi wharf. The **Museo
Marino** nearby is worth a
peek for its collection of
corals and seashells.

On weekends and holidays,
Golfito is flooded with Ticos
drawn to the Depósito Libre
(Free Trade Zone) shopping
compound created in 1990 to
revive the town's fortunes.

The forested hills east and
north of town are protected
within **Refugio Nacional de
Vida Silvestre Golfito**.

> 🏛️ **Museo Marino**
> Hotel Centro Turístico Samoa,
> just N of Pueblo Civíl. **Tel** 2775-
> 0233. 🕐 7am–11am daily.

> 🦋 **Refugio Nacional de Vida
> Silvestre Golfito**
> E of Golfito. 🕐 8am–4pm daily.
> 📷 with local operators.

Zancudo ⑰

Road Map F5. 6 miles (10 km) S of
Golfito (41 miles/66 km by road).
🚌 from Golfito. 🚤 water-taxi from
Golfito.

This hamlet on the east shore
of Golfo Dulce is known for
its stupendously beautiful

gray sand beach, caressed by
breezes and surf. The 4-mile
(6-km) long strip of sand is
a spit, projecting from the
shore. A mangrove swamp
inland of the beach is good
for spotting crocodiles,
caimans, and waterfowl.
Sportfishing centers offer
superb river-mouth and deep-
water fishing (see p299),
while tarpon and snook can
be hooked from the shore.

Pavones ⑱

Road Map B5. 7 miles (12 km)
S of Zancudo. ✈️ 🚌 from Golfito.
🚤 water-taxi from Golfito.

Known in the surfing world
for its consistent 0.5-mile
(1-km) 3-minute break, this
small fishing village has
blossomed due to the influx
of young surfers. The waves
peak between April and October. Coconut palms lean over
the beautiful, rocky coastline.

Environs

Marine turtles nest along the
shore. At **Punta Banco**, 6 miles
(10 km) south of Pavones, the
local community participates
in the Tiskita Foundation Sea
Turtle Restoration Project,
which has a nursery to raise
baby turtles for release. Nearby,
Tiskita Lodge (see p266) offers
fabulous vistas from its
hillside perch. This lodge is
part of a fruit farm that lures
a wealth of bird- and animal
life. Guided hikes are offered
into a private reserve, where
waterfalls tumble through
majestic rainforest.

Reserva Indígena Guaymí,
9 miles (14 km) south of
Punta Banco, is the remote
mountain home of the Guaymí.
Visits are discouraged.

A surfer wading ashore at Pavones

Parque Nacional Isla del Coco ⑲

Named a National Park in 1978, the world's largest uninhabited island is a UNESCO World Heritage Site. Of volcanic origin, the 9-sq-mile (23-sq-km) island is a part of the Galapagos chain. Torrential rainfall feeds spectacular waterfalls that cascade to the sea, while dense premontane moist forest carpets the land. The fragile ecosystem protects endemic fauna such as the Pacific dwarf gecko and Cocos anole, as well as 70 endemic plant species. A highlight is the huge colonies of seabirds, including magnificent frigate birds, noddies, and white terns. With waters of astounding clarity, the island is a world-renowned dive site (see p300).

VISITORS' CHECKLIST

310 miles (500 km) SW of mainland. 🚢 with dive operators (a 36-hr journey). ℹ 2256-7476 (Fundación Amigos de La Isla del Coco); @ islacoco@ns.minae.co. cr (Ranger station). Permit needed to step ashore, which dive operators can arrange. 📷 **Dive Operators** Undersea Hunter: 2228-6613; Okeanos Aggressor: see p253. **www**.cocosisland.org

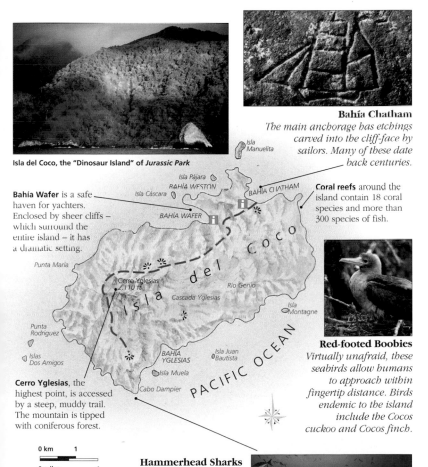

Isla del Coco, the "Dinosaur Island" of Jurassic Park

Bahía Chatham
The main anchorage has etchings carved into the cliff-face by sailors. Many of these date back centuries.

Bahía Wafer is a safe haven for yachters. Enclosed by sheer cliffs – which surround the entire island – it has a dramatic setting.

Coral reefs around the island contain 18 coral species and more than 300 species of fish.

Cerro Yglesias, the highest point, is accessed by a steep, muddy trail. The mountain is tipped with coniferous forest.

Red-footed Boobies
Virtually unafraid, these seabirds allow humans to approach within fingertip distance. Birds endemic to the island include the Cocos cuckoo and Cocos finch.

Hammerhead Sharks
Congregating in their hundreds, these sharks provide an exhilarating experience for scuba divers. Also drawn by the huge fish population around the island are white-tipped sharks.

Isla Manuelita
Isla Pájara
BAHÍA WESTON
Isla Cáscara
BAHÍA CHATHAM
BAHÍA WAFER
Punta María
Cerro Yglesias 2,110 ft
Río Genio
Cascada Yglesias
Isla Montagne
Isla del Coco
Punta Rodriguez
Islas Dos Amigos
BAHÍA YGLESIAS
Isla Juan Bautista
Isla Muela
Cabo Dampier
PACIFIC OCEAN

0 km   1
0 miles   1

KEY

-- Trail
☀ Viewpoint
△ Peak
ℹ Visitor information

TRAVELERS' NEEDS

WHERE TO STAY

Costa Rica has an excellent selection of accommodations covering the entire country, with a wide choice for every budget. Even the remotest corners have inexpensive *cabinas* (cabins). The country's forté is the wilderness nature lodge, many in extraordinary settings, where guests can view wildlife without leaving their hammocks. Also on offer are special-interest lodgings catering to a particular activity, such as surfing or sportfishing. Hotels range

Sign outside Orosi Lodge (see p253)

from self-catering *apartotels* (apart-hotels) to world-class luxury resorts and boutique hotels, which reflect the individuality of their owners. Backpackers' hotels are ever more numerous, and their quality is growing accordingly. Costa Rican hotels rarely use the star-grading system. Instead, the country has adopted the Certificate for Sustainable Tourism (CST) system, which grades hotels by their cultural and ecological sensitivity, such as level of energy efficiency.

A warmly welcoming room at the upscale Four Seasons (see p256)

CHAIN HOTELS

Costa Rica's many chain hotels span a range of prices. International chains such as **Best Western**, **Choice Hotels**, and **Quality Inn** are well represented in the low- and mid-range brackets. **Occidental** and **Marriott** offer reliable service and quality, while **Four Seasons** represents the deluxe end. **Hilton Hotels & Resorts** offers several all-inclusive options, in which all meals, entertainment, and facilities are provided for a set room rate at its Fiesta beach resorts.

Room cleaning and linen changing on a daily basis, and private bathrooms with showers are standard in most establishments, and all chain hotels have a restaurant and bar. However, visitors should be aware that standards among budget-oriented chain hotels vary considerably and may not conform to their equivalents in North America

or Europe. The more expensive options usually offer a gourmet restaurant, gym, and casino or nightclub, and sometimes tour agency and boutique shops.

BOUTIQUE HOTELS

A pleasant and more unusual accommodation option is the range of intimate boutique hotels, which are characterized

Capitán Suizo, one of Costa Rica's many boutique hotels (see p260)

by a charming originality and hospitality. Ranging from upscale, family-run bed-and-breakfasts to architectural stunners in the midst of coffee plantations to beach hotels inspired by a Balinese aesthetic, these exquisite lodgings can be found throughout the country.

Most of the boutique hotels are the creation of foreign entrepreneurs with artistic vision, and with few exceptions benefit from the owners' hands-on management. They are usually lower priced than many chain hotels of similar standard and represent excellent value. Many boutique hotels offer gourmet dining, a spa, and a range of activities and excursions.

WILDERNESS LODGES

Nature lovers can choose between more than 100 wilderness lodges in the country. The majority are located close to, or within, national parks and wildlife reserves, or otherwise offer immediate access to regions of natural beauty. Guided hikes and other wilderness-related activities are generally available at these lodges.

Accommodations range from basic to modestly upscale, although all have a degree of rusticity in common. The focus is on the nature experience, rather than the amenities offered. Several lodges have attained international fame; advance bookings are recommended

◁ **Hotel balcony in San José, with a lovely view of surrounding hills**

Bathroom in Shawandha Lodge at Puerto Viejo *(see p263)*

for these. Many of the more simple lodges, including those located within indigenous reserves, are run by community cooperatives. These offer opportunities to appreciate local culture and experience nature from the local perspective. **Cooprena** is a promotion and booking agent representing many such ecolodges.

BUDGET HOTELS

The country has thousands of simple budget accommodations called *cabinas*, which cater to the mass of Tico (Costa Rican) travelers and backpackers. Usually the term refers to a row of hotel rooms, but it is used loosely and can cover a variety of accommodation types. *Cabina* is at times used interchangeably with *albergue*, *hospedaje*, or *posada*, three terms for "lodging." *Albergue* normally refers to simple rural lodges, and *hospedaje* and *posada*

are usually akin to bed-and-breakfasts.

It is acceptable to ask to inspect rooms before taking them. Services and furnishings are minimal, and bathroom accouterments are usually limited to soap and towels; bring your own sink plug and wash cloth. Many cheaper *cabinas* require that visitors share bathrooms. Be prepared for cold water only; where hot water is available, it is typically heated by inefficient electric elements that can give you a shock if touched. You may be asked to place toilet paper in a basket to avoid blocking the toilet drain. Theft is a common problem in *cabinas*. Take a padlock, and check that doors and windows are secure and that there are no holes or cracks that can be used by peeping toms.

Several budget hotels operate as members of International Youth Hostel Federation (IYHF). Most are run to a very high standard and have clean, single-sex dormitories. Some also have co-ed dorms. **Hostelling International Costa Rica** is the representative of the IYHF in Costa Rica and can make reservations for hostels all over the country.

APARTOTELS AND MOTELS

Ticos are fond of *apartotels*, which are basic self-catering apartments with kitchens or kitchenettes and a small living and dining room; they are usually offered on long-term rentals. Rarely do they have

restaurants or other facilities. San José has a large number of *apartotels*; they are also found in other towns and the major beach resorts.

Motels should not be confused with their North American or European equivalents. Found across the nation, they are no-frills places of convenience used mainly by lovers and rented by the hour. Overnight stays are usually permitted, even for singles. Occasionally they can prove useful at night in locations where few other options exist.

Corcovado Adventures Tent Camp, featuring furnished tents *(see p264)*

CAMPING

Visitors can camp in many of the national parks and wildlife refuges, including at ranger stations, where water, toilets, and occasionally showers are usually available. Some ranger stations prepare meals by arrangement; if not, carry your own provisions. A mosquito net and waterproof tent are also essential items to carry.

Outside the reserves, camping facilities are few except at major beach resorts. On weekends and public holidays, Tico families flock to beaches, where they camp on the sands. Avoid this illegal practice and restrict your camping to designated sites. Hammocks can be bought or rented and hung almost anywhere. Campers always need to beware of theft and should never leave items unguarded.

Casa de Las Tías *(see p250)*, Escazú

Pool at Hotel Villa Caletas *(see p255)*, of the Small Distinctive Hotels

HOTEL GROUPS

Several local hotel groups represent member hotels that market themselves jointly based on their similarities. Eight of the finest boutique hotels of the country form the **Small Distinctive Hotels of Costa Rica**. This group offers a distinctive ambience in their excellent accommodations, which are located in diverse regions ranging from the capital city to remote mountains and beaches. **Greentique Hotels** represents three quality, nature-based hotels that operate according to sustainable practices. Several Swiss- and German-owned hotels are marketed collectively under the **Charming & Nature Hotels of Costa Rica** umbrella.

SPECIALIZED LODGING

Many places cater for a specific activity. Several nature lodges, for instance, are dedicated exclusively to sportfishing, and offer all-inclusive packages. Usually these are in remote locations accessible solely by boat. Other resorts specialize in scuba diving, and offer diving lessons for beginners. Visitors planning more advanced diving will need to provide proof of their qualifications. Budget-oriented "surf camps" are often found at Costa Rica's many beaches. Some are quite sophisticated and offer various options, from outdoor dormitories with hammocks to private air-conditioned rooms. There are also plenty of health-oriented hotels, which range from rustic lodges to luxurious yoga retreats.

Many tour operators offer specialist tours for those interested in a particular activity *(see p296)*. By far the largest focus is on nature tourism: packages usually include stays at wilderness lodges and pre-arranged hikes, birding, and similar nature excursions.

BOOKING

It is best to book your accommodation well ahead of your visit, particularly if you are traveling during the dry season (December–April). This is especially true around Christmas, New Year, and Easter, and during special local events, such as Carnaval in Puerto Limón. Reservations are also recommended for travelers following a pre-planned route. Advance bookings for *cabinas* are not as critical except at the peak times.

Many hotels in Costa Rica have a reputation for not honoring reservations, and for not issuing refunds. It is, therefore, advisable to make reservations through a travel agency or tour operator. If making a booking yourself, never send your request by mail, as the postal service is unreliable. Instead, use the phone or fax, or book online using the hotel websites. If a deposit is required you can pay by credit card. In all cases, make sure that you obtain a written confirmation of your reservation.

Los Sueños Marriott Ocean & Golf Resort *(see p256)*, set amid sprawling grounds in Playa Herradura

El Sano Banano Beach Hotel, part of Ylang Ylang Beach Resort *(see p255)*

PRICES AND PAYMENTS

Regardless of hotel type, prices will be higher in the dry season than in the wet season (May–November). The more expensive hotels usually charge an additional premium for the peak season, which is the Christmas–New Year holidays, as well as for Easter. Rates can also vary according to the type of room. Hotels that depend on business travelers often have reduced rates for weekends and long stays. Tour operators may also be able to offer special deals that you may find difficult to obtain yourself. Many hotels offer discount schemes, such as special rates for surfers.

A 16.39 per cent tax is added to lodgings in tourist hotels. This is not always included in the advertised rate. Traveler's checks and credit cards are accepted in most hotels, with the exception of many budget hotels, which will only accept cash. Most places accept payment in US dollars.

TIPPING

It is customary to leave a *propina* (tip) for the hotel staff at the end of your stay. The amount will depend on the type and quality of service, as well as the length of your stay. Use your discretion. In general, it is normal to tip bellboys $1 and chambermaids $1 or more. Visitors should be aware that hotel wages among service staff in Costa Rica are often quite low and that tips in dollars often amount to a significant part of such workers' livelihoods.

DISABLED TRAVELERS

Only the more recently built hotels have access and purpose-built facilities for disabled travelers, including bathrooms with wheelchair access. Many wilderness lodges have level trails designed for wheelchairs. Hotel staff in all parts of Costa Rica will do everything they can to assist disabled travelers. **Vaya con Silla de Ruedas** (Go With Wheelchairs) provides services for disabled travelers, including recommendations for appropriate lodgings.

An executive suite at Hotel Grano de Oro *(see p251)* in San José

DIRECTORY

CHAIN HOTELS

Best Western
Tel 800-780-7234.
www.bestwestern.com

Choice Hotels
Tel 0800-011-0517.
www.choicehotels.com

Four Seasons
Tel 2696-0000.
www.fourseasons.com/costarica

Hilton Hotels & Resorts
Tel 800-445-8667.
www.hilton.com

Marriott
Tel 888-236-2427.
www.marriott.com

Occidental
Tel 2248-2323.
www.occidental-hoteles.com

Quality Inn
Tel 0800-011-0517.
www.qualityinn.com

WILDERNESS LODGES

Cooprena
Tel 2290-8646.
www.turismoruralcr.com

YOUTH HOSTELS

Hostelling International Costa Rica
Ave 8 and Calle 41, 1002 San José.
Tel 2234-5486.
www.hihostels.com

HOTEL GROUPS

Charming & Nature Hotels of Costa Rica
www.charmingnaturehotels.com

Greentique Hotels
Tel 2560-0060.
www.greentiquehotels.com

Small Distinctive Hotels of Costa Rica
Tel 2258-0150.
www.distinctivehotels.com

DISABLED TRAVELERS

Vaya con Silla de Ruedas
Tel 2454-2810.
www.gowithwheelchairs.com

Choosing a Hotel

Most of the hotels and resorts in this guide have been selected across a wide price range for facilities, good value, and location. The prices listed are those charged by the hotel, although discounts may be available through agencies. The hotels are listed by area. For map references for San José, see pages 128–9.

PRICE CATEGORIES
For a standard double room per night in the tourist season, including tax and service:

$ Under $25
$$ $25–40
$$$ $40–80
$$$$ $80–140
$$$$$ Over $140

SAN JOSE

CITY CENTER Casa Ridgway
$
Calle 15 and Aves 6 bis/8 **Tel** 2233-2693 **Fax** 2222-1400 **Rooms** 13
Map 2 E4

Located close to the Museo Nacional in downtown San José, Casa Ridgway is a peaceful hostel operated by a Quaker organization. With spacious dorms and private rooms, as well as a communal kitchen, this hostel is good value for money. Also on offer is a library and a TV lounge. **www.amigosparalapaz.org**

CITY CENTER Costa Rica Backpackers
$
Calles 21/23 and Ave 6 **Tel** 2221-6191 **Rooms** 16
Map 2 F4

On the eastern edge of downtown, this secure backpackers' hostel is run to high standards by French owners. It has both private rooms and dorms, plus a self-service kitchen, TV lounge, Internet rooms, and tour planning facilities. Its swimming pool is set in a lush garden. **www.costaricabackpackers.com**

CITY CENTER Hostel La Casa del Parque
$$
Calles 19 and Ave 3 **Tel** 2233-3437 **Fax** 2258-7113 **Rooms** 4
Map 2 E2

This welcoming Costa Rican-run hostel, set in an Art Deco house in the northeastern corner of Parque Nacional, is convenient, has great views, and offers complimentary coffee, kitchen use, and storage. The owners are happy to arrange tours and car rentals on request. **www.hostelcasadelparque.com**

CITY CENTER Kap's Place
$$
Calle 19 and Aves 11/13 **Tel** 2221-1169 **Fax** 2256-4850 **Rooms** 23
Map 2 E2

In a quiet locality close to Barrio Amón, this rambling converted home has a cozy family atmosphere and is enlivened by colorful decor. Each room is distinct, and some have TVs. Guests can use the kitchen, and a terrace garden has hammocks to laze in. Free Internet access is available. **www.kapsplace.com**

CITY CENTER Britannia Hotel
$$$
Calle 3 and Ave 11 **Tel** 2223-6667 **Fax** 2223-6411 **Rooms** 23
Map 1 C2

This restored mansion in Barrio Amón dates from 1910 and was built by a Spanish coffee baron. Stained-glass windows, mosaic tile floors, and period furnishings help create a warm atmosphere. A modern annex is similarly decorated and has lush courtyards. **www.hotelbritanniacostarica.com**

CITY CENTER Gran Hotel
$$$
Calle 3 and Ave 2 **Tel** 2221-4000 **Fax** 2255-0139 **Rooms** 94
Map 1 C4

Built in 1899, the Gran Hotel is considered a historic monument. It boasts a fabulous location for sightseeing, but some of the rooms are less than impressive. The lobby casino offers non-stop excitement. Open round the clock, the patio café is a great place to watch the world go by. **www.granhotelcostarica.com**

CITY CENTER Hotel Don Carlos
$$$
Calle 9 bis and Ave 9 **Tel** 2221-6707 **Fax** 2258-1152 **Rooms** 36
Map 2 D2

Located in the heart of Barrio Amón and once the residence of two former presidents, Don Carlos is a part of San José's heritage. Its maze of quiet corridors, decorated with artwork and pre-Columbian motifs, lead into garden settings. There is a splendid souvenir store. **www.doncarloshotel.com**

CITY CENTER Hotel Kekoldi
$$$
Calles 5/7 and Ave 9 **Tel** 2248-0804 **Fax** 2248-0767 **Rooms** 10
Map 2 D2

Decorated in bright pastels and saturated with sunlight, this Art Deco house enjoys a fine location in the heart of historic Barrio Amón. Its elegant rooms are well appointed, and it has a small private Japanese garden. Tours, transfers, and car rentals can be arranged. **www.kekoldi.com**

CITY CENTER Hotel Presidente
$$$
Calles 7/9 and Ave Central **Tel** 2222-3022 **Fax** 2221-1205 **Rooms** 100
Map 2 D4

Steps away from Plaza de la Cultura, this hotel has a casino, rooftop Jacuzzi and sauna, and an excellent street-front café and restaurant. The best suite in the house offers an eight-person Jacuzzi, an open-air shower, and spectacular views from oversized windows. **www.hotel-presidente.com**

Key to Symbols see back cover flap

CITY CENTER Clarion Hotel Amón Plaza
P | ¶ | 🍷 | 🗐 | ♿ | TV $$$$

Calle 3 bis and Ave 11 **Tel** *2523-4600* **Fax** *2523-4614* **Rooms** *90*   **Map** *2 C2*

This modern hotel in Barrio Amón offers good service and excellent facilities. The elegant lobby is well appointed with objects of art. The hotel also has a disco, a conference center, a spa, and an upscale open-air roadside restaurant. All rooms have a wireless Internet connection. **www.hotelamonplaza.com**

CITY CENTER D'Raya Vida Villa
P | TV $$$$

Calle 15 bis and Ave 11 **Tel** *2223-4168* **Fax** *2223-4157* **Rooms** *4*   **Map** *2 E2*

This gracious Southern plantation-style mansion is now a bed-and-breakfast with stylish furnishings and splendid artwork. A quiet garden room with a fountain and a sunny, glass-enclosed den are ideal for relaxation. The hotel offers free transfers from the airport. **www.rayavida.com**

CITY CENTER Hotel Balmoral
P | ¶ | 🍷 | 🗐 | ♿ | TV $$$$

Calles 7/9 and Ave Central **Tel** *2222-5022* **Fax** *2221-1919* **Rooms** *112*   **Map** *2 D3*

The modern Balmoral hotel is suitable for business travelers and tourists. The decor is uninspired, but it is located close to major sights and offers a wide range of services, including a business center and conference rooms. There is a casino for those who want to try their luck. **www.balmoral.co.cr**

CITY CENTER Hotel Fleur de Lys
¶ | 🗐 | TV $$$$

Calle 13 and Ave 2 **Tel** *2223-1206* **Fax** *2221-6310* **Rooms** *31*   **Map** *2 E2*

A quaint Swiss-run boutique hotel, this converted mansion is mere steps from the main sights in downtown San José. Each bedroom is named for a flower and individually styled, with either wicker or wrought-iron beds. Musicians perform live in the wood-paneled Italian restaurant. **www.hotelfleurdelys.com**

CITY CENTER Hotel Santo Tomás
P | ¶ | 🏊 | 🗐 | TV $$$$

Ave 7, Calles 3/5 **Tel** *2255-0448* **Fax** *2222-3950* **Rooms** *19*   **Map** *1 A2*

Located on the cusp between downtown and Barrio Amón, this former colonial mansion offers lodgings with tasteful furnishings and a peaceful ambience. Rooms vary widely in size. The adjoining restaurant is one of the city's best and opens onto a garden with a whirlpool spa. **www.hotelsantotomas.com**

CITY CENTER Hotel Villa Tournon
P | ¶ | 🏊 | 🗐 | ♿ | TV $$$$

Barrio Tournon, E of "La Republica" **Tel** *2233-6622* **Fax** *2222-5211* **Rooms** *80*   **Map** *2 D1*

Located north of Barrio Amón, this modern hotel features modern artwork, polished hardwood floors, and rich fabrics in the guest rooms, all of which also have cable Internet connections. The piano bar and restaurant are excellent. A business center and conference rooms are also available. **www.costarica-hotelvillatournon.com**

CITY CENTER Hotel Aurola Holiday Inn
P | ¶ | 🏊 | 🍷 | 🗐 | ♿ | TV $$$$$

Calle 5 and Ave 5 **Tel** *2523-1000* **Fax** *2255-1171* **Rooms** *200*   **Map** *2 D3*

The Aurola Holiday Inn is a 17-story, modern building on Parque Morazán. Some of its rooms have breathtaking views of volcanoes and the city. The hotel has a spacious, elegant lobby, as well as a casino, gym, and sauna. Also on offer are facilities for business travelers. **www.aurola-holidayinn.com**

CITY CENTER Radisson Europa Hotel and Conference Center
P | ¶ | 🏊 | 🍷 | 🗐 | ♿ | TV $$$$$

Calle 3 and Ave 15 **Tel** *2257-3257* **Fax** *2257-8221* **Rooms** *210*   **Map** *1 C1*

This is a contemporary business hotel on the northern edge of downtown with international levels of service. The facilities on offer include a casino, gym, high-speed WiFi, six conference rooms, and shops. **www.radisson.com/sanjosecr**

EAST OF CITY CENTER Hostel Toruma
P | ¶ | 🏊 | TV $

Calles 29/31 and Ave Central **Tel** *2234-8186* **Fax** *2224-4085* **Rooms** *18*

The residence of a former president of Costa Rica, this youth hostel is spotlessly clean and run to high standards. Both dormitories and private rooms are available. Breakfast is included, and there is a guest kitchen. There is also an Internet café, a swimming pool, and a travel desk to assist visitors. **www.hosteltoruma.com**

EAST OF CITY CENTER Hotel 1492 Jade y Oro
P | ♿ | TV $$$

Calles 31/33 and Ave 1, No. 2985 **Tel** *2225-3752* **Fax** *2280-6206* **Rooms** *10*

Named after the year that Columbus landed in the New World, this is a charming, atmospheric bed-and-breakfast hotel in a Colonial-style house. Setting Hotel 1492 apart are its personalized service, a cozy lounge with a fireplace, and wine and cheese served on a garden patio. **www.hotel1492.com**

EAST OF CITY CENTER Hotel Milvia
P | ¶ | TV $$$

NE of Centro Comercial M&N, San Pedro **Tel** *2225-4543* **Fax** *2225-7801* **Rooms** *9*

Hotel Milvia is a small, intimate hotel housed in a 1930s wooden home in a quiet residential area. Sitting rooms and a tropical garden are great for relaxation. Hardwood floors, spacious rooms, and bathrooms featuring hand-painted decorative tilework add to its elegance. **www.hotelmilvia.com**

EAST OF CITY CENTER Boutique Hotel Jade
P | ¶ | 🏊 | ♿ | TV $$$$

N of Autos Subaru dealership, Barrio Dent **Tel** *2224-2455* **Fax** *2224-2166* **Rooms** *29*

Close to the Universidad de Costa Rica, this two-story hotel has public areas boasting lively contemporary decor. It features a cigar bar and a superb restaurant, Jürgen's Grill *(see p273)*. Each room offers Wi-Fi connectivity and a minibar. **www.hotelboutiquejade.com**

EAST OF CITY CENTER Hôtel Le Bergerac

P **11** **&** **TV** $$$$

Calle 35, S of Ave Central **Tel** *2234-7850* **Fax** *2225-9103* **Rooms** *19*

Set in a former colonial home in a quiet, residential part of San Pedro, this hotel exudes a classical European aesthetic and has a fine French restaurant. Many of the spacious, wood-floored rooms have their own private garden patios. The hotel has a reputation for excellent service. **www.bergerachotel.com**

ESCAZU Apartotel María Alexandra

P **11** **≅** **Y1** **≣** **&** **TV** $$$

NW of El Cruce, San Rafael de Escazú **Tel** *2228-1507* **Fax** *2289-5192* **Rooms** *14*

This offers modern apartments and twin-level units with elegant furnishings, close to the center of Escazú. The amenities include a swimming pool, sauna, fitness center, and mini-golf, as well as a travel agency, and Harley-Davidson authorized rentals for biking aficionados. **www.mariaalexandra.com**

ESCAZU Casa de Las Tías

P **TV** $$$

San Rafael de Escazú **Tel** *2289-5517* **Fax** *2289-7353* **Rooms** *5*

This bed-and-breakfast is housed in a sprawling Victorian-style cedar house, set amidst lush gardens within walking distance of Escazú. The atmosphere is cozy and tranquil. The hosts are a delight and provide gourmet breakfasts. **www.hotels.co.cr/casatias.html**

ESCAZU Costa Verde Inn

P **11** **≅** **&** **TV** $$$

Barrio Rosa Linda, San Miguel de Escazú **Tel** *2228-4080* **Fax** *2289-8591* **Rooms** *18*

Polished hardwoods are a feature of this delightful bed-and-breakfast hotel, which has a cozy lounge warmed by a log fire. Each room is individually decorated. Guests can take relaxing swims in the pool, and the lush garden is perfect for lazing in a hammock. **www.costaverdeinn.com**

ESCAZU Villa Escazú

≅ **P** $$$

W of Banco Nacional, San Miguel de Escazú **Tel** *2289-7971* **Fax** *2289-7971* **Rooms** *6*

This is a Swiss-style chalet with a veranda on three sides for great views. Surrounded by verdant gardens, it has a charming rustic atmosphere; log fires add to the cozy ambience inside. An upstairs veranda has rocking chairs, and the studio apartment has a kitchen and TV. **www.hotels.co.cr/vescazu.html**

ESCAZU Out of Bounds Hotel & Tourist Center

P **11** **≣** **&** **TV** $$$$

Carretera John F. Kennedy, San Rafael de Escazú **Tel** *2288-6762* **Fax** *2288-5747* **Rooms** *5*

Opened in 2007, this mid-range hotel on the road to Santa Ana offers spacious, contemporary-styled guest rooms with pine floors, split over two levels. Balconies offer magnificent views. The Italian-Canadian owners also provide a complete adventure-travel service. **www.bedandbreakfastcr.com**

ESCAZU Posada El Quijote

P **TV** $$$$

Off Calle del Llano, San Miguel de Escazú **Tel** *2289-8401* **Fax** *2289-8729* **Rooms** *10*

Exquisite gardens, complete with a brook running through them, and stupendous views through the floor-to-ceiling windows are the highlights of this contemporary hilltop hotel. Each of its eight rooms and two apartments has hand-crafted wood furniture and a private bath. No children allowed. **www.quijote.co.cr**

ESCAZU The Alta Hotel

P **11** **≅** **Y1** **≣** **&** **TV** $$$$

Alto de las Palomas, 2 miles (3 km) W of Escazú **Tel** *2282-4160* **Fax** *2282-4162* **Rooms** *23*

Set on a hillside with great views, this elegant hotel blends Colonial and contemporary styles. Graciously appointed rooms have deep Roman-style tubs. Its gourmet restaurant, La Luz *(see p274)*, is considered one of the region's finest. **www.thealtahotel.com**

ESCAZU Intercontinental Real Hotel & Club Tower

P **11** **≅** **Y1** **≣** **&** **TV** $$$$$

Autopista Prospero Fernández and Blvd Camino Real **Tel** *2208-2100* **Fax** *2208-2101* **Rooms** *372*

This opulent hotel, 1 mile (1.6 km) west of San Rafael de Escazú, offers deluxe amenities and is popular with business travelers. The spa includes a beauty salon, fitness center, and swimming pool. A floodlit tennis court, shops, tour agency, and a business center are among its other amenities. **www.ichotelsgroup.com**

WEST OF CITY CENTER Gaudy's Backpackers

≅ **P** $

Calles 36/38 and Ave 5 **Tel** *2248-0086* **Fax** *2258-2937* **Rooms** *13*

On a quiet residential street close to Paseo Colón, this clean backpackers' hostel is in a converted middle-class home. It has mixed dorms and private rooms with bathrooms. Also on offer are free tea and coffee, a lounge with cable TV, and a free Internet connection. There is no curfew. **www.backpacker.co.cr**

WEST OF CITY CENTER Mi Casa Hostel

& $

Calle 48, Sabana Norte **Tel** *2231-4700* **Fax** *2232-3928* **Rooms** *5*

Housed in a beautiful modernist home in a quiet, upscale residential district, this backpackers' hostel boasts a well-lit co-ed dorm and a women's dorm, as well as private rooms. Guests also enjoy access to a TV lounge, pool table, Internet café, kitchen, and a lovely garden. **www.micasahostel.com**

WEST OF CITY CENTER Apartotel La Sabana

P **≅** **Y1** **≣** **&** **TV** $$$

Calle 44, N of Avenida las Américas **Tel** *2220-2422* **Fax** *2231-7386* **Rooms** *25*

Located next to Parque Sabana, this modern *apartotel* offers rooms, studios, and apartments. As part of its Business Express service, it provides an office within the room, complete with ergonomic chair. Other amenities include babysitting services upon request and a sauna. **www.apartotel-lasabana.com**

Key to Price Guide *see p248* **Key to Symbols** *see back cover flap*

WEST OF CITY CENTER Hotel Cacts

`P` `ıı` `≋` `⅄` $$$

Calles 28/30 and Ave 3 bis, No. 2845 **Tel** *2221-2928* **Fax** *2221-8616* **Rooms** 33

In a hilly residential area, this rambling hotel has ultra-clean rooms with simple decor; those in a modern annex are gloomy. Some rooms have shared bathrooms, while the deluxe rooms have TVs. Breakfast is served on a rooftop terrace. The hotel also has a travel service. **www.hotelcacts.com**

WEST OF CITY CENTER Barceló Palma Real

`P` `ıı` `Ψ` `目` `TV` $$$$

200 yards N of ICE, Sabana Norte **Tel** *2290-5060* **Fax** *2290-4160* **Rooms** 65

Despite its ungainly rust-red post-modernist exterior, this business hotel has delightful rooms furnished in contemporary fashion and featuring state-of-the-art amenities. It also offers a gym, business center, and an elegant restaurant with outdoor dining. **www.barcelopalmareal.com**

WEST OF CITY CENTER Best Western Irazú Hotel & Casino

`P` `ıı` `≋` `目` `⅄` `TV` $$$$

Barrio La Uruca **Tel** *2290-9300* **Fax** *2520-2483* **Rooms** 214

Best Western Irazú is a comfortable modern hotel on the northwestern fringe of the city. Its amenities include tennis courts, a casino and bar, a travel agency, and a shopping mall. Shuttles connect the hotel to downtown and to the international airport. **www.bestwesterncostarica.com**

WEST OF CITY CENTER Days Hotel Centro Colón

`P` `ıı` `Ψ` `目` `⅄` `TV` $$$$

Calle 38 and Ave 3 **Tel** *2547-2323* **Fax** *2257-2582* **Rooms** 98

Located near Parque Sabana, this twin-tower high-rise hotel offers classy, contemporary elegance. Amenities include a casino, nightclub, and coffee shop, as well as a tour agency, business center, and souvenir shop. **www.dayshotelsanjose.com**

WEST OF CITY CENTER Hotel Occidental Torremolinos

`P` `ıı` `≋` `Ψ` `目` `⅄` `TV` $$$$

Ave 5 and Calle 6 **Tel** *2222-5266* **Fax** *2255-3167* **Rooms** 92

Close to Parque Sabana, this upscale two-story hotel is centered on a lush garden with swimming pool. The guest quarters have all modern conveniences and elegant furnishings. A courtesy bus shuttles guests to and from downtown San José. **www.occidental-hoteles.com**

WEST OF CITY CENTER Hotel Parque del Lago

`ıı` `目` `TV` $$$$

Calles 40/42 and Ave 2 **Tel** *2257-2000* **Fax** *2223-1617* **Rooms** 40

This is a well-kept modern establishment close to Parque Sabana. Popular with business travelers, it has an elegant bar-restaurant, and its public areas are decorated with tropical hardwoods, colonial tile work, and details from traditional Costa Rican architecture. **www.parquedellago.com**

WEST OF CITY CENTER Crowne Plaza Corobicí

`P` `ıı` `≋` `Ψ` `目` `⅄` `TV` $$$$$

Autopista General Cañas, Sabana Norte **Tel** *2232-8122* **Fax** *2231-5834* **Rooms** 213

A landmark hotel with dramatic architecture and soaring atrium, this is popular with business travelers. The hotel has spacious rooms and abundant facilities including a casino, two restaurants and a bar, a travel agency, and a free shuttle service. **www.crowneplaza.com**

WEST OF CITY CENTER Hotel Grano de Oro

`P` `ıı` `⅄` `TV` $$$$$

Calle 30 and Aves 2/4 **Tel** *2255-3322* **Fax** *2221-2782* **Rooms** 40

Combining exquisite decor and exemplary service with a peaceful location, this colonial-era mansion enjoys a loyal clientele. It has rooftop Jacuzzis and a splendid gourmet restaurant *(see p274)*. Well-managed by Canadian owners, it is a member of Small Distinctive Hotels of Costa Rica *(see p246)*. **www.hotelgranodeoro.com**

THE CENTRAL HIGHLANDS

ALAJUELA Hotel II Millenium B&B

`P` `⅄` `TV` $$$

Río Segundo de Alajuela, 1 mile (1.6 km) SE of Alajuela **Tel** *2430-5050* **Fax** *2441-2365* **Rooms** 12

A favorite of backpackers, this simple but well-run, pleasant hostel has private rooms with baths as well as dorms. The owners offer a free 24-hour airport pickup service. The hostel also arranges day trips to nearby places of interest. Internet facilities are available. **www.bbmilleniumcr.com**

ALAJUELA Orquideas Inn

`P` `ıı` `目` `目` `⅄` `TV` $$$$

Cruce de Grecia y Poás, 2 miles (3 km) W of Alajuela **Tel** *2433-7128* **Fax** *2433-9740* **Rooms** 26

At the base of Volcán Poás, this atmospheric hacienda-style building sits in sprawling lush grounds. The comfortable rooms vary greatly, but all have brightly colored decor. Fountains feed the pool, which has a wooden sundeck. The bar draws its own clientele. **www.orquideasinn.com**

ALAJUELA Pura Vida Hotel

`P` `ıı` `⅄` `TV` $$$$

Cruce de Tuetal Norte y Sur, 0.5 mile (1 km) N of Alajuela **Tel** *2430-2929* **Fax** *2430-2630* **Rooms** 7

Originally a coffee *finca* (farm) set amid verdant hillside gardens, this family-run bed-and-breakfast has independent *casitas* (cottages) in distinct styles. The open-air restaurant serves gourmet meals, and the lobby has free Internet and Wi-Fi. The owners' dogs have the run of the place. **www.puravidahotel.com**

ALAJUELA Xandari   🅿️ 🍴 ♨️ 🚿 📺 $$$$$

Tacacori, 3 miles (5 km) N of Alajuela **Tel** *2443-2020* **Fax** *2442-4847* **Rooms** *24*

A superb boutique hotel with visionary contemporary design set in its own coffee *finca* (farm) in the hills above Alajuela. Spacious guest villas have rippling ceilings, artwork, and fabulous views. In addition to a restaurant *(see p275)*, the hotel boasts a holistic spa. Trails lead through bamboo groves to a waterfall. **www.xandari.com**

ATENAS El Cafetal Inn   🅿️ 🍴 ♨️ 📺 $$$$

Santa Eulalia, 3 miles (5 km) N of Atenas **Tel** *2446-5785* **Fax** *2446-4850* **Rooms** *16*

This friendly country inn is located on a coffee *finca* with nature trails. The spectacular two-story house with rounded glass corner alcoves overlooks the Río Colorado valley and coffee and sugarcane fields. The live-in owners are charming conversationalists. Choose from rooms, cottages, or a two-story bungalow. **www.cafetal.com**

BAJOS DEL TORO Bosque de Paz Lodge   🅿️ 🍴 $$$$

9 miles (14 km) E of Zarcero **Tel** *2234-6676* **Fax** *2225-0203* **Rooms** *12*

A two-story riverstone-and-timber building on the edge of the rainforest, this lodge has terra-cotta floors and wrought-iron beds. There is also a library with natural history books and research documents on the reserve. Meals are included in the price. Reservations are required. **www.bosquedepaz.com**

BAJOS DEL TORO El Silencio Lodge & Spa   🅿️ 🍴 $$$$$

10 miles (16 km) E of Zarcero **Tel** *2234-6676* **Fax** *2225-0203* **Rooms** *16*

The most luxurious nature lodge in Costa Rica, this gorgeous hotel edges up to the thick forest. The lavishly appointed bungalows are eco-sensitive in every regard and offer fabulous views over lush rainforest. A holistic spa offers yoga, and the lounge has a cozy fireplace. **www.elsilenciolodge.com**

EL ROSARIO DE NARANJO Vista del Valle   🏊 🅿️ 🍴 ♨️ 🗒️ 🚿 $$$$

Calle Indio, El Rosario de Naranjo **Tel** *2450-1165* **Fax** *2451-1165* **Rooms** *22*

Sitting right on the edge of the Rio Grande Canyon, this American-run boutique hotel has a beautiful main house and Japanese-style cottages, with individual porches; condo-villas have also been added. The rooms are well equipped and the hotel has its own reserve with a waterfall and plenty of wildlife. **www.vistadelvalle.com**

HEREDIA Casa Holanda   🍴 🗒️ 📺 $$$

San Pablo de Heredia, 2 miles (3 km) E of Heredia **Tel** *2238-3241* **Rooms** *4*

This bed-and-breakfast in a quiet residential area is run by classical musician James Holland, who offers impromptu concerts and private tours, in addition to gourmet meals served alfresco in a patio garden. The guest rooms are uniquely and tastefully furnished. **www.casaholanda.com**

HEREDIA Hotel Bougainvillea   🅿️ 🍴 ♨️ 🚿 📺 $$$$

Santo Domingo de Heredia, 2 miles (3 km) SE of Heredia **Tel** *2244-1414* **Fax** *2244-1313* **Rooms** *81*

This reasonably priced hotel is managed to high standards. Original pieces of specially commissioned modern art are scattered through the hotel. Rooms have views either of the mountains or of the San José skyline. The hotel offers tennis, swimming, a jogging track, and a well-known restaurant *(see p275)*. **www.bougainvillea.co.cr**

HEREDIA Finca Rosa Blanca Coffee Plantation & Inn   🅿️ 🍴 ♨️ $$$$

Santa Barbara de Heredia, 4 miles (6 km) NW of Heredia **Tel** *2269-9392* **Fax** *2269-9555* **Rooms** *17*

This fabulous family-run hotel on a coffee farm is an architectural delight inspired by Spanish architect Antoni Gaudí. Each guest room has unique decor and gourmet meals are served *(see p275)*. Horseback rides are offered, along with guided tours of the estate's coffee farm. **www.fincarosablanca.com**

LA GARITA Hotel La Rosa de América   🅿️ 🍴 ♨️ 🚿 📺 $$$

Barrio San José, 3 miles (5 km) W of Alajuela **Tel** *2433-2741* **Fax** *2433-2741* **Rooms** *12*

Located at an elevation of 3,000 ft (915 m) between La Garita and Alajuela, La Rosa de América is an intimate, reasonably priced hotel. Rooms are available in cabins set amid lush gardens. The Canadian family who owns it keeps it spotlessly clean. **www.larosadeamerica.com**

LA GARITA Martino Resort & Spa   🅿️ 🍴 ♨️ 📺 🗒️ 📺 $$$$$

Hwy 3, 2 miles (3 km) E of Pan-Am Hwy **Tel** *2433-8382* **Fax** *2433-9052* **Rooms** *42*

Manicured lawns, sumptuous hardwoods, and Romanesque-style statuary are hallmarks of this gracious family-run hotel. Facilities include a casino, tennis court, a modern gym and full-service spa, and a cigar bar and gourmet restaurant *(see p276)*. **www.hotelmartino.com**

LOS ANGELES CLOUD FOREST RESERVE Villablanca Cloud Forest Hotel 🅿️ 🍴 🚿 📺 $$$$

Los Angeles, 7 miles (12 km) N of San Ramón **Tel** *2401-3800* **Fax** *2461-0302* **Rooms** *35*

Perched atop the Continental Divide at the edge of a cloud forest, this colonial-era farmstead has an elegant restaurant and offers charming deluxe cottages warmed by log fires. Horseback rides, hikes, and bird-watching tours over 5 sq miles (12 sq km) of dairy pasture and cloud forest are a specialty. **www.villablanca-costarica.com**

MONTE DE LA CRUZ Hotel Chalet Tirol   🅿️ 🍴 ♨️ 📺 🚿 $$$

6 miles (10 km) NE of Heredia **Tel** *2267-6222* **Fax** *2267-6373* **Rooms** *34*

Designed in the style of a Swiss alpine village, this mountain retreat has a fine restaurant *(see p276)*. Choose from modern hotel rooms or rustic yet cozy chalets. Trails lead into cloud forest, and its facilities include tennis courts, a sauna, and meeting and convention facilities. **www.hotelchaleteltirol.com**

Key to Price Guide *see p248* **Key to Symbols** *see back cover flap*

OROSI Orosi Lodge

`P` `11` `目` $$$

SW of the plaza, Orosi village **Tel** *2533-3578* **Fax** *2533-3578* **Rooms** *6*

This simple yet charming family-run hotel is a minute's walk from hot spring pools, and is well placed for other local attractions such as Casa el Soñador. It offers rooms with kitchenettes, private baths, and terraces. It is known for its excellent café, which also has Internet facilities *(see p276).* **www.orosilodge.com**

OROSI Hotel Río Perlas Spa & Resort

`P` `11` `≋` `&` `TV` $$$$

1 mile (1.6 km) W of Orosi **Tel** *2533-3341* **Fax** *2533-3085* **Rooms** *69*

Surrounded by lush gardens, the secluded valley setting is a plus point for this modern chain hotel resembling a village complete with chapel. Thermal waters feed the pool and spa. Fishing outings to the five ponds in the surrounding area can be organized for keen anglers. **www.rioperlasspaandresort.com**

POAS Siempre Verde Bed & Breakfast

`P` `11` `&` `TV` $$$

Doka Estate, 7 miles (11 km) N of Alajuela **Tel** *2449-5562* **Fax** *2239-0540* **Rooms** *4*

Scenically situated within a vast coffee plantation, this warm, friendly hotel is a peaceful retreat from the bustle of the cities. Siempre Verde provides breakfast, as well as meals for special events such as conferences and private parties. **www.siempreverdebandb.com**

SALSIPUEDES Finca Eddie Serrano

`≋` `P` `11` `&` $$$

Km 80 on the Pan-Am Hwy **Tel** *8381-8456 or 2200-5915* **Rooms** *16*

Quetzals are plentiful at Finca Eddie Serrano, also known as Albergue Mirador de Quetzales. Located near Genesis II, this rustic timber lodge has simple log cabins offering awesome views, and is perfect for keen birders. The rates include breakfast and dinner. **www.elmiradordequetzales.com**

SAN ANTONIO DE BELEN Costa Rica Marriott

`P` `11` `≋` `W` `目` `&` `TV` $$$$$

Ribera de Belén, 1 mile (1.6 km) E of San Antonio de Belén **Tel** *2298-0000* **Fax** *2298-0011* **Rooms** *290*

This deluxe hotel set amid coffee fields boasts a sensational location with splendid views toward the Talamanca mountains. Guest rooms are sumptuous, and the well-rounded facilities include swimming pool, gym, boutiques, and a choice of restaurants. **www.marriotthotels.com**

SAN GERARDO DE DOTA Trogon Lodge

`P` `11` $$$

5 miles (8 km) W of the Pan-Am Hwy **Tel** *2293-8181* **Fax** *2239-7657* **Rooms** *58*

Situated amid lush gardens at an elevation of 7,000 ft (2,135 m) in the Valle de San Gerardo, this wooden lodge enjoys a marvelous setting next to the clear waters of Río Savegre. It offers trout fishing, as well as hiking, horseback rides, and mountain biking, plus a zipline. **www.grupomawamba.com**

SAN GERARDO DE DOTA Dantica Lodge & Gallery

`≋` `P` `11` `&` `TV` $$$$$

2.5 miles (4 km) S of reserve entrance **Tel** *2740-1067* **Fax** *2740-1071* **Rooms** *10*

With its own private trails within the cloud forest, this colonial-style lodge has bungalows with modern interiors and large glass windows offering stunning views over the surrounding canopy. The forest is rich in bird species, and the lodge has all mod cons and a restaurant, as well as its own gallery of indigenous crafts. **www.dantica.com**

TURRIALBA Hotel Villa Florencia

`P` `11` `≋` `木` `目` `&` `TV` $$$$

4 miles (6 km) SE of Turrialba **Tel** *2557-3536* **Fax** *2556-2372* **Rooms** *11*

Opened in 2008, this converted villa is an excellent option for bird-watchers, given its hilltop setting overlooking sugarcane fields close to Lake Angostura. The spacious guest rooms feature such details as terra-cotta tiles and river stones. **www.villaflorencia.com**

TURRIALBA Hotel Casa Turire

`P` `11` `≋` `TV` $$$$$

Hacienda Atirro, 5 miles (8 km) SE of Turrialba **Tel** *2531-1111* **Fax** *2531-1075* **Rooms** *16*

Situated on the shores of Lake Angostura, this delightful boutique hotel has spacious rooms and an elegant restaurant *(see p277).* Activities include visits to sugarcane, coffee, and macadamia nut processing centers. It is a member of Small Distinctive Hotels of Costa Rica *(see p246).* **www.hotelcasaturire.com**

TURRIALBA Rancho Naturalista

`≋` `P` `11` $$$$$

Tuís, 9 miles (14 km) E of Turrialba **Tel** *2544-8100* **Fax** *2544-8101* **Rooms** *11*

Perched on a mountainside, this homely wilderness ranch run by Evangelicals, is considered one of the finest birding lodges in the country. They have an extensive trail system and resident guides. Visitors can choose between cottages or rooms. Meals and guided hikes are included in the price. **www.ranchonaturalista.net**

VARA BLANCA Poás Volcano Lodge

`P` `11` `&` $$$$

14 miles (22 km) N of Alajuela **Tel** *2482-2194* **Fax** *2482-2513* **Rooms** *11*

Remodeled in dramatic modernist fashion after being damaged by the 2009 earthquake, this farm-run hotel stands amid cattle pastures with stupendous views. Guests are offered log fires and down comforters. There is also a games room, a gift shop, a small library, and an art gallery. **www.poasvolcanolodge.com**

VARA BLANCA Peace Lodge

`P` `11` `≋` `TV` $$$$$

Montaña Azul,15 miles (24 km) N of Alajuela **Tel** *2482-2720* **Fax** *2482-2720* **Rooms** *17*

Located at the La Paz Waterfall Gardens, the lodge's dramatic deluxe decor includes natural wood beams, hardwood flooring, hand-crafted canopy beds, fireplaces, and garden bathrooms and riverstone showers in spacious rooms. Each room boasts a Jacuzzi and oversized balcony. **www.waterfallgardens.com**

VOLCÁN TURRIALBA Volcán Turrialba Lodge
P 11 ☰ & $$$$

12 miles (19 km) NW of Turrialba **Tel** 2273-4335 **Fax** 2273-0703 **Rooms** 22

This simple mountain lodge is situated between Turrialba and Irazú Volcanoes, perfect for horseback rides and hiking. Of particular interest are its volcano tours, which lead into the crater when the volcano is quiescent. A 4WD is required to access the lodge. **www.volcanturrialbalodge.com**

THE CENTRAL PACIFIC AND SOUTHERN NICOYA

ESTERILLOS Alma del Pacífico
P 11 ☲ ☰ & $$$$$

Esterillos Este, 10 miles (16 km) S of Jacó **Tel** 2778-7070 **Fax** 2778-7878 **Rooms** 21

This beachside property has gorgeous contemporary villas fronting a sweeping gray-sand beach, although many guests prefer to laze on their terraces or by the pool. The garden is studded with contemporary sculptures. It is managed by Rock Resorts. **www.almadelpacifico.com**

JACO Hotel Cocal and Casino
P 11 ☲ ☰ $$$

Calle Cocal **Tel** 2643-3067 **Fax** 2643-0036 **Rooms** 43

Conveniently located, this is a lively low-rise beachfront hotel. With two swimming pools and a poolside bar, an open-air restaurant that serves good international cuisine, and a casino, the hotel is popular with small tour groups. Children are not allowed. **www.hotelcocalandcasino.com**

JACO Hotel Poseidon
P 11 ☲ ☰ & TV $$$$

Calle Bohío **Tel** 2643-1642 **Rooms** 14

The gourmet restaurant *(see p277)* is the highlight of this two-story hotel with modest furnishings. The upstairs rooms are better. All rooms have minibars and Wi-Fi, and some have ceiling fans instead of air-conditioning. The hotel can arrange tours and activities. **www.hotel-poseidon.com**

JACO Vista Guapa Surf Camp
P ☲ ☰ $$$$

1 mile (1.6 km) NW of Jacó **Tel** 2643-2830 **Rooms** 6

Set on a hillside, this surfers' hotel has simply but comfortably furnished bungalows, with great views of the ocean. Guests can watch TV in the communal lounge. While there is no restaurant as such, breakfast and dinner are available in the main house. The hotel specializes in surfing packages. **www.vistaguapa.com**

JACO Hotel Club del Mar
P 11 ☲ ☰ & TV $$$$$

Hwy 34, 1 mile (1.6 km) S of Jacó **Tel** 2643-3194 **Fax** 2643-3550 **Rooms** 31

This upscale beachfront hotel has rooms and self-catering villas around a huge pool with a tapas bar. There is a lush garden, an open-air restaurant, and a full-service spa. The focus is on water sports, with swimming, surfing, and canoeing on offer. Kayaks can also be rented. **www.clubdelmarcostarica.com**

MALPAIS Malpaís Surf Camp & Resort
P 11 ☲ ☶ $

S of Carmen **Tel** 2640-0031 **Fax** 2640-0061 **Rooms** 16

This well-run surfers' camp has several types of accommodations, from camping and cabins with shared bathrooms to poolside rooms and rustic bungalows with their own facilities. It offers various forms of recreation, such as horseback riding, mountain biking, and surf fishing, as well as surfing tours. **www.malpaissurfcamp.com**

MALPAIS Moana Lodge
P 11 ☲ ☰ TV $$$$

2 miles (3 km) S of Carmen **Tel** 2640-0230 **Fax** 2640-0623 **Rooms** 10

Beautifully decorated according to an African safari theme, Moana Lodge offers log cabins and lavish suites that nestle right at the forest's edge. Huge showers are a highlight, and all lodgings have Wi-Fi. The gourmet open-air restaurant overlooks a landscaped pool. **www.moanalodge.com**

MALPAIS Star Mountain Eco-Resort
P 11 ☲ $$$$

1 mile (1.6 km) E of Malpaís **Tel** 2640-0101 **Fax** 2640-0102 **Rooms** 5

A family-run ecological lodge, Star Mountain Eco-Resort is surrounded by forests adjoining Parque Nacional Cabo Blanco. Highlights are the colorful decor and a delightful tropical ambience. The hotel's open-air restaurant looks over lush grounds that meld into the lodge's own forest reserve. **www.starmountaineco.com**

MALPAIS Florblanca Resort
P 11 ☲ ☶ ☰ TV $$$$$

Playa Santa Teresa, 3 miles (5 km) N of Carmen **Tel** 2640-0232 **Fax** 2640-0226 **Rooms** 10

A serene beachfront deluxe resort with a Balinese motif. Spacious villas feature bathrooms open to the sky and tasteful furnishings, while the alfresco Nectar Bar & Restaurante offers gourmet food *(see p277)*. Guests can learn yoga and martial arts. A member of Small Distinctive Hotels of Costa Rica *(see p256)*. **www.florblanca.com**

MALPAIS Hotel Milarepa
P 11 ☲ ☰ & $$$$$

Playa Santa Teresa, 3 miles (5 km) N of Carmen **Tel** 2640-0023 **Fax** 2640-0663 **Rooms** 4

This intimate beachfront hotel is operated by live-in French owners. With an Asian aesthetic, the bungalows sit on the sands and have antique four-poster beds, open, screened walls, and partly open-air bathrooms. The restaurant serves gourmet cuisine. **www.milarepahotel.com**

MANUEL ANTONIO Vista Serena Hostel [P] ❄ ♿ $

2 miles (3 km) SE of Quepos ***Tel*** *2777-5162* ***Rooms*** *12*

One of the best backpackers' hostels in Costa Rica, this hillside retreat is kept spotless by the mother-and-son team that owns and runs it. Guests socialize in the TV lounge and on the veranda with games and hammocks. Vista Serena also offers a mangrove tour. **www.vistaserena.com**

MANUEL ANTONIO Hotel Mono Azul 💳 [P] 🍴 🏊 🏋 ❄ [TV] $$$

1 mile (1.6 km) S of Quepos ***Tel*** *2777-2572* ***Fax*** *2777-1954* ***Rooms*** *32*

This homely hotel is run along ecological lines and offers an assortment of rooms (made by combining a few small hotels and villas), which are all well equipped. There are also three swimming pools, wireless Internet access (for a small fee) and a good restaurant. Family friendly. **www.monoazul.com**

MANUEL ANTONIO Arenas del Mar [P] 🍴 🏊 ❄ ♿ $$$$$

4 miles (6.5 km) S of Quepos ***Tel*** *2777-2777* ***Fax*** *2777-2777* ***Rooms*** *38*

Arenas del Mar is a deluxe retreat with an enviable location at the north end of Playa Espadilla and access to its own private beach. The stylish suites all feature whirlpool spas on balconies overhanging the beach. Gourmet dishes are served in an airy thatched restaurant. **www.arenasdelmar.com**

MANUEL ANTONIO Hotel La Mariposa [P] 🍴 🏊 ❄ $$$$$

3 miles (5 km) S of Quepos ***Tel*** *2777-0355* ***Fax*** *2777-0050* ***Rooms*** *66*

A venerable hotel with a magnificent hilltop setting, Hotel La Mariposa has fantastic views of the ocean and the rainforests of Parque Nacional Manuel Antonio. Rooms vary from Mediterranean-style cottages to contemporary suites. The restaurant is renowned *(see p278)*. Free shuttles to the beach. **www.hotelmariposa.com**

MANUEL ANTONIO Hotel Si Como No Resort [P] 🍴 🏊 🏋 ❄ ♿ $$$$$

3 miles (5 km) S of Quepos ***Tel*** *2777-0777* ***Fax*** *2777-1093* ***Rooms*** *61*

This is an ecologically sensitive upscale contemporary hotel with a choice of restaurants *(see p278)*. It boasts a multimedia theater, Internet café, spa, two pools, and a host of activities. The original rooms are spacious, but the newer ones are more stylish. The hotel offers ecological tours. **www.sicomono.com**

MANUEL ANTONIO Makanda by the Sea [P] 🍴 🏊 $$$$$

3 miles (5 km) S of Quepos ***Tel*** *2777-0442* ***Fax*** *2777-1032* ***Rooms*** *11*

Makanda offers great forest and ocean views from spacious deluxe villas in harmony with their surroundings. Forest trails lead to a secluded beach with pre-Columbian fish traps. There is an infinity pool, and a romantic open-air restaurant serves gourmet cuisine *(see p278)*. **www.makanda.com**

MONTEZUMA Horizontes de Montezuma 💳 [P] 🍴 🏊 $$$

1 mile (1.6 km) N of Montezuma ***Tel*** *2642-0534* ***Fax*** *2642-0625* ***Rooms*** *7*

A gracious plantation-style hilltop lodging with a huge veranda, this German-run hotel has delightful, sparkling-white decor. It offers intensive as well as short-term Spanish language courses. The hotel can make arrangements with local tour operators for various activities. **www.horizontes-montezuma.com**

MONTEZUMA Nature Lodge Finca Los Caballos 💳 [P] 🍴 🏊 $$$$

2 miles (3 km) N of Montezuma ***Tel*** *2642-0124* ***Fax*** *2642-0664* ***Rooms*** *12*

Run by a German-Costa Rican couple, the Nature Lodge was built by local craftsmen using wood, stone and terra-cotta. Some of the rooms have outdoor showers with wonderful Pacific views, and breakfast is included in the price. Horse riding, full moon beach tours, and birding are specialities. **www.naturelodge.net**

MONTEZUMA Ylang Ylang Beach Resort 🍴 🏊 $$$$$

Playa Grande, 0.5 mile (1 km) E of Montezuma ***Tel*** *2642-0636* ***Fax*** *2642-0631* ***Rooms*** *20*

Set amid lush palm-shaded gardens, this attractive hotel is reached by a beach walk. It features various types of accommodations, including the El Sano Banano Hotel, safari tents, beach suites, and bungalows, all with an exquisite and creative aesthetic. The landscaped pool and gourmet restaurant are highlights. **www.ylangylangresort.com**

PLAYA HERMOSA Cabinas Las Arenas [P] 🍴 $$

Hwy 34 ***Tel*** *2643-7013* ***Fax*** *210-764-5675* ***Rooms*** *10*

Sitting over the shore, this surfers' guesthouse has charming wooden cabins and also permits camping. The restaurant is appealingly rustic, and there is a souvenir shop. Various tour reservations are offered. **www.cabinaslasarenas.com**

PLAYA HERMOSA Terraza del Pacífico [P] 🍴 🏊 ❄ [TV] $$$$

1 mile (1.6 km) S of Jacó ***Tel*** *2440-6862* ***Fax*** *2430-7571* ***Rooms*** *62*

Although it promotes itself as a surfers' hotel, Terraza del Pacifico is a modern beachfront option with broad appeal. It offers rooms and suites (with kitchenettes), as well as a pool for children. Canopy tours and dolphin-watching trips can be arranged. **www.terrazadelpacifico.com**

PLAYA HERRADURA Hotel Villa Caletas [P] 🍴 🏊 🏋 ❄ [TV] $$$$$

2 miles (3 km) N of Playa Herradura ***Tel*** *2637-0505* ***Fax*** *2637-0404* ***Rooms*** *36*

Combining a sublime mountaintop location and stunning decor, this French-run hotel exudes luxury. Its restaurants are acclaimed *(see p278)*, and it has a full-service spa. Live concerts are held in the classical amphitheater set in the cliff-face. A member of Small Distinctive Hotels of Costa Rica. **www.hotelvillacaletas.com**

PLAYA HERRADURA Los Sueños Marriott Ocean & Golf Resort   🅿️ 🍴 🏊 🍽️ 🗐 ⚙️ 📺 $$$$$
1 mile (1.6 km) W of Hwy 34   **Tel** *2630-9000*   **Fax** *2630-9090*   **Rooms** *201*

This grand beachfront hotel boasts a marina, a golf course in the lap of nature, a casino, business facilities, and a choice of restaurants *(see p279)*. Tastefully done-up suites have superb views of the ocean and mountains surrounding the resort, as well as minibars and 24-hour service. **www.marriott.com/sjols**

PLAYA HERRADURA Zephyr Palace   🅿️ 🍴 🏊 🍽️ 🗐 ⚙️ 📺 $$$$$
2 miles (3 km) N of Playa Herradura   **Tel** *2637-0505*   **Fax** *2637-0404*   **Rooms** *12*

The country's most luxurious hotel enjoys the same sublime views as the adjoining Hotel Villa Caletas *(see p255)*. Inspired throughout by the grandeur of Imperial Rome, Zephyr Palace offers sumptuous suites on a range of themes, including African safari and Ancient Egypt. **www.zephyrpalace.com**

PUNTARENAS Hotel Tioga   🅿️ 🍴 🏊 🗐 ⚙️ 📺 $$$$
Calles 17/19 and Ave 4   **Tel** *2661-0271*   **Fax** *2661-0127*   **Rooms** *52*

Established in 1959, this venerable hotel facing the Gulf of Nicoya is close to several good restaurants and bars. Rooms are adequate rather than inspired; some have only cold water. Hotel Tioga has a small casino, and the enclosed pool in the atrium courtyard has an island with a large tree. **www.hoteltioga.com**

PUNTARENAS Doubletree Resort by Hilton Puntarenas   🅿️ 🍴 🏊 🍽️ 🗐 ⚙️ 📺 $$$$
Playa Puntarenas, 5 miles (8 km) E of Puntarenas   **Tel** *2663-0808*   **Fax** *2663-0856*   **Rooms** *230*

This lively beach resort has a casino and several pools, bars, and restaurants. Sports facilities include tennis, volleyball, mini-golf, and water sports. Also on offer are live entertainment at night and a kids' club. The resort has stylish guest rooms and gets crowded on weekends. **www.doubletree1.hilton.com**

QUEPOS Wide Mouth Frog   🅿️ 🏊 🗐 ⚙️ $
100 yards (100 m) E of the bus station   **Tel** *2777-2798*   **Rooms** *24*

British and New Zealand partners run this highly regarded backpackers' hostel in the heart of Quepos. Maintained to high standards, Wide Mouth Frog has tastefully decorated dorms and private rooms around a courtyard with pool. Facilities include an Internet station and self-catering kitchen. **www.widemouthfrog.org**

SAVEGRE Rafiki Safari Lodge   🏊 🅿️ 🍴 🏊 $$$$$
19 miles (30 km) SE of Quepos   **Tel** *2777-2250*   **Fax** *2777-5327*   **Rooms** *10*

Set in a deep river valley, this African-style lodge has luxurious safari tents with fully appointed bathrooms. The lodge offers nature trips, as well as kayaking and whitewater rafting. A highlight is its South African *braai* (barbecue) in a thatched open-air restaurant. **www.rafikisafari.com**

TAMBOR Tambor Tropical   🅿️ 🍴 🏊 $$$$$
0.5 (1 km) SW of the airstrip   **Tel** *2683-0011*   **Fax** *503-371-2471*   **Rooms** *20*

A modern beachside hotel, Tambor Tropical features hexagonal two-story hardwood cabins in tranquil landscaped grounds. The hotel offers a spa and yoga classes. Among the many activities available for guests are boat trips, sportfishing, and horseback riding. **www.tambortropical.com**

TAMBOR Tango Mar Resort   🅿️ 🍴 🏊 🗐 ⚙️ 📺 $$$$$
3 miles (5 km) SW of Tambor   **Tel** *2683-0001*   **Fax** *2683-0003*   **Rooms** *35*

Tango Mar boasts a cliffside setting overlooking a splendid beach. Choose from amongst modern hotel rooms, romantic thatched cabins, and villas. The resort has a nine-hole golf course, stables, and a yoga and spa center, as well as a choice of two restaurants. **www.tangomar.com**

GUANACASTE AND NORTHERN NICOYA

BAHIA CULEBRA Four Seasons Resort at Papagayo Peninsula   🅿️ 🍴 🏊 🍽️ 🗐 ⚙️ 📺 $$$$$
Punta Mala, 27 miles (43 km) W of Liberia   **Tel** *2696-0000*   **Fax** *2696-0510*   **Rooms** *155*

Visitors get the best of all worlds at this deluxe chain resort: a fabulous hilltop location, excellent facilities, and fine service. It offers three swimming pools, a full-service spa, tennis, and a championship golf course designed by Arnold Palmer. **www.fourseasons.com/costarica**

BAHIA SALINAS Eco-Playa Resort   🅿️ 🍴 🏊 🗐 ⚙️ 📺 $$$$
Playa La Coyotera, 10 miles (16 km) W of La Cruz   **Tel** *2228-7146*   **Fax** *2289-4536*   **Rooms** *36*

Home to an advanced windsurfing center, this beachfront resort has a windswept location and spacious, well-appointed rooms. Guests can visit nearby Refugio Nacional de Vida Silvestre Isla Bolaños by kayak or boat. Also on offer are tours to Nicaragua's colonial cities and to Lake Nicaragua. **www.ecoplaya.com**

CAÑAS Hacienda La Pacífica   🅿️ 🍴 🗐 ⚙️ $$$$
2.5 miles (4 km) N of Cañas   **Tel** *2669-6050*   **Rooms** *19*

This historic property is situated at the heart of a working cattle estate and reforestation project. Oak furnishings evoke a suitably rustic feel, but guests rooms have Wi-Fi and cable TV, although the beds are far from comfortable. A homey restaurant serves traditional fare. **www.pacificacr.com**

Key to Price Guide *see p248* **Key to Symbols** *see back cover flap*

ISLITA Hotel Punta Islita [P] 🍴 🏊 🍸 ❄ [TV] $$$$$

Punta Islita, 10 miles (16 km) S of Carrillo ***Tel*** *2656-3036* ***Fax*** *2656-2202* ***Rooms*** *32*

This remote hillside deluxe hotel provides a variety of accommodations. Most of them have canopy beds and great views. The hotel has the gourmet 1492 Restaurante *(see p279)*, a spa, and a beach club, and offers kayaking, canopy tours, and an ATV adventure ride along mountain trails. **www.hotelpuntaislita.com**

LIBERIA Best Western Hotel & Casino El Sitio [P] 🍴 🏊 🍸 ❄ ♿ [TV] $$$

Hwy 21, W of Pan-Am Hwy ***Tel*** *2666-1211* ***Fax*** *2666-2059* ***Rooms*** *52*

This modern hotel has spacious rooms around an atmospheric courtyard with two pools. It also has gift stores, a tour desk, and a casino for those who wish to try their luck. It is the perfect jumping-off point for visiting Pacific beaches, national parks, and volcanoes. **www.bestwestern.com**

LIBERIA Bed & Breakfast El Punto [P] 🍴 ❄ ♿ $$$$

1 mile (1.6 km) S of Liberia ***Tel*** *2665-2986* ***Rooms*** *6*

Owner Mariana Estreda has transformed a former school into a cleverly designed boutique hotel with lively color schemes and contemporary furnishings. Shaded balconies face a lush garden, and there is also a stylish restaurant with a sushi bar and outdoor deck. **www.elpuntohotel.com**

MONTEVERDE Pensión Santa Elena 🏊 $$

Santa Elena, E of bus stop ***Tel*** *2645-5051* ***Fax*** *2645-5051* ***Rooms*** *24*

In the heart of Santa Elena, this popular and friendly budget hotel appeals to backpackers. Bright and inviting private rooms, deluxe rooms, and budget dorms are available. The hotel offers a short cut tour to Volcán Arenal, and also has a tourist information bureau. **www.pensionsantaelena.com**

MONTEVERDE Arco Iris Lodge [P] $$$

Santa Elena, NE of bus stop ***Tel*** *2645-5067* ***Fax*** *2645-5022* ***Rooms*** *12*

Albergue Arco Iris is a superbly run budget hotel in the center of Santa Elena. Amid well-tended lawns are a dozen delightful stone-and-timber cottages built by craftsmen using locally available material. The hotel is well placed for both the Monteverde and Santa Elena Reserves. **www.arcoirislodge.com**

MONTEVERDE El Sapo Dorado [P] 🍴 $$$$

Cerro Plano, 0.5 mile (1 km) E of Santa Elena ***Tel*** *2645-5010* ***Fax*** *2645-5180* ***Rooms*** *30*

This hillside hotel has accommodations in lovely stone-and-timber cottages. Some suites offer the coziness of a fireplace, while others have open-air terraces overlooking the Gulf of Nicoya. El Sapo Dorado also boasts one of Monteverde's premier restaurants *(see p280)*. **www.sapodorado.com**

MONTEVERDE Monteverde Lodge [P] 🍴 ♿ $$$$

SE of Santa Elena ***Tel*** *2257-0766* ***Fax*** *2257-1665* ***Rooms*** *27*

A contemporary hotel set in exquisite gardens at the edge of Costa Rica's best known cloud forest, Monteverde Lodge offers spacious, luxuriously furnished rooms, a family size Jacuzzi, and fine dining. Operated by Costa Rica Expeditions, it specializes in birding and nature hikes. **www.costaricaexpeditions.com**

NOSARA Hotel Café de Paris [P] 🍴 🏊 ❄ $$$

Beaches of Nosara, 4 miles (6 km) S of the airstrip ***Tel*** *2682-0087* ***Fax*** *2682-0089* ***Rooms*** *17*

What started as a great French-run bakery has expanded into an open-air restaurant, bar, and hotel featuring a range of accommodations, including deluxe villa suites. The architecture of the hotel makes the most of the tropical breezes. A selection of activities is available. **www.cafedeparis.net**

NOSARA Lagarta Lodge [P] 🍴 🏊 $$$

Punta Nosara, 2 miles (3 km) S of Boca Nosara ***Tel*** *2682-0035* ***Fax*** *2682-0135* ***Rooms*** *6*

A Swiss-run hilltop hotel whose main appeal lies in the wonderful coast or hill vista that every room offers, as well as the restaurant and bar. Rooms are comfortable, although uninspired. Trails lead into Reserva Biológica Nosara, and canoeing, and bird- and turtle-watching trips are offered. **www.lagarta.com**

NOSARA Harmony Hotel [P] 🍴 🏊 ❄ ♿ $$$$

Playa Guiones, Beaches of Nosara ***Tel*** *2682-4114* ***Fax*** *2682-4113* ***Rooms*** *24*

This hotel is located just a stone's throw from the beach and has a hip contemporary aesthetic. It offers a choice of rooms and bungalows with Wi-Fi and colorful furnishings. The landscaped pool is set in lush grounds, and activities such as tennis and yoga are available. **www.harmonynosara.com**

NOSARA L'Acqua Viva Hotel & Spa [P] 🍴 🏊 🍸 ❄ ♿ [TV] $$$$$

2 miles (3 km) S of Boca Nosara ***Tel*** *2682-1087* ***Fax*** *2682-0420* ***Rooms*** *35*

This fashionable Indonesian-themed resort opened in 2009 in the midst of a forest a 15-minute walk from the beach. Soaring thatched structures include a dramatic main lodge overlooking a multilevel swimming pool. Oriental furnishings abound throughout. Road noise is a drawback, so ask for a poolside room. **www.lacquaviva.com**

PLAYA AVELLANAS JW Marriott Guanacaste Resort & Spa [P] 🍴 🏊 🍸 ❄ ♿ [TV] $$$$$

Hacienda Pinilla, 3 miles (5 km) S of Tamarindo ***Tel*** *2681-2000* ***Fax*** *2681-2001* ***Rooms*** *310*

The Marriott chain opened this deluxe hotel in 2009 at the heart of a residential complex with a championship golf course. Sumptuous throughout, the Guanacaste Resort exudes an atmosphere of pampered comfort. Facilities include a spa, gym, tennis, and stables. **www.marriott.com**

PLAYA CARRILLO El Sueño Tropical   `P` `▯▮` `≋` `目` $$$

1 mile (1.6 km) SE of Puerto Carrillo **Tel** *2656-0151* **Fax** *2656-0152* **Rooms** *12*

Set amid vast beautiful gardens, this comfortable hotel run by a Tica-US couple has two swimming pools, a dozen rooms, and a thatched hilltop restaurant. Each room is decorated with bamboo and tropical pastels. Free transfers to Playa Carrillo's airstrip are available. **www.elsuenotropical.com**

PLAYA CONCHAL Westin Playa Conchal Beach & Spa   `P` `▯▮` `≋` `▥` `目` `&` `TV` $$$$$

Playa Brasilito, 2 miles (3 km) SW of Flamingo **Tel** *2654-3500* **Fax** *2654-4181* **Rooms** *406*

This deluxe resort nestles up to a sparkling white beach and is renowned for its championship golf course. The spacious rooms are gorgeously appointed, with contemporary styling and state-of-the-art amenities. Activities on offer include water sports. **www.westin.com**

PLAYA FLAMINGO Mariner Inn   `P` `▯▮` `≋` `目` `TV` $$$

By the marina, central Playa Flamingo **Tel** *2654-4081* **Fax** *2654-4024* **Rooms** *12*

A favorite of yachting enthusiasts, this small two-story inn is conveniently located next to the marina. The lively open-air Spreader Bar has great views and is where anglers, divers, and surfers can relax and watch the activity at the marina from the comfort of leather rockers. **marinerinn@racsa.co.cr**

PLAYA FLAMINGO Flamingo Marina Resort   `P` `▯▮` `≋` `目` `TV` $$$$

Atop hill, S of central Playa Flamingo **Tel** *2654-4141* **Fax** *2654-4035* **Rooms** *123*

This rambling hotel is perched on a lush hilltop close to the unspoiled expanse of Playa Flamingo. In addition to tropical breezes and spectacular views, it offers comfortable rooms, swimming pools, bars, and restaurants. It also has a boutique, dive shop, and activity center. **www.flamingomarina.com**

PLAYA GRANDE Hotel Bula Bula   `P` `▯▮` `≋` `目` `&` `TV` $$$$

S of El Mundo de la Tortuga, S end of Playa Grande **Tel** *2653-0975* **Fax** *2653-0978* **Rooms** *10*

This low-rise hotel offers intimate rooms with delightful decor and private baths. The open-air restaurant is run by a professional chef and opens on to lush gardens *(see p281)*. Also on offer are turtle tours and aquatic activities, as well as visits to Guaitil and Arenal and Rincón de la Vieja Volcanoes. **www.hotelbulabula.com**

PLAYA GRANDE Hotel Las Tortugas   `P` `▯▮` `≋` `目` $$$$

N end of Playa Grande **Tel** *2653-0423* **Fax** *2653-0458* **Rooms** *11*

Situated right next to Parque Nacional Marino Las Baulas, this ecologically sensitive hotel is popular with surfers. Rooms vary greatly – some are rather lackluster and in need of refurbishing. However, the amiable atmosphere and excellent restaurant make up for this *(see p281)*. **www.lastortugashotel.com**

PLAYA HERMOSA Hotel La Finisterra   `P` `▯▮` `≋` `目` $$$$

Atop hill, W of main road, S end of Playa Hermosa **Tel** *2672-0227* **Fax** *2672-0293* **Rooms** *10*

Known for its fine dining *(see p281)*, this hilltop hotel also offers the best views in the region. The spacious rooms include private bathrooms. Breakfast is included in the price. Among other activities, guests can tour Río Bebedero in Parque Nacional Palo Verde in a *panga* (water-taxi) or explore the Río Tempisque estuary. **www.lafinisterra.com**

PLAYA HERMOSA Villas del Sueño   `P` `▯▮` `≋` `目` `&` `TV` $$$$

W of main road, S end of Playa Hermosa **Tel** *2672-0026* **Fax** *2672-0026* **Rooms** *14*

Friendly Canadian hosts oversee this well-run hotel. It offers both spacious rooms and self-contained villas. There is gourmet dining in the open-air restaurant, which offers live music *(see p281)*. Activities include hiking, kayaking, rafting, and visits to Guaitil. **www.villadelsueno.com**

PLAYA HERMOSA Hotel Playa Hermosa   `P` `▯▮` `≋` `目` `&` `TV` $$$$$

0.5 mile (1 km) W of the main road in Playa Hermosa **Tel** *2672-0046* **Fax** *2672-0019* **Rooms** *32*

Once quite simple, this beachfront hotel was totally renovated and upgraded in 2008/9 and now boasts a series of two-story Balinese-style units around a landscaped pool shaded by venerable trees. The massive suite is utterly sumptuous, and the restaurant is one of the region's finest. **www.hotelplayahermosa.com**

PLAYA NEGRA Pablo's Picasso   `P` `▯▮` `目` `&` $$

S of Los Pargos **Tel** *2658-9158* **Rooms** *11*

Located near one of the premier surfing spots of Costa Rica and aimed at surfers and backpackers, this budget hotel offers dorms and simple *cabinas (see p235)*. It also has a restaurant *(see p281)* and a bar with a pool table and videos. The rates include breakfast. Tamarindo is a short drive away. **www.playanegrapablos.com**

PLAYA NEGRA Café Playa Negra   `P` `▯▮` `目` $$$

200 yards (200 m) S of the soccer field **Tel** *2652-9351* **Rooms** *6*

The beach may be a 15-minute walk away, yet this small hotel in the village is the nicest for miles. Run by a friendly Peruvian owner-chef, it offers tasteful offbeat furnishings in colorful rooms. Downstairs, a lively bar-restaurant *(see p281)* serves an eclectic menu and has Internet service. **www.playanegracafe.com**

PLAYA OCOTAL El Ocotal Beach Resort & Marina   `P` `▯▮` `≋` `目` `&` `TV` $$$$$

2 miles (3 km) SW of Playas del Coco **Tel** *2670-0321* **Fax** *2670-0083* **Rooms** *71*

Commanding a hilltop with spectacular views, this modern hotel specializes in scuba diving and sportfishing but is a splendid option for everyone. Also on offer are snorkeling, mountain biking, kayaking, tennis, and horseback riding. **www.ocotalresort.com**

Key to Price Guide *see p248* **Key to Symbols** *see back cover flap*

PLAYA OSTIONAL Tree Tops Bed & Breakfast 📠 🅿 $$$$

San Juanillo, 3 miles (5 km) N of Ostional **Tel** 2682-1334 **Fax** 2682-1334 **Rooms** 1

The owners rent out one sparsely furnished room in their thatched home overlooking a cove surrounded by wildlife-rich forest. Guests are welcomed as family, and the meals served are delicious. Activities include swimming with turtles, riding, and sportfishing. **www.costaricatreetopsinn.com**

PLAYAS DEL COCO Hotel Puerta del Sol 🅿 🍴 ≋ 🍷 🗐 🕭 📺 $$$$

SE of the plaza **Tel** 2670-0195 **Rooms** 22

Decorated in warm tropical pastels, this small, intimate hotel is run with panache by its Italian owners. It is acclaimed for Sol y Luna, its open-air gourmet restaurant *(see p281)*. Just a few minutes away from Playas del Coco fishing village, the hotel offers diving, sportfishing, and boat tours. **www.lapuertadelsolcostarica.com**

PLAYAS DEL COCO Rancho Armadillo 🅿 ≋ 🍷 🗐 📺 $$$$

1 mile (1.6 km) SE of Playas del Coco **Tel** 2670-0108 **Fax** 2670-0441 **Rooms** 6

This hacienda-style hotel offers a tranquil setting amid expansive grounds. There is delightful decor in the spacious rooms, all of which have "rainforest" showers. The owner, a former chef, prepares meals by request and rents out the entire complex to groups. **www.ranchoarmadillo.com**

PLAYAS DEL COCO Café de Playa Beach & Dining Club 🅿 🍴 ≋ 🗐 🕭 $$$$$

600 yards (600 m) E of the village center **Tel** 2670-1621 **Rooms** 5

Guests at this deluxe boutique hotel can enjoy the best of all worlds: a beachfront locale, a gourmet restaurant, a sushi bar, a canopy-shaded swimming pool, and hip contemporary furnishings in the individually styled bedrooms. A Hobie-Cat takes guests out on the bay. **www.cafedeplaya.com**

RINCON DE LA VIEJA Aroma de Campo 🅿 🍴 🗐 🕭 $$$

Curubandé, 11 miles (18 km) E of Pan-Am Hwy **Tel** 2665-0008 **Fax** 2665-0011 **Rooms** 4

The Belgian owners of this charming hillside hotel, dramatically located at the base of the Rincón de la Vieja volcano, pamper guests with gourmet meals served on an open-air patio. Furnishings are simple yet colorful and romantic. Friendly dogs and other animals abound. **www.aromadecampo.com**

RINCON DE LA VIEJA Buena Vista Mountain Lodge & Adventure Center 🅿 🍴 🕭 $$$

17 miles (27 km) NE of Liberia via Cañas Dulces **Tel** 2665-7759 **Fax** 2665-7759 **Rooms** 80

This ecolodge, a former cattle ranch, is known for the range of activities it offers, including a water slide, canopy trail, and zipline. Accommodation is in stone-and-timber cabins, and a rustic open-air restaurant serves *típico* (typical) meals, made using the lodge's own produce. **www.buenavistalodgecr.com**

RINCON DE LA VIEJA Hacienda Lodge Guachipelín 🅿 🍴 ≋ 📺 $$$

14 miles (22 km) NE of Liberia via Curubandé **Tel** 2666-8075 **Fax** 2665-2178 **Rooms** 40

At the center of a working cattle and horse farm, this down-to-earth, cozy hotel is perfectly situated for exploring Parque Nacional Rincón de la Vieja on horseback. The hotel's wide, inviting verandas are great for spending a somnolent afternoon. There are many activities on offer. **www.guachipelin.com**

RINCON DE LA VIEJA Rincón de la Vieja Lodge 🅿 🍴 ≋ $$$

17 miles (27 km) NE of Liberia via Curubandé **Tel** 8708-0238 **Fax** 2666-2441 **Rooms** 22

Close to the park entrance, and the nearest hotel to the volcano, this nature lodge has rustic wooden dorms, cabins, and bungalows spread throughout landscaped grounds. About 70 percent of the lodge's vast grounds are part of a reserve. The rates include meals. **www.hotelrincondelavieja.com**

SAMARA Flying Crocodile Lodge 🅿 🍴 ≋ 🗐 🕭 $$$

Playa Buena Vista, 5 miles (8 km) N of Sámara **Tel** 2656-8048 **Fax** 2656-8049 **Rooms** 8

One of Costa Rica's most eclectic hotels, the German-run Flying Crocodile Lodge doubles as an ultralight flight center. The cabins, each simple yet distinct, are bold statements of artsy design infused with Moroccan, Indian, and other exotic influences. **www.flying-crocodile.com**

SAMARA Hotel Belvedere 🅿 🍴 ≋ 🗐 🕭 📺 $$$

Playa Sámara, NE of soccer field **Tel** 2656-0213 **Fax** 2656-0213 **Rooms** 12

This cozy hotel on the hillside, close to the beach, has Swiss-style chalets, some with air-conditioning and king-size beds. The lush gardens contain a Jacuzzi and a swimming pool, which look out on to the ocean. Breakfast, included in the rate, is served on the terrace. **www.belvederesamara.net**

SAMARA Hotel Casa del Mar 🅿 🍴 🗐 $$$

Playa Sámara, E of soccer field **Tel** 2656-0264 **Fax** 2656-0129 **Rooms** 17

This small, two-story bed-and-breakfast is run to high standards by its French-Canadian owners. The rooms have simple furnishings. There are hammocks and lounge chairs for relaxing in the tropical garden or by the Jacuzzi. Nearby is a 5-mile (8-km) long beach for quiet walks. **www.casadelmarsamara.net**

SANTA CRUZ Hotel La Calle de Alcala 🅿 🍴 ≋ 🗐 🕭 📺 $$$

SE of Plaza de los Mangos **Tel** 2680-0000 **Fax** 2680-1633 **Rooms** 29

Hotel La Calle de Alcala is an intimate modern hotel with delightful decor and an appealing open-air bar and restaurant. The air-conditioned rooms have attached bathrooms. Among the amenities it offers are a swimming pool and Jacuzzi, and two conference rooms. **hotelalcala@hotmail.com**

TAMARINDO Hostel La Botella de Leche 💳 [P] ▤ ♿ $$

Across from the gym, Tamarindo ***Tel*** *2653-2061* ***Fax*** *2653-0189* ***Rooms*** *12*

This hostel for surfers and backpackers offers exceptional value for money. Guests can choose from dorms or private rooms. There is a communal kitchen, lockers, and Internet access. The hostel also offers surfboard rental and surfing lessons. **www.labotelladeleche.com**

TAMARINDO Hotel Arco Iris 💳 🍴 🍸 $$

E of Parque Central ***Tel*** *2653-0330* ***Fax*** *2653-0330* ***Rooms*** *5*

New owners have infused this formerly offbeat hotel with a dynamic 21st-century look, including stone-walled bathrooms. The highlights are a wood-and-stone sundeck and a gourmet restaurant serving Mediterranean-inspired cuisine. **www.hotelarcoiris.com**

TAMARINDO Luna Llena [P] 🍴 ≋ ▤ $$$$

SE of Iguana Surf ***Tel*** *2653-0082* ***Fax*** *2653-0120* ***Rooms*** *13*

This brightly colored, intimate hotel is run to professional standards by its Italian owners. Stone pathways run between conical thatched cottages, whose comfortable rooms exude good taste. All the cottages have private bathrooms. **www.hotellunallena.com**

TAMARINDO Capitán Suizo [P] 🍴 ≋ $$$$$

0.5 mile (1 km) SW of Plaza Colonial ***Tel*** *2653-0075* ***Fax*** *2653-0292* ***Rooms*** *31*

This luxurious beachfront hotel is set in lush gardens that have a free-form swimming pool. The elegant rooms use plenty of natural stone and hardwood. The open-air restaurant is one of the area's finest *(see p282)*. The hotel is a member of Small Distinctive Hotels of Costa Rica *(see p246)*. **www.hotelcapitansuizo.com**

TAMARINDO Hotel Jardín del Eden [P] 🍴 ≋ ▤ [TV] $$$$$

200 yards inland of Tamarindo Diría ***Tel*** *2653-0137* ***Fax*** *2653-0111* ***Rooms*** *36*

A delightful hillside hotel with lush grounds, the Jardin del Eden has a Mediterranean exterior that belies the deluxe rooms, which are furnished in globe-spanning fashions, including influences from Tunisia and Japan. The thatched restaurant and bar serves gourmet fusion fare and overlooks a tiered pool. **www.jardindeleden.com**

TAMARINDO Sueño del Mar Bed & Breakfast [P] 🍴 ≋ ▤ $$$$$

Playa Langosta, 0.5 mile (1 km) S of Tamarindo ***Tel*** *2653-0284* ***Fax*** *2653-0558* ***Rooms*** *6*

This colonial-era home has been converted into a gracious family-run bed-and-breakfast. Rooms boast timber beams, terra-cotta tiles, and exquisite furnishings. Delicious breakfasts are served in the garden, which opens onto the beach. **www.sueno-del-mar.com**

TAMARINDO Tamarindo Diría [P] 🍴 ≋ ▤ ♿ [TV] $$$$$

E of Plaza Colonial ***Tel*** *2653-0031* ***Fax*** *2653-0208* ***Rooms*** *182*

With a beachfront location in the center of Tamarindo, this upscale resort has a beautiful aesthetic. The restaurant is set under a tall *matapalo* tree on Tamarindo beach. The hotel also has two bars and a small casino. Among other activities, it offers tennis, golf, turtle-watching, and jungle boat rides. **www.tamarindodiria.com**

TILARAN Hotel El Sueño [P] 🍴 [TV] $$

N of the plaza ***Tel*** *2695-5347* ***Fax*** *2695-5347* ***Rooms*** *15*

This is a clean, well-run hotel with a friendly ambience and no-frills rooms at bargain prices. It is well placed as a pleasant stop en route to and from Laguna de Arenal. Rooms, all on the second floor, surround a skylit courtyard. No meals are offered, but there's a restaurant below.

THE NORTHERN ZONE

BIJAGUA Celeste Mountain Lodge [P] 🍴 $$$$

3 miles (5 km) NE of Bijagua ***Tel*** *2278-6628* ***Fax*** *2278-6628* ***Rooms*** *18*

This French-run ecolodge has a dramatic contemporary design, with open walls angled for shade. Rooms with walls of louvered glass guarantee vistas of both Tenorio and Miravalles volcanoes. The lodge also has a whirlpool. A special rickshaw allows handicapped guests to explore mountain trails. **www.celestemountainlodge.com**

CAÑO NEGRO Hotel de Campo [P] 🍴 ≋ $$$

NW of Caño Negro village ***Tel*** *2471-1012* ***Fax*** *2471-1490* ***Rooms*** *14*

This sportfishing lodge on the edge of Lago Caño Negro has spacious modern cabins set in a former citrus orchard. In addition to sportfishing packages, the lodge offers horseback tours and nature excursions. A souvenir shop is located on the grounds, and fishing tackle is available for sale. **www.canonegro.com**

CHACHAGUA Hotel Bosque de Chachagua [P] 🍴 ≋ $$$$

6 miles (10 km) SE of La Fortuna ***Tel*** *2468-1010* ***Fax*** *2468-1020* ***Rooms*** *31*

At the base of a mountain range, the Chachagua Rainforest Lodge is housed in a working cattle ranch located in a private rainforest reserve. Comfortable and spacious cabins are set amid lovely gardens, and an open-air restaurant overlooks a corral. **www.chachaguarainforesthotel.com**

Key to Price Guide *see p248* **Key to Symbols** *see back cover flap*

LA FORTUNA Gringo Pete's Hostel
SE of the plaza **Tel** 2479-8521 **Fax** 2479-8521 **Rooms** 5

This rambling backpackers' hostel has colorful decor, and offers both dorms (one open-air) and private rooms. Guests can use the communal kitchen, and there's a barbecue grill. Facilities include lockers, hammocks and sofas in a simple lounge, as well as a travel service. **www.gringopeteshostel.com**

LA VIRGEN DE SARAPIQUI Rancho Leona
On the banks of Río Sarapiquí **Tel** 2761-1019 **Rooms** 5

Appealing to backpackers, this simple, offbeat hotel hangs over the banks of Río Sarapiquí. Some of the rooms have bunks. The lodge boasts a small spa. The main activity here is kayaking, with the owner leading kayak trips. Spanish language courses are also offered. **www.rancholeona.com**

LA VIRGEN DE SARAPIQUI SarapiquíS Rainforest Lodge
N of La Virgen de Sarapiquí **Tel** 2761-1004 **Fax** 2761-1415 **Rooms** 36

Part of a broad-based ecological center *(see p205)*, this classy contemporary hotel boasts architecture inspired by traditional indigenous building techniques, and corresponding earthy interiors. The fine open-air restaurant and bar has the rainforest close at hand. **www.sarapiquis.org**

LAGUNA DE ARENAL Chalet Nicholas
1 mile (1.6 km) W of Nuevo Arenal **Tel** 2694-4041 **Fax** 2695-5387 **Rooms** 3

This bargain-priced, three-story, non-smoking bed-and-breakfast offers intimate rooms. Chalet Nicholas is run by welcoming hosts, who serve organic meals and arrange horseback rides. Trails lead into an adjacent forest reserve. **www.chaletnicholas.com**

LAGUNA DE ARENAL Lake Coter Eco-Lodge
4 miles (6 km) NW of Nuevo Arenal **Tel** 2289-6060 **Fax** 2288-0123 **Rooms** 46

This nature lodge is known for its wide range of activities, including kayaking, canoeing, freshwater fishing, hiking, horseback riding, and bird-watching. The duplex cabins are preferred over standard rooms, particularly for the views of Volcán Arenal as well as Arenal and Coter Lakes. **www.ecolodgecostarica.com**

LAGUNA DE ARENAL Mystica Lodge
10 miles (16 km) W of Nuevo Arenal **Tel** 2692-1001 **Rooms** 6

The charming Italian owners tend this intimate hotel with care. Rooms have a romantic aesthetic, and verandas offer splendid views. Gourmet meals are served at the restaurant, which is dominated by a baker's oven *(see p282)*. There is also a small souvenir shop. **www.mysticaretreat.com**

LAGUNA DE ARENAL Villa Decary
2 miles (3 km) E of Nuevo Arenal **Tel** 2694-4330 **Fax** 2694-4330 **Rooms** 8

Originally a coffee farm, this modern bed-and-breakfast hotel overlooking tranquil Lake Arenal has a pleasing home-away-from-home feel. It is popular with birders as well as gay travelers. Bird books and binoculars are available for guests. **www.villadecary.com**

LAGUNA DE ARENAL Hotel La Mansion Inn
5 miles (8 km) E of Nuevo Arenal **Tel** 2692-8018 **Fax** 2692-8019 **Rooms** 17

This deluxe option, with a spectacular hillside location, boasts an elegant restaurant. Rooms are graciously appointed, and have broad verandas with rocking chairs. The suites and deluxe rooms have TVs and minibars. Horseback rides are included in the rates, and rowboats are available. **www.lamansionarenal.com**

LAS HORQUETAS Rara Avis
9 miles (14 km) W of Las Horquetas **Tel** 2764-1111 **Fax** 2764-1114 **Rooms** 18

One of Costa Rica's original nature lodges and private rainforest reserves *(see p209)*, Rara Avis is deep in the rainforest. The rustic accommodations include a bare-bones treetop cabin. Rates are for a two-night stay and include meals and transfers by tractor-pulled rig. **www.rara-avis.com**

MONTERREY Leaves and Lizards Arenal Volcano Cabin Retreat
Monterrey **Tel** 2478-0023 **Rooms** 8

Built of ecologically sourced timber, Leaves and Lizards has six deluxe cabins and two houses perched on a hillside offering views of the volcano. The surrounding land is being reforested, and the friendly owners can arrange birding, riding, fishing, and hiking tours. Meals are served in the family dining room. **www.leavesandlizards.com**

MUELLE Tilajari Resort Hotel and Country Club
12 miles (19 km) NW of Ciudad Quesada **Tel** 2462-1212 **Fax** 2462-1414 **Rooms** 76

An expansive multifaceted resort on the banks of the Río San Carlos, Tilajari Resort Hotel and Country Club is popular for business meetings. The hotel has a wide range of excursions and facilities, including a gift shop, tennis courts, and botanical and butterfly gardens. **www.tilajari.com**

PARQUE NACIONAL VOLCAN ARENAL Arenal Observatory Lodge
5 miles (8 km) SE of park entrance **Tel** 2479-1070 **Fax** 2479-1074 **Rooms** 35

Spectacularly located on the flanks of Volcán Chato, this modern ecolodge offers dramatic views of Volcán Arenal from its rooms as well as its pleasant restaurant *(see p283)*. Accommodations range from standard rooms to a four-bedroom farmhouse. Guided hikes are offered. **www.arenalobservatorylodge.com**

PARQUE NACIONAL VOLCAN ARENAL Arenal Nayara   P ⅰ ⅈ ⅷ ≣ & TV $$$$$
5 miles (8 km) W of La Fortuna **Tel** *2479-1600* **Fax** *2479-1601* **Rooms** *24*

The fabulous Arenal Nayara hotel combines a hillside location offering outstanding volcano views with luxurious and colorful furnishings reminiscent of a Balinese theme. Its restaurant is acclaimed, and there is also a full-service spa. **www.arenalnayara.com**

PN VOLCAN ARENAL Montaña de Fuego Resort & Spa   P ⅰ ≋ ≣ & TV $$$$
4 miles (6 km) W of La Fortuna **Tel** *2460-1220* **Fax** *2479-1240* **Rooms** *50*

The comfortable wooden cabins of this luxury hotel have large picture windows opening to the volcano. Trails lace the lush gardens. Helicopter tours are available, as well as activities such as horseback riding and whitewater rafting. The resort has a souvenir shop and a full-service spa. **www.montanadefuego.com**

PN VOLCAN ARENAL The Arenal Springs Resort & Spa   P ⅰ ≋ ⅷ ≣ & TV $$$$$
6 miles (10 km) W of La Fortuna **Tel** *2401-3313* **Fax** *2401-3319* **Rooms** *42*

The largest hotel in the region, this resort takes up six levels on a hillside with splendid volcano views. Landscaped thermal pools and cascades, a casino, spa, multiple restaurants, an activity center, and a wildcat refuge are among its many draws. The resort also has villas. **www.thespringscostarica.com**

PUERTO VIEJO DE SARAPIQUI Posada Andrea Cristina   ≣ P ⅰ & $$
0.5 mile (1 km) W of Puerto Viejo **Tel** *2766-6265* **Fax** *2766-6265* **Rooms** *4*

This comfortable bed-and-breakfast is set in a forested garden, which draws varieties of wildlife. The lodge is run to high standards by an active conservationist and his wife, who cooks excellent meals on request. The naturalist owner takes guests on informative tours to nearby attractions. **www.andreacristina.com**

PUERTO VIEJO DE SARAPIQUI La Selva Biological Station   P ⅰ $$$$
2 miles (3 km) S of Puerto Viejo **Tel** *2766-6565* **Fax** *2766-6535* **Rooms** *10*

The lodge at this well-known biological station *(see p208)*, operated by the Organization of Tropical Studies (OTS), offers dormitories as well as private rooms. The rates include set meals at fixed hours. Reservations are essential at La Selva, which appeals mainly to nature lovers. **www.ots.ac.cr**

PUERTO VIEJO DE SARAPIQUI Selva Verde   P ⅰ $$$$$
5 miles (8 km) W of Puerto Viejo **Tel** *2766-6800* **Fax** *2766-6011* **Rooms** *40*

A world-renowned ecolodge and private reserve *(see p206)*, Selva Verde specializes in birding and nature hikes. The adventure activities have educational components, and there are conservation programs for student or teacher groups. The spacious rooms have canopied verandas, and the room rate includes food. **www.selvaverde.com**

THE CARIBBEAN

BARRA DEL COLORADO Río Colorado Fishing Adventure Lodge   ⅰ ≣ TV $$$$$
W of Barra del Colorado Sur airstrip **Tel** *2232-4063* **Fax** *2231-5987* **Rooms** *18*

Built on stilts at the mouth of Río Colorado, this sportfishing lodge offers well-equipped fiberglass fishing boats with knowledgeable guides and a well-stocked tackle shop. Among its other attractions are a small zoo, games room, and boat tours into the nearby rainforest. **www.riocoloradotarponfishing.com**

BARRA DEL COLORADO Silver King Lodge   ⅰ ≋ $$$$$
W of Barra del Colorado Sur airstrip **Tel** *8381-1403* **Fax** *2711-0708* **Rooms** *10*

Adjoining Río Colorado Lodge and rising over a swampy riverfront, this all-wood sportfishing lodge has spacious cabins linked by boardwalks. Several fishing packages are on offer. The lodge is closed mid-June through August, and also from mid-November through December. **www.silverkinglodge.net**

CAHUITA Alby Lodge   ≣ P $$
SE of bus stop and plaza **Tel** *2755-0031* **Fax** *2755-0031* **Rooms** *4*

Run by an Austrian couple, the lodge is situated amid lawns close to the beach. It features charming thatched and stilt-legged cabins, spaced well apart for privacy. Each small, simply-appointed cabin has a hammock, plus mosquito nets over the bed. Guests can make use of a communal kitchen. **www.albylodge.com**

CAHUITA El Encanto Bed & Breakfast Inn   P ⅰ & $$$
Playa Negra, 0.5 mile (1 km) N of Cahuita village **Tel** *2755-0113* **Fax** *2755-0432* **Rooms** *7*

Set in a serene garden infused with a Buddhist aesthetic, this is a delightful family-run hotel. Tasteful fabrics and art pieces grace the rooms, which vary in size. The hotel organizes several activities such as kayak tours, horseback riding, snorkeling, scuba diving, and dolphin-watching. **www.elencantobedandbreakfast.com**

CAHUITA Kelly Creek Cabins   P $$$
E of bus stop, next to Kelly Creek ranger station **Tel** *2755-0007* **Rooms** *4*

Located adjacent to the entrance of Parque Nacional Cahuita, this Spanish-run beachfront hotel has spacious yet sparsely furnished wooden cabins with broad verandas. Kelly Creek does not offer a restaurant service, but a dozen or so eating venues are located just a stone's throw away. **www.hotelkellycreek.com**

Key to Price Guide *see p248* **Key to Symbols** *see back cover flap*

CAHUITA La Diosa [P] 🍴 🏊 ❄ ♿ [$][$][$]

1 mile (1.6 km) N of Cahuita village ***Tel*** *2755-0055* ***Fax*** *2755-0321* ***Rooms*** *10*

An inviting palm-shaded beachfront location is a major draw to this charming and colorful hotel, whose owner offers yoga classes. Rooms are cozy, and two of the cabins even boast whirlpool tubs. La Diosa is set in lovely palm-shaded gardens sloping down to the beach. **www.hotelladiosa.net**

CAHUITA Magellan Inn [P] 🍴 🏊 ❄ [$][$][$]

Playa Negra, 3 miles (5 km) N of Cahuita village ***Tel*** *2755-0035* ***Fax*** *2755-0035* ***Rooms*** *6*

The exquisite grounds are the top draw at this family-run hotel at the far north end of Cahuita. All rooms have verandas overlooking a sunken pool and the beautiful gardens with pool, and the owner prepares gourmet dinners for the guests. The clean beaches of Cahuita are within walking distance. **www.magellaninn.com**

GUAPILES Casa Río Blanco Ecolodge 💳 [P] 🍴 [$][$][$]

Río Blanco, 4 miles (6 km) W of Guápiles ***Tel*** *2710-4124* ***Fax*** *2710-4124* ***Rooms*** *6*

This delightful riverside bed-and-breakfast at the edge of the forest is run by a charming South African couple. Cabins boast rich and calming decor. It offers nature trails and splendid wildlife viewing – over 300 species of birds have been recorded in the surrounding forests. **www.casarioblanco.com**

PUERTO LIMON Hotel Park [P] 🍴 ❄ [TV] [$][$][$]

Calle 1 and Ave 3 ***Tel*** *2758-3476* ***Fax*** *2758-4364* ***Rooms*** *32*

This clean, well-run hotel has one of the town's best restaurants plus secure parking (a requirement in this town). Although fairly simple, the rooms are adequate. It's worth paying extra for an oceanfront room with balcony. Locals are drawn to the bar. **parkhotellimon@ice.co.cr**

PUERTO VIEJO DE TALAMANCA Pagalú Hostel [P] ❄ [$]

100 yards inland and 50 yards E of the bank ***Tel*** *2750-1930* ***Rooms*** *8*

A stand-out surfers' and backpackers' hostel, this airy, contemporary two-story structure is kept clinically clean. Dorms and rooms have lovely bathrooms and many thoughtful amenities, such as halogen bedside reading lamps. On the west side of town, it is only a few minutes' walk from major services and restaurants. **www.pagalu.com**

PUERTO VIEJO DE TALAMANCA Rockings J's [P] 🍴 [$][$]

E of the Puerto Viejo bus stop, on the road to Manzanillo ***Tel*** *2750-0657* ***Rooms*** *10*

This is a well-run and popular surfers' hostel with a choice of accommodations, including camping, canopied hammocks, dorms, and private rooms. The ambience is lively and colorful, with ceramic murals throughout. Surf boards and bicycles can be rented. **www.rockingjs.com**

PUERTO VIEJO DE TALAMANCA La Costa de Papito [P] ♿ [$][$][$]

Playa Cocles, 1 mile (1.6 km) E of Puerto Viejo ***Tel*** *2750-0080* ***Fax*** *2750-0704* ***Rooms*** *10*

Located in front of the white expanse of Playa Cocles and surrounded by tropical gardens on the edge of a forest, this hotel has spacious hardwood cabins with endearing jungly decor, huge verandas, and attached baths. A calypso band sometimes performs in the airy, thatched restaurant. **www.lacostadepapito.com**

PUERTO VIEJO DE TALAMANCA Shawandha Lodge [P] 🍴 ♿ [$][$][$][$]

Playa Chiquita, 3 miles (5 km) E of Puerto Viejo ***Tel*** *2750-0018* ***Fax*** *2750-0037* ***Rooms*** *11*

Gracious contemporary decor in spacious thatched cabins highlight this romantic French-run resort, which extends up to the rainforest. The open-air restaurant is acclaimed for its French-inspired cuisine *(see p284)*. **www.shawandhalodge.com**

PUERTO VIEJO DE TALAMANCA Cameleón Boutique Resort [P] 🍴 🏊 ❄ ♿ [$][$][$][$][$]

Playa Cocles, 1.5 miles (2.5 km) S of Puerto Viejo ***Tel*** *2750-0501* ***Fax*** *2750-0501* ***Rooms*** *23*

The hippest hotel on the Caribbean coast, this chic deluxe resort opened in 2009. Guest rooms with state-of-the-art amenities are aglow with whites highlighted by colorful pillows. Uniquely for this region, it also has TVs. The Cameléon has a spa and a trendy bar-restaurant. **www.lecameleonhotel.com**

PUERTO VIEJO DE TALAMANCA Samasati Nature Retreat [P] 🍴 [$][$][$][$][$]

Hone Creek, 2 miles (3 km) W of Puerto Viejo ***Tel*** *2756-8015* ***Fax*** *2224-5032* ***Rooms*** *18*

Nestled high in forested hills, this rustic hotel specializes in yoga and holistic practices. Choose from simple cabins with shared bathrooms, bungalows, or self-contained two-story houses. Wildlife viewing is fabulous. A 4WD is required to get there. **www.samasati.com**

SELVA BANANITO RESERVE Selva Bananito Lodge 💳 [P] 🍴 [$][$][$][$][$]

16 miles (26 km) SW of Puerto Limón ***Tel*** *2253-8118* ***Fax*** *2280-0820* ***Rooms*** *11*

Close to Reserva Biológica Hitoy-Cerere, this rustic rainforest lodge has stilt-legged cabins, splendid for nature viewing and active adventures, such as tree climbing and waterfall rappeling. Basic meals, included in rates, are served family style. A 4WD is essential for access. **www.selvabananito.com**

TORTUGUERO Casa Marbella B&B ❄ ♿ [$][$]

100 yards (100 m) N of the public dock ***Tel*** *2709-8011* ***Fax*** *2709-8094* ***Rooms*** *5*

The Canadian owner of this simple yet well-maintained bed-and-breakfast lodge overlooking the lagoon is knowledgeable about the entire region and offers a selection of interesting tours. Guests enjoy full use of a kitchen and TV lounge. **http://casamarbella.tripod.com**

TORTUGUERO Miss Junie's

🔲 🕮 $$

N of public dock, Tortuguero village **Tel** *2709-8102* **Rooms** *12*

A simple two-story hotel run by a delightful hostess who serves Caribbean soul food (*see p284*). Set close to the lagoon, the rooms have wicker furnishings, ceramic floors, shuttered windows with screens, and ceiling fans. Each has hot water in private bathrooms. **www.iguanaverdetours.com**

TORTUGUERO Tortuga Lodge & Gardens

🕮 ≋ $$$$

3 miles (5 km) N of Tortuguero village **Tel** *2257-0766* **Fax** *2257-1665* **Rooms** *27*

Spacious and stylish rooms are on offer at this well-run eco- and sportfishing lodge with lush grounds. Top-class nature guides are on hand to take guests on turtle- or other wildlife-watching trips. It has gourmet dining and a romantic open-air lounge bar. Various packages are available. **www.costaricaexpeditions.com**

TORTUGUERO Laguna Lodge

🕮 ≋ ♿ $$$$$

1 mile (1.6 km) N of Tortuguero village **Tel** *2709-8082* **Fax** *2709-8081* **Rooms** *80*

This riverside ecolodge specializing in nature excursions has butterfly and botanical gardens, and an atmospheric restaurant overhanging the waters. Package rates include transfers, buffet meals, and nature tours. Fishing trips with experienced guides are available on request. **www.lagunatortuguero.com**

THE SOUTHERN ZONE

BAHIA DRAKE Corcovado Adventures Tent Camp

🕮 $$$

Playa Caletas, 3 miles (5 km) S of Agujitas **Tel** *8384-1679* **Rooms** *10*

Close to Parque Nacional Corcovado, this beachfront camp exudes a safari-style jungle atmosphere. Bathrooms are shared, and guests eat in a simple restaurant under a thatched roof. Meals are included in the room rate. Horseback rides are a popular activity. **www.corcovado.com**

BAHIA DRAKE Finca Maresia

🅿 ▤ $$$

1 mile (1.6 km) E of Agujitas **Tel** *2775-0279* **Rooms** *7*

A charming Spanish couple runs this modernist hotel surrounded by luxuriant forest on the road to Los Patos. Guests can choose from various lodging options, including a dorm and individual cabins with Japanese-style screened sliding doors that look onto verandas. **www.fincamaresia.com**

BAHIA DRAKE Jinetes de Osa

🕮 $$$$

S of Agujitas **Tel** *2231-5806* **Fax** *2231-5806* **Rooms** *9*

Specializing in scuba diving, this hotel stands amid rainforest on the beach. The rooms, although simple, are clean and comfortable. Rates include meals in an open-air restaurant, and fresh bread and fresh produce supplement the hotel's Mexican and Italian cuisine. **www.costaricadiving.com**

BAHIA DRAKE Aguila de Osa Inn

🕮 $$$$$

0.5 mile (1 km) S of Agujitas **Tel** *2296-2190* **Fax** *2232-7722* **Rooms** *13*

Tucked away in a canyon at the mouth of Río Agujitas, this lodge specializes in scuba diving and sportfishing. Spacious yet simply furnished rooms stairstep a steep hillside. Included in the room rate are quality meals served at the open-air restaurant (*see p284*). **www.aguiladeosainn.com**

BAHIA DRAKE La Paloma Lodge

🕮 ≋ $$$$$

Playa Cocalito, 1 mile (1.6 km) S of Agujitas **Tel** *2293-7502* **Fax** *2239-0954* **Rooms** *11*

La Paloma is a deluxe family-run clifftop hotel set amidst lush grounds with dramatic sunset views. The spacious and cozy cabins have wide balconies with hammocks; villas are also available. A range of activities are offered, including night hikes, all of which are covered by the room rate. **www.lapalomalodge.com**

CABO MATAPALO Bosque del Cabo

🅿 🕮 ≋ $$$$$

12 miles (19 km) S of Puerto Jiménez **Tel** *2735-5206* **Fax** *2735-5206* **Rooms** *12*

This family-run clifftop hotel combines simplicity with luxury. The surrounding forest abounds in wildlife, and scarlet macaws nest on the property. The open-air, solar-powered restaurant serves delicious food, which is included in the room rate. Yoga, a canopy tour, and various excursions are on offer. **www.bosquedelcabo.com**

CABO MATAPALO Lapa Ríos

🔲 🅿 🕮 ≋ $$$$$

9 miles (14 km) S of Puerto Jiménez **Tel** *2735-5130* **Fax** *2735-5179* **Rooms** *16*

Set in a private nature reserve, this deluxe jungle lodge is superb for birding and wildlife viewing. The lodge offers breathtaking ocean vistas and the airy and open bamboo bungalows have great romantic appeal. The gourmet restaurant (*see p284*) is set beneath a *palenque* (soaring circular thatched cover). **www.laparios.com**

CARATE Lookout Inn

🅿 🕮 ≋ $$$$

0.5 mile (1 km) E of Carate **Tel** *2735-5431* **Fax** *2735-5043* **Rooms** *18*

This three-story hotel has a splendid hillside location good for spotting scarlet macaws. A wooden staircase takes guests up the mountainside to spectacular ocean views. Lodgings include hotel rooms, beach bungalows, and jungle cabins. A range of activities is offered. Room rates include meals. **www.lookout-inn.com**

Key to Price Guide see p248 **Key to Symbols** see back cover flap

CARATE Luna Lodge   P 🍴 ♨ $$$$$

0.5 mile (1 km) N of Carate **Tel** *8380-5036* **Rooms** *15*

This peaceful rainforest lodge offers guests a choice of airy thatched cabins and safari-style tents. A traditional, conical, thatched restaurant-bar enjoys a spectacular setting. Meals are included in the rates. A variety of tours are available. A 4WD is required for access. **www.lunalodge.com**

CIUDAD NEILY Hotel Andrea   P 🍴 🗒 📺 $$

23 miles (37 km) E of Golfito **Tel** *2783-3784* **Fax** *2783-1057* **Rooms** *45*

Located in the heart of Ciudad Neily, this modern Colonial-style hotel has comfortable rooms and a fine restaurant *(see p284)*. The room rates are a bargain considering the amenities the hotel offers. **elhotelandrea@hotmail.com**

DOMINICAL Cabinas San Clemente   🏠 P 🍴 $$

W from the soccer field **Tel** *2787-0026* **Fax** *2787-0055* **Rooms** *12*

This is a friendly hostel aimed at surfers, located just a few steps away from the beach. Some rooms have air-conditioning and hot water, and some have wraparound verandas. Fully furnished houses are also offered. Avoid the barebones budget rooms. The hostel's popular bar and grill *(see p284)* is a short walk away.

DOMINICAL Refugio Nacional de Vida Silvestre Barú   P 🍴 ♿ $$$

2 miles (3 km) N of Dominical **Tel** *2787-0003* **Fax** *2787-0057* **Rooms** *6*

This wildlife refuge *(see p230)* has modestly furnished cabins, each with a beautiful view of the forest and located within a short walk of the beach. A wide selection of activities is available, from night tours in the jungle to bird-watching hikes. **www.haciendabaru.com**

DOMINICAL Hotel Roca Verde   P 🍴 ♨ 🗒 ♿ $$$$

0.5 mile (1 km) S of Dominical **Tel** *2787-0036* **Fax** *2787-0013* **Rooms** *10*

The highlights of this small hotel near the beach are the charming *cabinas* (cottages) and an open and airy bar and restaurant with frequent live music, very popular with the surf crowd. Kayaking, canopy tours, sportfishing, and biking are on offer. **www.rocaverde.net**

DOMINICAL Cascadas Farallas   P 🗒 $$$$$

Platanillo, 5 miles (8 km) E of Dominical **Tel** *2787-8378* **Fax** *2787-8378* **Rooms** *3*

This deluxe, family-run riverside lodge at the edge of dense forest seamlessly blends into nature. Inspired by Balinese themes, it exudes a Zen-like peace. Rivestones and bamboo feature prominently in the design, and the three two-bedroom suites have balconies fronting the forest. Yoga is offered. **www.waterfallvillas.com**

DOMINICAL Cuña del Angel   P 🍴 ♨ 🗒 ♿ $$$$$

5 miles (8 km) S of Dominical **Tel** *2787-8012* **Fax** *2787-8015 (ext. 304)* **Rooms** *16*

A gracious, Italian-themed hotel that is a member of the Small Distinctive Hotels of Costa Rica, this colorful property offers a varied selection of rooms and villas. The elegant restaurant is first-rate. Cuña del Angel also has a spa, and sportfishing is a specialty. **www.cunadelangel.com**

ESCALERAS The Necochea Inn   P 🍴 ♨ 🗒 $$$$

4 miles (6 km) SE of Dominical **Tel** *2787-0155* **Rooms** *6*

Perched in the mountains inland of Dominical, this delightful and deluxe B&B with ocean views is reached via a steep and sometimes muddy dirt road. One suite has a wraparound deck; two others share a bathroom. Amenities include a library and a games room. **www.thenecocheainn.com**

GOLFITO Hotel Centro Turístico Samoa   P 🍴 ♨ 🗒 ♿ 📺 $$$

N of Pueblo Civil **Tel** *2775-0233* **Fax** *2775-0573* **Rooms** *14*

This clean and modestly furnished waterfront hotel has spacious rooms. The hotel marina has facilities for sailboats and sportfishing boats. The lively bar and restaurant have excellent views of the marina and the surrounding gulf *(see p285)*. The hotel also contains the Museo Marino *(see p240)*. **www.samoadelsur.com**

GOLFITO Banana Bay Marina   P 🍴 🗒 ♿ 📺 $$$$

S of the plaza **Tel** *2775-0838* **Fax** *2775-0735* **Rooms** *4*

Located on the edge of tropical rainforest, Banana Bay Marina is a small contemporary hotel with delightful decor. Its quiet, comfortable rooms look out on to the marina and have private bathrooms. The hotel also offers Internet access. **www.bananabaymarina.com**

GOLFITO Casa Roland Marina Resort   P 🍴 ♨ 📺 🗒 ♿ $$$$$

Zona Americana **Tel** *2775-0180* **Rooms** *53*

Although located inland, at a considerable distance from a marina, this hotel bills itself as a sportfishing resort. Festooned throughout with contemporary art, it also has a fine (albeit windowless) restaurant. Rooms, which come in three different types, are rather on the gloomy side. **www.fishingmarinaresort.com**

LAS CRUCES Las Cruces Biological Station   P 🍴 ♿ $$$$

4 miles (6 km) S of San Vito **Tel** *2524-0628* **Fax** *2524-0629* **Rooms** *12*

This research center *(see p227)* has spacious and airy wooden cabins overlooking lush forest. All cabins have balconies and private baths. There are refectory-style meals in a dining room with views of the Talamanca Mountains. Guided nature hikes are on offer. Reservations are essential. **www.ots.ac.cr**

OJOCHAL Finca Bavaria
`P` `11` `≋` `&` $$$

0.5 mile (1 km) E of Playa Ballena **Tel** *8355-4465* **Rooms** *5*

This German-run property is set in hilltop gardens. The spacious rooms have bamboo decor and a romantic aesthetic. Ocean views can be enjoyed from the terraces. There are nature trails for guests who wish to enjoy the solitude of the surroundings. **www.finca-bavaria.de**

OJOCHAL Villas Gaia
`P` `11` `≋` `&` $$$

Playa Tortuga, 0.5 mile (1 km) W of Ojochal **Tel** *2786-5044* **Fax** *2786-5004* **Rooms** *14*

Providing easy access to Playa Tortuga and the Terraba-Sierpe mangrove ecosystem, this colorful property offers scuba diving and other activities, plus a gourmet restaurant *(see p285)*. The hilltop swimming pool offers spectacular views of ocean sunsets. **www.villasgaia.com**

OJOCHAL The Lookout at Turtle Beach
`▣` `P` `11` `≋` `TV` $$$$$

Playa Tortuga, 0.5 mile (1 km) W of Ojochal **Tel** *2786-5074* **Rooms** *12*

This luxury option is set in lovely landscaped hilltop grounds. There is delightful pastel decor in the *casitas* (cottages), which have private patios and splendid views. Delicious breakfasts are included in the price, and a range of activities is available. **www.hotelcostarica.com**

PARQUE INTERNACIONAL LA AMISTAD Finca Anael
`▣` `P` `11` $$

Reserva Biológica Durika, 11 miles (18 km) E of Buenos Aires **Tel** *2730-0657* **Fax** *2730-0657* **Rooms** *9*

A simple lifestyle is the hallmark of this ecologically sustainable mountain farm. Accommodation is in rustic cabins, with meals being included in the room rates. The *finca* (farm) can arrange guided nature hikes. A 4WD is required for access, but the daunting drive is best left to jeep-taxis. **www.durika.org**

PAVONES Cabinas La Ponderosa
`▣` `P` `11` `≋` `&` `TV` $$$

2 miles (3 km) S of Pavones, on the road to Punta Banco **Tel** *2776-2076* **Rooms** *6*

This is a popular beachfront surfers' hostel with comfortable, casual cabins. All cabins have private bathrooms, outdoor sitting area, and either fans or air-conditioning; there are also villas and suites. Volleyball, basketball, horseback rides, and forest trails are also available. **www.laponderosapavones.com**

PAVONES Casa Siempre Domingo Bed & Breakfast
`▣` `P` `11` `≋` `≣` $$$$

1 mile (1.6 km) S of Pavones **Tel** *2776-2185* **Rooms** *4*

A bargain-priced family-run bed-and-breakfast set in lush gardens. The elevation and open interiors allow for constant breezes and the tropical decor adds to the ambience. Miles of secluded beaches lend themselves to quiet walks, and trails lead into rainforest. **www.casa-domingo.com**

PAVONES Tiskita Lodge
`P` `11` `≋` $$$$$

Punta Banco, 3 miles (5 km) S of Pavones **Tel** *2296-8125* **Fax** *2296-8133* **Rooms** *16*

This rustic hilltop ecolodge is part of a fruit farm and forest reserve fabulous for viewing wildlife. "Rainforest" bathrooms are made of river stones. Meals, served family-style in the open-air farmstead, and guided nature hikes are included. Closed mid-September to mid-October. **www.tiskita-lodge.co.cr**

PIEDRAS BLANCAS Agua Dulce Lodge & Resort
`11` `≣` $$$$$

Playa Preciosa, 9 miles (14 km) W of Golfito **Tel** *8817-2850* **Rooms** *2*

Backed by pristine rainforest, this intimate two-story beachfront ecolodge is constructed of native hardwoods and furnished with rattan and wicker pieces. Accommodation is in upscale two-bedroom villas with air-conditioning and balconies. Access is by boat only. **www.aguadulcelodge.com**

PIEDRAS BLANCAS Esquinas Rainforest Lodge
`P` `11` `≋` $$$$$

Las Gambas, 6 miles (10 km) NE of Golfito **Tel** *2741-8001* **Fax** *2741-8001* **Rooms** *14*

Adjoining Parque Nacional Piedras Blancas, this pleasant community-run ecolodge has comfortable rooms with private bathrooms and terraces. Guided nature hikes, Golfo Dulce kayak tours, and other activities are offered. The rates include meals made from the hotel's own fresh produce. **www.esquinaslodge.com**

PIEDRAS BLANCAS Playa Nicuesa Rainforest Lodge
`11` $$$$$

Playa Nicuesa, 9 miles (14 km) NW of Golfito **Tel** *2258-8250* **Rooms** *8*

A member of the Small Distinctive Hotels of Costa Rica, this is an atmospheric ecolodge nestled between ocean and rainforest reserve. All rooms have canopied beds and garden showers. Electricity is provided by solar power. Rates include meals. Access is only by boat – a 20-minute journey from Golfito. **www.nicuesalodge.com**

PLAYA PLATANARES Iguana Lodge
`P` `11` `≋` $$$$$

2 miles (3 km) E of Puerto Jiménez **Tel** *8848-0752* **Fax** *2735-5436* **Rooms** *14*

This lovely property has luxurious rooms with travertine-clad bathrooms, plus bamboo-and-log bungalows; some have garden showers. A beachfront restaurant has live music on Fridays. The lodge also has a Japanese bathhouse, a yoga deck, and a lap pool. **www.iguanalodge.com**

PLAYA SAN JOSECITO Casa Corcovado Jungle Lodge
`11` `≋` $$$$$

8 miles (13 km) S of Bahía Drake **Tel** *2256-3181* **Fax** *2256-7409* **Rooms** *14*

Close to the northern border of Corcovado, this luxurious jungle-themed hotel has thatched cabins with exquisite decor. Excursions and gourmet meals are offered. Access is solely by boat. Closed September to mid-November. **www.casacorcovado.com**

Key to Price Guide *see p248* **Key to Symbols** *see back cover flap*

PUERTO JIMENEZ Cabinas Jiménez
100 yards (100 m) N of the soccer field **Tel** *2735-5090* **Rooms** *10*

Under a US owner, this once-mediocre shorefront property now offers the nicest accommodations in town. Comfortable and delightfully furnished, the rooms open onto verandas with bay vistas. Several restaurants are a short walk away. A variety of tours can be arranged. **www.cabinasjimenez.com**

RINCON Suital Lodge
4 miles (6 km) NE of Rincón **Tel** *8826-0342* **Fax** *8826-0342* **Rooms** *3*

This is a rustic wooden lodge with individual stilt-legged cabins set in a forest clearing. All have private bathrooms and balconies. Close by are about 3 miles (5 km) of forest trails and a peaceful beach. Other activities include kayaking on Río Esquinas and horseback riding. **www.suital.com**

SAN GERARDO DE RIVAS Cabinas Roca Dura
9 miles (14 km) NE of San Isidro **Tel** *2742-5071* **Rooms** *9*

Roca Dura is a backpackers' delight. Built into the rock-face and named accordingly, the hotel has basic and draughty yet distinctive rooms. The bedrock makes up one of the walls at the entrance, as well as in some of the bedrooms. The hotel also has a simple restaurant.

SAN GERARDO DE RIVAS Río Chirripó Retreat
8 miles (13 km) NE of San Isidro **Tel** *2742-5109* **Rooms** *8*

A fabulous riverside location, rich decor, and tasteful furnishings combine to make this bargain-priced bed-and-breakfast an irresistible option. All rooms have private baths and a deck overlooking the river. There are also some roofed camping platforms for the more adventurous, and a yoga dojo. **www.riochirripo.com**

SAN GERARDO DE RIVAS Monte Azul Boutique Hotel
Chimirol de Rivas, 4 miles (6 km) SW of San Gerardo de Rivas **Tel** *2742-5222* **Rooms** *6*

A sensational boutique hotel with a lush valley setting, Monte Azul also acts as an art retreat. Guests are welcomed with home-made goat's cheese and bread, and the restaurant serves a nightly gourmet meal. Trails wind through the landscaped gardens. A sumptuous villa has its own pool. **www.monteazulcr.com**

SAN ISIDRO DE EL GENERAL Rancho La Botija
4 miles (6 km) NE of San Isidro de El General **Tel** *2770-2146* **Fax** *2770-2146* **Rooms** *11*

This charming family-run hotel is set within coffee plantations and orchards. The land falls within an archaeological zone, and a Tour of the Trails is offered. A 19th-century *trapiche* (sugarcane press) dominates the atmospheric restaurant. There is also an observatory. **www.rancholabotija.com**

SIERPE Veragua River Lodge
1 mile (1.6 km) NE of Sierpe **Tel** *2788-1460* **Fax** *2786-1460* **Rooms** *7*

Veragua River Lodge is a peaceful and isolated riverside hotel with whimsical charm. The Italian artist owner has converted the two-story house into an intimate hotel with delightful tropical decor. All the rooms are comfortable and spacious. **www.hotelveragua.com**

UVITA Toucan Hotel
100 yards E of Hwy 34, Central Uvita **Tel** *2743-8140* **Rooms** *10*

This is a well-run budget hostel near Parque Nacional Marino Ballena. Some of the rooms have private baths and air-conditioning, the others share facilities. Guests have the use of a communal kitchen, laundry, and TV room. Free Internet and Wi-Fi are available, as are live music and open-air films. **www.tucanhotel.com**

UVITA Las Terrazas de Ballena
0.75 mile (1 km) NE of Uvita **Tel** *2743-8034* **Rooms** *3*

Perched on the forested hillside with views along the Costa Ballena, this intimate hotel provides accommodation in three thatched, stone-walled cabins with huge balconies. The Balinese-style restaurant is the best for miles *(see p285)*. A 4WD is required for access. **www.terrazasdeballena.com**

ZANCUDO Cabinas Sol y Mar
1 mile (1.6 km) S of Zancudo village **Tel** *2776-0014* **Rooms** *5*

This charming American-run hotel is always abuzz with karaoke, beach golf, and other activities. The restaurant specializes in Californian cuisine. The rooms are enlivened by Guatemalan fabrics. Camping is permitted, and a two-bedroom house can also be rented. Closed October. **www.zancudo.com**

ZANCUDO Oceano
400 yards (400 m) S of Zancudo village **Tel** *2776-0921* **Rooms** *2*

This small, simple hotel is run by a charming US couple who lavish attention on their guests. Although simple, the two rooms feature such thoughtful touches as flashlights and umbrellas. The open-air restaurant is the best around *(see p285)*. Guests get free use of bicycles and Internet. **www.oceanocabinas.com**

ZANCUDO The Zancudo Lodge
N of Zancudo village **Tel** *2776-0008* **Fax** *2776-0011* **Rooms** *20*

This highly respected sportfishing lodge enjoys a windswept oceanfront setting. The rooms are comfortable and well tended, and there are a swimming pool and large hot tub close to the ocean. The lodge provides tackle and lure for anglers, as well as fly rods. **www.zancudolodge.com**

WHERE TO EAT

Remarkably cosmopolitan, the restaurants in San José and tourist enclaves offer a wealth of dining options. These span the globe, from Peruvian to Indian, with French and Italian cuisine being well represented. In the countryside, food is based on traditional staples – rice and beans, accompanied by pork or chicken and tropical vegetables. Regional variations are prevalent, especially along the nation's eastern seaboard, where Afro-Caribbean

A chef at San José's Hotel Grano de Oro

dishes are infused with coconut milk and spices. Hot spices are rarely used elsewhere in Costa Rica. Small snack shops, called *sodas*, are found throughout the country, as are fast-food chain outlets, both US and local. Roadside fruit stalls are ubiquitous, with fresh fruits being an important part of the local diet *(see p270)*. Some vegetarian restaurants exist in San José and other major cities, and most other establishments will feature at least one vegetarian dish.

The dining room at the Restaurant Grano de Oro *(see p274)*, San José

RESTAURANTS AND BARS

The capital city offers by far the greatest choice of places to eat, with a variety of cuisines for every budget and taste. Many of the finest gourmet restaurants are in deluxe hotels. There are a number of internationally renowned eateries presided over by award-winning chefs. Most of these specialize in conventional international cuisine. Hotels usually have their own restaurants, which in wilderness areas may be the only places to eat in the vicinity. In *hospedajes* (B&Bs), the owners may be willing to prepare meals for an extra fee. The cheapest places to eat local dishes are the family-run *sodas*, small snack counters serving fixed-price menus and *casados* (set lunches, often referred to as *plato del día, plato ejecutivo, or comida corrida*).

Working-class males visit *cantinas* – neighborhood bars often identified by their Wild West-style swing doors – where *bocas (see p270)* are served. These bars can be quite rough and women will generally not feel comfortable in these places. Visitors should stick to recommended bars in urban areas. Hotel staff can advise you of places to avoid.

CHAIN RESTAURANTS

All the principal American fast-food chains are conspicuous in Costa Rica, including Burger King, KFC, Pizza Hut, and McDonald's. There are also several homegrown companies, such as Burguí and Rosti Pollo, which compete with their US counterparts.

The main cities have a good selection of chain cafés, which serve light snacks and sometimes inexpensive buffets. An excellent option is Spoons, found in larger cities in the Central Highlands – it offers a wide range of sandwiches, salads, and hot meals at low prices. Musmanni is a nationwide *panadería* (bakery) chain selling freshly baked breads, confectionery, and sandwiches. Mexican fare is the specialty of Antojitos, which has outlets around San José. Bagelman's features bagels, sandwiches, and breakfast specials, while Pops is the local ice cream chain.

LOCAL EATING HABITS

For the most part, Ticos (Costa Ricans) follow North American eating habits, with some differences. The typical *desayuno* (breakfast) consists of *gallo pinto (see p270)* served with fresh fruit juice and milky coffee. Males often take a shot of whisky with their breakfast. Extended families usually come together on weekends for brunch. Many businesses close at noon for *almuerzo* (lunch), which might last as long as 2 hours. The *merienda* (mid-afternoon coffee break) is still

A bar in the village of Ojochal, near Dominical

El Sano Banano Village Restaurant & Café *(see p278)*, Montezuma

popular. Most restaurants close by 11pm, as the local preference is for early dining. Ticos are leisurely in their dining, and often linger at the table after finishing their meal, which can be frustrating if the restaurant is full. Many eateries close on Sunday.

Ticos rarely invite friends and acquaintances to dine at home, and prefer to extend invitations to restaurants. They seldom arrive at an appointed hour, except for important businesses occasions, and it is considered rude to arrive on time if invited for *cena* (dinner) in a private home.

PAYING AND TIPPING

Fixed-price menus such as *casados* normally offer better value than their à la carte equivalents. At *sodas*, it is possible to have a wholesome cooked meal for around 800 colones. In elegant restaurants, a three-course dinner with wine might cost around 13,000 colones per person. *Sodas* have no tax – in other places, the prices shown on menus usually include a 13 per cent sales tax. An additional 10 per cent service charge is often automatically added to your bill. Feel free to challenge this charge if service has been poor, and tip extra only for exceptional service.

Credit cards are accepted by most restaurants in cities and major resorts, but expect to pay in cash in rural areas, small restaurants, and *sodas*. VISA is the widely accepted card, followed by MasterCard

and American Express, few places take Diners Club or traveler's checks.

FOOD HYGIENE

Food is normally of a high standard nationwide, and tap water in most regions is trustworthy. If in any doubt, it is worth taking precautions by drinking only bottled water, fruit juices, or processed drinks. Bottled water is sold in all restaurants, hotels, and supermarkets. In restaurants and bars, order drinks without ice *(sin hielo)*.

Salads, vegetables, and fruits pose little problem, except in the Caribbean, Puntarenas, and Golfito, where hygiene can be questionable. To play safe, avoid salads and uncooked vegetables, and peel all fruits, especially those bought from open-air markets and urban fruit stalls. Across the nation, milk, and dairy products are pasteurized and are no cause

Cocktail menu, Ricky's Bar, Cahuita

for concern. Take care to avoid undercooked shellfish, meat, and fish.

CHILDREN

Costa Ricans love children and most restaurants welcome them. High-chairs are usually available, and many restaurants offer child portions; some even have special kids' menus. Many eating places, especially fast-food outlets and rural roadside cafés, have children's playgrounds.

ALCOHOL

Restaurants are usually licensed to sell beers and spirits, including *guaro*, the popular alcohol of choice. The more elegant restaurants serve a variety of international wines, although outside the Central Highlands quality often suffers due to poor storage. Sale of alcohol is not permitted during election periods and three days (Thu–Sat) before Easter; nonetheless, Ticos stock up in advance, and the days before elections see heavy drinking.

SMOKING

Smoking is popular in Costa Rica. There are laws requiring non-smoking areas in restaurants, but these are rarely in separate rooms. In addition, enforcement is rare. Indeed, it is common for diners to light up between, or even during, courses.

The kitchen of the Iguana Lodge, Playa Platanares *(see p266)*

The Flavors of Costa Rica

At Costa Rica's *ferias de agricultores* (farmers' markets), stalls are piled with glistening fruit, including exotics such as guayaba, marañón, and papaya. Tomatoes, peppers, and squash add their own bouquets and hues, as does a potpourri of herbs and spices. Pasture-fed cattle provide beef and fresh milk, while poultry roams free until ready for the pot. The warm waters off Costa Rica's shores deliver fresh fish and crustaceans glistening with brine. Caribbean and Creole are the main culinary styles.

Ripe papayas

One of the many *sodas* (foodstalls) found all over Costa Rica

CARIBBEAN CUISINE

Making the most of local spices, cuisine along Costa Rica's Atlantic seaboard bears the zesty imprimatur of Jamaica, thanks to the many islanders who settled in the region. The sea's fresh bounty, such as shrimp and lobster, finds its way into curries and stews enlivened with chilies, ginger, and Scotch bonnet peppers. In Tortuguero, green turtle has long been a favorite meat, popularly used in stews, along with mackerel. *Pargo* (red snapper) is often "jerked" – spiced up with mouth-searing peppers and grilled over coals.

The milk of the versatile coconut forms a base ingredient for cooking and in cocktails, while providing invigorating refreshment when drunk fresh from the shell. Local fruits such as citrus, papaya, and guava are jellied and candied with sugar, coconut, and cocoa.

Mackerel | **Mahimahi**

Lobster

Shrimps | **Red snapper**

A selection of fresh seafood available in Costa Rica

COSTA RICAN DISHES AND SPECIALTIES

Gallo pinto (fried rice and black beans) is the dish most associated with Costa Rica. It is commonly served as breakfast with scrambled eggs and slabs of local Monteverde cheese. At lunch it becomes *arroz con pollo*, with lightly seasoned stewed chicken or pork. This forms the basis of *casados* (set meals), served with vegetables such as carrots, yucca, cabbage, onions, *plátanos* (fried plantain), and a simple salad of lettuce, tomatoes, and hearts of palm. Rice dishes are enlivened by a splash of Salsa Lizano, a mildly spicy sauce made of vegetables. Countryfolk still favor traditional stews such as *sopa de mondongo*, made from tripe and vegetables, and a spicy meatball soup called *sopa de albóndigas*, from Guanacaste. Main meals are often preceded by *bocas*, tasty tidbits such as tortillas with cheese. Turtle eggs on offer may have been illegally harvested.

Scotch bonnet peppers

Ceviche *is raw chunks of white fish marinated in citrus juice with garlic, onion, and red and green peppers, served on crackers or lettuce leaves.*

Well-stocked grocery store in San José

GUANACASTECAN SPECIALTIES

From the heartland of *comida criolla* (Creole cuisine), Guanacastecan fare revolves around *maíz* (sweet corn), introduced in pre-Columbian times by indigenous peoples. Succulent yellow sweet corn is eaten as a vegetable – cooked, boiled, or grilled – and, following ancient recipes, is ground into flour to form the base for tortilla and *tamale* dough. *Arroz* (rice) was brought by the Spanish from Asia. Today, it is a major crop in the lowlands and forms the chief accompaniment to the nation's cuisine, usually served alongside black beans, also grown in the lowlands. Brahma cattle graze the pastures, producing highly prized steaks and ground beef. The seas off Nicoya are famous for game

Vegetables at a *feria de agricultores* (farmers' market)

fish, such as the flavorful dorado or mahimahi. Playas del Coco, Quepos, and Tamarindo are the main centers for sportfishing, while the port town of Puntarenas has a large shrimping and commercial fishing fleet.

ON THE MENU

Arreglados (nationwide). Puff pastries filled with cheeses and/or meats.

Akee and codfish (Caribbean). Akee, blended with salted codfish and served with *callaloo* (similar to spinach) and fried dumplings called Johnny Cakes.

Cajetas (nationwide). A thick, nougat-like dessert made of coconut milk, sugar, orange peel, and other fruits.

Chorreadas (Guanacaste). Large corn tortillas served like pancakes and topped with *natilla* (sour cream).

Empanadas (nationwide). Turnover pastries filled with minced meat, potatoes, and onions, or cheese and beans.

Pan bon (Caribbean). Dark bread spiced with nutmeg and sweetened with caramelized sugar and candied fruits.

Rundown (Caribbean). Mackerel simmered in coconut milk with vegetables.

Tamales (nationwide). Steamed corn-dough pastries stuffed with minced beef and wrapped in banana leaves.

Filete de pescado grillé, *grilled fillet of* corvina *(sea bass), is traditionally served with* ajo *(buttered garlic), rice, and mixed vegetables.*

Olla de carne, *a dish from Guanacaste, is a meat-and-vegetable stew with pumpkin-like chayote, corn, plantain, potatoes, and yuca.*

Tres leches *comprises layers of dense sponge cake soaked in condensed milk, evaporated milk, and cream, and topped with whipped cream.*

Choosing a Restaurant

The restaurants in this guide have been selected, as far as possible, for the quality of the food and atmosphere. However, in some parts of Costa Rica there are few restaurants that can be recommended. In such cases, places have been suggested that offer at least good value. For map references for San José, see pages 128–9.

PRICE CATEGORIES
For a three-course meal for one (excluding wine), including tax and service:

$ Under $10
$$ $10–15
$$$ $15–20
$$$$ $20–30
$$$$$ Over $30

SAN JOSE

CITY CENTER La Criollita
$

Calles 7/9 and Ave 7 **Tel** *2256-6511*
Map 2 D3

This delightful eatery on the edge of Barrio Amón is suffused with sunlight filtering through a *vidriera* (stained-glass panel). Songbirds visit the lush outdoor patio. The large menu includes full breakfasts, snack lunches, and simple but well-executed entrées. It is popular with a business clientele at lunch. Closed Sunday.

CITY CENTER Mama's Place
$

Calles Central/2 and Ave 1 **Tel** *2223-2270*
Map 1 B3

Attracting workers at lunchtime, this small, no-frills family-run diner in the heart of downtown specializes in filling *casados* (set meals) and Italian pastas and salads. *Tipico* (typical) dishes are displayed behind glass, cafeteria-style. The Italian family running the place fusses over their clientele. Closed Sunday.

CITY CENTER Restaurante Vishnu
$

Calles 1/3 and Ave 1 **Tel** *2223-4434*
Map 1 C3

This is a splendid budget option for vegetarians, with an extensive menu and large portions. It focuses on health food, including vegetarian burgers, salads, fruit juices, and filling *casados*. The owners have similar restaurants downtown and throughout San José. The eatery is kept spotlessly clean.

CITY CENTER Café de la Posada
$$

Calle 17 and Ave 2 **Tel** *2258-1027*
Map 2 E4

A delightful bohemian café-restaurant run by Argentinians. Creative fare includes *empanadas* (stuffed turnovers), salads, quiches, and omelettes, as well as cappuccinos and delicious desserts, enjoyed to the accompaniment of jazz and classical music. Diners can sit outside under large umbrellas in a pleasant pedestrian precinct.

CITY CENTER Spoon
$$

Calles 5/7 and Ave Central, plus various other locations throughout San José **Tel** *2217-2600*
Map 1 C3

Clean and simple cafeteria-style venue popular for its bargain-priced *casados* and various dishes such as salads, sandwiches – including *lapices* (submarines) – and local favorites. Delicious baked goods attest to the chain's origins as a bakery.

CITY CENTER Balcón de Europa
$$$

Calle 9 and Aves Central/1 **Tel** *2221-4841*
Map 2 D3

An informal, timeless restaurant in the heart of downtown, with wood-paneled walls and serving hearty pastas and other dishes conjured up by the French-born chef-owner. The decor includes framed proverbs and historical prints. Closed Saturday.

CITY CENTER Gourmet
$$$

Parque Mora Fernández, Ave 2 **Tel** *2221-4000*
Map 1 C4

An inviting 24-hour patio restaurant known for its splendid position in front of the Teatro Nacional, and for the comings and goings of itinerant musicians and hawkers. The simple *arroz con pollo* (chicken with rice) is cheap and filling, and a buffet is offered. Usually, there is a pianist playing.

CITY CENTER Kalú
$$$

Calle 7 and Ave 11, Barrio Amón **Tel** *2221-2081*
Map 2 D2

Chef Camille Ratton oversees this fantastic dining venue, which is part-café, part-art gallery, and part-store. The decor is avant-garde, the mood casual, and the eclectic nouvelle fusion cuisine is sensational. A raised deck provides the perfect location for warm nights. Closed Sunday.

CITY CENTER La Cocina de Leña
$$$

Centro Comercial El Pueblo, Barrio Tournon **Tel** *2256-5353*
Map 2 D1

Tucked away amidst the narrow alleys of the El Pueblo complex, this invitingly rustic restaurant is decorated in the style of a quintessential Costa Rican farmstead and is considered *the* place to enjoy traditional fare. The menu also includes corn dishes.

Key to Symbols *see back cover flap*

CITY CENTER Restaurante Casa China

            🛇 🎵 V $$$

Calle 25 and Aves 8/10 **Tel** *2257-8392*   **Map** 2 F3

Located in the Asociación China de Costa Rica, this refectory-style restaurant is like a piece of Shanghai transported to the center of San José. The menu offers a varied and seemingly endless list of authentic Chinese dishes at unbeatable prices. Parking is available.

CITY CENTER Tin Jo

            🕏 🍸 V $$$

Calle 11 and Aves 6/8 **Tel** *2221-7605*   **Map** 2 D4

This homely restaurant spans the Orient with its wide-ranging menu featuring regional dishes from China, India, Indonesia, Japan, and Thailand. The cuisine is filling and tasty, rather than gourmet. The decor bears minimal Asiatic motifs, but the moodily dark ambience is appealing and the prices are right.

CITY CENTER La Esquina de Buenos Aires

     🛇 🎵 🍸 V $$$$

Calle 11 and Ave 6 **Tel** *2223-1909*   **Map** 2 D4

Re-creating the ambience of a Buenos Aires bodega, this warm and inviting restaurant is run by an Argentinian who delivers hearty meat dishes from the homeland. Also on offer is seafood, such as filet of sole in blue cheese with boiled potatoes. The large wine list is – unsurprisingly – heavy on Malbecs.

EAST OF CITY CENTER Bagelmen's

                    🍴 V $

Calle 33 and Ave 2 **Tel** *2212-1314*

Specializing in sandwiches, bagels, and baked goods, this clean modern option resembles a tastefully decorated fast-food restaurant in ambience. The breakfasts, including *gallo pinto (see p270)*, are an attractive bargain, but the menu also features omelettes and other American favorites. There are also outlets in Escazú and San Pedro.

EAST OF CITY CENTER Café Ruiseñor

            🕏 🍽 V $$

Calles 41/43 and Ave Central **Tel** *2225-2562*

Separated from the buzz of traffic by a wide grassy strip, this airy brasserie in the Los Yoses district is an excellent place to lunch on soups, salads, and nouvelle seafood and meat dishes. The cappuccinos and espressos are good. Choose indoor or shaded patio dining. Closed Sunday.

EAST OF CITY CENTER Olio

            🛇 🍸 V $$$

Calle 33, Aves 3/5, Barrio Escalante **Tel** *2281-0541*

This tapas restaurant exudes a bohemian atmosphere and draws a trendy and sophisticated clientele. Exposed brick walls and dark wainscoting paneling add to the romantic ambience. The expansive menu spans the Mediterranean, from Spain to the Levantine.

EAST OF CITY CENTER Marbella

     🕏 🛇 🍸 V $$$$

Ave Central, San Pedro **Tel** *2224-9452*   **Map** 1 A3

Considered the finest Spanish restaurant in San José, this elegant establishment is situated at the rear of the Centro Comercial de la Calle Real. Chef Emilio Machado is especially renowned for his superb paellas. Marbella has a large wine list.

EAST OF CITY CENTER Jürgen's Grill

       🕏 🍸 V $$$$$

Boutique Hotel Jade, N of Autos Subaru dealership, Barrio Dent **Tel** *2283-2239*

Situated in the Boutique Hotel Jade *(see p249)*, this fashionable restaurant exudes contemporary elegance. The menu of predominantly nouvelle dishes is invitingly creative and the ambience appealing, although the service is somewhat formal and a dress code applies. The bar has a cigar lounge. Closed Sunday.

ESCAZU Giacomin

           🕏 🍽 V $$

Calle del Llano, San Rafael de Escazú **Tel** *2288-3381*

Light snacks and baked goods, from croissants to *paninis*, are offered at this café specializing in exquisite home-made chocolates and gourmet coffees. Enjoy your temptations in the air-conditioned café or on a terrace overlooking a landscaped garden. Closed Sunday.

ESCAZU Taj Mahal

      🍴 🛇 🍸 V $$$$

0.5 mile (1 km) W of Paco Plaza **Tel** *2228-0980*

Costa Rica's only Indian restaurant, the Taj Mahal serves *biryanis*, *tandoor* dishes, *tikka masala*, *naan* bread, and other authentic specialties from northern India. The menu accommodates both vegetarians and meat eaters, and the food is cooked as "hot" as you like. The rack of lamb is not to be missed. Closed Monday.

ESCAZU Capital Grill

                 🍸 V $$$$

Tara Resort Hotel, San Antonio de Escazú **Tel** *2288-6362*

This renowned restaurant is a magnet for Costa Rica's social elite. Walls of glass offer sensational views, while the menu features well-known Continental favorites, from lobster tail to corn-fed Angus steaks and Alaskan king crab.

ESCAZU Cerutti

                         $$$$$

100 yards N of Plaza Atlantic, San Rafael de Escazú **Tel** *2228-4511*

This supremely elegant Italian restaurant draws Costa Rica's A-listers to dine in an ambience that marries stylish contemporary fittings to a Colonial-era mansion with a well-worn terra-cotta floor. Superb service and gourmet dishes all contribute to the sublime experience. Closed Sunday.

ESCAZU La Luz
🍸 🇻 $$$$$

The Alta Hotel, Alto de las Palomas, 2 miles (3 km) W of Escazú **Tel** *2282-4160*

High ceilings and elegant contemporary decor in mock-Tudor style characterize this upscale restaurant in the Alta Hotel *(see p250)*. Inventive nouvelle gourmet cuisine makes the most of local ingredients, although the food quality has famously gone through periods of ups and downs. La Luz is favored for Sunday brunch.

ESCAZU Le Monastère
🚶 🎵 🍴 🍸 🇻 $$$$$

4 miles (6 km) W of Escazú **Tel** *2288-8515*

Located high above Escazú, this fashionable restaurant in a former chapel plays on the monastic theme. Waiters dress as monks, and Gregorian music fills the historic hallways and dining rooms. The French cuisine includes *escargot*, and sea bass with crab, caviar, and champagne. Closed Sunday.

ESCAZU Saga
🍽 ♿ 🇻 $$$$$

Ave Excazú **Tel** *2289-6615*

A trendy restaurant renowned for its food, ambience, and superb service. The menu features international dishes including chicken in peanut sauce served with chutney, and seafood risotto with coconut. The deep-fried calamari is a great appetizer. Don't miss the restaurant's own bread or its great desserts, such as rice pudding with strawberries.

WEST OF CITY CENTER Sabor Nicaragüense
🍽 🚶 🍴 🇻 $

Calle 20 and Aves Central/1 **Tel** *2248-2547*

Situated close to the Coca Cola bus terminal, this clean and well-run family-operated restaurant serves Nicaraguan fare, as well as Costa Rican staples at budget prices. Although air-conditioned, it also has a small outdoor area facing the tumultuous street.

WEST OF CITY CENTER Antojitos
🚶 🎵 🇻 $$

W of Sabana Oeste, Rohrmoser **Tel** *2231-5564*

A lively Mexican restaurant serving all the traditional favorites, along with steaks and grilled meats, as well as excellent margaritas. Mariachis sometimes entertain diners. Antojitos has outlets throughout the city. The chain is extremely popular with locals and can get noisy.

WEST OF CITY CENTER Marisquería La Princesa Marina
♿ $$

Sabana Oeste, SW corner of Parque Sabana **Tel** *2296-7667*

Good, simple dishes from the sea are served at this no-frills restaurant on the west side of Parque Sabana. This canteen-style option is always lively and very popular with the working-class crowd for its filling portions. The *ceviche* appetizer is recommended, as is the *corvina al ajillo* (garlic sea bass) as a main dish.

WEST OF CITY CENTER Fogo de Brasil
🚶 ♿ 🎵 🍸 🇻 $$$

Ave las Américas, Calles 40/42 **Tel** *2248-2526*

Carnivores are in heaven at this huge Brazilian restaurant, where waiting staff dress in gaucho gear and deliver all-you-can-eat charcoal-broiled meats to your table. A buffet table includes sushi, and there is also a pasta bar. Free hotel shuttles are provided.

WEST OF CITY CENTER Lubnan
🎵 🍸 🇻 $$$

Calles 22/24 and Paseo Colón **Tel** *2257-6071*

Small and popular Lebanese restaurant with authentic Levantine dishes such as falafel and *shish kebabs*, served by waiters wearing red vests and fezes. Hookahs are passed around and prove popular with the young crowd, which flocks here for the quasi-party atmosphere. Closed Monday.

WEST OF CITY CENTER Machu Picchu
🇻 $$$

Calle 32 and Aves 1/3 **Tel** *2283-3679*

Extremely popular seafood restaurant with superb service. The fare includes quality Peruvian dishes, from *ceviche* (marinated raw fish or shellfish) to the *picante de mariscos* seafood casserole. Meals are best accompanied with the *pisco sour* house drink. Peruvian art enlivens the place. Closed Sunday.

WEST OF CITY CENTER La Bastille
🇻 $$$$

Calle 22 and Paseo Colón **Tel** *2255-4994*

A long-standing fixture, this elegant and semi-formal restaurant on a busy thoroughfare serves highly regarded French cuisine from the hands of Chef Hans Pulfer. Service, however, is aloof, and although not required, a jacket and other dressy attire is not out of place. Closed Sunday.

WEST OF CITY CENTER Park Café
♿ 🍴 🇻 $$$$$

Calle 44, Sabana Norte **Tel** *2290-6324*

Perhaps the finest dining experience in San José is to be had at this intimate restaurant in the courtyard garden of an antique shop. England's Michelin-starred chef Richard Neat delivers mouthwatering dishes, including tapas, that draw on influences from around the world. Reservations essential.

WEST OF CITY CENTER Restaurant Grano de Oro
🍴 🍸 🇻 $$$$$

Hotel Grano de Oro, Calle 30 and Aves 2/4 **Tel** *2255-3322*

One of the city's finest restaurants, this elegant option is in San José's premier boutique hotel *(see p251)* and attracts the social and business elite. Superb French-inspired dishes blend Costa Rican influences, and the desserts alone justify dining here. The filling breakfasts include healthy options. The staff are efficient and courteous.

Key to Price Guide *see p272* **Key to Symbols** *see back cover flap*

THE CENTRAL HIGHLANDS

ALAJUELA Jalapeños Comida Tex-Mex
V $

Calle 2 and Aves Central/1 **Tel** 2430-4027

This lively restaurant draws a loyal clientele of local expatriate residents. The menu ranges from hamburgers and omelettes to Tex-Mex staples such as *tostadas* (tortillas with fillings), corn nachos, and *huevos rancheros* (a breakfast favorite made with tortillas and eggs). Closed Sunday.

ALAJUELA Xandari
V $$$$

Tacacori, 3 miles (5 km) N of Alajuela **Tel** 2443-2020

Magnificent views across the valley from the open-air balcony are a highlight at this romantic restaurant, located in a superlative boutique hotel set amid coffee plantations *(see p252)*. Gourmet health-conscious dishes using fresh local ingredients are complemented by a robust wine list and estate-grown coffee.

ATENAS Mirador del Cafetal
V $$$

Hwy 3, 5 miles (8 km) W of Atenas **Tel** 2446-7361

Tasty, simple food is served at this roadside restaurant with magnificent views over coffee fields and mountain valleys. The vast menu features filling breakfasts, plus indigenous dishes such as *tamales (see p271)*, as well as smoothies, cappuccinos, and daiquiris. There is also a well-stocked gift store.

CIUDAD CARIARI Antonio Ristorante Italiano
V $$$

6 miles (10 km) NW of San José **Tel** 2293-0622

An elegant and modern restaurant, Antonio Ristorante Italiano specializes in well-prepared Italian dishes, from gnocchi to a splendid spaghetti with squid. Inexpensive *casados* (set meals) are a lunchtime bargain. The service is excellent. It has a piano bar.

CIUDAD CARIARI Sakura
V $$$$

Ribera de Belén, 0.5 (1 km) SE of San Antonio de Belén **Tel** 2209-9800 (ext. 7060)

Quality Japanese fare is served in authentically Oriental surroundings adjoining the Ramada Herradura Hotel. It has a sushi bar, teppanyaki grills where guests can watch their food being prepared, and tatami rooms with private chefs. An indoor pond is stocked with koi.

HEREDIA Spoon
V $

Plaza Heredia, Calle 9 and Ave 6 **Tel** 2263-2159

This small yet clean café on the edge of downtown is noted for its inexpensive *casados*, salads, snacks, desserts, and delicious baked goods, all served cafeteria-style. It is highly popular with university students as a breakfast and lunch spot.

HEREDIA La Lluna de Valencia
V $$$

San Pedro de Heredia, 2 miles (3 km) NW of Heredia **Tel** 2269-6665

With his flamboyant command of the open kitchen, Vicente Aguilar, the Catalan owner, is reason enough to visit this restaurant. At night Aguilar joins live musicians on stage, in addition to overseeing the making of superb paellas and other Spanish dishes, best washed down with sangría. The venue is a centenary wooden home.

HEREDIA Le Petit Paris
V $$$

Calle 5 and Aves Central/2 **Tel** 2262-2524

In the heart of town, this compact and intimate restaurant occupies a converted home. The traditional French cuisine – chicken *à la Normandie* is typical – is well-prepared and tasty, and the wide-ranging menu includes salads, sandwiches, and pastries. Crêpes are a specialty. Live music is hosted on Fridays and Sundays.

HEREDIA Restaurante Don Próspero
V $$$

Santa Lucía, 0.5 mile (1 km) N of Heredia **Tel** 2260-2748

Part of the Café Britt coffee processing site *(see p142)*, this informally elegant open-air restaurant has a health-conscious menu featuring organically grown vegetables, plus delicious desserts and a wide variety of coffee drinks. Although best enjoyed as part of an inclusive tour, casual diners are also welcome.

HEREDIA Vitrales
V $$$

Santo Domingo de Heredia, 2 miles (3 km) SE of Heredia **Tel** 2244-1414

This clean and well-lit restaurant in Hotel Bougainvillea *(see p252)* is adorned with appealing artwork. It serves Continental dishes along with local fare of superior quality. The service is always professional, overseen by a conscientious and capable owner. The weekend brunch is popular with locals in the know.

HEREDIA El Tigre Vestido
V $$$$

Santa Barbara de Heredia, 4 miles (6 km) NW of Heredia **Tel** 2269-9392

Gourmet meals served at Finca Rosa Blanca Coffee Plantation & Inn *(see p252)* can be enjoyed alfresco. Their accomplished chef uses estate-grown ingredients in nouvelle temptations of award-winning quality. The menu includes Central American dishes, such as *pupusas* (stuffed flat breads). Dinner by reservation.

LA GARITA Fiesta del Maíz   Ⓥ   Ⓢ
Hwy 3, 0.5 mile (1 km) W of Pan-Am Hwy **Tel** *2487-5757*

This popular roadside restaurant specializes in traditional corn-based items, such as *chorreadas* (corn fritters) and *tamales (see p271)*, served in a no-frills environment. A favorite of locals, it gets packed on weekends, when *gallo pinto (see p270)* and other local favorites are also offered. Closed Monday.

LA GARITA Restaurante La Focaccia   🏃♫🖅Ⓨ Ⓥ   ⓈⓈⓈⓈ
Martino Resort & Spa, Hwy 3, 2 miles (3 km) E of Pan-Am Hwy **Tel** *2433-8382*

This sumptuous restaurant is situated in the Martino Resort & Spa *(see p252)* and features a curved balcony overlooking the pool that offers an option for outdoor dining. The health-conscious Italian fare on the menu utilizes fresh vegetables and fruits from the hotel's own gardens.

MONTE DE LA CRUZ Baalbek Bar & Grill   🍽♿♫Ⓨ Ⓥ   ⓈⓈⓈ
Los Angeles de San Rafael, 2 miles (3 km) S of Monte de la Cruz **Tel** *2267-6683*

A favorite of San José's upper crust, this Levantine-themed restaurant combines superb views over the valley with a big dose of ambience and top-class cuisine. Baba ghanoush and other Mediterranean favorites feature on the menu. At the end of your meal, you can enjoy a hookah in intimate upstairs booths.

MONTE DE LA CRUZ Los Tiroleses   🏃Ⓨ Ⓥ   ⓈⓈⓈⓈ
Monte de la Cruz, 6 miles (10 km) NE of Heredia **Tel** *2267-6222*

Located in the Swiss-inspired Hotel Chalet Tirol *(see p252)*, this cozy, wood-beamed alpine restaurant has a log fire and candlelit dining at night. While the focus is on traditional French dishes, the menu also features creative dishes using Costa Rican ingredients, such as shrimp in fennel and Pernod sauce.

OROSI Orosi Lodge   🖅 Ⓥ   Ⓢ
SW of the plaza, Orosi village **Tel** *2533-3578*

Located in a small lodge *(see p253)* tucked into the southeast corner of the village, this small café has a charming ambience. It serves light breakfasts, pizzas, snacks, and cookies and ice cream sundaes. A juke box and table football are on hand for rainy days. It also offers Internet connectivity. Closed Sunday.

OROSI Restaurant Coto   🍽🏃♿🖅Ⓥ   ⓈⓈⓈ
On the N side of the plaza **Tel** *2533-3032*

This traditional open-air restaurant exudes ambience thanks to its wood-fired oven. Roast chicken and pork dishes feature prominently on the menu, which also offers garlic sea bass, plus trout from nearby streams. Cheap *casados* (set lunches) ensure this restaurant is busy round the clock.

SABANA REDONDA Restaurante Jaulares   🏃♫🖅Ⓨ   ⓈⓈ
12 miles (19 km) N of Alajuela **Tel** *2482-2155*

This restaurant on the cool mid-elevation slopes of Volcán Poás, designed as a rustic farmstead, serves traditional dishes, steaks, and seafood. Pizzas are fired in a traditional wood-burning *horno* (oven). Take a sweater for chilly nights. Live music on weekends draws in the crowds.

SAN ANTONIO DE BELEN El Rodeo   🏃🖅Ⓥ   ⓈⓈⓈ
4 miles (6 km) S of Alajuela **Tel** *2293-3909*

An appealing rusticity, with saddles and other equestrian paraphernalia, lend this airy timber-beamed restaurant a unique ambience. Authentic Costa Rica cuisine, such as corn tortillas with sliced tongue, and more imaginative dishes such as tenderloin in jalapeño cream, draw an appreciative clientele.

SAN GERARDO DE DOTA Comida Típica Miriam   🏃♿Ⓥ   ⓈⓈⓈ
2 miles (3 km) NE of San Gerardo de Dota **Tel** *2740-1049*

Offering a real *campesino* (peasant) experience, this delightful little family-run restaurant on the mountain road above Dantica Lodge *(see p253)* serves hearty country fare, including freshly caught trout. A tiny cast-iron stove provides warmth.

SAN JOSE DE LA MONTANA Las Ardillas   🖅Ⓨ Ⓥ   ⓈⓈⓈ
6 miles (10 km) N of Heredia **Tel** *2266-0015*

This wood-and-stone lodge set amid pines has a delightfully rustic ambience enhanced by a huge hearth with blazing logs on chilly days and at night. It specializes in roasted meat dishes, prepared in a wood-burning oven, and seafood, but also has local favorites. It gets chilly here, so bring a sweater or jacket.

SAN PABLO DE LEON CORTES Bar Restaurante Vaca Flaca   🍽Ⓨ Ⓥ   ⓈⓈ
25 miles (40 km) SE of San José **Tel** *2546-3939*

Situated in a pine forest along the Ruta de los Santos *(see p147)*, this rustic restaurant has a wonderful warm ambience. The decor includes cowhide seats, cowboy hats, mounted deer heads, and old rifles. Simple traditional dishes are served, as are burgers, sandwiches, and the restaurant's own brand of coffee.

SANTA ANA Bacchus   🍽🖅   ⓈⓈⓈⓈ
Santa Ana **Tel** *2282-5441*

Housed in a refurbished 100-year-old house, this stylish bistro, which has modern art on the walls, serves French and Italian dishes including baked mushroom-and-polenta ragout and pizza cooked in a wood-fired oven. There is an extensive wine list and exceptional desserts. Wonderful service. Closed Monday.

Key to Price Guide *see p272* **Key to Symbols** *see back cover flap*

SANTA MARIA DE DOTA La Casona de Sara `V` `$`

E of Beneficio Coopedota **Tel** 2541-2258

Overseen by a charming matriarch, this simple family-run restaurant serves hearty *tipico* fare from the open kitchen, where you are welcome to peek into the simmering pots to make your selection. Be sure to try the fresh fruit *batidos*, also called *refrescos* (shakes).

SARCHI Restaurante Las Carretas `$$$`

Adjacent to Fábrica de Carretas Joaquín Chaverrí, Sarchí Sur **Tel** 2454-1633

A homely and airy restaurant in the heart of this artisans' center melds a rustic charm with a contemporary setting. The extensive menu ranges from soups, salads, and burgers to Italian dishes and local favorites. Outdoor dining is an option on sunny days.

TURRIALBA Hotel Casa Turire `$$$$`

Hacienda Atirro, 5 miles (8 km) SE of Turrialba **Tel** 2531-1111

Opening on to a lavishly landscaped courtyard with fountains, this elegant restaurant in a classy boutique hotel *(see p253)* has a wide-ranging menu of locally inspired dishes highlighted by scrumptious desserts and estate-grown coffee. Dishes are creatively presented and filling, albeit not gourmet.

VARA BLANCA Restaurante Colbert `$$`

14 miles (22 km) N of Alajuela **Tel** 2482-2776

Views down the mountain are reason enough to dine at this French-run bakery and café, which serves crêpes, light snacks, confections, and nouvelle Costa Rican cuisine *à la français*, such as tilapia fish in tomato sauce. Sitting atop the Continental Divide, it is often shrouded in clouds.

THE CENTRAL PACIFIC AND SOUTHERN NICOYA

JACO Bar Restaurante Colonial `$$`

Calle Bohío and Ave Pastro Díaz **Tel** 2643-3326

A spacious and airy tropical-themed restaurant with a skylight, a large bar, and shaded outdoor dining. It offers an ambitious menu with light fare, including bar snacks, and fresh seafood with a nouvelle twist – mussels in garlic and olive oil are typical.

JACO Clarita's Sports Bar & Grill `$$$`

Off Ave Pastor Díaz, at the N end of Jacó **Tel** 2643-2615

One of very few dining options actually on the beach, this open-air US-style diner serves many North American favorites, from omelettes to burgers and burritos. The all-female waiting staff are chosen for their looks, and live music and beauty contests are regularly hosted.

JACO Taco Bar `$$$`

Behind Multicentro Costa Rica, off Ave Pastor Díaz **Tel** 2643-0222

This casual, Israeli-run open-air establishment is a tremendous bargain for its all-you-can-eat buffet and Japanese-inspired fare, including sashimi and such main dishes as citrus-teriyaki chicken. It specializes in custom-made fish tacos, including spicy coconut shrimp. Taco Bar also has free Wi-Fi.

JACO Hotel Poseidon Bar y Restaurante `$$$$`

Hotel Poseidon, Calle Bohío **Tel** 2643-1642

Located in Hotel Poseidon *(see p254)*, this restaurant is known for its hearty breakfasts and creative fusion fare, such as filet mignon with a Béarnaise-jalapeño sauce. Oriental throw rugs, wooden carvings, and stone walls provide a warm ambience, enhanced by live jazz. The open-wall plan lets in the tropical breezes.

JACO Restaurant Hicacos `$$$$`

Calle Hicaco **Tel** 2643-3226

This elegant restaurant with an enviable breeze-swept oceanfront setting serves delicious seafood and has an all-you-can-eat lobster buffet on Wednesday nights, accompanied by live calypso music. There is an extensive wine list, and a lounge bar where diners can relax by playing chess and other games.

MALPAIS Rancho Itauna `$$$`

Playa Santa Teresa, 1 mile (1.6 km) N of Carmen **Tel** 2640-0095

Renowned for its full moon and New Year parties, this small, unpretentious, and colorful restaurant serves international cuisine from around the globe, but with an emphasis on Brazilian dishes. It occasionally has live music and parties, and hosts a traditional barbecue every Thursday evening.

MALPAIS Nectar Bar and Restaurante `$$$$`

Florblanca Resort, Playa Santa Teresa, 3 miles (5 km) N of Carmen **Tel** 2640-0232

Outstanding menu and atmosphere at the fashionable Florblanca Resort *(see p254)*. Gourmet, Asian-inspired fusion dishes are presented with flair, and the airy beachfront setting is enhanced at night by candlelight. The curvilinear bar serves sushi and plays a wide variety of music, from classical to jazz.

MANUEL ANTONIO Ronnie's Place   🔲 V $$

1 mile (1.6 km) W of Marlintini's **Tel** *2777-5120*

A simple open-air restaurant that serves traditional Costa Rican dishes alongside seafood specialties and international favorites, Ronnie's Place boasts a hilltop setting with spectacular ocean vistas. It makes delicious sangria and desserts such as caramelized pumpkin in cane juice. Popular with tour groups.

MANUEL ANTONIO Café Milagro   🔲 V $$$

3 miles (5 km) S of Quepos **Tel** *2777-0794*

A small roadside café with a charming ambience and simple furnishings in various tropical pastels. Sandwiches and pastries and a large selection of coffees and teas can be enjoyed on the shady patio to the rear. The café also has a souvenir store. Closed Sunday and during evenings in the low season.

MANUEL ANTONIO Restaurante Gato Negro   🔲🎵🔲🍸V $$$

Hotel Casitas Eclipse, 3 miles (5 km) S of Quepos **Tel** *2777-0408*

Situated in an elegant hotel, the airy restaurant has a warm, romantic ambience with splendid views. With a large wine list, the eating place has a Mediterranean-inspired menu. The choice of pastas is extensive, and many Italian favorites (such as tagliatelle) are featured.

MANUEL ANTONIO Karola's   🔲🎵🍸V $$$$

Los Altos Beach Resort, 3 miles (5 km) S of Quepos **Tel** *2777-8880*

One of Manuel Antonio's top picks for fine dining, Karola's is situated in a breeze-swept locale overlooking the Pacific Ocean and open to the elements. Its chic ambience includes dark slate floors. On the menu, diners will find delicious pan-Pacific fusion dishes.

MANUEL ANTONIO Marlintini's   🔲🔲🎵🔲🍸V $$$$

1 mile (1.6 km) S of Quepos, on the road to Manuel Antonio **Tel** *2777-7474*

Marlintini's specializes in fresh seafood, but it also has many Continental favorites, such as pork chops and steaks. Bring in your catch, and resident chef Art Lander will prepare it to your specifications. The lively bar features more than two dozen Martini-based cocktails and has live music.

MANUEL ANTONIO Claro Que Si   🔲🔲🍸V $$$$$

Hotel Sí Como No Resort, 3 miles (5 km) S of Quepos **Tel** *2777-0777*

This fine-dining restaurant with contemporary sophistication is located in an upscale hotel *(see p255)*. An engaging seafood menu, combining local ingredients with Caribbean and international flavors, is complemented by a large wine list. Healthy, mouthwatering winners include the avocado salad and the seafood and spinach ravioli.

MANUEL ANTONIO La Mariposa   🔲🍸V $$$$$

Hotel La Mariposa, 3 miles (5 km) S of Quepos **Tel** *2777-0355*

Located in a venerable hotel *(see p255)*, this acclaimed restaurant serves French-inspired cuisine in the open air, with unsurpassed views over the national park. Ranging from local staples such as *gallo pinto*, to tempting entrées, including chicken breast in mustard and French wine sauce, the inventive menu has plenty of appeal.

MANUEL ANTONIO Sunspot Poolside Bar and Grill   🔲🔲🍸V $$$$$

Makanda by the Sea, 3 miles (5 km) S of Quepos **Tel** *2777-0442*

Acclaimed and intimate open-air gourmet restaurant with a romantic poolside setting located in a deluxe hotel with dramatic decor and ocean vistas *(see p255)*. Fresh ingredients and creative flare are hallmarks of the nouvelle menu, with many dishes prepared on the grill. Gourmet pizzas are a signature dish. Closed Monday.

MONTEZUMA Bakery Café   🔲🔲V $

200 yards (200 m) E of the village square **Tel** *2642-0458*

Located close to the main beach entrance, this simple café pleases vegetarians and vegans alike with its creative range of organic dishes, including delicious banana breads and soy burgers. A wooden deck provides an alfresco dining space beneath the shade of trees.

MONTEZUMA El Sano Banano Village Restaurant & Café   🔲🔲V $$$

W side of the plaza **Tel** *2642-0638*

This natural-food restaurant in the heart of the village boasts an international menu and is known for its fresh fruit juices. The scrambled tofu breakfast and curried veggies are popular items, as are *batidos* (iced fruit shakes). Movies, free with dinner, are screened nightly. The restaurant prepares boxed lunches.

PLAYA HERRADURA Steve N' Lisa's Paradise Café   🔲🎵🔲V $$

1 mile (1.6 km) S of Parque Nacional Carara **Tel** *2637-0954*

Situated on a perch beside Highway 32, this long-standing and popular open-air roadside diner offers a large menu of light snacks and international dishes that includes burgers, tuna melt sandwiches, and cooked meals from pastas to seafood.

PLAYA HERRADURA El Mirador and El Anfiteatro   🔲🎵🔲🍸V $$$$$

Hotel Villa Caletas, 2 miles (3 km) N of Playa Herradura **Tel** *2637-0505*

The sublime mountaintop setting at the renowned Hotel Villa Caletas *(see p255)* sets these two fine-dining eateries apart. Gourmet nouvelle dishes evoke the best of fusion cuisine and the classical-themed mood is inviting. A patio with fine views is suited to breakfasts and luncheons. Live concerts are offered in a classical amphitheater.

Key to Price Guide *see p272* **Key to Symbols** *see back cover flap*

PLAYA HERRADURA El Nuevo Latino ⛱ 🍸 [V] [$][$][$][$][$]

Los Sueños Marriott Ocean & Golf Resort, 1 mile (1.6 km) W of Hwy 34 ***Tel*** *2630-9000*

Seafood and gourmet Latin fusion dishes highlight the menu in this elegant, yet informal, restaurant with pool views at the Los Sueños Marriott Ocean & Golf Resort *(see p256)*. Recommended appetizers include lobster and shrimp croquettes, followed perhaps by imaginative entrées such as plantain-crusted red snapper.

PUNTARENAS La Yunta Steakhouse ⛱ 🍸 [V] [$][$][$]

Paseo de los Turistas ***Tel*** *2661-3216*

A venerable two-story wooden home on the main oceanfront drag, this restaurant has a shaded windswept veranda overlooking the Gulf of Nicoya. The menu includes grilled steaks, as well as seafood such as the signature *corvina tropical* (sea bass with tropical fruit sauce), all well prepared and offered in filling portions.

QUEPOS El Patio Café 🚫 🚸 ♿ ⛱ [V] [$]

On the shorefront road in town ***Tel*** *2777-4982*

This colorful and airy café is a favorite local gathering spot for breakfasts such as granola with fruit and yogurt, or traditional *gallo pinto* (fried rice and black beans). El Patio bakes its own breads and desserts, and it also serves delicious fruit shakes, plus lattes, cappuccinos, etc.

QUEPOS Dos Locos 🚫 🚸 ⛱ 🍸 [V] [$][$]

W of the bus station ***Tel*** *2777-1526*

This Mexican restaurant has lively decor playing on the cactus and sombrero theme. Open walls lend an airy tropical feel. Its acclaimed regional fare includes expected staples, from *chimichangas* (deep-fried burritos) and *flautas* (cylindrical stuffed tortillas) to *quesadillas*. American breakfasts are also served.

QUEPOS El Gran Escape 🚸 🍸 [V] [$][$][$][$]

W of the bus station ***Tel*** *2777-0395*

Immensely popular and often packed restaurant in an old two-story wooden building open to refreshing tropical breezes. The wide-ranging menu goes from light snacks to fresh seafood, steaks, and locally inspired coconut curry chicken. Closed Tuesday.

TAMBOR Restaurante Arrecife ⛱ 🍸 [V] [$][$][$][$]

Hotel Costa Coral, 1 mile (1.6 km) W of the airstrip ***Tel*** *2683-0105*

This clean restaurant boasts colorful contemporary decor. It has an extensive menu of light snacks and seafood, from *ceviche* and *corvina* with heart-of-palm sauce to burgers and chicken in orange sauce. The bar has karaoke and a large-screen TV.

GUANACASTE AND NORTHERN NICOYA

CAÑAS Hacienda La Pacífica 🚸 ♿ [V] [$]

2.5 miles (4 km) N of Cañas ***Tel*** *2669-6050*

This restaurant housed in a historic hacienda offers a fabulous traditional ambience combining rusticity and elegance. Locally grown organic rice accompanies such international dishes as jumbo garlic shrimps and tenderloin pepper steak. Diners would be wise to bring mosquito repellent.

CAÑAS Restaurante Rincón Corobicí 🚸 ⛱ 🍸 [V] [$][$]

Pan-Am Hwy, 3 miles (5 km) N of Cañas ***Tel*** *2669-6262*

Overhanging Río Corobicí, this airy, multidecked roadside restaurant offers a fine vantage point to watch whitewater rafters. The broad-ranging menu features local staples, including seafood – the garlic sea bass is particularly good. The home-made lemonade is a perfect antidote to the mid-summer heat.

ISLITA 1492 Restaurante 🚸 ⛱ 🍸 [V] [$][$][$][$][$]

Hotel Punta Islita, 6 miles (10 km) S of Carrillo ***Tel*** *2656-2020*

A romantic and elegant gourmet restaurant under soaring thatch at the deluxe Hacienda Punta Islita resort *(see p257)* enjoys a fabulous hilltop setting and coastal vistas. Chef Lizbeth Molina Muñoz conjures local ingredients into mouthwatering treats influenced by Pacific Rim and European tastes. The service is excellent.

LIBERIA Café Europa 🚸 ⛱ [V] [$][$]

Hwy 21, 12 miles (19 km) W of Liberia ***Tel*** *6268-1081*

Small roadside café-bakery offering delicious pastries and breads baked onsite by the German owner. Burgers and German-inspired hot dishes such as breaded veal cutlets are also served. The restaurant can get stuffy; if the weather permits, opt to sit outside.

LIBERIA Casa Verde Restaurant & Lounge Bar ♿ 🎵 🍸 [V] [$][$][$]

Pan-Am Hwy, 100 yards S of Ave Central ***Tel*** *2665-5037*

A total contrast to its colonial city surrounds, this spacious restaurant is furnished in contemporary style, with black leather lounge chairs atop the glazed concrete floor. Sunlight pours in through walls of glass. The fusion menu spans the globe. There is a sushi bar and a special five-course dinner with live music on Fridays.

LIBERIA Restaurante Paso Real   🏃🌴☂️Ⓥ $$$
Calles Central/2 and Ave Central **Tel** *2666-3455*

Situated over the plaza, this spacious restaurant offers quality seafood, including calamari and lobster dishes, along with *casados* (set meals) and more. A small balcony permits outdoor dining. Service is prompt and courteous. The lively bar has a large-screen TV.

MONTEVERDE Café Caburné   ☂️Ⓥ $$$
Paseo de Estella, 2 miles (3 km) E of Santa Elena **Tel** *2645-5020*

Argentinian owner Susana Salas and her husband craft handmade chocolates and truffles in this spacious restaurant incorporating a chocolate museum. Chocolate drinks are served, along with sandwiches, wraps, and entrées such as rubbed steak. Diners can eat inside or on the veranda.

MONTEVERDE Restaurant Morphos   Ⓥ $$$
Santa Elena village **Tel** *2645-5607*

In the heart of Santa Elena, this restaurant is built with natural stones and timbers, and has furniture made of rough-hewn logs. It has *casados* (set meals), but the menu also offers burgers, salads, and sea bass Dijon, as well as ice cream sundaes and fresh fruit *batidos* or *refrescos* (shakes). It can be packed, day or night.

MONTEVERDE Garden Restaurant   ☂️Ⓥ $$$$
Monteverde Lodge, SE of Santa Elena **Tel** *2645-5057*

Airy restaurant overlooking lush gardens. The menu highlights creative Costa Rican cuisine, such as shredded duck *empanadas* (stuffed turnovers), and coconut and macadamia-crusted sea bass, supported by a large wine list. A cozy bar with a log fire adjoins the restaurant. Service is swift and efficient.

MONTEVERDE El Sapo Dorado   🏃🎵☂️☂️Ⓥ $$$$$
Cerro Plano, 0.5 mile (1 km) E of Santa Elena **Tel** *2645-5010*

Recognized for its wholesome health-food dishes, this elegant restaurant attached to the El Sapo Dorado hotel *(see p257)* has a delightful ambience and an open-air terrace. The inventive menu includes dishes such as tofu with vegetarian primavera, and shrimp in Sambuca sauce, as well as delicious desserts.

MONTEVERDE Sofia   🍽️♿🎵Ⓥ $$$$$
Opposite the medical clinic, 1 mile (1.6 km) E of Santa Elena **Tel** *2645-7017*

Chef-owner Karen Nielsen raised the bar a notch when she opened this fine-dining restaurant serving fusion dishes that combine Costa Rican ingredients with inspirations from around the globe. Live music ranges from classical to jazz ensembles.

NOSARA Pizzería Giardino Tropicale   🍽️🏃☂️Ⓥ $$
Beaches of Nosara, 4 miles (6 km) S of the airstrip **Tel** *2682-0258*

A rustic thatched restaurant with several wooden decks beneath shade trees. As the name suggests, it is known for its pizzas fired in a traditional wood-fired oven, but the menu also features seafood, including carpaccio of *corvina* (sea bass) and daily specials.

NOSARA Luna Bar and Grill   🍽️☂️☂️Ⓥ $$$
Playa Pelada, Beaches of Nosara **Tel** *2682-0122*

Tucked in a cove, this atmospheric beachfront bar with a hip groove offers gourmet snacks such as sushi rolls and lentil soup. It has a west-facing terrace for enjoying the spectacular sunsets. World music draws patrons on to the dance floor.

NOSARA Marlin Bill's   ☂️Ⓥ $$$
Beaches of Nosara, 4 miles (6 km) S of the airstrip **Tel** *2682-0458*

Situated at the main junction of the unpaved coast road, this elevated open-air eatery highlights American favorites, from pork loin chops and blackened tuna salad to Key lime pie. It is very popular with locals, who congregate at the bar, which also has a TV.

NOSARA Restaurante Vista del Paraíso   🍽️♿☂️Ⓥ $$$$
In the hills, 1 mile (1.6 km) E of Beaches of Nosara **Tel** *2682-0637*

As the name suggests, this ridgetop restaurant offers sensational views up and down the coast. The Texan owner is a French-trained chef who serves a continental menu that includes such treats as baked goat's cheese salad and Napoleon of beef tenderloin. Candlelit dining can be enjoyed on a terrace.

PLAYA CONCHAL Outback Jack's Australian Road Kill Grill   🍽️☂️☂️Ⓥ $$$
Hotel Brasilito, NW corner of the plaza, Brasilito **Tel** *2654-4596*

Open to the elements, this windswept restaurant in the Hotel Brasilito is splendidly situated just a few steps from the beach. A huge international menu includes Aussie fish and chips, and shrimp on the barbie. The place for breakfasts, it offers warm croissants, *huevos rancheros* (a breakfast favorite made with tortillas and eggs), and more.

PLAYA FLAMINGO Marie's Restaurante   🏃☂️Ⓥ $$$
Centro Comercial La Plaza, W of the marina **Tel** *2654-4136*

Now in elegant surroundings, this venerable restaurant caters to sailors with a menu of international favorites – from fish and chips to burritos – served under a huge thatched ceiling. A wide choice of coffee drinks and ice cream sundaes are reason enough to choose Marie's, named after the English-born hostess.

Key to Price Guide *see p272* **Key to Symbols** *see back cover flap*

PLAYA FLAMINGO Angelina's

🖼️ 🖼️ 🍷 V $$$$$$$$$$

Centro Comercial La Plaza, W of the marina **Tel** 2654-4839

With its trendy decor and creative fusion menu, this restaurant has upped the level of sophistication in Playa Flamingo. Start and end your Angelina experience at the stylish lounge bar, with its sumptuous leather sofas. Bear in mind that prices are steep and that management can be haughty toward guests.

PLAYA GRANDE The Great Waltini's

🚶 🖼️ V $$$$$$$$

Hotel Bula Bula, S of El Mundo de la Tortuga, S end of Playa Grande **Tel** 2653-0975

This small restaurant in delightful Hotel Bula Bula *(see p258)* has a shaded deck overlooking a landscaped garden. Snacks and gourmet fusion dishes from the hands of a professional chef are served. Consider the shrimp and crabcakes followed by duckling with red wine and raspberry reduction. Closed Monday.

PLAYA GRANDE Hotel Las Tortugas

🚶 🖼️ V $$$$$$$$

W of El Mundo de la Tortuga, N end of Playa Grande **Tel** 2653-0423

Situated close to the beach within Hotel Las Tortugas *(see p258)*, this restaurant serves light meals such as burgers and salads, as well as steaks and seafood. The owners boast of their apple pie and ice cream, and with good reason. There is a shaded wooden deck, and the service and mood are relaxed and friendly.

PLAYA HERMOSA The Bistro

🖼️ 🍷 V $$$$$$$$

Atop the hill, W of the main road, S end of Playa Hermosa **Tel** 2670-0227

Recherché French-Costa Rican cuisine served on the hilltop terrace of Hotel La Finisterra *(see p258)*. Dishes such as filet mignon with peppercorn sauce have earned the chef a regional reputation for excellence. Sushi is served on Friday evenings. Closed Tuesday.

PLAYA HERMOSA Villas del Sueño

🎵 🖼️ 🍷 V $$$$$$$$

S end of Playa Hermosa **Tel** 2672-0026

Elegance is a keyword at this open-air restaurant of the well run Villas del Sueño *(see p258)*. Live bands perform in high season. Gourmet meals focus on fresh seafood such as mahimahi and shrimp in cream sauce, but also include such dishes as tenderloin in brandy and three-pepper sauce.

PLAYA NEGRA Café Playa Negra

🖼️ 🖼️ V $$$$

S of Los Pargos Plaza **Tel** 2652-9143

Small, charming Internet café in the village center, a short walk from the beach. The Peruvian-born owner-chef offers a wide selection of light food, from pancakes and French toast to *ceviche* (marinated raw fish or shellfish), quiches, and pastas. Leave room for the lemon pie or an iced fresh fruit *batido* (shake).

PLAYA NEGRA Pablo's Picasso

🖼️ 🍷 $$$$

S of Los Pargos **Tel** 2652-9158

Located in a budget hotel *(see p258)*, this rustic restaurant with a barefoot ambience serves jumbo burgers, pastas, and *tipico* (typical) dishes plus filling American breakfasts, including pancakes. It boasts a pool table and movies at the bar with oversize wooden chairs. Popular with the surfing crowd.

PLAYA OCOTAL Father Rooster Bar & Grill

🚶 🎵 🖼️ 🍷 V $$$$

2 miles (3 km) W of Playas del Coco **Tel** 2670-1246

Situated on the sands, this rustic restaurant is centered on a lively bar of rough-hewn timbers, which serves killer cocktails. The menu focuses on bar foods, such as burgers and *quesadillas* (stuffed fried tortillas). Activities include volleyball, and the mood is almost always party-hearty.

PLAYAS DEL COCO Restaurante Sol y Luna

🖼️ 🍷 V $$$$

Hotel Puerta del Sol, SE of the plaza **Tel** 2670-0195

Opening on to an exquisitely landscaped garden in Hotel Puerta del Sol *(see p259)*, this intimate restaurant has Romanesque decor and a menu of Italian staples prepared by a professional chef. An extensive wine list and delicious coffee drinks and desserts, including tiramisu, round off the menu. Closed Tuesday.

PLAYAS DEL COCO Café de Playa

🖼️ ♿ 🖼️ V $$$$$$$$

0.5 mile (1 km) E of the village center **Tel** 2670-1621

Facing the bay, the breeze-swept Café de Playa has a lovely contemporary elegance, but the main draw is its eclectic international menu of gourmet fusion dishes, from penne pastas to jumbo shrimp in rum sauce, and even sushi. There is also an impressive wine list.

PLAYAS DEL COCO Citrón

♿ 🖼️ 🍷 V $$$$$$$$

Plaza Pacífico **Tel** 2670-0942

Fashionable styling adds to the elegance of this sophisticated restaurant run by Venezuelan chef David Posner, a graduate of the Culinary Institute of America. His Latin-American fusion dishes focus on fresh seafood, such as the stir-fried poached sea bass. Dining on the wide, tree-shaded deck is a delight on balmy nights. Closed Sunday.

SAMARA Restaurante Las Brasas

🖼️ ♿ 🖼️ V $$$$

On the NE corner of the soccer field **Tel** 2656-0546

Las Brasas is an atmospheric open-air Mediterranean restaurant made entirely of glazed hardwoods and thatch. The menu is laden with Spanish specialties such as gazpacho and paella, but a wide range of seafood, steak, and pasta dishes also feature on the menu.

TAMARINDO Lazy Wave ⟨🏃 🖥 V⟩ ⟨$⟩⟨$⟩
Hotel Pasatiempo, S of Plaza Colonial **Tel** 2653-0737

With a dead tree at its heart, this open-air restaurant draws a young, high-energy crowd. The seafood menu favors the health-conscious and offers a daily selection of fusion dishes, such as wasabi-crusted tuna. Eclectic dishes such as *jambalaya* (a kind of paella) are also available. Live music includes an open mic on Tuesdays.

TAMARINDO Panadería La Laguna del Cocodrilo ⟨📋 🖥 V⟩ ⟨$⟩⟨$⟩
E of Tamarindo Diría and Plaza Colonial **Tel** 2653-0255

Situated in front of a lagoon with crocodiles, this congenial bakery-café produces superb pastries and *empanadas* (stuffed turnovers) and is known for its all-you-can-eat breakfast buffet. The French owners deliver consistently light croissants and sweet and savory tarts.

TAMARINDO Capitán Suizo ⟨🏃 🎵 🖥 V⟩ ⟨$⟩⟨$⟩⟨$⟩⟨$⟩
0.5 mile (1 km) SW of Plaza Colonial **Tel** 2653-0075

Fine nouvelle cuisine served in an airy, colorful, and tranquil beachfront restaurant with a poolside bar, located within the luxurious Capitán Suizo hotel *(see p260)*. Creative dishes fuse European influences and Costa Rican ingredients – sea bass in mango sauce and tilapia fish in caper sauce are typical of the menu, which changes daily.

TAMARINDO Dragonfly ⟨♿ 🖥 ⟐ V⟩ ⟨$⟩⟨$⟩⟨$⟩⟨$⟩
100 yards (100 m) NE of Hotel Pasatiempo **Tel** 2653-1506

Patrons have been known to travel from as far away as San José simply to dine on the inspired Latin-Asian fusion cuisine at the acclaimed restaurant of chef-owner Tish Tomlinson. The romantic open-air dining area has a canvas sail roof supported by twisting columns. Closed Sunday.

TAMARINDO El Jardín del Eden ⟨🏃 🖥 ⟐ V⟩ ⟨$⟩⟨$⟩⟨$⟩⟨$⟩
SE of Tamarindo Diría and Plaza Colonial **Tel** 2653-0137

Overlooking a landscaped swimming pool, floodlit at night, this thatched restaurant in the Hotel Jardín del Eden *(see p260)* is appealing for its romantic atmosphere. Gourmet Mediterranean-inspired dishes include lobster in lemon sauce, and jumbo shrimp in whiskey. Fresh-baked pastries and *gallo pinto (see p260)* are served at breakfast.

THE NORTHERN ZONE

LA FORTUNA Choza de Laurel ⟨🖥 🏃 V⟩ ⟨$⟩⟨$⟩
400 yards (400 m) NW of the church **Tel** 2479-7063

A rustic restaurant in the style of an old farmhouse, with a wood-fired *horno* (oven) and beams adorned with cloves of garlic. Inexpensive *casados* (set meals) and local dishes are the focus, as well as rotisserie chicken and other grilled meats. The *plato especial* (mixed plate) is popular.

LA FORTUNA Rancho La Cascada ⟨🏃 🎵 🖥 ⟐ V⟩ ⟨$⟩⟨$⟩⟨$⟩
NW corner of the plaza **Tel** 2479-9145

With a huge circular thatched roof, La Cascada dominates the town square. Open-sided and airy, it has a pleasingly informal ambience. Mid-priced Western favorites are served, as are pastas, pizzas, and Costa Rican staples, from *gallo pinto* to *corvina al ajillo* (garlic sea bass). An upstairs bar has a large-screen TV and disco.

LA FORTUNA Restaurante Luigi ⟨🏃 🎵 🖥 ⟐ V⟩ ⟨$⟩⟨$⟩⟨$⟩
Luigi's Hotel, 2 blocks W of the plaza **Tel** 2479-9636

Flambée dishes are a specialty of this elegant restaurant, but the menu also includes local seafood and other internationally recognized dishes, such as beef stroganoff, along with pizzas and pastas. Attached to a hotel, this spacious eatery opens onto a pleasant roadside terrace.

LAGUNA DE ARENAL Tom's Pan German Bakery ⟨🖥 V⟩ ⟨$⟩⟨$⟩
Nuevo Arenal, SE of the plaza **Tel** 2694-4547

This rustic, German-run bakery-café on the main drag in town serves baked dishes hot from the oven. It also offers international favorites, including American breakfasts, as well as lasagne and sauerkraut. There are only a few tables and chairs on the shaded terrace out front, and German tour groups often fill the place.

LAGUNA DE ARENAL Mystica Lodge ⟨🏃 🖥 V⟩ ⟨$⟩⟨$⟩⟨$⟩
10 miles (16 km) W of Nuevo Arenal **Tel** 2692-1001

Located in the intimate Mystica Lodge *(see p251)*, this Italian restaurant is colorful by day and romantic by night. It has exquisite decor: informally elegant place settings, rough-hewn timber furniture, tropical pastels, and flowers on every table. Pizzas are the specialty, but the raviolis and other dishes, prepared in the open kitchen, are all top-notch.

LAGUNA DE ARENAL Gingerbread ⟨🏃 ♿ 🖥 ⟐ V⟩ ⟨$⟩⟨$⟩⟨$⟩⟨$⟩
2 miles (3 km) E of Nuevo Arenal **Tel** 2694-0039

Themed after a Tuscan villa, this restaurant is attached to a boutique hotel whose Israeli owner proves extremely proficient in the kitchen. His daily fusion menu can range from sushi to jumbo shrimp with couscous and lentils. Opt to dine on the shaded patio or in private booths in the cool interior.

Key to Price Guide *see p272* **Key to Symbols** *see back cover flap*

LAGUNA DE ARENAL Restaurante Willy's Caballo Negro

$$$$

1 mile (1.6 km) W of Nuevo Arenal Tel 2694-4515

The owner's German origins show in the menu of this delightful café overlooking a pond with waterfowl. Its schnitzels are well known, but eggplant Parmesan and veal cutlet in spicy onion and bell pepper sauce exemplify more inventive fare. Its art store, the Lucky Bug Gallery, is renowned.

PARQUE NACIONAL VOLCAN ARENAL Arenal Observatory Lodge

$$$$

5 miles (8 km) SE of the park entrance Tel 2479-1070

Spectacular views of Volcán Arenal are the main draw of this restaurant, which is located in a modern ecolodge *(see p251)* on the upper flanks of Volcán Chato. Its menu mixes international influences with local ingredients: the chicken in curry sauce and the various tilapia dishes are recommended. Service is courteous and efficient.

TABACON Ave del Paraíso

$$$

8 miles (13 km) W of La Fortuna Tel 2460-6229

Situated over steaming hot springs with dramatic volcano views at Balneario Tabacón, this airy restaurant offers Costa Rican staples and a wide choice of quality international dishes, from *gallo pinto* to burgers and French onion soup. The *corvina* in apple and chile pepper sauce is recommended. Service is efficient.

TABACON Los Tucanes

$$$$

6 miles (10 km) W of La Fortuna Tel 2479-2000

Located in the grounds of the deluxe Tabacón Grand Spa Thermal Resort, this chic restaurant looks onto the landscape swimming pool, with views of the Arenal Volcano beyond. The nouvelle Costa Rican menu includes such delights as roasted salmon with truffle oil-flavored mash potatoes.

THE CARIBBEAN

CAHUITA Miss Edith's

$$

NW of Cahuita Plaza Tel 2755-0248

Spicy Caribbean classics such as "rundown" *(see p271)* are featured at this colorful restaurant attached to the home of the eponymous owner. The family prepares meals in an open kitchen, and patrons dine on a shaded and colorful terrace. Home-made ice cream is served on weekends, and the herb teas are worth trying

CAHUITA Café Cocorico

$$$

50 yards (50 m) N of the plaza Tel 2755-0409

Gauzy curtains, colorful cushions, and Arab-style ceiling drapes predominate at this small, open air, Italian-run restaurant, which draws patrons for screened movies as much as it does for its delicious food. Gnocchi, pastas, and pizzas all feature alongside seafood dishes and home-made ice cream. Closed Wednesday.

CAHUITA Cha Cha Cha

$$$

W of Cahuita Plaza Tel 2755-0476

A wide-ranging menu spans the globe at this charmingly rustic restaurant painted white with blue trim and lit by candles and fairy-lights. Grilled squid salad, fajitas, and spicy coconut honey wings are typical appetizers. Entrées range from filet mignon to sea bass with shrimp and basil sauce. Service is relaxed to a fault. Closed in low season.

GUACIMO Restaurant Río Palmas

$$

Hwy 32, 1 mile (1.6 km) E of Guácimo Tel 2760-0330

The special feature of this welcoming roadside restaurant are its forest trails good for spotting poison-dart frogs. The menu features the standard Costa Rican fare, as well as international dishes. The dining is in the open air beneath a red-tile roof, but is set back from the busy highway.

MANZANILLO Bar y Restaurante Maxi

$

Manzanillo village Tel 2759-9086

This no-frills restaurant in a two-story wooden structure draws a young party crowd and is always lively, even at lunch. Quality seafood snacks and dishes cooked Caribbean-style as well as filling *típico* (typical) dishes are served, including on the beach by request.

PLAYA COCLES La Pecora Nera

$$$$$

1 mile (1.6 km) E of Puerto Viejo Tel 2750-0490

An unpretentious yet world-class restaurant where mouthwatering gourmet Italian fare belies the offbeat locale. Delicious gnocchi, bruschetta, pizzas, and calzones feature on the wide-ranging menu. The Italian owner-chef Ilario Giannono and his family fuss over patrons. Closed Monday and in low season.

PUERTO LIMON Restaurante Brisas del Caribe

$$

Calles 0/1 and Ave 2 Tel 2758-0138

This clean and airy downtown restaurant, on the north side of Parque Vargas, is the best in town. It is known for its seafood dishes but the locals flock there especially for its lunchtime *casados* and for its large buffet of *típico* fare, served cafeteria-style.

PUERTO VIEJO DE SARAPIQUI Veronica's Place [V] $$

Above Color Caribe, on the main street ***Tel*** *2750-0263*

Full of colorful Caribbean atmosphere, this charming and spacious restaurant is located on the upper floor of a creaky clapboard mansion. Breakfasts include pancakes, omelets, and *gallo pinto* (rice and beans). Other typical Costa Rican and Caribbean dishes are served at lunch and dinner. Veronica's also offers cookery classes.

PUERTO VIEJO DE TALAMANCA Café Rico ⛱ 🚸 🍴 [V] $$

50 yards (50 m) W of Casa Verde Lodge ***Tel*** *2750-0510*

This rustic open-air café in a two-story structure of rough-hewn timbers serves hearty, health-conscious breakfasts and lunches on the palm-fringed ground floor. This is the place for granola with fruit and yogurt, sandwiches and scrambles, or *huevos rancheros* (a breakfast favorite made with tortillas and eggs). Closed Thursday.

PUERTO VIEJO DE TALAMANCA Soda Miss Sam's ♿ [V] $$

Two blocks SE of Hot Rocks on the main road ***Tel*** *2750-0108*

Run by local senior citizen Hazel Miller on the porch of her home, Soda Miss Sam's serves classic Caribbean cuisine, such as rice and beans, as well as wonderful chicken and fish dishes. Diners should be aware that the casual, family-style atmosphere means that service is inevitably slow.

PUERTO VIEJO DE TALAMANCA Salsa Brava 🚸 🍴 🍸 [V] $$$

E of Puerto Viejo village ***Tel*** *2750-0241*

This informal rainbow-hued thatched restaurant has a lovely beachfront setting and an international menu featuring *ceviche* (marinated raw fish or shellfish), Caesar salad with chicken teriyaki, ice cream sundaes, and sangría. The Spanish owners provide filling portions. It has counter dining and a roadside patio. Closed Monday.

PUERTO VIEJO DE TALAMANCA Shawandha Lodge 🚸 🍴 🍸 [V] $$$$

Playa Chiquita, 3 miles (5 km) E of Puerto Viejo ***Tel*** *2750-0018*

A delightful ambience pervades this classy restaurant attached to a romantic lodge *(see p263)*. The Tico chef fuses tropical flavors into tantalizing French-Caribbean dishes. A typical dinner might comprise avocado and palmito salad, lobster *à la Normandie*, and mango mousse.

TORTUGUERO Miss Junie's ⛱ 🍴 [V] $$

N of the public dock, Tortuguero village ***Tel*** *2709-8102*

Named for a village matriarch who serves delicious Caribbean dishes, such as jerk chicken, and lobster in curry and coconut milk, this restaurant is now enclosed and air-conditioned. Also on the menu are *pan bon* (bread laced with caramelized sugar) and ginger cakes. Not open for breakfast. Reservations needed.

THE SOUTHERN ZONE

BAHIA DRAKE Aguila de Osa Inn 🍴 [V] $$$

0.5 mile (1 km) S of Agujitas ***Tel*** *8840-2929*

This circular, thatched restaurant of the Aguila de Osa Inn *(see p264)* is perhaps the best in the area, and most dishes are filling and flavorful, albeit not gourmet. Seafood, including sushi, dominates the menu, which also ranges to pastas. It has splendid bay views, best enjoyed from the relaxing sofas with a cocktail in hand.

CABO MATAPALO Brisas Azul 🚸 🍴 🍸 [V] $$$$$

9 miles (14 km) S of Puerto Jiménez ***Tel*** *2735-5130*

This soaring *palenque* restaurant with an eclectic gourmet menu is a feature of the acclaimed Lapa Rios ecolodge *(see p264)*. The chefs are locals trained to exacting standards. Pineapple honey ginger salad, coconut crusted fish, and delicious coffee cake are typical of the rotating menu. Spiral stairs lead to a lookout with spectacular views.

CIUDAD NEILY Hotel Andrea 🚸 🍴 🍸 [V] $$$

23 miles (37 km) E of Golfito ***Tel*** *2783-3784*

Set within a Colonial-style hotel *(see p265)* in the heart of town, this clean and well-run restaurant, open to the tropical breezes, offers the best dining for miles. Breakfast is excellent, with *huevos rancheros*, pancakes with honey, and more. The lunch and dinner menu offers international favorites, from onion soup to filet mignon.

DOMINICAL Confusione 🚸 ♿ ♫ 🍴 [V] $$$

400 yards (400 m) S of the police station ***Tel*** *2787-0244*

Attached to a mediocre hotel, this Italian restaurant delivers consistently delicious gourmet cuisine in an airy, elegant setting. The creative dishes include penne with shrimps and capers in a vodka sauce. Live classical music and acoustic guitar liven things up four nights a week.

DOMINICAL San Clemente Bar and Grill 🍴 🍸 [V] $$$

S of the soccer field ***Tel*** *2787-0055*

This informal bar and grill serves American and Tex-Mex favorites, as well as seafood such as mahimahi with honey and orange sauce. Owner Mike McGinnis makes his own searingly hot sauces. The lively bar is festooned with surf boards, and has a pool table and sports TV. The place also runs a hostel a short walk away *(see p265)*.

Key to Price Guide *see p272* **Key to Symbols** *see back cover flap*

GOLFITO Le Coquillage

Hotel Centro Turístico Samoa, N of Pueblo Civil **Tel** *2775-0233*

This airy restaurant at the Centro Turístico Samoa *(see p265)* encircles a bar in the shape of a ship's prow. It offers international favorites and a wide selection of seafood, including *corvina al ajillo* (garlic sea bass). Bar games include pool, table soccer, and darts.

OJOCHAL Citrus

200 yards (200 m) E of the Costanera Sur **Tel** *2786-5175*

This sublime eatery, a sibling to Restaurant Exótica *(see below)*, raises local dining to previously unimagined heights. Stylish 21st-century decor provides an uplifting setting for award-winning fusion dishes. Musical events include flamenco and belly-dancing. Closed Sunday and Monday.

OJOCHAL Villas Gaia

Playa Tortuga, 0.5 mile (1 km) W of Ojochal **Tel** *2786-5044*

Attached to the small Villas Gaia *(see p266)*, this open-air roadside restaurant has colorful, casual decor, and a vast international menu with a selection of soups, salads, and light snacks, as well as exotic cooked dishes, such as macadamia-crusted fish fillet. The eatery features an extensive children's menu, and Friday is tapas night.

OJOCHAL Restaurant Exótica

Ojochal village **Tel** *2786-5050*

This small and intimate restaurant is acclaimed for its creative tropical nouvelle cuisine that draws upon the best of Continental influences – fish filet with banana curry sauce, for example. The outdoor candlelit dining offers tremendous romantic appeal, and the wine list is extensive. Closed Sunday.

PUERTO JIMENEZ Restaurante Carolina

SE of the soccer field **Tel** *2735-5185*

Located on the main street and popular with the backpacking crowd, this budget restaurant is the best breakfast spot in town. It offers well-prepared and filling *típico* (typical) dishes, including variations on *gallo pinto*, and seafood served alfresco. International influences are present in the likes of chicken cordon bleu.

PUERTO JIMENEZ Juanita's Mexican Bar and Grill

SE of the soccer field **Tel** *2735-5056*

Filling Tex-Mex fare and a genuine Mexican ambience in an atmospheric *cantina (see p268)* that is the liveliest place in town. Choose from expected staples such as taco salads, burritos, and *chimichangas* (deep-fried burritos). Entertainment includes hula hoop contests and live crab races, the fun being assisted by giant margaritas.

PUERTO JIMENEZ Perla de Osa

Iguana Lodge, Playa Platanares, 2 miles (3 km) E of Puerto Jiménez **Tel** *8848-0752*

A colorful beachfront restaurant with hammocks and a delightful barefoot ambience. Dishes include Caesar salad, *empanadas* (stuffed turnovers), and grilled chicken club sandwiches. It has pasta night on Fridays, with live music as an accompaniment. The hardwood bar serves fresh fruit smoothies and exotic tropical cocktails.

SAN ISIDRO DE EL GENERAL Taquería México Lindo

Calle Central and Ave 2 **Tel** *2771-8222*

Situated on the northwest side of the plaza, this Mexican restaurant offers a full menu of regional fare at exceptional prices. The chef hails from Mexico, and the burritos, enchiladas, and vanilla flans are as authentic as anywhere in Costa Rica. The place is festooned with *piñatas* (papier-mâché vessels) and other Mexican decor. Closed Sunday.

SAN ISIDRO DE EL GENERAL Café Trapiche

Rancho La Botija, 4 miles (6 km) SE of San Isidro **Tel** *2770-2146*

This rustic farmstead at Rancho La Botija *(see p267)* has endearing country decor, such as antique farm implements. The simple menu of *típico* and international dishes includes pastas, garlic sea bass, and steaks. It is open only for breakfast and lunch. Closed Monday.

SAN VITO Pizzería Liliana

NW of the plaza **Tel** *2773-3080*

Splendid pizzas and other Italian staples attest to the heritage of the owners at this simple restaurant located in the center of town. The cooking is homely rather than gourmet, and great value for money. Diners can eat alfresco on a small patio.

UVITA Las Terrazas de Ballena

0.75 mile (1 km) NE of Uvita **Tel** *2743-8034*

The sensational views are reason enough to dine here. Perched on a forested hillside, this open-air candlelit restaurant has a sumptuous Balinese-style lounge. Choose from burgers and sandwiches to such exotic dishes as jumbo shrimp marinated in orange juice, ginger, and honey served with a sweet chili sauce.

ZANCUDO Oceano

400 yards (400 m) S of Zancudo village **Tel** *2776-0921*

Located in a popular beach village with few dining options, this tiny open-air restaurant stands out for its charming diced-log tables. The live-in expatriate owners prepare burgers, *huevos rancheros*, and similar North American staples, plus ice creams. There are special theme nights, plus a popular Sunday brunch.

SHOPPING IN COSTA RICA

For many visitors, shopping is one of the thrills of a trip to Costa Rica. The range of quality *artesanías* (crafts) has grown rapidly in recent years, and most hotels have stores selling coffee, beautiful earthenware pottery in pre-Columbian style, handwoven hammocks, and souvenirs such as bowls and animal figures made of exotic hardwoods. San José has several art galleries, craft stores that stock a range of products including *molas* (reverse-appliqué cloth) from

Saddle, Ciudad Quesada

Bahía Drake and Sarchí leather rockers, and city malls that offer a vast choice of boutiques and jewelry stores. Across the country, bustling *mercados* (markets) are full of trinkets, piles of spices and herbs, *talabarterías* (saddle-makers) and *zapaterías* (shoe-makers), while colorful roadside stalls are piled high with fruits and vegetables. Indigenous crafts are increasingly appearing on the market. Note that it is illegal to buy or export pre-Columbian artifacts.

Palm-leaf baskets and hats for sale at a roadside stall

OPENING HOURS

Shops in San José are usually open from 8am to 6pm, Monday to Saturday. Large US-style malls are open on Sundays, but may close on Mondays. Outside San José, many *tiendas* (shops) close for lunch, typically between noon and 1:30pm. Shops in many tourist resorts remain open all week long, often until 9 or 10pm. Department stores and supermarkets everywhere stay open during lunchtime and often into the evening. Street markets and *mercados* usually open at around 6am and close by 2 or 3pm, although street stalls often stay open late.

PAYING AND PRICES

Cash will be needed to pay for goods bought directly from craftsmen and at street stalls and markets. However,

most stores accept VISA, and to a lesser degree, MasterCard and American Express, as well as US dollars. Credit card payments are sometimes subject to a small surcharge. Torn dollar bills are usually refused by shopkeepers. Some shops accept traveler's checks. A 13 percent sales tax will be added to the cost of most consumer goods in shops.

While leather goods are less expensive here than in most other countries, in general prices are relatively high. Items in galleries and hotel gift stores are sold at a fixed price. However, a certain amount of bargaining is expected at craft markets and *mercados*. The local artisans' cooperative markets have the best prices, and being government-regulated, ensure that a large slice of the profit goes directly to the craftsman. In general, larger stores and local export companies will arrange to have purchases shipped to the buyer's home.

ART GALLERIES

San José has numerous art galleries selling paintings, sculptures, prints, and other artworks by leading artists. Many of the best are found in the area around Parque Morazán *(see p116)* and **Centro Comercial El Pueblo**, which has over a dozen galleries. Two good outlets are the **Andrómeda Gallery** and **Kandinsky**. For more avant-garde art works, try **TeoréTica**, in Barrio Amón, which has a comprehensive selection, or **Galería 11–12**, which is located in the upscale western suburb of Escazú.

Many professional artists live in Monteverde. Manco Tulio Brenes sells his lovely paintings and sculptures at **Artes Tulio**. In the Caribbean lowlands, it is worth dropping in at Patricia Erickson's **Gallery at Home** *(see p214)*, from where the artist sells her vibrant Afro-themed paintings.

Centro Comercial El Pueblo, San José

Shelves of colorful objects in a San José craft store

CRAFT STORES

The variety of *artesanías* available in Costa Rica is quite large. Quality craft stores sell a range of products, from woodworks, which are created out of exotic hardwoods such as rosewood, ironwood, and purpleheart, to nature-themed books and tapes to Guatemalan weavings and embroideries.

The town of Sarchí *(see p136)* in the Central Highlands is the main source of crafts, and produces leather rocking chairs, handmade furniture with bas-relief carvings, and brightly painted miniature *carretas* (oxcarts; *see p137*). Here, the **Fábrica de Carretas Joaquín Chaverrí** has the largest and best selection of crafts. Nearby, the **Plaza de la Artesanía** also has several craft shops.

Many store owners pride themselves on seeking out the finest quality crafts. One such place worth seeking

Toad Hall sign, Lake Arenal

out is **Lucky Bug Gallery** *(see p200)*, on the north shore of Lake Arenal. A huge array of crafts are displayed at shops along Highway 21, not far from Liberia's Daniel Oduber International Airport.

In San José, the **Boutique Annemarie**, in the Hotel Don Carlos, has a fabulous array of crafts at fair prices, as does **La Casona**, a two-story building with several stores selling a varied range of Central American crafts.

Visitors who like browsing open-air markets should head to the **Mercado de Artesanías Nacionales**. This artisans' market houses a broad range of craft stalls under one roof. The most concentrated crafts shopping, however, is in the northeastern suburb of Moravia, where Calle de la Artesanía is lined with crafts stores. Here, the **Mercado de Artesanía Las Garzas** has several dozen stores. Competition is intense, and bargaining is normal.

INDIGENOUS CRAFTS

Although Costa Rica does not have as strong an indigenous craft tradition as other Latin American nations, it has many unique handicrafts to offer visitors. The Boruca tribe of **Reserva Indígena Boruca** *(see p232)* make balsa-wood masks and bas-relief wall hangings, available at a discount if bought directly from the artists. When buying directly from the craftsmen, bear in mind that their margin of profit is usually quite low. Many of the finest examples of Boruca art are also available in quality crafts stores in San José, and at **Coco Loco Art Gallery and Café** *(see p282)* in Chachagua near La Fortuna. Coco Loco also sells some fabulous contemporary pottery and marble carvings by leading artists.

Intriguing indigenous pottery comes from **Guaitíl** *(see p193)*, where ocher vases, bowls, plates, and animals emblazoned with traditional Chorotega motifs are sold at the potters' roadside stalls. Many venues also sell the colorful hand-stitched *molas* of the Kuna Indians of the San Blas islands of Panama. At **Molas y Café**, in Atenas, you can sometimes see Kuna members at work.

The two best commercial outlets for indigenous arts and crafts are **Galería Dantica** and **Galería Namu**, which sells an excellent selection of palm-leaf baskets, Boruca masks, Huetar carvings, and colorful, embroidered Guaymí clothing.

Pottery wares lining a street in Santa Ana, near San José

WOODWORKS

Popular items sold in stores specializing in woodwork include figurines, kitchen utensils, bowls, and jewelry boxes. Some of the finest wooden bowls and boxes are produced by **Barry Biesanz Woodworks** *(see p125)* – it is possible to buy directly from his Escazú studio. Biesanz's works have been gifted by the government of Costa Rica to many visiting dignitaries.

Gold jewelry on sale, Museo del Oro Precolombino store

JEWELRY

Skilled goldsmiths craft exquisite jewelry using both modern designs and pre-Columbian motifs such as frogs and birds, often incorporating semi-precious stones such as lapis lazuli, onyx, and jade. It is best to buy from reputable stores, such as San José's **Esmeraldas y Diseños**, which also offers demonstrations of jewelry design. Most deluxe hotels and large malls also have jewelry stores. For good-quality jewelry in 14-carat gold, the Museo del Oro Precolombino store *(see p113)* is worth a visit. Items sold at streetside jewelry stalls are usually gold-washed, not pure gold.

COFFEE

Several *beneficios* (coffee-processing factories) are open to visitors and will ship bulk purchases of vacuum-packed coffee. Among these are the Café Britt airport gift stores and the Café Britt *beneficio (see p142)*, which has a well-stocked craft store. Many regional varieties of coffee are sold at hotel gift shops, where traditional Costa Rican coffee-strainers called *chorreadores* are also often available. Domestic-quality

coffee is sold at shops in San José's **Mercado Central** *(see p108)*, where it is roasted on the spot; ask for *granos puros* (whole beans) rather than *café traditional*, which is coffee ground very fine and mixed with sugar.

GARMENTS

Traditional Guanacasteco (from Guanacaste) dresses and blouses, such as those worn by dancers of Fantasía Folklórico *(see p293)*, are sold at the Mercado Central *(see p108)* in San José. The **Museo Comunitario Boruca** sells colorful indigenous skirts, while Fundación Neotrópica's **Tienda de la Naturaleza**, in the suburb of Curridabat, sells good-quality T-shirts. There are no factory outlets selling discounted designer clothes.

OTHER SPECIALTY STORES

The suburb of Moravia in San José is known for its leatherwork. Belts and purses are an excellent buy, as are cowboy boots, which range in design from classical to trendy. A wide selection

of cowboy boots is sold by *zapaterías* (shoemakers) in Barrio México, northwest of downtown San José. Ciudad Quesada (San Carlos) *(see p204)* is the best place to go if you are looking for ornate saddles – a wide variety is available. It is worth keeping in mind that leather costs significantly less than in Europe or North America.

The capital city has several cigar outlets, which stock Cuban cigars. The **Cigar Shoppe**, in the city center, and the **Tobacco Shop**, in the Centro Comercial El Pueblo, are recommended. Don't buy cigars on the street; the boxed cigars may look genuine, but they are almost always cheap fakes. However, US citizens should note that it is illegal for them to bring home Cuban products, even if bought in Costa Rica.

Beautiful orchids in sealed vials are available at airport gift shops and in various botanical gardens such as **Jardín Botánico Lankester** *(see p143)*, near Cartago.

Many artists produce stunning *vidriera* (stained glass). Good sources are Escazú's **Creaciones Santos** and **Rancho Leona** *(see p261)*.

One of the many specialty leather stores in Costa Rica

Stalls selling fresh produce and other articles at Mercado Central, San José

MARKETS AND MALLS

Every town has its *mercado central* (central market), selling everything from cowboy hats to medicinal herbs. Good buys at San José's Mercado Central include embroidered *guayabero* shirts (summer shirts for men), and cowboy boots made of exotic leathers. Town markets can be dark warrens, and quite crowded, especially on Saturdays; shoppers should watch out for pickpockets. Not many shopkeepers speak English. Most towns also have *ferias de agricultores* (farmers' markets) on weekends, which sell all kinds of fresh produce. These usually start at dawn and are frequented by locals.

Malls are found only in big towns. **Mall San Pedro** in San José and **Multiplaza** in Escazú have many boutiques.

DIRECTORY

ART GALLERIES

Andrómeda Gallery
Calle 9 and Ave 9,
Barrio Amón,
San José.
Tel 2223-3529.

Artes Tullo
Monteverde.
Tel 2645-5567.

Centro Comercial El Pueblo
Barrio Tournon.
Tel 2221-9434.

Galería 11–12
Plaza Itzkatzu,
Escazú.
Tel 2288-1975.

Kandinsky
Centro Comercial,
Calle Real,
San Pedro, San José.
Tel 2234-0478.

TeoréTica
Calle 7 and Aves 9/11,
San José.
Tel 2233-8775.

CRAFT STORES

Boutique Annemarie
Calle 9 and Ave 9,
San José.
Tel 2221-6707.

La Casona
Calle Central and
Ave Central, San José.
Tel 2222-7999.

Mercado de Artesanía Las Garzas
Calle 8 and Ave 2 bis,
Moravia.
Tel 2236-0037.

Mercado de Artesanías Nacionales
Calle 11 and Ave 4,
San José.

Plaza de la Artesanía
Sarchí Sur, Sarchí.
Tel 2454-3430.

INDIGENOUS CRAFTS

Galería Dantica
Lighthouse Plaza,
Playa Herradura.
Tel 2740-1067.

Galería Namu
Calles 5/7 and Ave 7,
San José.
Tel 2256-3412.

Molas y Café
Atenas.
Tel 2466-5155.

JEWELRY

Esmeraldas y Diseños
Sabana Norte, San José.
Tel 2231-4808.

GARMENTS

Museo Comunitario Boruca
Boruca Village.
Tel 2514-0045.

Tienda de la Naturaleza
Ave Central, Curridabat.
Tel 2253-1230.

OTHER SPECIALTY STORES

Cigar Shoppe
Calle 5 and Ave 3,
San José.
Tel 2257-5021.

Creaciones Santos
Calles 1/3 and Ave 3,
San Miguel de Escazú.
Tel 2228-6747.

Tobacco Shop
Centro Comercial
El Pueblo, San José.
Tel 2223-0873.

MARKETS AND MALLS

Mall San Pedro
Ave Central and
Circunvalación,
San José.

Multiplaza
Autopista Prospero
Fernández, Escazú.
Tel 2201-6025.

What to Buy

Wall hanging

With a wide selection of quality items sold in shops and galleries throughout the country, there is no shortage of mementos to take home. Hand-crafted objects made from tropical hardwoods, such as bowls, boxes, and kitchen articles, as well as aromatic coffee beans and coffee products of various kinds, are must-buys. Ceramics are excellent, as is jewelry, particularly gold necklaces and pendants that replicate pre-Columbian designs. T-shirts with wildlife motifs, and cuddly sloths, curling snakes made of wood, and other such toys, are popular choices.

FORBIDDEN ITEMS

Objects made from various protected species are commonly sold at local markets. It is illegal to buy anything made from turtle shells, furs such as ocelot and jaguar skins, or feathers of quetzals and other endangered bird species. Conservation groups also discourage buying items made of coral, as well as framed butterflies.

HANDICRAFTS

Costa Rica's skilled artisans are concentrated in Sarchí, famous for its miniature oxcarts painted in gaudy patterns and colors, and for homespun rocking chairs of wood and leather. Dozens of artisans' studios produce a dizzying variety of crafts, which find their way into stores throughout the country. Moravia, near San José, is another center of crafts, particularly leather goods.

Leather Goods
Cowboy boots, purses, and attaché cases exude quality and are relatively inexpensive. Those made of caiman and snake skins should be avoided for conservation reasons.

Wooden bowl and spoons

Painted wooden box

Carved box

Colorful wooden earrings

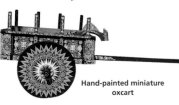

Hand-painted miniature oxcart

Wooden Items
Costa Rica's precious hardwoods yield a wealth of objects. They include statuettes, animal figurines, carved boxes, and notably, lathe-turned bowls, some thin enough to be transparent when held up to the light.

Hammocks
Hammocks made of colored hemp rope, in a variety of designs, are sold on the sea shores. Roomy two-person models are also available.

Jewelry
Delicate brooches, necklaces, and earrings in 14-carat gold, often in combination with corals and semi-precious stones, are popular. Street hawkers sell bright necklaces of shells, hardwoods, and seeds.

Brooch

Pearl earrings

Necklace in gold and semi-precious stone

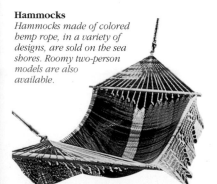

Seed necklace

INDIGENOUS CRAFTS

Items made by Indian tribes can be bought at quality craft stores and, preferably, in indigenous reserves where income goes directly to the artists. Traditional weavings, carved gourds, painted masks, and musical instruments are often imbued with spiritual symbols.

Carved Gourds
Decorated with wildlife motifs, carved gourds are lightweight and can be used as vases.

Painted mask

Boruca mask

"Devil" Masks
Made of balsa wood, these masks made by the Boruca tribe should be bought directly from the carver. Other indigenous wooden goods include wall hangings.

Ocher Pottery
Pottery adorned with traditional Chorotega motifs are produced in Guaitil, using traditional firing methods. Pots, plates, and vases of varying shapes and sizes can be bought at roadside stalls and cooperatives throughout Guanacaste.

Coffee liqueur

Organic coffee

A regional variety of coffee

Chocolate-coated coffee beans

COFFEE

Coffee products range from gourmet roasted whole beans to coffee liqueurs. Be sure to buy export-quality coffee, as coffees sold for the domestic market are often of inferior quality and, if sold pre-ground, adulterated with large amounts of sugar.

SOUVENIRS

All manner of trinkets, utensils, and miscellaneous artistic creations are for sale at gift stores nationwide, from candles to stained-glass pendants. Typically, they are emblazoned with images of wildlife or rural scenes. The store at San José's international airport has a good selection.

Bright brooch

Candle

Ceramic plate

Painted metal jug

Stained-glass item

ENTERTAINMENT IN COSTA RICA

Cultural activities and live entertainment in Costa Rica have traditionally been somewhat restrained by the standards of many other Latin American countries. Nonetheless, Ticos have a tremendous love of music and dance, and recent years have witnessed a blossoming of entertainment venues. Nightlife, especially in San José, is excitingly diverse. Theater and classical concerts are an integral part of San José's social life, and even smaller

Guanacaste National Band poster

cities usually have theater spaces and *glorietas* (bandstands) where live musicians perform. Music festivals are staged both indoors and outdoors, and country fairs called *ferías* are in full swing year-round. Every town has numerous discos, and karaoke bars are popular with lower-income Ticos. Entertainment in country towns revolves around *topes* (horsemanship shows) and *retornos* (rodeos) that spill onto the streets with traditional live music and dance.

INFORMATION

A calendar of major events is carried in Spanish and English on the website of the Instituto Costarricense de Turismo (Costa Rican Tourism Institute, or ICT; *see p304*). The website also has addresses of theaters, nightclubs and similar venues. *Tico Times* (*see p309*), which is available in many hotels, also provides listings of artistic events and entertainment, as do the "Tiempo Libre" and "Viva" sections of the *La Nación* daily newspaper. *San José Volando* is a free monthly publication that contains information about live concerts, shows, nightclubs, and other entertainment.

I·C·T

Costa Rican Tourism Institute logo

THEATER

Costa Rica has a long tradition of producing great theater, and Josefinos are passionate theatergoers. San José has several small theaters, which offer everything from mainstream and experimental theater, to comedy and puppet shows, at affordable prices. Most productions are in Spanish and are typically restricted to Thursday–Sunday evenings. Mime performances are the main attraction at **Teatro Chaplin**. The country's oldest theater company, the English-language **Little Theatre Group**, performs at the **Teatro Laurence Olivier**,

which doubles as a lively cultural center and has a jazz club and movie theater. The Teatro Eugene O'Neill, located inside the **Centro Cultural Costarricense-Norteamericano** (Costa Rican-North American Cultural Center), also hosts theater performances, plus monthly musical concerts on weekends.

CLASSICAL MUSIC, BALLET, DANCE, AND OPERA

Costa Rica's middle class are enthusiastic lovers of classical music. The nation's foremost venue for classical and ballet performances is San José's **Teatro Nacional** (*see pp110–11*). It was inaugurated to great national pride in 1897 with a performance of *El Fausto de Gournod* by the

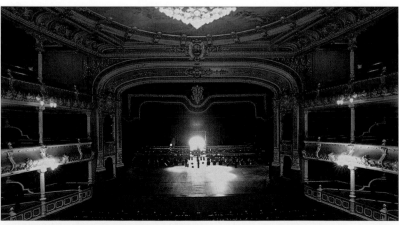

The opulent interior of the auditorium of Teatro Nacional

A lively traditional dance in progress in Pueblo Antiguo, San José

Paris Opera. The theater hosts the **Orquestra Sinfónia Nacional**, founded in 1970, which performs a series of concerts each year between April and December. It also holds performances by the **Compañía de Lírica Nacional** (National Lyric Opera Company), the country's only opera company, from June to August. The companies feature many of the world's best-known works in their repertoires. International orchestras and singers also perform in the Teatro Nacional. Evening performances at the theater are considered an occasion to dress up for. Prices in the *galería* (galleries) are generally below $5, depending on the particular performance in question.

Theater production in Costa Rica has a long tradition, boosted in the early 1900s when a number of South American dramatists settled here, and drama was introduced to the high school curriculum. The **Teatro Mélico Salazar** *(see p108)* stages drama, musicals, classical concerts, and occasional performances of traditional Costa Rican singing and dancing. The theater is also the principal venue of Costa Rica's **Compañia Nacional de Danza** (National Dance Company), a world-class organization founded in 1979, which has an extensive repertoire of contemporary and classical works.

It is advisable to book in advance, which you should do directly with the venue or event organizers.

JAZZ

Jazz clubs have grown in number in recent years, and jazz trios play in several hotel lobbies and bars. The main venue is San José's **Jazz Café**, a red-brick structure with a classic bohemian ambience. Leading international performers such as Chucho Valdés and Irakere have played here. Jazz Café also has a venue in Escazú. San José's jazz buffs also frequent the Shakespeare Gallery in the **Sala Garbo**, which hosts live jazz on Monday evenings.

TRADITIONAL MUSIC

Rather limited in form and style, the country's popular music is a more restricted version of the *marimba* cultures of Nicaragua and Guatemala. The *marimba* (xylophone), *quijongo* (single-string bow with gourd resonator), and guitar provide the backing for such traditional folk dances as the *punto guanacasteco*, the national dance *(see p295)*. Live *marimba* music is performed at *ferias*, a few tourist venues, and city plazas on weekends. A good place to experience traditional music and dance is **Pueblo Antiguo** *(see p125)*. Indigenous communities perform ritual dances accompanied by drums, rattles, and ceramic flutes.

The Teatro Mélico Salazar, one of San José's popular cultural venues

Dancing the night away at a beach resort nightclub

NIGHTCLUBS AND DISCOS

San José and key tourist resorts have swanky dance clubs. Many of the best nightclubs are associated with leading hotels, and several larger beach resorts feature discos. Less sophisticated venues are everywhere, catering to the dance-crazy Ticos. The predominant music is Latin: *cumbia*, salsa and, especially, merengue, often interspersed with reggae and world-beat tunes.

In San José, the well-to-do can be found at the various bars and clubs along San Pedro's Avenida Central, and in San Rafael de Escazú. **Discoteque Planet Mall**, popular with teenagers, claims to be the largest disco in Central America. A more down-to-earth and always crowded option is **El Cuartel de la Boca del Monte**, with an earthy atmosphere, eclectic patrons, and live music by many of Costa Rica's leading bands. Several discos and bars can be found in the alleyways comprising **El Pueblo**, while the Los Yoses and San Pedro districts have many bars and clubs catering to students and well-off young Ticos. Calle de la Amargura (Street of Bitterness), leading to the university, is lined with student bars, and draws few foreigners. Bars in "Gringo Gulch," a red-light area of

central San José, mostly cater to an older foreign clientele, including the city's large number of expatriate residents. Take care with whom you interact in this locality, and always use taxis at night.

Most of the clubs don't begin to liven up until midnight, and many don't close until dawn. Attire is usually quite casual, with jeans permitted; shorts are generally not allowed, except at beach resorts.

CASINOS

Costa Rica has dozens of casinos, concentrated in the capital city. They are mostly associated with large, expensive hotels. Several casinos are clustered in the infamous Gringo Gulch. Some casinos are open

24 hours. The most popular games are craps, *tute* (a version of poker), canasta, which resembles roulette, and *veinte un* (21), a variant of blackjack. Visitors should be aware that the odds are far more favorable to the house than they are in the US.

DANCE SCHOOLS

Many visitors come to Costa Rica to learn to dance. Several reputable *academias de baile* (dance schools) offer residential courses where you can pick up some fancy foot skills in hip-swiveling *cumbia*, merengue, salsa, and whatever the latest Latin dance craze may be. Most classes are typically in Spanish. The well-known **Merecumbé** has several schools in San José and major highland cities.

FESTIVALS

Costa Rica's annual calendar is full of festivals, large and small *(see pp32–5)*. Many of them celebrate the country's diverse cultures, such as the Fiesta de los Diablitos *(see p232)* of the Borucas and Puerto Límon's extravagant Caribbean-style Carnaval *(see p215)*. Costa Rica's best-known music festivals include the nationwide **International Festival of Music**, which is held at half a dozen venues throughout the country. Many of the towns in Catholic Costa Rica honor their patron saints on specific days of the year.

A Caribbean-style performance in a resort in Guanacaste

THE PUNTO GUANACASTECO

The national dance is the *punto guanacasteco*, a toe-and-heel dance performed in traditional regional costumes. The women wear white bodices and colorful frilly satin skirts. The men wear white shirts and pants, satin sashes, and cowboy hats. The slow, twirling *baile típico* (typical dance) features the tossing of hats and scarves, as males interrupt the proceedings in turn to shout rhyming verses aimed at winning over a love interest.

Dancers performing the *punto guanacasteco*

Nationally, the most important religious festival is the Día del Virgen de los Angeles, which is celebrated in Cartago's Basílica de Nuestra Señora de los Angeles *(see pp144–5)* in August. Nicoya's Fiesta de la Yeguita *(see p192)*, held in December, is one of the nation's most colorful regional festivals.

CINEMA

Most cities have cinemas, although those in smaller towns are often ramshackle. San José and other large cities have modern multiplex cinemas up to the standards of North America and Western Europe. **Cinepolis** and others show first-run Hollywood and international movies, which are usually subtitled in Spanish. Dubbed films are advertised with the phrase *hablado en español*. International art-house movies are shown at **Sala Garbo**. Costa Rica has no major cinema industry of its own.

PEÑAS

San José's intellectuals enjoy *peñas* (circles of friends), bohemian get-togethers that evolved from Latin America's Leftist revolutionary movement of the 1970s. Poetry is recited and plaintiff *nueva trova* music is performed at *peñas*, also called *tertulias*. They are leading outlets for experimental music and literature by such avant-garde performers as Esteban Monge and Canto America. Typical venues are private homes and cafés. An active venue is **TeoréTica**, a hip art gallery that hosts literary readings, round-table discussions, and other cultural events.

DIRECTORY

THEATER AND CULTURAL CENTERS

Centro Cultural Costarricense-Norteamericano
San Pedro, San José.
Tel 2225-9433.
www.centrocultural.cr

Little Theatre Group
Tel 8858-1446.
www.littletheatregroup.org

Teatro Chaplin
Calles 11/13 and Ave 12,
San José.
Tel 2221-0812.
www.teatrochaplin.com

Teatro Laurence Olivier
Calle 28 and Ave 2,
San José. **Tel** 2223-1960.

CLASSICAL MUSIC, BALLET, DANCE, AND OPERA

Compañía de Lírica Nacional
Tel 2240-3333.
www.mcjdcr.go.cr/musica/compania_lirica.html

Compañía Nacional de Danza
Tel 2222-2974.
www.mcjdcr.go.cr

Orquestra Sinfónia Nacional
Tel 2240-0333.
www.osn.go.cr

JAZZ

Jazz Café
Calle 7 and Ave Central,
San Pedro, San José.
Tel 2253-8933.

Plaza Itzkatzú,
Autopista Prospero
Fernández, Escazú.
Tel 2288-4740.
www.jazzcafecostarica.com

Sala Garbo
Calle 28 and Ave 2,
San José.
Tel 2222-1034.

NIGHTCLUBS AND DISCOS

Discoteque Planet Mall
Mall San Pedro, San José.
Tel 2280-4693.

El Cuartel de la Boca del Monte
Calles 21/23 and Ave 1,
San José. **Tel** 2221-0327.

El Pueblo
Ave Central, Barrio
Tournón, San José.
Tel 2221-9434.

DANCE SCHOOLS

Merecumbé
Tel 2224 3531.
www.merecumbe.net

FESTIVALS

International Festival of Music
Tel 2282-7724.
www.costaricamusic.com

CINEMA

Cinepolis
Autopista a Cartago,
San José.
Tel 2518-0002.

Sala Garbo
See Jazz.

PEÑAS

TeoréTica
Calle 7 and Aves 9/11,
San José.
Tel 2233-8775.
www.teoretica.org

OUTDOOR ACTIVITIES AND SPECIALTY VACATIONS

The varied terrain, salubrious climate, and diversity of wilderness reserves in Costa Rica combine to afford a wealth of outdoor activities. Some of these, which have been spawned by the tourist boom of the past two decades, are unusual – canopy tours, for example, are a staple of the rain- and cloud forest reserves. Others are more conventional. Ample opportunities for hiking are provided by the trails that lace the superb national parks and

Sign, Playa Flamingo

reserves. Costa Rica is also well-geared for biking and horseback riding. Both coasts offer fabulous surfing, and windsurfing is world class, with dedicated facilities at Lake Arenal and Bahía Salinas. Whitewater rafting is highly developed, while scuba divers and anglers are in for a treat. Wherever you are in the nation, the great outdoors is close at hand. A handy resource is *Costa Rica Outdoors*, a bimonthly publication available nationwide.

The range of activities offered at Selva Verde Lodge

ORGANIZED TOURS

A plethora of tour operators in Costa Rica cater to visitors interested in particular activities. Companies offering a range of specialized tours include **Costa Rica Expeditions**, **Costa Rica's Temptations**, and **Costa Rica Sun Tours**. Operators dedicated to a specific activity are listed in the relevant subsection.

NATIONAL PARKS AND WILDLIFE RESERVES

Costa Rica has about 190 national parks, wildlife reserves, and related protected areas, with a combined area of almost 6,000 sq miles (15,500 sq km). Dozens of other privately owned reserves protect additional

natural habitats. Protected areas continue to be created to link individual parks and reserves with the purpose of creating uninterrupted migratory corridors for wildlife. The national parks and reserves are organized into "conservation areas" administered by the **SINAC** (Sistema de Areas de Conservación/System of Conservation Areas), which is a division of MINAE (Ministerio de Ambiente y Energía/Ministry of Atmosphere and Energy).

La Amistad, covering an area of 749 sq miles (1,940 sq km), is the largest national park *(see p227)*. This is also the most remote and inaccessible one, and hiking can be challenging. The most visited park is Parque Nacional Volcán Poás, which lies within a 2-hour drive of San José and has the most developed facilities *(see p140)*. Also popular is Parque Nacional Manuel Antonio, which offers

the advantage of easy access and an assortment of attractions, including beautiful beaches *(see pp168–9)*. Parque Nacional Cahuita, on the Caribbean coast, features similar attractions *(see p218)*. Parque Nacional Chirripó *(see pp228–9)* and Parque Nacional Rincón de la Vieja *(see p182)* offer fabulous mountain hiking – Rincón has the added enticement of fumaroles and boiling mud pools. Guided boat tours make the rainforests and swamps of Parque Nacional Tortuguero accessible *(see p217)*. A more challenging but no less rewarding destination is Parque Nacional Corcovado, perhaps the nation's premier rainforest environment *(see p239)*. Reserva Biológica Bosque Nuboso Monteverde is the top cloud forest reserve *(see p177)*. A useful source of information on various reserves is **Fundación de Parques Nacionales**.

Boat tour in Parque Nacional Tortuguero

Bird-watchers in Parque Nacional Manuel Antonio

WILDLIFE-VIEWING

Viewing animals and birds in the wild is the prime attraction for the majority of visitors to Costa Rica. It's easily done, even without visiting protected reserves, as wildlife is literally everywhere outside city limits. Morpho butterflies, toucans, monkeys, and coatis can be seen from your hotel porch, depending on location. However, most species are well disguised or reclusive, and spotting them often requires a combination of patience and planning. Hiring a naturalist guide is recommended – their trained eyes and knowledge of where and when to look for certain species will greatly increase your success rate. Guides can be hired through Costa Rica Expeditions, which also offers nature trips of its own. A particularly good way to view wildlife is to take a natural history cruise aboard a small ship, with daily excursions ashore. Leading companies include **National Geographic Expeditions**.

On a nature trip, dress in greens and browns to blend in with the surroundings. Silence is imperative. Bring a pair of binoculars. Laminated spotters' charts are available at book- and souvenir stores. Companies specializing in birding include **Horizontes**.

HIKING

For those who like to experience nature on foot, Costa Rica is a dream come true. Thousands of miles of trails traverse the countryside, offering opportunities to explore the most remote terrain. Many trails are well marked and easy to hike, while others provide a rugged challenge to even the most experienced hikers. **Librería Universal** and the **Instituto Geográfico Nacional** sell detailed topographic maps.

The majority of trails are associated with the national parks and wildlife reserves, where facilities are usually restricted to the ranger stations and/or private lodges near the entrances. Many of the larger parks have only basic huts, sometimes a full day's hike from each other – hikers will need to be self-sufficient in terms of camping equipment and food. Always inquire about the distance to the next hut, and the difficulty of the hike. You will need to get permission to camp anywhere other than at designated campsites. For overnight hikes, always report to a ranger station at the beginning and end of your trip. Permits and local guides are essential for certain hikes, such as those across the remote Talamancas.

Look out for venomous snakes – never leave your tent or cabin door open (see p.307). Hikers in Parque Nacional Corcovado and other lowland rainforest reserves may come across bands of aggressive wild pigs called peccaries. If threatened, climb a tree and wait until the animals depart. Otherwise, the best bet is usually to stand still: most charges are bluffs.

Lightweight yet sturdy waterproof hiking shoes are essential, as is a water bottle and a backpack with room for a waterproof jacket with hood. Apart from sunscreen and insect repellent, other recommended items are a first aid kit, as well as a flashlight and spare batteries. Pack your gear in a plastic bag before placing it in your backpack to ensure that it remains dry. Clean up the campsite before leaving – only footprints should be left behind.

CANOPY TOURS

With its soaring trees and deep valleys, it is no surprise that Costa Rica has dozens of canopy tours to whisk you between treetops and across gorges (see pp24–5). Zipline tours provide an adrenalin-packed ride, but don't expect to see much wildlife. The **Original Canopy Tour** has four locations around the country.

Zipline canopy tour, Arenal Rainforest Reserve

Horseback riding on one of Costa Rica's many beaches

HORSEBACK RIDING

Costa Rica affords numerous opportunities for equestrian pursuits. Tour operators and hotels can make all the necessary arrangements for rides, which are usually on the small, mild-tempered local *criollo* horse.

Guanacaste province has several ranches specializing in horse riding. **Hacienda Guachipelín** *(see p259)* is an excellent location, as is the **Buena Vista Lodge** *(see p259)*. Another good place is **Club Hípico La Caraña**, near Escazú.

CYCLING

Touring the country by bicycle is an excellent way to meet local people and to enjoy the spectacular scenery. However, many roads are potholed and cycling in highland areas requires caution due to fog, blind bends, and speeding traffic. Several companies specialize in bicycle tours: **Backroads**, in North America, and **Coast to Coast Adventures**, in Costa Rica, are two reputable outfits. Most international airlines will let you bring your own

bicycle as checked luggage, if properly packed.

Costa Rica's rugged terrain is particularly suited to mountain biking, and Ticos (Costa Ricans) are enthusiasts of the sport. Several hotels and local tour agencies rent mountain bikes and offer short mountain-biking excursions.

GOLF AND TENNIS

The country has six 18-hole courses, as well as four 9-hole ones. Additional courses are in the offing. In the Nicoya Peninsula, the leading greens are at the **Four Seasons Resort** *(see p256)* and the **Reserva Conchal Golf Club**. The best of

the Central Highlands courses are at the **Cariari Country Club** and **Parque Valle del Sol**.

Many hotels and beach resorts have tennis courts available free of charge to guests. Non-guests are usually allowed to play on these courts for a fee.

WHITEWATER RAFTING AND KAYAKING

Costa Rica's high rainfall and mountain terrain combine to provide ideal conditions for whitewater rafting *(see p152)*. The Reventazón and Pacuare Rivers of the Central Highlands are renowned, but every region has world-class whitewater. Tumbling from the country's highest mountain, Río Chirripó (Class III–IV) creates dozens of explosive rapids. It merges with Río General (Class III–IV), known for its challenging rapids. Río Corobicí (Class I–II) is fed by dam-released waters and flows between tree-lined banks in the heart of Guanacaste. It offers a float perfect for families, as wildlife is plentiful and easily seen. Río Savegre (Class III–V) flows out of the mountains of the Central Pacific. The steep upper section is a demanding thriller; the river slows lower down as it passes through African oil palm plantations.

The rafting industry is well regulated, and operators conform to international standards. Life jackets and helmets are mandatory. Trips cost between $70 and $100 per day, including transport, meals, and equipment. Overnight trips involve camping or stays at remote riverside

The serene Parque Valle del Sol golfing greens

Kayaking in Lake Angostura, near Turrialba

lodges. Numerous companies offer rafting trips, including **Ríos Tropicales**. Take sunscreen and suitable attire. A warm jacket for mountain runs is a good idea. Expect to get wet – pack a set of dry clothes and shoes.

Sea kayaks are an ideal means of exploring the mangrove systems of the coasts. One of the major rafting operators, Ríos Tropicales, also features trips on kayaks. Various other nature tour operators offer kayaking trips, and many resort hotels rent kayaks for exploring sheltered bays. With luck, dolphins may appear alongside. If you plan on kayaking alone, *The Rivers of Costa Rica: A Canoeing, Kayaking and Rafting Guide*, by Michael W. Mayfield and Rafael E. Gallo, is indispensable; it is available from San José's **7th Street Books**.

SURFING AND WINDSURFING

Thousands of visitors flock to Costa Rica each year to ride the waves that wash ashore along both the Pacific and Caribbean coastlines. Some of the best surfing beaches are in Northern Nicoya *(see p187)*. Most airlines permit you to check a surfboard as luggage free of charge. However, there is no shortage of surf shops at key surf spots such as Tamarindo, Jacó, and Puerto Viejo de Talamanca. Playa Pavones *(see p240)* is another excellent location, but you will need to bring your own equipment. Dedicated surf camps give

their own meaning to the term "bed and board."

Bahía Salinas *(see p180)* and Laguna de Arenal *(see pp200–2)* are marvelous for windsurfing, thanks to consistently high winds. Both have windsurf centers.

SPORTFISHING

The challenge of landing a world-record catch draws hundreds of anglers to Costa Rica's waters every year. Most sportfishing is on a catch-and-release basis. The Pacific coast *(see p167)* is fabulous for deep-sea fish, such as sailfish, tuna, dorado, and swordfish. Marlin are the big prize: the fish run off Nicoya in November–March; the central and southern Pacific are best in August–December.

On the Caribbean side, anglers use light tackle in rivers, lakes, and lagoons to hook tarpon, snook, and garfish. Caño Negro, as well as the rivermouths of the San Juan and Colorado Rivers, feature some of the world's best tarpon fishing: the best time is December–March. Trout fishing is popular in mountain streams, particularly on the northern slopes of the Talamancas. Laguna de Arenal is renowned for massive rainbow bass; **Rain Goddess** offers fishing trips here *(see p202)*. Permits required for freshwater fishing are organized by the

Sportfishing charter sign

Fishing yacht anchored at Bahía Drake

operators. Several sportfishing lodges cater exclusively to anglers. Boat charters offered from sportfishing centers, such as Flamingo, Quepos, Tamarindo, Golfito, and Zancudo, typically cost $250–400 for a half day and $350–650 for a full day. Fishing tackle is sold and rented at **La Casa del Pescador**. Excellent sources of angling information are **Club Amateur de Pesca** and local fishing expert Jerry Ruhlow's weekly column in the *Tico Times*.

SPIRITUAL RETREATS

A non-profit spiritual community off the beaten track, **PachaMama** offers a sweat lodge and classes in subjects like meditation, yoga, health and well-being, and tantra.

Surfing on the high waves off Playa Jaco

Scuba Diving in Costa Rica

The warm waters off Costa Rica provide splendid opportunities for divers. The country's prime site is Isla del Coco, which offers some of the world's finest scuba diving for seeing marine animals. Other dive spots include the Murciélagos Islands in Northern Nicoya; the coral reefs of Playa Manuel Antonio, Parque Nacional Ballena Marina, and Isla del Caño on the

Scuba diver

Pacific side; and Gandoca-Manzanillo and Cahuita on the Caribbean. Marine turtles and moray eels can be spotted everywhere. Other commonly seen large marine creatures include manta rays, grouper, tuna, jewfish, and several types of sharks and whales. However, visibility is less than high at most dive sites, especially during the rainy season when river runoff clouds the oceans.

Getting ready *for a dive involves careful checking of all equipment, especially the breathing apparatus.*

While underwater, *it is wise to swim in a group so as to assist each other in times of need.*

Starfish can be seen creeping slowly atop the reefs.

Tropical fish of varied hues and shapes inhabit the waters.

Corals, generally poorly developed in Costa Rica, are at their most colorful here.

ISLA DEL CAÑO

This island boasts the largest coral formations in Costa Rica, attracting a rainbow of tropical fish. Also seen here are octopus, sea horses, and starfish. Dolphins cavort in near-shore waters. Diving trips are offered from Bahía Drake *(see p238).*

Several angelfish species, such as king, queen, and French angelfish, are found around Isla del Caño *(see p232).*

At Punta Gorda, *off Playa Ocotal, scuba divers are sure to see a vast number of eagle rays flap past. Also seen are golden rays, as well as stone fish and sea horses.*

Isla del Coco (see p241) *is said to be a site of hidden gold, but its real treasure lies underwater, and includes huge schools of hammerhead sharks. Accessed by live-aboard boats, this is only for experienced divers.*

Islas Murciélagos, *the most favored dive site in the northwest, is renowned for white tip sharks, marlin, and other giant pelagics. Several outfitters in Playas del Coco (see p186) offer trips.*

SWIMMING

Most large hotels, and many smaller ones, have swimming pools. Ocean water temperatures typically range between 25 and 30° C (77–87° F). However, extreme caution is required when swimming in the oceans: Costa Rica averages about 200 drownings a year due to riptides. These fast-moving water currents are typically associated with beaches with high volumes of incoming surf and where retreating water funnels into a narrow channel that can drag you out to sea. Many of the most popular beaches have riptides. If you get caught in one, do not struggle against the current or try to swim to shore: this will quickly exhaust you. Swim parallel to the shore to exit the current. Avoid swimming near river estuaries, where crocodiles may lurk, and in ocean waters off beaches where marine turtles nest, as sharks are often present.

SCUBA DIVING

Almost all the beach resorts near the prime dive sites have scuba operators. You can rent or buy gear here, and at **Mundo Aquático**, in San José. **El Ocotal Diving Safaris** and **Rich Coast Diving** are two respected dive

Divers about to go underwater off Costa Rica's Pacific coast

operators based at Playa Ocotal and Playas del Coco, respectively (see p186). Trips to Isla del Coco, for experienced divers, are offered aboard the **Okeanos Aggressor**, which sails from Puntarenas on 8-, 9-, and 10-day voyages.

DIRECTORY

TOUR OPERATORS

Costa Rica Expeditions
Calle Central/2 and Ave 3, San José. **Tel** 2257-0766.
www.costaricaexpeditions. com

Costa Rica Sun Tours
Edificio Cerro Chato, La Uruca, San José.
Tel 2296-7757.
www.crsuntours.com

Costa Rica's Temptations
PO Box 1199-1200, San José.
Tel 2508-5000.
www.crtinfo.com

NATIONAL PARKS AND WILDLIFE RESERVES

Fundación de Parques Nacionales
Barrio Escalante, San José.
Tel 2257-2239.
@ fpncr@ice.go.cr

SINAC
Calle 25 and Ave 8/10, San José. **Tel** 2248-2451.
www.sinac.go.cr

WILDLIFE-VIEWING

Horizontes
Tel 2222 7022.
www.horizontes.com

National Geographic Expeditions
1145 17th Street NW, Washington, D.C. 20037, USA.
Tel 888-966-8687.
www.nationalgeographic expeditions.com

HIKING

Instituto Geográfico Nacional
Calles 9/11 and Ave 20, San José.
Tel 2523-2000 (ext. 2630).

Librería Universal
Calles Central/1 & Ave Central, San José.
Tel 2222-2222.

CANOPY TOURS

Original Canopy Tour
Tel 2291-4465.
www.canopytour.com

HORSEBACK RIDING

Club Hípico La Caraña
Tel 2282-6754.
www.lacarana.com

CYCLING

Backroads
801 Cedar St, Berkeley, CA 94710, USA.
Tel (510) 527-1555.
www.backroads.com

Coast to Coast Adventures
P.O. Box 2135-1002, San José.
Tel 2280-8054.
www.ctocadventures. com

GOLF

Cariari Country Club
Tel 2293-3211.
www.clubcariari.com

Parque Valle del Sol
Tel 2282-9222.
www.vallesol.com

Reserva Conchal Golf Club
Tel 2654-3000.
www.reservaconchal.com

WHITEWATER RAFTING AND KAYAKING

Ríos Tropicales
Tel 2233-6455.
www.riostropicales.com

7th Street Books
Calle 7 and Ave Central/1, San José.
Tel 2256-8251.
@ marroca@racsa.co.cr

SPORTFISHING

Club Amateur de Pesca
Tel 2232-3430.
www.clubamateur pescacr.com

La Casa del Pescador
Calle 2 and Ave 16/18, San José.
Tel 2222-1470.

SPIRITUAL RETREATS

PachaMama
Apartado 110, Boca de Nosara, Nicoya.
Tel 8785-8949
www.pachamama.com

SCUBA DIVING

El Ocotal Diving Safaris
Tel 2670-0321 (ext. 120).
www.ocotaldiving.com

Mundo Aquático
109 yd (100 m) N of Mas X Menos, San Pedro, San José.
Tel 2224-9729.
@ mundoac@racsa.co.cr

Okeanos Aggressor
Tel 800-348-2628.
www.aggressor.com

Rich Coast Diving
Tel 2670-0176.
www.richcoastdiving.com

SURVIVAL
GUIDE

PRACTICAL INFORMATION

Signs advertising local attractions

It is possible to visit all but the most remote parts of Costa Rica with relative ease, either with a rented vehicle or by public transport. The country has a superb tourist infrastructure, especially in the realms of ecotourism and adventure travel. Rarely will visitors be far from tourist facilities. National tourist offices are found only in San José; in smaller towns and beach resorts, travel agencies and tour operators double as tourist information bureaus. On the whole, tour operators are extremely professional. However, many aspects of day-to-day life in Costa Rica are slow and often bureaucratic. Some patience and flexibility are required to help cope with the minor frustrations.

WHEN TO GO

Costa Rica is best visited in the dry season, which runs from December to April. However, there are regional variations (see p36) – the Caribbean and Southwest Pacific, for example, receive torrential rains year-round.

The wet season is also the hottest time of the year, and it can be torrid, especially in Guanacaste. Many dirt roads become impassable during this time. However, prices are lower than during the dry season, when many hotels are booked solid.

VISAS AND PASSPORTS

All visitors need a valid passport, a return or onward ticket, and adequate finances to support themselves for the duration of their stay. Some visitors need visas. Entry requirements are prone to change so check before travel. A tourist card will be issued on arrival; valid for 90 days, this can be extended at a *migración* (immigration) office in any major city.

If transiting via the USA, you must apply for the Electronic System for Travel Authorization (**ESTA**) before traveling.

CUSTOMS INFORMATION

Buying or exporting archaeological artifacts is illegal and subject to harsh penalties, so be sure to buy only certified reproductions. Items covered by the Convention on International Trade in Endangered Species (CITES) are also prohibited. Visit www.cites.org for more information.

The Chamber of Tourism in Santa Elena, Monteverde

TOURIST INFORMATION

Brochures and maps are available free of charge at the **Instituto Costarricense de Turismo (ICT)** bureaus at the two international airports (see p310). Outside San José, visit tour agencies for information on the local area. Backpacker hostels, hotel tour desks, and websites are other useful sources of information.

ADMISSION PRICES AND OPENING HOURS

Entry prices vary considerably, although most public museums and art galleries are free or charge only a minimal fee. Most national parks cost between $6 and $10. Private reserves and nature centers are typically more expensive, but they often include guided tours and/or activities.

Museum opening hours vary. Bear in mind that many museums close for lunch and on Mondays. National parks are typically open daily from 8am until 4pm.

For opening hours of shops and banks, see p286 and p308.

LANGUAGE

The official language of Costa Rica is Spanish, which is spoken without the Castilian lisp. A basic knowledge of this language is an advantage, though virtually everybody working in the tourism and service industries speaks English. Traditional languages also exist, but most indigenous people speak Spanish.

ETIQUETTE AND SMOKING

Courtesy is greatly valued in Costa Rica. It is normal to shake hands or kiss on one cheek when greeting. Use proper titles such as *señor, señora,* and *señorita. Quedar bien* (to appear well) is a form of behavior intended to leave a good impression, but be aware that it can also involve making false promises simply to please the listener. It is a good idea to ask more than one person for directions.

There are laws requiring non-smoking areas in restaurants and public spaces, but enforcement is rare.

TAXES AND TIPPING

Hotels and restaurants add a 13 percent sales tax, which is also applicable to most store purchases. In addition, restaurants add a 10 percent service charge to all bills.

It is the norm to tip hotel service staff; taxi drivers are optional *(see p314)*. Tour guides should be tipped depending on the quality of their service and presentation; $2 per person per day is the norm for group tours. Additional tips are usually given only for exceptional service. See also Where to Stay *(p247)* and Where to Eat *(p269)*.

TRAVELERS WITH SPECIAL NEEDS

Some airports and the newer hotels and restaurants provide wheelchair ramps and adapted toilets. Few wildlife parks have accessible trails or toilets, although the situation is improving. **Vaya con Sillas de Ruedas** provides transportation within Costa Rica for wheelchair-bound visitors.

TRAVELING WITH CHILDREN

Costa Ricans are very fond of children, and most restaurants have high chairs and special kids' menus *(see p269)*. Hotels permit children under 16 to stay at no extra charge if they share a room with their parents. Many tour companies and eco-lodges provide special family programs, while most museums and private attractions offer free entry for children under the age of

six, and discounts for those aged between six and 12. Car rental companies do not offer children's car seats, so remember to bring your own. Baby foods, diapers, and all other necessities are widely available in local stores.

Parents should consult with their doctor about any recommended vaccinations. The **Hospital Nacional de Niños** in San José is the local children's hospital.

GAY AND LESBIAN TRAVELERS

Costa Ricans are tolerant of homosexuality, although public displays of affection between members of the same sex may provoke strong reactions, especially in rural areas. San José has several gay nightclubs and gay-only hotels, as does Manuel Antonio, the most popular destination for gay travelers.

TRAVELING ON A BUDGET

Costa Rica is popular with budget travelers, who can find affordable accommodations at *cabinas*, backpacker hostels, and surf camps. It is possible to eat well and inexpensively at *sodas* (food stalls) or by ordering *casados* (set menus). Bus travel is also cheap, and most tourist attractions offer discounts to students and seniors.

TIME AND ELECTRICITY

Costa Rica is 6 hours behind Greenwich Mean Time (GMT) and 1 hour behind New York's Eastern Standard Time

(EST). The country has not adopted daylight saving time.

Electrical current is 100 volts, but many hotels in remote areas generate their own power, with a nonstandard voltage.

RESPONSIBLE TOURISM

There are positive attitudes to responsible tourism throughout Costa Rica, as shown by the many conservation schemes. Travelers can contribute to local welfare by buying crafts directly from artisans, hiring local guides, and patronizing community ecotourism projects. Consider volunteering with programs that help save endangered wildlife or contribute to the development of impoverished communities. **Costa Rica Expeditions**, for example, has a program that lets guests at Tortuga Lodge teach English to local children.

Tortuga Lodge, where guests can take part in an English-teaching program

Personal Security and Health

Police department badge, San José

Generally regarded as a safe destination, Costa Rica has a stable democracy and a reputation for neutrality. This can lull visitors into a sense of security that may occasionally prove to be false. Tourists can be targets for theft, scams, and even violent crime, so it is wise to take a few basic safety precautions.

The country has a relatively advanced health system, and you will rarely be far from medical assistance in times of need. Keep an eye out for venomous snakes and other potentially harmful creatures that inhabit the wild. It is also wise to be aware of the country's natural hazards, including dangerous riptides and the sun's powerful tropical rays.

Tourist police patroling the beach at Tamarindo, on the Pacific coast

POLICE

Costa Rican police officers are professional, usually polite, and happy to help tourists. Their standard uniform is dark blue. The bicycle police, wearing white shirts and blue shorts, patrol major cities and tourist centers on bike, while *Tránsitos* (traffic police) patrol the highways, using radar guns to catch speeders.

Attempts by individual police officers to extract *mordidas* (bribes) are fairly rare. To make a complaint against an officer, note their name and badge number and report them to the **Organismo de Investigación Judicial (OIJ)**.

WHAT TO BE AWARE OF

Keep photocopies of your passport and other important documents in the hotel safe, along with your valuables. Be aware of your surroundings at all times, especially on city streets. Avoid wearing jewelry in public and do not leave your belongings unattended. Be especially cautious of scams involving your rental car *(see p315)* and of anyone offering unsolicited assistance of any kind, especially if you have tire problems; a common distracting ploy involves would-be thieves deflating your tires, then offering to help. Women should avoid dark and isolated areas. Never hitchhike. If you are a victim of serious crime, contact the OIJ's **Victim Assistance Office**.

Pedestrians do not have the right of way in Costa Rica, and extreme care is required when crossing the road. Always look both ways, even on one-way streets, since buses are allowed to travel in both directions on many roads, and the direction of traffic may change at certain times of day. Be careful at junctions too, as many drivers ignore stop signs and even red lights. When walking, keep your eyes open for deep holes and uneven sidewalks. When driving, watch for livestock and massive potholes, which are often indicated by a stick placed inside them.

IN AN EMERGENCY

Costa Rica has a single number for **emergencies**: 911. If things go wrong, your first port of call should be your embassy; depending on the circumstances, they may be able to help.

Most major towns and tourist centers have a **Cruz Roja** (Red Cross) station with an ambulance service. This is supplemented by private ambulance services on 24-hour call. However, in remote areas, you may find it quicker to take a taxi to the nearest clinic or hospital.

LOST AND STOLEN PROPERTY

In the event of loss or theft of belongings, inform the police within 24 hours; you will need an official police report for insurance purposes. If your passport is lost or stolen, contact your embassy or consulate at once. Loss or theft of credit cards should be reported to the relevant company *(see p308)*.

HOSPITALS AND PHARMACIES

Costa Ricans are served by the state-run Instituto Nacional de Seguridad (INS) hospitals, which also provide an emergency service to tourists for a nominal fee *(see p315)*. Most public hospitals are well run, if over-crowded, but rural clinics are often poorly equipped. Private hospitals – such as San José's **Hospital Clínica Bíblica** and Escazú's **Hospital CIMA** – conform to North American and European standards. Hotels and embassies usually have a list of reliable doctors. Most tourist centers also have private dental clinics.

Farmacias or *boticas* (pharmacies), numerous in

Red Cross logo

Exterior of a *farmacia* (pharmacy) in San José

cities nationwide, sell an extensive range of drugs over the counter, including some that require a doctor's prescription in the US, Canada, and Europe. However, visitors with prediagnosed conditions are advised to bring their own medication.

MINOR HAZARDS

The tropical sun can be fierce; always use sunscreen and a hat when outdoors. Drink plenty of fluids to guard against dehydration. Heat and high humidity may cause heatstroke – if you suffer from thirst, nausea, fever, and dizziness, consult a doctor. Wash and dry clothes often to prevent prickly heat and athlete's foot.

Cover up well and use lots of insect repellent to avoid diseases such as dengue fever, which is spread by mosquitoes. Symptoms include fever, headaches, and joint pains, usually lasting about 10 days, after which a month-long recovery is normal. Insect repellents and *espirales* (coils) can be bought locally. Minor insect bites can be treated with antihistamines, but if they become infected, you should seek the advice of a local doctor. If you get bitten by a venomous snake or a wild animal that may carry rabies do not panic, try not to move, and seek immediate medical attention.

Insect repellent and a mosquito coil for protection against bites

Shun tap water if possible, and follow basic precautions with food *(see p269)* to avoid diarrhea and parasitic infections such as giardiasis. For diarrhea, drink lots of bottled water and see a doctor if the condition becomes chronic.

TRAVEL AND HEALTH INSURANCE

Tour and travel agencies sell a wide range of insurance policies, covering baggage loss, theft, and trip cancellation. Ideally, however, travel insurance should also cover medical expenses, since public health care is not always adequate, and treatment in private hospitals and clinics can be expensive. You may need to pay for treatment while in Costa Rica and then make a claim on your insurance when you return home. Prior to departure, check whether your domestic health insurance policies cover you while abroad.

VACCINATIONS

No specific vaccinations are required to enter Costa Rica. Malaria can be found along the southern Caribbean coast, and antimalarial medication is therefore recommended for visitors to that area. It is also wise to be immunized against typhoid and hepatitis A and B, and to make sure that your polio and tetanus vaccinations are up to date.

NATURAL DISASTERS

In the event of an earthquake, move away from tall structures. Do not use elevators. If you are indoors, the safest place is usually in a doorway. Keep a flashlight and shoes near your bed at night.

Obey all instructions at volcanic parks, such as Poás, Arenal, and Turrialba, which became active in 2009 after being dormant for a long time. Arenal is especially volatile, and visits to the immediate area – notably Tabacón *(see p198)* – are always risky. Never hike in restricted zones.

Beware of riptides, which are strong currents that can drag swimmers out to sea *(see p298)*. Flash floods are common during heavy rainfall, when waterfalls and rivers must be avoided.

Banking and Currency

The Costa Rican currency is the colón, but US dollars are also widely accepted. Only larger banks are able to exchange other foreign currencies; however, most tourist hotels will change money at rates similar to those offered by the banks. Large hotels, restaurants, and shops usually take major credit cards, whereas traveler's checks are rarely accepted. It is wise to have small-denomination dollar notes, since stores rarely take $50 and $100 bills, due to the prevalence of counterfeit bills in circulation.

BANKS, ATMS, AND EXCHANGE BUREAUS

The largest banks are the **Banco de Costa Rica** and **Banco Nacional**, both with branches countrywide. Most banks are open on weekdays from 8am to 4pm, but avoid visiting them on a Friday, which is payday for many Costa Ricans. In rural areas, you may have to wait in line for a considerable time to transact any business.

Many of the bigger banks provide *cajeros automáticos* (ATMs), which accept major bank and credit cards to withdraw cash. Be aware of your surroundings when using an ATM, and avoid counting your money in public.

The country's two international airports and the major border crossings *(see p311)* have *casas de cambio* (foreign exchange bureaus), but you will receive a better rate of exchange at banks and hotels. Any other establishment offering to change your currency is doing so illegally. Many tourists are swindled by unofficial money-changers on the street; be sure to steer clear of these touts.

CREDIT AND DEBIT CARDS

The most widely accepted credit cards are **VISA**, **MasterCard**, and, to a lesser extent, American Express and Diners Card. A VISA card (and sometimes a MasterCard)

allows you to obtain cash advances at banks. Many hotels will also offer cash advances on your credit card.

TRAVELER'S CHECKS

Buy traveler's checks at your local bank at home or via the websites of **Thomas Cook** and **Barclays Bank**. These checks are generally more secure than credit cards, and in the event of loss or theft, you can claim a refund. Traveler's checks can be exchanged for cash at banks for a commission; however, few places accept them as currency.

CURRENCY

The Costa Rican currency is the colón (¢), which is often called *peso*. Money is sometimes colloquially referred to as *plata* or *pista*, and cash as *efectivo*. Always carry some coins and small-denomination bills for tips and minor purchases in small establishments.

DIRECTORY

BANKS

Banco de Costa Rica
Calles 4/6 and Ave 2, San José.
Tel 2284-6600.

Banco Nacional
Calles 2/4 and Ave 1, San José.
Tel 2212-2000.

CREDIT & DEBIT CARDS

MasterCard
Tel 0800-011-0184 *(lost cards).*
www.mastercard.com

VISA
Tel 0800-011-0030 *(lost cards).*
www.visa.com

TRAVELER'S CHECKS

Barclays Bank
www.barclays.com

Thomas Cook
www.thomascook.co.uk

1,000 colones

2,000 colones

5,000 colones

10,000 colones

Bank Notes and Coins
Bank notes come in denominations of 1,000, 2,000, 5,000, and 10,000 colones, which are nicknamed rojo *(red),* dos rojos *(two reds),* tucán *(toucan), and* jaguar *respectively.*
Costa Rican coins come in denominations of 5, 10, 20, 25, 50, 100, and 500 colones. Coins minted a while ago are in silver; the newer ones are golden in color. Loose change is sometimes called menudo.

50 colones

100 colones

500 colones

Media and Communications

Telecommunications in Costa Rica are highly developed. *Ticos* are avid users of cell phones, despite reception being erratic in many areas. The postal service, however, is slow and unreliable. As well as several international channels, Costa Rica has 12 local TV channels and more than 100 radio stations. There are three major Spanish newspapers and a few English-language publications.

An Internet café and photocopying center in Cahuita

COSTA RICAN ADDRESSES

Although most towns are organized into *avenidas* and *calles* (streets), few buildings have numbers, and people rarely know their own street address. Mail deliveries are usually made to *apartados* (post office boxes).

NEWSPAPERS AND MAGAZINES

Costa Rica's three big Spanish-language daily newspapers – *La Nación, La Prensa*, and *La República* – are sold at streetside stalls, hotel gift stores, and a few newsagents in major cities. *The Tico Times* is an English-language weekly covering news and events.

TELEVISION AND RADIO

Most hotels, with the exception of wilderness lodges and budget *cabinas*, offer in-room TVs. Upscale establishments often have a cable or satellite service, with stations such as CNN and MTV, some key European channels, and Costa Rican stations. Large business hotels also offer pay-per-view films.

The country has more than 120 radio stations, which broadcast mainly in Spanish. Super Radio (102.3 FM) has music and news in English.

INTERNATIONAL AND LOCAL TELEPHONE CALLS

There are public telephones on main streets and plazas in every Costa Rican town. In remote villages, they are often found at a *pulpería* (grocery store), where the owner may place the call and charge by the minute. Most public phones require a *tarjeta telefónica* (phonecard), available from supermarkets, stores, and banks. Cards such as Colibrí 197 (for domestic calls) and Viajero 199 (for international calls) can be used with any phone. Simply key in 197 or 199, as relevant, followed by the PIN number on the back of the card.

Making calls from your hotel room is expensive, but you can save money by calling the operator at companies such as **AT&T**, **Worldcom**, and **Sprint** and charging the call to

your credit card. A cheaper alternative is to use a call center. Many Internet cafés offer free Skype.

CELL PHONES

North American cell phones usually work within Costa Rica, but European phones do not. Cell phones are useful when traveling in remote areas, but coverage may be patchy.

INTERNET AND EMAIL

Usually, large hotels have business centers, and budget hotels have Wi-Fi or broadband plug-in modems in a communal area. Internet cafés are found in every town and in many small villages too. Service can be slow and erratic.

POSTAL SERVICES

Most towns and villages have *oficinas de correos* (post offices), which are usually open 8am–4pm Monday to Friday. The mail service in Costa Rica is slow, inefficient, and subject to theft, so send any important documents and valuable items via an international courier service such as **DHL**. Major hotels allow you to drop off postcards and letters at the front desk.

DIALING CODES

- Costa Rica's country code is 506.
- Costa Rican telephone numbers have eight digits; there are no area codes.
- Dial 113 for information. International operators speak English.

DIRECTORY

INTERNATIONAL TELEPHONE CALLS

AT&T
Tel 0800-011-4114.

Sprint
Tel 163 or 0800-013-0123.

Worldcom
Tel 0800-014-4444.

POSTAL SERVICES

DHL
Calles 30/32 and Paseo Colón, San José. *Tel 2209-6000.*

NEWSPAPERS AND MAGAZINES

The Tico Times
www.ticotimes.net

TRAVEL INFORMATION

Most visitors to Costa Rica arrive at San José's Juan Santamaría International Airport, near Alajuela. An ever-larger number of international flights land at Daniel Oduber International Airport, 7 miles (11 km) west of Liberia, which is the airport of choice of most major US carriers. The country is also served by several bus companies, and some visitors travel from North America by car. Cruise ships berth on both the Pacific and Caribbean coasts, bringing passengers on day excursions.

Tourist bus laden with luggage

Costa Rica's domestic transportation system includes small planes serving regional airstrips and buses of varying quality. Rental vehicles are a practical alternative to public transport and grant maximum freedom. Most places in the country are within a day's drive of San José. However, the highway system is dilapidated in parts, and driving can be a challenge in certain areas, especially during the wet season. Costa Rica's train service is limited to commuter trains between San José and Heredia.

The terminal at San José's Juan Santamaría International Airport

ARRIVING BY AIR

Leading US airlines, such as **American Airlines**, **Frontier**, **Delta**, **JetBlue**, **Spirit Airlines**, **United**, and **US Airways**, offer scheduled direct flights to Costa Rica. **Grupo Taca**, the regional airline of Central America, has scheduled flights from several cities in the US. Services are either direct or routed via gateways such as Dallas or Miami; others make one or more stops en route in El Salvador, Mexico City, or Managua, in Nicaragua. Both **Air Canada** and Grupo Taca offer a service from Canada.

From Europe, **Air France** and **Iberia** operate direct scheduled flights, while **British Airways** and other carriers connect via Miami. **Condor** has charters from Germany. There are no direct flights from Australia or New Zealand; however, visitors from these countries can catch a connecting flight from Los Angeles.

TICKETS AND FARES

Flights to Costa Rica often sell out, especially during the dry season, so book well in advance; the earlier you buy, the lower the fare. It is worth comparing the airlines' fares against those available at travel websites such as **Travelocity**, **Expedia**, and **Orbitz**. Round-trip tickets tend to cost less than one-way fares, and traveling midweek is usually cheaper than at the weekend. Charter flights offer a better deal than scheduled flights, although more restrictions apply. If you are after a beach holiday, an inclusive flight-and-hotel package with a charter airline or tour operator will likely work out cheaper than independent travel.

ON ARRIVAL

Present your tourist card and customs form (both issued by your airline; *see p304*). The baggage-claim area at Juan Santamaría has an ATM and a foreign exchange bureau that offers poor rates. An official tourist information bureau and a number of car-rental agencies are located immediately beyond the Customs Hall. Daniel Oduber Airport has similar facilities.

GETTING TO SAN JOSE

There are usually taxis outside Customs at Juan Santamaría International. First, pick up a ticket from the dispatcher, being sure to double-check the fixed price to your chosen destination; then, confirm the rate with your driver before departure, as many use crafty ruses to charge more. **Taxi Aeropuerto**, which operates the orange airport taxis, takes reservations. Some hotels provide a shuttle service, either free or for a fee. Budget travelers can use the **Tuasa** public buses, which link the airport to San José and Alajuela.

If driving to San José, try to recover from jetlag before renting a car. There have been instances of rental cars being hijacked on the main highway, so be vigilant.

DEPARTURE TAX

All travelers flying out of Costa Rica must pay a departure tax of $26. You can pay this in advance, upon arrival, at the check-in hall, or at banks and tour agencies at any time during your stay.

ARRIVING BY LAND

There are three border crossings for vehicles: at Peñas Blancas (between Costa Rica and Nicaragua), and at Paso Canoas and Sixaola (both between Costa Rica and Panama). Pedestrians can also cross to/from Nicaragua at the town of Los Chiles. Visas are not necessary to enter either Nicaragua or Panama, as temporary tourist visas are issued at the border. Transit permits and insurance can be arranged through **Sanborn's**. Note that rental cars may not be taken across borders.

Many visitors travel to and from Costa Rica by bus. Companies such as **Transnica** and **Ticabus**, both with terminals in San José, provide bus services between various Central American countries. Another option is to cross the border on foot and catch onward buses on the other side. Keep a close eye on your personal belongings on bus trips.

Visitors driving between the US and Costa Rica should allow at least two weeks for the 2,300-mile (3,700-km) road journey.

Enjoying a waterfall tour on the Reventazón River

ARRIVING BY SEA

Several cruise ships include Puerto Caldera (on the Pacific) and Puerto Limón (Caribbean) on their itineraries, and allow passengers to disembark for day-long excursions.

ORGANIZED TOURS

Companies such as **Costa Rica Connection** and **Costa Rica Experts**, in North America, and **Journey Latin America**, in the UK, offer a wide range of special-interest vacations, as well as customized tour arrangements. Nature-oriented trips geared toward bird-watching and other wildlife-viewing are especially popular. Other special-interest vacations include bicycling, whitewater rafting, kayaking, sportfishing, surfing, and scuba diving *(see pp296–301)*. **National Geographic Expeditions'** nature-themed cruise-tours offer a unique way of exploring several hard-to-reach destinations.

DIRECTORY

ARRIVING BY AIR

Air Canada
Tel 1-888-247-2262.
www.aircanada.com

Air France
Tel (33) 0820-320-820.
www.airfrance.com

American Airlines
Tel 1-800-433-7300.
www.aa.com

British Airways
Tel 0844 493 0787.
www.british-airways.
co.uk

Condor
Tel (49) 0180-5-707 202.
www.condor.com

Delta
Tel 800-321-1212.
www.delta.com

Frontier
Tel 1-800-432-1359.
www.frontierairlines.com

Grupo Taca
Tel 1-800-400-8222.
www.taca.com

Iberia
Tel (34) 902-400-500.
www.iberia.com

JetBlue
Tel 800-539-2583.
www.jetblue.com

Spirit Airlines
Tel 800-772-1717.
www.spiritair.com

United
Tel 1-800-864-8331.
www.united.com

US Airways
Tel 1-800-428-4322.
www.usairways.com

TICKETS AND FARES

Expedia
www.expedia.com

Orbitz
www.orbitz.com

Travelocity
www.travelocity.com

GETTING TO SAN JOSE

Taxi Aeropuerto
Tel 2222-6865.
www.taxiaeropuerto.com

Tuasa
Ave 2 and Calles 12/14,
San José.
Tel 2222-5325.

ARRIVING BY LAND

Sanborn's
Tel 1-800-222-0158.
www.sanborns
insurance.com

Ticabus
Tel 2248-9636.
www.ticabus.com

Transnica
Tel 2223-4242.
www.transnica.com

ORGANIZED TOURS

Costa Rica Connection
P.O. Box 15832,
San Luis Obispo,
CA 93401.
Tel 1-800-345-7422.
www.crconnect.com

Costa Rica Experts
Tel 1-800-827-9046.
www.costarica
experts.com

Journey Latin America
Tel 020 8747 8315.
www.journey
latinamerica.co.uk

National Geographic Expeditions
Tel 1-888-966-8687.
www.nationalgeographic
expeditions.com

Getting Around Costa Rica

Local bus terminal

Despite Costa Rica's compact size, traveling overland can take quite a long time due to the varying conditions of the road network. On the plus side, buses are inexpensive and can be combined with local jeep-taxi services to reach the more isolated spots. Air travel is especially convenient for people on a tight schedule and those who wish to visit remote regions or several attractions that are spaced far apart. Reaching Isla Tortuga and some sights in Golfo Dulce and the Osa Peninsula involves the use of a ferry or boat service. Hitchhiking is not common or safe in Costa Rica. For more on driving, see pp314–15.

GREEN TRAVEL

Consider ways to reduce your impact on the environment when making travel arrangements. If possible, rent a hybrid vehicle. When exploring national parks and wetlands by boat, choose tour companies and private guides that use canoes or non-polluting four-stroke, not two-stroke, engines. Consider flying with **Nature Air**, which claims to be the world's first carbon-neutral airline and offsets emissions from every flight with a contribution to rainforest protection. Finally, travel with local guides and businesses as much as possible to ensure that your money stays within local communities.

DOMESTIC FLIGHTS

Scheduled domestic flights from San José's Juan Santamaría International Airport are offered by **Sansa**. The company links the capital with 16 domestic airstrips, using 22- and 35-passenger Cessnas. Sansa's published itineraries change frequently and are not 100 percent reliable. A slightly superior service is offered by Nature Air, which flies to the same destinations from Tobias Bolaños Airport, located about 1.2 miles (2 km) west of Parque Sabana in San José. Nature Air offers children's discounts.

Note that the baggage allowance is 30 lb (14 kg) for Sansa and 15–40 lb (7–18 kg)

A twin-engine airplane flying over Quepos, on the Pacific coast

for Nature Air, depending on fare class. This is considerably less than for international flights, so be sure to plan your baggage accordingly.

Airplane tickets can be purchased through travel agents and tour operators, or directly from the airlines. Reservations should be made as far in advance as possible, especially for travel during peak times, such as Christmas, Easter, and the dry season (Dec–Apr). The timetables vary between wet and dry seasons (see pp32–7).

Private companies offer an on-demand charter service to airstrips nationwide using 4- to 8-seater aircraft. You need to charter the entire aircraft, including the return journey, if no additional passengers sign up.

LOCAL BUSES AND TERMINALS

More than a dozen private companies offer a bus service linking San José to towns and villages nationwide. Services between large cities are usually aboard comfortable air-conditioned vehicles with reclining seats. Shorter trips between smaller towns and villages are typically on older, more basic second-class buses. The ICT (see p305) publishes a bus schedule.

For intercity travel, *directo* buses offer a fast and often nonstop service, while the *corriente*, or normal, service is slower, with more stops en route. The fares are rarely more than $10. Advance reservations are recommended for intercity travel, especially on Fridays and Saturdays, when demand peaks. If you can, avoid traveling at the weekend. Arrive at the bus station well ahead of your departure time to secure a good seat. Travel with as little baggage as possible, and guard your belongings at all times against theft. Rural buses can be waved down at *paradas* (bus stops) along their routes.

In most towns, the bus terminal is close to the main plaza. Some towns have more than one; for example, there are two large bus terminals in San José, with additional bus stations all around downtown. Buses to the Caribbean leave from Gran Terminal Caribe, and those to most other parts of the country from a series of bus stops concentrated in an area called "Coca Cola", located west of downtown. The Coca Cola terminal has a reputation for pickpockets and muggings, so be on your guard in this area.

A shuttle bus run by Interbus

A *colectivo* (pickup truck) heading for Puerto Jiménez

TOURIST BUSES AND ORGANIZED TOURS

A direct shuttle service linking the most popular tourist destinations is offered by **Interbus** and **Grayline**; both also have shuttles between San José and Juan Santamaría Airport. Interbus offers door-to-door pickup and dropoff, while Grayline has discounts for children and seniors.

Sightseeing bus tours give useful overviews of Costa Rica or specific regions; some focus on nature-viewing and other activities. Leading operators include Grayline and Costa Rica Expeditions *(see p315)*.

TAXIS AND COLECTIVOS

Taxis can be found around the central plazas in most towns. In San José, you can also call one of several taxi companies *(see p317)*. Licensed taxis are red (though airport taxis are orange), with a white triangle on the front door showing the license number. For journeys under 8 miles (12 km), drivers are required to use their *marias* (meters), but many

will make an excuse not to do so in order to be able to charge more. The rates for longer journeys are negotiable. Never take an unlicensed private taxi – several tourists have been robbed by the drivers or their accomplices. Many taxis lack functioning seat belts. Make sure yours works before setting off.

Jeep-taxis serve many communities that are difficult to reach due to mountainous or unpaved roads. The most remote communities and tourist destinations are also served by *colectivos*, usually open-bed pickup trucks with seats and awnings. They follow fixed routes and can be flagged down anywhere along the route. *Colectivos* normally charge a flat fee, regardless of distance.

For more information on taxis, see p316.

COMMUTER TRAINS

Operated by **Tuasa**, *trenes interurbanos* (commuter trains) link downtown San José to Heredia, with seven stops along the 6-mile

(10-km) route. The fare for the 30-minute journey is 355 colones ($0.70). A commuter train linking San José and Cartago is also planned.

BOATS AND FERRIES

Car and passenger ferries link Puntarenas with Naranjo and Paquera, in Nicoya. There is also a water-taxi service between Puntarenas and Paquera, Jacó and Montezuma, and Sierpe and Bahía Drake, along the Tortuguero Canal, and throughout Golfo Dulce. Visitors can also go on boat trips along Costa Rica's many rivers, canals, and swamps.

Passengers waiting to board a boat at Isla Tortuga

Traveling by Car

License plate

Driving is the best way of exploring Costa Rica, as a car grants relatively easy access to some of the country's most remarkable scenery. Roads between towns are usually paved, but you still need to watch out for potholes. Minor roads are often dirt and gravel, turning into muddy quagmires during the wet season. A four-wheel drive vehicle is essential for exploring the countryside. Conditions are often hazardous, so take precautions. Do not drive at night, and carry a road atlas published by a reputable company rather than one bought locally. The use of seat belts is compulsory, but few Costa Ricans wear them, and laws are rarely enforced. If you're traveling with young children, bring a child seat, as car rental agencies do not supply them.

A busy street in San José

ROADS AND TOLLS

Only 20 percent of Costa Rica's 18,650 miles (30,000 km) of highway are paved, with the Central Highlands taking up a large chunk of the total. The percentage of unpaved roads increases as you travel away from San José. Three major highways, linking San José to Cartago, San Ramón, and Orotina via the new Autopista del Sol, are toll expressways.

It is difficult to find accurate maps, but the National Geographic Adventure Map and the detailed Costa Rica Nature Atlas are recommended.

Costa Ricans drive on the right-hand side of the road, and the speed limits are 50 mph (80 km/h) on major highways, and 37 mph (60 km/h) on secondary roads. *Tránsitos* (traffic police) patrol the highways in blue cars and on motorcycles, using radar guns to catch speeders. They are not allowed to collect money, though occasionally a corrupt official may try to extract a bribe *(see p306)*. Fines should be paid at a bank or at the car rental agency.

DIRECTIONS AND SIGNS

Major highways are well signposted. Although most towns also have street signs, the majority of Costa Ricans continue to refer to well-known landmarks when giving directions.

Road signs use international symbols. *Alto* means "stop," *ceda* means "yield," and *mantenga su derecha* means "keep right." *Túmulo* indicates a road bump ahead, while *derrumbe* denotes a landslide or falling rocks.

ROAD HAZARDS

Drive slowly to avoid bending a wheel on a pothole. Watch for people and animals in the road, especially outside towns, where few roads have sidewalks. During the wet season, mountain roads are often foggy and subject to landslides, while lowland roads are prone to flooding.

Beware drivers running stop signs, overtaking when there is barely enough room to do so, or driving too close to the vehicle in front. Costa Ricans often use their left-turn signal to indicate to drivers behind that it is safe to overtake. Be careful, though: the vehicle may actually be turning left.

In the event of an accident, call **Tránsitos**. Do not leave your vehicle, and do not let the other party move theirs. If possible, obtain the *cédulas* (identification) and license number of the other driver. If anyone is injured, call the Cruz Roja *(see p307)*. Rental cars have a red triangle; place this in the road a safe distance from your accident site, or make a small pile of stones and branches to warn other drivers. If you own the vehicle, report the accident to the **Instituto Nacional de Seguridad (INS)**, which handles all insurance claims.

PARKING

Car break-ins are common throughout Costa Rica. Never leave any items in a parked vehicle, especially in beach locations, where signs warn of the severity of the threat of theft from parked cars. Avoid parking on the street overnight; instead, use one of the many inexpensive parking lots with security guards.

GAS STATIONS

Unleaded gas, or *gasolina*, is sold as either super or regular; the latter is lower-octane and less expensive. Diesel is cheaper still. *Gasolineras* (gas stations) are plentiful in towns, but much scarcer in rural areas, especially in Nicoya.

A road sign indicating the route and the distance to several destinations

It is wise to refill whenever the tank drops to half-full. In remote areas, gasoline is usually available at *pulperías* (grocery stores), where it may cost twice as much as at gas stations.

Gas stations are typically open from 6am to midnight, but some operate round the clock. They are not self-service, and most will accept credit cards.

BREAKDOWN SERVICES

In the event of a breakdown, call your car rental agency, which will send a repairman. All reputable agencies have a 24-hour service for such emergencies. Major cities, plus *gasolineras* on major highways, have tow-truck services. Elsewhere, you may need to find a local farmer and tractor to haul you out of a troublesome situation, such as being stuck in mud.

CAR AND MOTORCYCLE RENTAL

Most car rental agencies ask that drivers be at least 25 years old, but some will rent to people aged over 21. You will need a valid driver's license and a credit card for paying a deposit and settling your bill. If you wish to stay for more than three months, you will need a domestic driver's license.

International car rental firms such as **Alamo**, **Budget**, and **Hertz** have local franchises at the international airports. San José and a few leading tourist centers also offer some local agencies. Prices are generally lower during the wet season, and unlimited-mileage options tend to work out the cheapest.

When pre-booking, always get a written confirmation. Liability insurance to cover damages to other vehicles or persons is mandatory. Check if it is included in the quote; if so, get it confirmed in writing. It is also wise to purchase additional coverage for the vehicle, although some rental agencies may

A four-wheel drive vehicle on a dirt road near Ojochal, southern Costa Rica

accept your domestic auto insurance. Check with your insurance or credit card company whether your policy covers travel in Costa Rica.

Before signing the contract, ensure that the vehicle is in good condition and keep a note of any scratches or other faults. You may be asked to sign a blank credit card slip, which is torn up when the car is returned intact. When returning the car, bring a trusted friend, if possible: unscrupulous agency employees may tamper with the vehicle if you leave it unattended while settling your bill. Check the final bill for any questionable charges, which you may dispute.

A four-wheel drive (4WD) vehicle is vital for rural areas, where extra traction is required. Companies such as **U-Save** have a wide variety of 4WD vehicles, while Costa Rica's Temptations *(see p301)* offers pre-planned self-drive tours. All-terrain vehicles (ATVs), scooters and bicycles can be rented at many beach resorts. **María Alexander Tours** rents Harley Davidson motorcycles and arranges tours for people aged 25 or older. Helmets are mandatory.

OFF-ROAD DRIVING

A 4WD vehicle is essential for exploring Costa Rica beyond the main cities. A manual-shift vehicle is preferable to an automatic for handling the steep, rock-strewn tracks that lead to many national parks

and eco-lodges. Keep your speed down on corrugated and loose-gravel roads, where it is easy to lose traction.

Some rivers require fording, especially in western Nicoya and the Osa Peninsula. Use caution in the wet season, when rivers can be too deep or fast-flowing to ford. Ask the locals about current conditions. Edge slowly into the river, as rushing forward can flood and stall the engine. If necessary, wade the river in advance to ascertain the best route across. In wet season, it's easy to get stuck in mud.

Stop sign ALTO

DIRECTORY

ROAD HAZARDS

Instituto Nacional de Seguridad (INS)
Tel 800-800-80000.

Tránsitos
Tel 117 or 911 or 222-9330.

CAR AND MOTORCYCLE RENTAL

Alamo
Tel 2233-7733.
www.alamocostarica.com

Budget
Tel 2436-2000.
www.budget.co.cr

Hertz
Tel 2221-1818.
www.costaricarentacar.net

María Alexander Tours
Tel 2289-5552.
www.costaricamotorcycles.com

U-Save
Tel 2430-4647.
www.usavecostarica.com

Getting Around San José

Public bus

Most places of interest in Costa Rica's capital are centrally located, and within walking distance of one another and of many hotels and restaurants. The best way to explore central San José is on foot, though you will need to rely on some form of transport to reach the suburbs and outlying areas. The city's public transportation network is crowded, but an efficient taxi system eases the burden of traveling around by bus. It is not advisable to drive around San José, especially during the morning and afternoon rush hours, when the roads become extremely congested.

Traffic on a busy thoroughfare in downtown San José

BUSES

Running from 5am to 10pm, buses in San José are cheap but tend to be overcrowded. There is no central terminal for city buses, and routes are identified not by number but by destination, shown above the front window. Free route maps are available from the ICT office at Juan Santamaría International Airport.

An important bus route is Sabana-Cementerio, which links the city center to Parque Sabana *(see p124)*, running eastbound along Avenida 10 and westbound along Avenida 3. Public buses to the airport depart from Avenida 2, Calles 12/14. Buses to San José's suburbs fill up fast, and you should board at the original departure point.

Pay your fare (130–360 colones) by dropping the money into the electronic counter upon boarding. Do not stand by the counter, which also records passengers; if it registers you twice, you

will have to pay twice. Watch out for pickpockets when traveling by bus. It is a good idea to wear your money belt inside your clothes.

WALKING

The most practical way to explore the heart of San José is by walking, since being on foot permits you to enjoy the city at close quarters. The city center is laid out in an easy-to-understand grid pattern that makes for convenient strolling. However, the sidewalks are narrow and crowded, and pedestrians are often forced to step into the street. Take great care, as downtown streets are thronged with traffic. Do not assume that vehicles will stop at pedestrian crossings or give way to pedestrians on the road when traffic lights turn to green. Be especially careful of buses, which often drive onto the sidewalks

Paseo de los Estudiantes, one of San José's few pedestrianized streets

when turning corners. There are usually cafés close at hand, allowing you to escape the heat and noise. Be prepared for late-afternoon showers, especially during the rainy season, when you will certainly need an umbrella. These can be bought at roadside stalls.

Beware of pickpockets, especially in crowded places. Avoid wearing jewelry and carry your valuables in a money belt. Hold your camera in front of you, with the strap over your neck rather than on your shoulder. Keep to busy, well-lit areas at night, when you should avoid the streets northwest of the Mercado Central *(see p108)* and southwest of Parque Central *(see p106)*, as well as Parque Nacional *(see pp118–19)* and Parque Morazán *(see p116)*.

TAXIS

Taxis are numerous, but they can be in short supply during rush hour and heavy rains. They can be hailed on the street or summoned by phone or via your hotel concierge. The main taxi rank in San José is around Parque Central. Licensed taxis are red; an illuminated sign on the roof indicates that the taxi is available. Most taxis take four passengers.

TG 106 502010 NICOYA

Sign on a local taxi

You can pay in colones or dollars. Fares begin at 530 colones and rise by 380 colones for every kilometer. Taxis are good value by US and European standards – rarely does a fare within the city center cost more than $5. Taxis are required by law to use their *marias* (meters) for journeys of less than 8 miles (12 km). Many drivers decline to do so, hoping to be able to charge you extra. Taxi drivers do not expect tips, but a 10 percent gratuity is appreciated.

Many private drivers offer an unlicensed taxi service. They usually charge more than licensed taxis and have a reputation for being unsafe. Never take an unlicensed taxi, however trustworthy you believe the driver to be.

Red taxis near San José's Catedral Metropolitana

DRIVING

Even if you are used to driving in cities, exploring San José by car can be a nerve-racking experience and one that is best avoided. *Josefinos* are aggressive drivers and often display a marked lack of consideration for other road users. Many drivers will proceed through red lights if no traffic is coming the other way, especially at night, when extreme care is needed. The speed limit on urban streets is 18 mph (30 km/h).

Route 39, also known as the Circunvalación, runs around the west, south, and east of the city. Avenida Central leads east to the University of Costa Rica and the busy suburb of San Pedro *(see p121)*. To the west, Paseo Colón links the city center to Parque Sabana and the Autopista General Cañas, which leads to the airport and Alajuela. Another

freeway, the Autopista Prospero Fernández, runs west from Parque Sabana to the town of Escazú *(see p125)*, where it becomes the Autopista del Sol, leading to the Pacific lowlands. Traffic normally flows in both directions along Paseo Colón, except 7–9am Monday to Friday, when it is one-way eastbound, and 8am–5pm on Sundays, when it is closed to traffic altogether.

The one-way system and grid pattern in the city center help lubricate traffic flow, but congestion can persist throughout the day. During rush hour, Avenidas 8 and 9 are usually the best routes to follow when traveling westbound; Avenida 10 is recommended for those who are heading east.

Non-commercial vehicles are banned from the city between 6am and 7pm Monday to Friday under a *pico y placa* ("rush hour and license plate") scheme. The specific days are assigned according to the last digit of each vehicle's license plate, and the numbers rotate every six months. Tourist rental cars are exempt.

There are many parking lots in San José's city center and you should have no trouble finding one. At most, you need to pay an attendant

Cautionary sign for seat belts

to watch over your car. They may require you to leave your ignition keys. Be sure to never leave anything inside the car, even in secure, guarded parking lots.

ROAD NAMES AND ADDRESSES

Within the city center, even-numbered *avenidas* lie north of Avenida Central, while odd-numbered ones are to the south; even-numbered *calles* are west of Calle Central, and odd-numbered ones are to the east as far as the Circunvalación. Avenida Central is pedestrianized between Calle 6 and Calle 7, as are Calle 2 between Avenidas 2 and 3, and Calle 17 (Bulevar Ricardo Jiménez) between Avenidas 1 and 8. Streets are poorly signposted *(see p314)*, and traffic lights, which are normally suspended over the center of junctions, are often difficult to see.

DIRECTORY

TAXIS

Coopetaxi
Tel 2235-9966.

Coopetico
Tel 2224-7979.

Avenida 2 is one of San José's main thoroughfares

General Index

Acknowledgments

Dorling Kindersley would like to thank the following people whose contributions and assistance have made the preparation of this book possible:

Main Contributor
Christopher P. Baker was born and raised in Yorkshire, England, and received his B.A. with Honours (1976) in Geography from the University of London. While there, his travels included two Sahara research expeditions. Baker holds two Masters' degrees – in Latin American Studies and in Education. He has made his living as a full-time professional travel writer/photographer since 1983.

Baker's numerous books include guides to Cuba, Costa Rica, and Jamaica, and *Mi Moto Fidel: Motorcycling Through Castro's Cuba*. He has had chapters and articles published in several books and more than 150 newspapers, magazines, and journals worldwide. He has won many prestigious awards for travel writing, addressed prominent entities such as the National Geographic Society, the National Press Club, and the World Affairs Council, and escorted group tours to Korea, New Zealand, Hong Kong, Cuba, and England. Baker also teaches travel-writing classes, appears on radio and TV shows, and lectures aboard cruise ships.

Fact Checker
Ana Voiculescu.

Proofreader
Sonia Malik.

Indexer
Jyoti Dhar.

Dorling Kindersley, London
Publisher
Douglas Amrine.
Publishing Manager
Jane Ewart.
Senior Editor
Christine Stroyan.
Senior Cartographic Editor
Casper Morris.
Senior Dtp Designer
Jason Little.

Editorial and Design Assistance
Brigitte Arora, Uma Bhattacharya, Tessa Bindloss, Nadia Bonomally, Louise Cleghorn, Hannah Dolan, Conrad Van Dyk, Anna Freiberger, Vinod Harish, Mohammad Hassan, Huw Hennessy, Claire Jones, Jasneet Kaur, Juliet Kenny, Vincent Kurien, Maite Lantaron, Carly Madden, Alison McGill, Sonal Modha, Harry Pariser, Helen Peters, Marisa Renzullo, Ellen Root, Simon Ryder, Sands Publishing Solutions, Azeem Siddiqui, Susana Smith, Dora Whitaker.

DK Picture Library
Hayley Smith, Romaine Werblow.

Production Controller
Wendy Penn.

Additional Special Photography
Christopher P. Baker, Alan Briere, Jonathan Buckley, Martin Camm, Geoff Dann, Greg & Yvonne Dean, Phillip Dowell, Hanne & Jens Erik-esen, Neil Fletcher, Frank Greenaway, Josef Hlasek, Johnny Jensen, Colin Keates, Dave King, Mike Linley, Ray Moller, David Murray, Stephen Oliver, Brian Pitkin, Alex Robinson, Rough Guides/Greg Roden, Clive Streeter, Harry Taylor, Tropical Birding/Nick Athanas, Mathew Ward, Laura Wickenden, Peter Wilson, Jerry Young.

Special Assistance
Many thanks for the invaluable help of the following individuals and establishments: Adolfo Rodríguez Herrera; Mrs. Dora Sequeira, Alejandra Jimenez Solis, and Andrea Bolaños Waters, Museo del Oro Precolombino; Dr. Luis Diego Gómez, Organización para Estudios Tropicales at La Selva; Mauricio P. Aymerich, Small Distinctive Hotels; Michael Snarskis.

Photography Permissions
Dorling Kindersley would like to thank the following for their assistance and kind permission to photograph at their establishments: Café Britt; Centro Costarricense de Ciencias y Cultura, San José; Costa Rica Expeditions; Fábrica de Carretas Joaquín Chaverrí, Sarchí; Museo del Oro Precolombino, San José; Museo Nacional, San José; Teatro Nacional, San José; Zoo Ave Wildlife Conser-vation Park; and all other cathedrals, churches, museums, hotels, restaur-ants, shops, galleries, national and state parks, and other sights too numerous to thank individually.

Picture Credits
Key – a-above, b-below/bottom, c-center, f-far, l-left, r-right, t-top.

The publishers would like to thank the following individuals, companies, and picture libraries for their kind permission to reproduce their photographs:

AKG IMAGES: 40crb; ALAMY IMAGES: 16b; Arco Images 71cb, /C.Steimer 83br; Arco Images GmbH; Maxime Bessieres 309cl; blinckwinkel/Layer 91bl, /Schmidbauer 77cra; Rick & Nora Bowers 95tr; Caro/Kruppa 94tr; Howard Cheek 67clb; Loetscher Chlaus 67br; Sylvia Cordaiy Photo Library Ltd/Richard Wareham 182bc; Lee Dalton 72br, 75cla; Danita Delimont/Kevin Schafer 20bl, 53bc, 76tl, /Keith and Rebecca Snell 20br, 60br, / Christian Ziegler 207tc; O. Digoit 68bl; FLPA/NULL 77clb; Frans Lanting Studio 65cb, 65br, 72–3, 77tl; Chris Fredriksson 269tl; Bob Gibbons 21cr; Michelle Gilders 61c; Eirik Grønningsæter 72bc; Göran Gustafson 60bl; Paul Harrison 20clb; Hemis/Franck Guiziou 54tr, 304cra, 306tl; ImageSync Ltd 20crb; Huw Jones 309cla; Michael J. Kronmal 75tl; Kuttig – Animals 66clb; Yadid Levy 313tr; Lonely Planet Images/Christer Fredriksson 219bl; LOOK Die Bildagentur der Fotografen GmbH/ Knorad Wothe 92br; Oyvind Martinsen 56tc, 95tl; Neil McAllister 93tc; McPHOTO/SCO/ blickwinkel 66br; Michael Patrick O'Neill 71bc; Papilio/Robert Pickett 89clb; Stuart Pearce 67tl; Photoshot Holdings Ltd 219cra; Anthony Pierce 80cla, 80br; Prisma Bildagentur AG/Newman Mark 72clb; Robert Harding Picture Library Ltd/Pearl Bucknall 227br; Kevin Schafer 73cra; Stephen Frink Collection/Masa Ushioda 71tl, /James D Watt 87tl; Martin Strmiska 49b; ticopix 258cla; Dave and Sigrun Tollerton 163cra; Visual&Written SL/ VWPICS/Kike Calvo 71br; WaterFrame 70clb, 70bc; WILDLIFE GmbH 21cb; WorldFoto 60cla; AM COSTA RICA LINK: 32cl, 291tr; JOHN ANDERSON: 18t, 119crb, 120tr, 167cb, 180tr; ARDEA: M. Watson 51tr; AXIOM, LONDON: Ian Cumming 35bc, 215br.

BANCO CENTRAL DE COSTA RICA: 260cl; 308cl, 308clb, 308cr, 308crb(a), 308crb(c), 308bl, 308br; BRUCE COLEMAN PICTURE LIBRARY: Michael Fogden 20crb.

CAFÉ BRITT: 28br; CHRIS BAKER COMPOSITIONS: Christopher P. Baker 29bc, 29bcr, 32tc, 44bcr, 57tr, 57br, 82bl, 90crb, 94cl, 94c, 107tl, 113cb, 119tl, 120bl, 120crb, 121tl, 125cl, 135cla, 142cr, 142bc, 147cra, 147clb, 147bc, 154cla, 155tl, 164tl, 181cl, 187crb, 187clb, 203bc, 211b, 216clb, 225cr, 233br, 291c(a), 291c(b), 291c(c), 293t, 312cl, CORBIS: 41tr,

42br, 87cra, Theo Allofs 75clb; Tony Arruza 34b, 167cl; Bettman 7c, 41cb, 42crb, 43clb, 44tr, 44cb, 45clb, 185bc; Gary Braasch 22cl, 22clb, 25br, 26cl, 56b, 157b, 218tl, 234-5; Tom Brakefield 63tl, 63cr, 64cla; Christie's Images 192bl; Ralph A. Clevenger 207cb, 207bl, 241cra; W. Perry Conway 65bc; Michael and Patricia Fogden 1c, 20br, 21bca, 61tl, 66cr, 74, 75br, 83tl, 89br, 95c, 96tc, 163cb, 163br, 175br, 177tc, 179c, 179bc, 207 cr, 214tl; D. Robert & Lorri Franz 77br; Stephen Frink 184tr, 206bc; Gallo Images/Martin Harvey 73bc; Bill Gentile 45bl; Derek Hall/Frank Lane Picture 237tc; Gray Hardel 300c; Jan Butchofsky-Houser 15b, 183ca; Dave G. Houser 29cla, 195b; Hulton-Deutsch Collection 303 (inset); Johnér Images/Lars-Olof Johansson 60clb; Wolfgang Kaehler 53tr, 241br; Kit Kittle 295tc; Bob Krist 55tr; Blue Lantern Studio 243 (inset); Frans Lanting 62, 63crb, 76cra; Joe McDonald 83cr; Mary Ann McDonald 64bc; Michael Maslan Historic Photograph 43bl; Stephanie Maze 17br; moodboard 96cb; Amos Nachoum 21cra, 81clb, 222, 241crb, 300bl, 300bc; David A. Northcott 89tl; Sergio Pitamitz 85cb; Radius Images 93br; Jose Fuste Raga 317b; Carmen Redondo 27cra, 191bl; Robert Harding World Imagery/Marco Simoni 61br; Martin Rogers 18bl, 19cr, 28cra, 101bl, 171b, 213cr, 292tc; Jeffrey L. Rotman 100crb, 300br; Kevin Schafer 8br, 12cl, 20clb, 23br, 26tr, 27tl, 53c, 54bl, 63br, 68cr, 89cra, 138-9, 173t, 188-9, 191br, 207clb, 208tl, 225cra, 228cla, 229cr, 241cla; Science Faction/ Norbert Wu 163cla; Paul A. Souders 80clb, 204tl; Brian A. Vikander 21cr, 141tr; Visuals Unlimited/Thomas Marent 82cr; Stuart Westmorland 87crb, 242-3; Jim Zuckerman 58; CORBIS SYGMA: C. Rouvieres 191cla, 191bl; CORCOVADO ADVENTURES TENT CAMP: 245cr; COST RICA EXPERTS: 309tr; COSTA RICA EXPEDITIONS: 50tc, 50br, 304bl, 309tl; COSTA RICA PHOTO ALBUM: © Rodrigo Fernandez and Millard Farmer 4crb, 9tr, 15ca, 16tl, 17tr, 17c, 19tc, 19br, 33tl, 35tl, 101tl, 146bc, 152cla, 197tl, 199tl, 200tl, 200br, 201cr, 203tc, 203clb, 203bl, 203br, 229ca, 287br, 297br, 298tl, 298br, 299br.

DANTICA LODGE AND GALLERY: 146t.

EL SANO BANANO HOTEL: 247tl, 269tl, 294tl.

RODRIGO FERNANDEZ: 34tc, 144br, 270cla, 271tl, 290tl, 290c, 290cb, 290crb(a), 290crb(b), 291cb, 291crb, 291bl, 291bc, 291br, 294br, 308bc, 308br, 308tbr, 309bc; FLPA: Minden Pictures/Gerry Ellis 73br, /

Konrad Wothe 92bc, /Marcel van Kammen 94tl, /Mark Moffett 207br, /Michael & Patricia Fogden 88clb, 92cla, 92crb, /Piotr Naskrecki 46–7; Jurgen & Christine Sohns 97tr; FOREST LIGHT: Alan Watson 146t; FOUR SEASONS: 146cla.

GETTY IMAGES: AFP/Daniel Garcia 95cr, / Mayela Lopez 50, /Yuri Cortez 97tl; DEA/G. DAGLI ORTI 93tc; Digital Vision/Tom Brakefield 64br, 65cr; Gallo Images/Danita Delimont 76crb; The Image Bank/Marco Simoni 90cla; Minden Pictures/Michael & Patricia Fogden 59b; National Geographic/ Brian J. Skerry 70cla, 70br, 71cr, /Roy Toft 69bl, 93cb, Photodisc/Tom Brakefield 97cr, /Paul E Tessier 91tl; Purestock 96cl; Riser/ Kevin Schafer 61bl; RF/Jeremy Woodhouse 67cra; Stone/Stuart Westmorland 90bl; Visuals Unlimited, Inc./Thomas Marent 69tr; PHILIP GREENSPUN: 33br; GREENTIQUE HOTELS OF COSTA RICA: Santa Juana Mountain Tour 165tr.

INTERBUSES UNO DE COSTA RICA SA: 310br. LONELY PLANET IMAGES: Chris Barton 28clb, Tom Boyden 184cla, Charlotte Hindle 312br; Ralph Lee Hopkins 2-3; Luke Hunter 184bl, 223b, 236bl; Eric L. Wheater 14.

MARY EVANS PICTURE LIBRARY: 42tc, 47 (inset), 99 (inset); Explore/Courau 38; JEAN MERCIER: 23cb, 140cr, 140br, 208bl; MASTERFILE; Alberto Biscaro 98-9, 114-15, 170, 286cla, 288br, 302-3; Peter Christopher 156; MUSEO DE CULTURA INDÍGENAS: 5c, 30tr, 30-31c, 31tc, 31cb, 31clb, 31bl, 31br, 32br, 205clb, 221bc, 221br, 232bc, 290bc, 291tc, 291cra; MUSEO DEL ORO PRECOLOMBINO: 112ca, 113bl, 113tl, 288cla, 290br; Alejandro Astorga 31cra.

Courtesy THE NATURAL HISTORY MUSEUM LONDON: 217br. Courtesy THE NATIONAL BIRDS OF PREY CENTRE, GLOUCESTERSHIRE: 228tl; NATURE AIR: 310c; NATUREPL.COM: Edwin Giesbers 73tl; Mary McDonald 88cr; Pete Oxford 71bl; Shattil & Rozinski 73cb; Lynn M.

Stone 56cla; NHPA/PHOTOSHOT: Tony Crocetta 85cra; Melvin Grey 97tc; Adrian Hepworth 84-5t; James Carmichael JR 88cla; John Shaw 76br.

PHOTOLIBRARY: Age fotostock/Eric Baccega 65bl, /Georgie Holland 81cr; All Canada Photos/Wayne Lynch 86ca; Animals Animals/Lynn Stone 72cla, /Stephen Ingram 93cra; Bios/Jean-Claude Carton 84bl, / Olivier Digoit 83cl, /Sylvain Cordier 73bl; Michael Boyny 48; Franck & Christine Dziubak 93bc; Jon Arnold Travel/John Coletti front endpaper tc, 194; Thierry Montford 65; Oxford Scientific (OSF) 88br, 94cr, /David B Fleetham 70-1, /Michael Fogden 66cla, /Roy Toft 20c, /Konrad Wothe 92–3, 93bl; Peter Arnold Images/ Gerard Lacz 64crb, /Doug Perrine 87bl, / Heinz Plenge 64–5; WaterFrame – Underwater Images/Masa Ushioda 86bl; SERGIO PUCCI: 20cb, 21cl, 21bl, 21bc.

REUTERS: Juan Carlos Ulate 29cra.

SKY PHOTOS: 23crb, 24cl, 25tl, 25cr, 100clb, 174tr, 174cl, 174clb, 199br, SMALL DISTINCTIVE HOTELS: 20cr, 200tl, 244bc, 299tl.

UNICORN MULTIMEDIA, INC.: Jan Csernoch 10t, 191cra, 193br, 228bl, 229tl, 229bc.

FRONT ENDPAPER: CORBIS: Amos Nachoum bc; MASTERFILE: Alberto Biscaro tl; Peter Christopher cl.

JACKET: Front – ALAMY IMAGES: Niebrugge Images; BACK - CORBIS: Blaine Harrington III tl; DORLING KINDERSLEY: Greg and Yvonne Dean bl; Greg Roden clb; ROBERT HARDING PICTURE LIBRARY: Marco Simoni cla.

All other images © Dorling Kindersley. For more information see **www.dkimages.com**

SPECIAL EDITIONS OF DK TRAVEL GUIDES

DK Travel Guides can be purchased in bulk quantities at discounted prices for use in promotions or as premiums. We are also able to offer special editions and personalized jackets, corporate imprints, and excerpts from all of our books, tailored specifically to meet your own needs.

To find out more, please contact:
(in the United States) **SpecialSales@dk.com**
(in the UK) **TravelSpecialSales@uk.dk.com**
(in Canada) DK Special Sales at
general@tourmaline.ca
(in Australia)
business.development@pearson.com.au

Phrase Book

Costa Rican Spanish is essentially the same as the Castilian spoken in Spain, although there are some differences in vocabulary and pronunciation. The most noticeable is the pronunciation of the soft "c" and the letter "z" as "s" rather than "th." Costa Ricans tend to be formal, and often use *usted* (rather than *tú*) for "you," even if they know the person well. Common courtesies of respect are expected. Always say *buenos días* or *buenas tardes* when boarding a taxi, and address taxi drivers and waiters as *señor*. Many colloquialisms exist, such as *¡upe!*, which is used to announce your presence outside someone's home when the door is open. *Buena suerte* ("good luck") is often used to wish someone well on parting.

The most common term throughout the country is *pura vida* ("pure life"), used as a common reply to questions about your wellbeing and as an expression that everything is great. *Tuanis*, popular with youth, is another phrase meaning things are positive. If you hear a Costa Rican referring to *chepe*, he or she is speaking about San José. If you wish to decline goods from street vendors, a polite shake of the head and a *muchas gracias* will usually suffice. Adding *muy amable* ("very kind") will help to take the edge off the refusal.

In an Emergency

Help!	¡Socorro!	soh-**koh**-roh
Stop!	¡Pare!	pah-reh
Call a doctor!	¡Llame a un médico!	yah-meh ah oon meh-dee-koh
Fire!	¡Fuego!	foo-**eh**-goh
Could you help me?	¿Me podría ayudar?	meh poh-**dree**-yah ah-yoo-**dahr**
policeman	policía	poh-lee-**see**-ah

Communication Essentials

Yes	Sí	see
No	No	noh
Please	Por favor	pohr fah-**vohr**
Thank you	Gracias	**grah**-see-ahs
Excuse me	Perdone	pehr-**doh**-neh
Hello	Hola	**oh**-lah
Good morning	Buenos días	bweh-nohs **dee**-ahs
Good afternoon	Buenas tardes	bweh-nahs **tahr**-dehs
Good night	Buenas noches	bweh-nahs **noh**-chehs
Bye (casual)	Chao	**cha**-oh
Goodbye	Adiós	ah-dee-**ohs**
See you later	Hasta luego	ah-**stah** loo-**weh**-goh
Morning	La mañana	lah mah-**nyah**-nah
Afternoon	La tarde	lah **tahr**-deh
Night	La noche	lah **noh**-cheh
Yesterday	Ayer	ah-**yehr**
Today	Hoy	oy
Tomorrow	Mañana	mah-**nyah**-nah
Here	Aquí	ah-**kee**
There	Allá	ah-**yah**
What?	¿Qué?	keh
When?	¿Cuándo?	kwahn-doh
Why?	¿Por qué?	pohr-keh
Where?	¿Dónde?	dohn-deh
How are you?	¿Cómo está usted?	koh-moh ehs-**tah** oos-**tehd**
Very well, thank you	Muy bien, gracias	mwee bee-**ehn grah**-see-ahs
Pleased to meet you	Mucho gusto	moo-choh **goo**-stoh
I'm sorry	Lo siento	loh see-**ehn**-toh

Useful Phrases

That's fine	Está bien	ehs-**tah** bee-ehn
Great/fantastic!	¡Qué bien!	keh bee-ehn
Where does this road go?	¿Adónde va esta calle?	ah-**dohn**-deh bah ehs-tah kah-yeh
Do you speak English?	¿Habla inglés?	ah-blah een-glehs
I don't understand	No comprendo	noh kohm-**prehn**-doh
I want	Quiero	kee-**yehr**-oh

Useful Words

big	grande	**grahn**-deh
small	pequeño/a	peh-**keh**-nyoh/nyah
hot	caliente	kah-lee-**ehn**-teh
cold	frío/a	**free**-oh/ah
good	bueno/a	bweh-noh/nah
bad	malo/a	mah-loh/lah
open	abierto/a	ah-bee-**ehr**-toh/tah
closed	cerrado/a	sehr-**rah**-doh/dah
left	izquierda	ees-key-**ehr**-dah
right	derecha	deh-**reh**-chah
near	cerca	**sehr**-kah
far	lejos	**leh**-hohs
up	arriba	ah-ree-bah
down	abajo	ah-**bah**-hoh
early	temprano	tehm-**prah**-noh
late	tarde	**tahr**-deh
now/very soon	ahora/ahorita	ah-ohr-ah/ah-ohr-ee-tah
more	más	mahs
less	menos	**meh**-nohs
very	muy	mwee
a little	(un) poco	oon poh-koh
opposite	frente a	frehn-teh ah
below/above	abajo/arriba	ah-**bah**-hoh/ehn-**trah**-dah
entrance	entrada	ehn-**trah**-dah
exit	salida	sah-**lee**-dah
stairs	escaleras	ehs-kah-**leh**-rahs
elevator	el ascensor	ehl ah-sehn-**sohr**
toilets	baños/servicios sanitarios	bah-nyohs/sehr-vee- see-yohs sah-nee-**tah**-ree-ohs
women's	de damas	deh **dah**-mahs
men's	de caballeros	deh kah-bah-**yeh**-rohs
sanitary napkins	toallas sanitarias	toh-ah-yahs sah-nee-**tah**-ree-yahs
tampons	tampones	tahm-**poh**-nehs
condoms	condones	kohn-**doh**-nehs
toilet paper	papel higiénico	pah-**pehl** hee-**hyen**-ee-koh
(non-)smoking area	área de (no) fumar	ah-ree-ah deh (noh) foo-**mahr**
camera	la cámara	lah kah-mah-rah
(a roll of) film	(un rollo de) película	(oon roh-yoh deh) peh-**lee**-koo-lah
batteries	las pilas	lahs **pee**-lahs
passport	pasaporte	pah-sah-**pohr**-teh
visa	visa	**vee**-sah

Post Offices and Banks

post office	oficina de correos	oh-fee-**see**-nah deh kohr-**reh**-ohs
stamps	estampillas	ehs-tahm-**pee**-yahs
postcard	una postal	oo-nah pohs-**tahl**
postbox	apartado	ah-pahr-**tah**-doh

English	Spanish	Pronunciation
cashier	cajero	kah-**heh**-roh
ATM	cajero automático	kah-**heh**-roh ahw-toh-**mah**-tee-koh
bank	banco	**bahn**-koh
What is the dollar rate?	¿A cómo está el dolar?	ah **koh**-moh ehs-**tah** ehl doh-**lahr**

Shopping

How much does this cost?	¿Cuánto cuesta esto?	kwahn tohkwehs-tah ehs-toh
Do you have?	¿Tienen?	tee-**yeh**-nehn
Do you take credit cards/ traveler's checks?	¿Aceptan tarjetas de crédito/ cheques de viajero?	ahk-**sehp**-tahn tahr-**heh**-tahs deh **kreh**-dee-toh/**cheh**-kehs deh vee-ah-**heh**-roh
discount	un descuento	oon dehs-koo-**ehn**-toh
expensive	caro	**kahr**-oh
cheap	barato	bah-**rah**-toh
clothes	la ropa	lah **roh**-pah
size, clothes	talla	**tah**-yah
size, shoes	número	**noo**-mehr-oh
bakery	panadería	pah-nah-deh **ree**-ah
bookstore	librería	lee-breh-**ree**-ah
grocer's	pulpería	pool-peh-**ree**-ah
market	mercado	mehr-**kah**-doh
shoe store	la zapatería	lah sah-pah-teh-**ree** ah
supermarket	el supermercado	ehl soo-pehr-mehr-**kah**-doh
travel agency	la agencia de viajes	lah ah-**hehn**-see-ah deh vee-**ah**-hehs

Sightseeing

bay	bahía	bah-**ee**-ah
beach	playa	**plah**-yah
building	edificio	eh-dee-**fee**-see-oh
cathedral	catedral	kah-teh-**drahl**
church	iglesia	ee-**gleh**-see-ah
farm	finca	**feehn**-kah
forest	bosque/selva	**bohs**-keh/**sehl**-bah
garden	jardín	hahr-**deen**
lake	lago	**lah**-goh
mangrove	manglar	mahn-**glahr**
mountain peak	cerro	**seh**-roh
mountain range	cordillera	kohr-dee-**yeh**-rah
museum	museo	moo-**seh**-oh
neighborhood	barrio	**bah**-ree-oh
port	puerto	poo-**her**-toh
ranger station	puesto de guardia	poo-ehs-toh deh goo-**ahr**-dee-ah
river	río	**ree**-oh
trail	sendero	sehn-**deh**-roh
theater	teatro	teh-**ah**-troh
tourist information office	oficina de turismo	oh-fee-**see**-nah deh too-**rees**- moh
viewpoint	mirador	mee-rah-**dohr**
ticket	el boleto/ la entrada	ehl boh-**leh**-toh lah ehn-**trah**-dah
guide (person)	el/la guía	ehl/lah **gee**-ah
guide (book)	la guía	lah **gee**-ah
guided tour	una visita guiada	oo-nah vee-**see**-tah gee-**ah**-dah
map	el mapa	ehl **mah**-pah

Health

I feel ill	Me siento mal	meh seh-**ehn**-toh mahl
We need a doctor	Necesitamos un médico	neh-seh-see-**tah**-mohs oon meh-dee-koh
drug store	farmacia	fahr-**mah**-see-ah
medicine	medicina	meh-dee-**see**-nah

ambulance	ambulancia	ahm-boo-**lahn**- see-ah
mosquito coils	espirales	ehs-pee-**rah**-lehs

Transportation

When does the… leave?	¿A qué hora sale el…?	ah keh oh-rah sah-leh ehl
Is there a bus to…?	¿Hay un bus a…?	eye oon boohs ah…
bus station	la estación de autobuses	lah ehs-tah-see-**ohn** deh aw-toh-**boo**-sehs
ticket office	la boletería	lah boh-leh-teh-**ree**-ah
airport	aeropuerto	ah-ehr-oh-poo-**ehr**-toh
customs	la aduana	lah ah-doo-**ah**-nah
taxi stand/rank	la parada de taxis	lah pah-**rah**-dah deh **tahk**-sees
car rental	rent a car	**rehn**-tah cahr
motorcycle	la moto(cicleta)	lah moh-toh(sec-**kleh**-tah)
bicycle	la bicicleta	lah bee-see-**kleh**-tah
4WD	doble tracción	**doh**-bleh trahk-siohn
water-taxi	una panga/ un bote	oo-nah **pahn**-gah/ oon **boh**-teh
aerial tram	teleférico	teh-leh-**feh**-ree-koh
insurance	los seguros	lohs seh-**goo**-rohs
gas station	gasolinera	gah-soh-leen **ehr**-ah
garage	taller de meránica	tah-**yehr** deh meh-**kahn**-ee-kah
I have a flat tire	Se me ponchó la llanta	seh meh pohn-**shoh** lah **yahn**-tah

Staying in a Hotel

I have a reservation	Tengo una reservación	tehn-goh **oo**-nah reh-sehr-vah-see-**ohn**
Do you have a vacant room?	¿Tienen una habitación libre?	tee-eh-nehn oo-nah ah-bee-tah-see ohnlee breh
double room	habitación doble	ah-bee-tah-see-**ohn doh**-bleh
single room	habitación sencilla	ah-bee-tah-see-**ohn** sehn-**see**-yah
room with a bath	habitación con baño	ah-bee-tah-see-**ohn** kohn **bah**-nyoh
shower	la ducha	lah **doo**-chah
The … is not working	No funciona el/la…	noh foon-see-oh-nah chl/lah
Where is the dining-room/bar?	¿Dónde está el restaurante/ el bar?	**dohn**-deh ehs-**tah** ehl rehs-toh-**rahn**-teh/ehl **bahr**
hot/cold water	agua caliente/ fría	ah-goo-ah kah-lee-**ehn**-teh/**free**-ah
soap	el jabón	ehl hah-**bohn**
towel	la toalla	lah toh-**ah**-yah
key	la llave	lah **yah**-veh

Eating Out

Have you got a table for …	¿Tienen mesa para …?	tee-eh-nehn meh-sah pah-**rah**
I want to reserve a table	Quiero reservar una mesa	kee-eh-roh reh-sehr-**vahr** oo-nah meh-sah
The bill, please	La cuenta, por favor	lah **kwehn**-tah pohr fah-**vohr**
I am a vegetarian	Soy vegetariano/a	soy veh-heh-tah-**ree**-ah-no/na
waiter/waitress	mesero/a	meh-**seh**-roh/rah
menu	la carta	lah **kahr**-tah
fixed-price menu	menú del día	meh-**noo** dehl **dee**-ah
wine list	la carta de vinos	lah **kahr**-tah deh **vee**-nohs

glass	un vaso	oon vah-soh
bottle	una botella	oo-nah boh-teh-yah
knife	un cuchillo	oon koo-chee-yoh
fork	un tenedor	oon teh-neh-dohr
spoon	una cuchara	oo-nah koo-chah-rah
breakfast	el desayuno	ehl deh-sah-yoo-noh
lunch	almuerzo	ahl-moo-ehr-soh
dinner	la cena	lah seh-nah
main course	el plato fuerte	ehl plah-toh foo-ehr-teh
starters	las entradas	lahs ehn-trah- das
dish of the day	el plato del día	ehl plat- toh dehl dee-ah
rare	término rojo	tehr-mee-noh roh-hoh
medium	término medio	tehr-mee-noh meh-dee-oh
well done	bien cocido	bee-ehn koh-see-doh
chair	la silla	lah see-yah
napkin	la servilleta	lah sehr-vee-yeh-tah
Is service included?	¿El servicio está incluido?	ehl sehr-vee-see-oh ehs-tah een-kloo-ee-doh
ashtray	cenicero	seh-nee-seh-roh
cigarettes	los cigarros	lohs see-gah-rohs
food stall	una soda	oo-nah soh-dah
neighborhood bar	una cantina/ un bar	oo-nah kahn-tee-nah/oon bahr

Menu Decoder *(see also pp222-3)*

el aceite	ah-see-eh-teh	oil
las aceitunas	ah-seh-toon-ahs	olives
el agua mineral	ah-gwa mee-neh-rahl	mineral water
el arroz	ahr-rohs	rice
el azúcar	ah-soo-kahr	sugar
una bebida	beh-bee-dah	drink
boca	boh-kah	a type of snack
el café	kah-feh	coffee
la carne	kahr-neh	meat
el cerdo	sehr-doh	pork
la cerveza	sehr-veh-sah	beer
el chocolate	choh-koh-lah-teh	chocolate
la ensalada	ehn-sah-lah-dah	salad
la fruta	froo-tah	fruit
el helado	eh-lah-doh	ice cream
el huevo	oo-eh-voh	egg
el jugo	ehl hoo-goh	juice
la leche	leh-cheh	milk
la mantequilla	mahn-teh-kee-yah	butter
la manzana	mahn-sah-nah	apple
los mariscos	mah-rees-kohs	seafood
el pan	pahn	bread
las papas	pah-pahs	potatoes
las papas a la francesa	pah-pahs ah lah frahn-seh-sah	French fries
las papas fritas	pah-pahs free-tahs	potato chips
el pastel	pahs-tehl	cake
el pescado	pehs-kah-doh	fish
picante	pee-kahn-teh	spicy
la pimienta	pee-mee-yehn-tah	pepper
el pollo	poh-yoh	chicken
el postre	pohs-treh	dessert
el queso	keh-soh	cheese
el refresco	reh-frehs-koh	soft drink/soda
la sal	sahl	salt
la sopa	soh-pah	soup
el sánguche	sahn-goo-she	sandwich
el té negro	teh neh-groh	tea
la torta	tohr-tah	burger
las tostadas	tohs-tah-dahs	toast
el vino blanco	vee-noh blahn-koh	white wine
el vino tinto	vee-noh teen-toh	red wine

Culture and Society

campesino	cahm-peh-see-noh	peasant
canton	cahn-tohn	county
carreta	cah-reh-tah	oxcart
cumbia	coom-bee-ah	Columbian music
Josefino	hoh-seh-fee-noh	resident of San José
marimba	mah-reem-bah	kind of xylophone
merengue	meh-rehn-geh	fast-paced Dominican music
sabanero	sah-bah-neh-roh	cowboy
salsa	sahl-sah	Cuban dance music
Tico/ costarricense	tee-coh/cohs-tah-ree-sehn-seh	Costa Rican

Numbers

0	cero	seh-roh
1	uno	oo-noh
2	dos	dohs
3	tres	trehs
4	cuatro	kwa-troh
5	cinco	seen-koh
6	seis	says
7	siete	see-eh-teh
8	ocho	oh-choh
9	nueve	nweh-veh
10	diez	dee-ehs
11	once	ohn-seh
12	doce	doh-seh
13	trece	treh-seh
14	catorce	kah-tohr-seh
15	quince	keen-seh
16	dieciséis	dee-eh-see-seh-ees
17	diecisiete	dee-eh-see-see-eh-teh
18	dieciocho	dee-eh-see-oh-choh
19	diecinueve	dee-eh-see-nweh-veh
20	veinte	veh-een-teh
30	treinta	treh-een-tah
40	cuarenta	kwah-rehn-tah
50	cincuenta	seen-kwehn-tah
60	sesenta	seh-sehn-tah
70	setenta	seh-tehn-tah
80	ochenta	oh-chehn-tah
90	noventa	noh-vehn-tah
100	cien	see-ehn
500	quinientos	khee-nee-ehn-tohs
1,000	mil	meel
1,001	mil uno	meel oo-noh
5,000	cinco mil	seen-koh meel

Time

one minute	un minuto	oon mee-noo-toh
one hour	una hora	oo-nah oh-rah
Monday	lunes	loo-nehs
Tuesday	martes	mahr-tehs
Wednesday	miércoles	mee-ehr-koh-lehs
Thursday	jueves	hoo-weh-vehs
Friday	viernes	vee-ehr-nehs
Saturday	sábado	sah-bah-doh
Sunday	domingo	doh-meen-goh
January	enero	eh-neh-roh
February	febrero	feh-breh-roh
March	marzo	mahr-soh
April	abril	ah-breel
May	mayo	mah-yoh
June	junio	hoo-nee-oh
July	julio	hoo-lee-oh
August	agosto	ah-gohs-toh
September	setiembre	seh-tee-ehm-breh
October	octubre	ohk-too-breh
November	noviembre	noh-vee-ehm-breh
December	diciembre	dee-see-ehm-breh

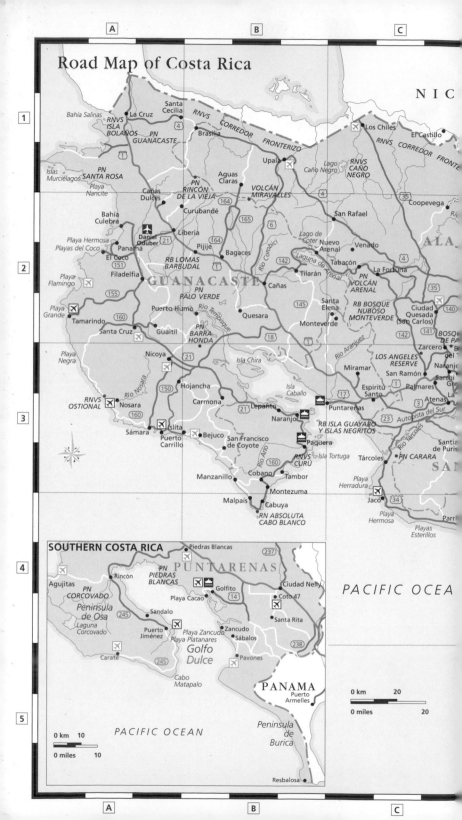